Influence without Arms

How does nuclear technology influence international relations? While many books focus on countries armed with nuclear weapons, this volume puts the spotlight on those that have the technology to build nuclear bombs but choose not to. These weapons-capable countries, such as Brazil, Germany, and Japan, have what is known as nuclear latency, and they shape world politics in important ways. Offering a definitive account of nuclear latency, Matthew Fuhrmann navigates a critical yet poorly understood issue. He identifies global trends, explains why countries obtain nuclear latency, and analyzes its consequences for international security. *Influence without Arms* presents new statistical and case evidence that nuclear latency enhances deterrence and provides greater influence but also triggers conflict and arms races. The book offers a framework to explain when nuclear latency increases security and when it incites instability, and generates far-reaching implications for deterrence, nuclear proliferation, arms races, preventive war, and disarmament.

Matthew Fuhrmann is a professor of political science in the Bush School of Government and Public Service at Texas A&M University. He has been a Stanton Nuclear Security Fellow at the Council on Foreign Relations (2010–11) and held visiting positions at Harvard University (2007–08), Stanford University (2016–17), and Yale University (2023–24). He is the author of *Atomic Assistance: How 'Atoms for Peace' Programs Cause Nuclear Insecurity* (2012) and co-author of *Nuclear Weapons and Coercive Diplomacy* (Cambridge, 2017). He was named an Andrew Carnegie Fellow by the Carnegie Corporation of New York in 2016. His research has been mentioned in national media outlets such as *The New York Times, The New Yorker, CNN,* and *NPR.*

Influence without Arms

The New Logic of Nuclear Deterrence

Matthew Fuhrmann

Texas A & M University

CAMBRIDGE
UNIVERSITY PRESS

CAMBRIDGE
UNIVERSITY PRESS

Shaftesbury Road, Cambridge CB2 8EA, United Kingdom

One Liberty Plaza, 20th Floor, New York, NY 10006, USA

477 Williamstown Road, Port Melbourne, VIC 3207, Australia

314–321, 3rd Floor, Plot 3, Splendor Forum, Jasola District Centre,
New Delhi – 110025, India

103 Penang Road, #05–06/07, Visioncrest Commercial, Singapore 238467

Cambridge University Press is part of Cambridge University Press & Assessment,
a department of the University of Cambridge.

We share the University's mission to contribute to society through the pursuit of
education, learning and research at the highest international levels of excellence.

www.cambridge.org
Information on this title: www.cambridge.org/9781108843201
DOI: 10.1017/9781108915106

First published 2024

A catalogue record for this publication is available from the British Library

Library of Congress Cataloging-in-Publication Data
Names: Fuhrmann, Matthew, 1980- author.
Title: Influence without arms : the new logic of nuclear deterrence /
    Matthew Fuhrmann.
Other titles: New logic of nuclear deterrence
Description: New York, NY : Cambridge University Press, [2024] |
    Includes bibliographical references and index.
Identifiers: LCCN 2024006396 (print) | LCCN 2024006397 (ebook) |
    ISBN 9781108843201 (hardback) | ISBN 9781108824071 (paperback) |
    ISBN 9781108915106 (epub)
Subjects: LCSH: Nuclear weapons. | Deterrence (Strategy) |
    Security, International. | Nuclear arms control.
Classification: LCC U263 F84 2024 (print) | LCC U263 (ebook) |
    DDC 355.02/17–dc23/eng/20240306
LC record available at https://lccn.loc.gov/2024006396
LC ebook record available at https://lccn.loc.gov/2024006397

ISBN 978-1-108-84320-1 Hardback
ISBN 978-1-108-82407-1 Paperback

Contents

Acknowledgments

During the 2010–11 academic year, the mathematician and nuclear engineer Paul Nelson contacted me with an intriguing idea. He suggested collaborating on a grant proposal to collect data on the international spread of sensitive nuclear technology. Despite widespread awareness that uranium enrichment plants and plutonium reprocessing facilities were the most sensitive from a nuclear proliferation standpoint, we did not yet have comprehensive open-source information about their global spread. We wanted to provide it, and the US Department of Energy gave us funding to do so (NEUP-3149). The collaboration with Paul, which also included Garill Coles at the Pacific Northwest National Laboratory, led to the creation of the Nuclear Latency (NL) dataset – a database that provided details about more than 250 sensitive nuclear facilities built globally.

The database enabled new research about the role of nuclear technology in international relations. My initial plan was to write a journal article or two using the NL dataset, and then move on to other projects. However, as time passed, I became convinced that scholars and policymakers needed to understand more deeply how nuclear technology – not just weapons – influenced peace, stability, and international order. I received a grant from the Carnegie Corporation of New York in 2016 that helped make this book possible (G-F-16-53706). The grant enabled me to work on the book for two years as an Andrew Carnegie Fellow.[1]

I wrote this book while at three universities. I began my work in earnest while I was a Visiting Associate Professor at Stanford University's Center for International Security and Cooperation (CISAC) in 2016–17. CISAC was a terrific place to begin thinking more deeply about the role of nuclear technology in world politics. After my time at Stanford, I continued working on the book at Texas A&M University, my permanent academic home since 2011. My department at Texas A&M provided a supportive environment and a steady stream of research assistants,

[1] The statements made and views expressed are solely the responsibility of the author.

helping me throughout the entire process. I finished the book while I was a Visiting Professor at Yale University in 2023–24. I am grateful for the opportunity to bring the book across the finish line at Yale. Outside my time at universities, I made key progress while temporarily living out of a tiny house on a subsistence farm in Gig Harbor, Washington, and in some of Atlanta's finest coffee shops.

Writing this book was exciting but also deeply challenging. At times, the problems I faced in trying to get to the truth about the role of nuclear technology in world politics seemed intractable. Many friends and colleagues provided feedback at critical junctures, helping me find a path forward and identify the parts of the book that needed a course-correction.

For help and constructive feedback, I am grateful to: Daniel Altman, Paul Avey, Ryan Bakker, David Bearce, Jeffrey Berejikian, Philip Bleek, Allison Carnegie, Don Casler, Terrence Chapman, Sunil Chirayath, William Clark, Garill Coles, Scott Cook, Eric Crahan, Andrew Coe, Toby Dalton, Alexandre Debs, Christopher Dunlap, Bryan Early, Jennifer Erickson, Christine Fair, James Fearon, Nikhar Gaikwad, Erik Gartzke, Rebecca Gibbons, Andrea Gilli, Sigfried Hecker, Stephen Herzog, David Halloway, Michael Horowitz, Colin Kahl, Jeffrey Kaplow, Joshua Kertzer, Jason Lindo, Jeffrey Knopf, Andrew Kydd, Michael Nacht, Rupal Mehta, Jeffrey Knopf, Matthew Kroenig, Alexander Lanoszka, Ariel Levite, Nicholas Miller, Theo Milonopoulos, Eric Min, Manuela Muñoz, Vipin Narang, Paul Nelson, George Perkovich, Joe Pilat, William Potter, Tyler Pratt, Didac Queralt, Robert Reardon, Jonathan Renshon, Toby Rider, Brad Roberts, Maria Rost Rublee, Scott Sagan, Kenneth Schultz, John Schuessler, Todd Sechser, Alastair Smith, Jesse Sowell, William Spaniel, Matias Spektor, Adam Stulberg, Jaroslav Tir, Harold Trinkunas, Jane Vaynman, Tristan Volpe, Rachel Wellhausen, Rachel Whitlark, Guy Whitten, Scott Wolford, and Amy Zegart.

Anonymous reviewers were also insightful and guided me to the places where the theory and evidence needed major surgery. I am thankful for their feedback, as it helped me produce a better book. I am also grateful to John Haslam, my editor at Cambridge University Press, for his enthusiasm and support from a very early stage – and for his flexibility and understanding throughout the process.

I was fortunate to receive lots of helpful feedback at workshops organized by the Carnegie Endowment for International Peace, Columbia University, George Washington University, the Middelbury Institute for International Studies at Monterey, Stanford University, Texas Tech University, University of Colorado at Boulder, University of Florida,

University of Georgia, University of Texas at Austin, University of Nebraska at Lincoln, the Woodrow Wilson Center for International Scholars, and Yale University. I thank everyone who attended these workshops and engaged with my work-in-progress.

Numerous research assistants helped me during my work on this project. I am grateful for assistance from Joshua Alley, Molly Berkemeier, Lauren Bondarenko, Swarup Das, Duncan Espenshade, Ali Kagawala, Yewon Kwon, Kyung Suk Lee, Benjamin Tkach, Hankyeul Yang, Joowon Yi, and Chamseul Yu.

Despite my efforts to keep track, there are undoubtedly others who aided me with this book. My apologies to anyone I unintentionally failed to mention. Of course, I alone bear all responsibility for the book's remaining shortcomings.

Portions of Chapter 4 were previously published as Fuhrmann, Matthew. 2019. "Explaining the Proliferation of Latent Nuclear Capabilities," pages 289–315 of: Joseph Pilat (ed.), *Nuclear Latency and Hedging: Concepts, History, and Issues*. Washington, DC: Woodrow Wilson Center for Scholars. I thank the Wilson Center for granting permission to reproduce the relevant sections here. Chapter 3 has the same main title as a 2015 article I published with Benjamin Tkach ("Almost Nuclear"), but the chapter does not reproduce any of the material from that article word-for-word.

My biggest debt is to my family, who provided a bedrock of support throughout this process. My wife, Lauren, and three kids – Kate, Adrienne, and Holden – serve as a constant reminder that there is more to life than a book, or work more generally. In helping to keep me balanced, I believe they enabled me to write a better book.

In February 2021, my then-8-year-old daughter Kate, who knew about the book I was writing, came into my home office and said, "Daddy, I wrote you a poem." It was titled "Deterence" and opened with the lines, "Deterence is boring. boring. Boring, BORING." After laughing at how uninteresting she thought my work was, I realized that she wasn't necessarily wrong. The study of deterrence in scholarship had become a bit stale, despite its importance in the real world, as most of the major contributions had been written during the Cold War. I hope this book interjects some fresh thinking to the study of deterrence in international relations. Kate may never be convinced, but I hope the book helps somebody out there think about an old problem in a slightly new way.

Introduction

On August 6, 1945, an American B-29 bomber named the *Enola Gay* dropped an atomic bomb on the Japanese city of Hiroshima, killing at least 70,000 people and damaging virtually every building within three miles of the blast site.[1] Three days later, the United States carried out a second nuclear attack, killing another 40,000 people and destroying large swaths of Nagasaki.[2] At the time of the nuclear bombings, the United States and Japan had been at war for almost four years – since the surprise Japanese attack at Pearl Harbor on December 7, 1941. Just days after the destruction of Hiroshima and Nagasaki, the Japanese government surrendered, bringing an end to World War II.[3]

Other countries soon began to pursue this new, potentially game-changing weapon. The American nuclear monopoly ended when the Soviet Union detonated a nuclear explosion, code-named "Fast Lightning," at its Semipalatinsk Test Site in Kazakhstan on August 29, 1949. The United Kingdom followed suit in October 1952, becoming the world's third nuclear power. Many feared that the proverbial floodgates were now open, paving the way for droves of other countries to obtain nuclear weapons. In a speech before the United Nations on December 8, 1953, US President Dwight D. Eisenhower acknowledged the possibility of wholesale nuclear weapons proliferation, saying that "the knowledge now possessed by several nations will eventually be shared by others, possibly all others."[4] Nuclear weapons could have become a fixture of any modern military, similar to tanks, bombers, or missiles.

However, the pace of nuclear weapons proliferation turned out to be slower than many feared. Seventy-five years into the atomic age, just

---

[1] US Department of Energy (N.D.a).

[2] US Department of Energy (N.D.b).

[3] Whether the nuclear bombings definitively caused the Japanese surrender is still debated in scholarship. Wilson (2007), for example, argues that the Soviet entry into the war against Japan on August 9, 1945 – not the nuclear bombings – led to the Japanese surrender.

[4] These remarks occurred during Eisenhower's so called Atoms for Peace address. See Eisenhower (1953).

ten countries have built nuclear weapons.[5] And only one new nuclear weapons state, North Korea, has emerged since India and Pakistan tested nuclear weapons in 1998.

At the same time, many countries have the technological capacity to build nuclear weapons if they so desired. These weapons-capable countries have what is known as "nuclear latency."[6] Countries with nuclear latency – also known as "latent nuclear powers" – could arm quickly because they already possess the building blocks for bomb-making. Nuclear technology is dual-use in nature: The same nuclear plant could be used for energy production or bomb-making. Countries with "peaceful" nuclear programs, therefore, have the potential foundation for making nuclear weapons. Journalists and other commentators sometimes say that Japan is merely a "screwdriver's turn away" from a bomb.[7] Japan is a prominent latent nuclear power in the world today, but it is hardly alone. Countries such as Canada, Brazil, Germany, and Iran have developed the technological capacity to make nuclear weapons.

Many policymakers believe nuclear latency brings a country greater foreign policy influence, an idea I call "latent nuclear deterrence."[8] American officials have long recognized that countries can use latent nuclear forces as a "bargaining chip" to influence allies and adversaries.[9] Mohamed ElBaradei, the former head of the International Atomic Energy Agency (IAEA), echoed this view in a 2004 interview. "If you are really smart," ElBaradei said, "you don't need to develop a weapon, you just develop that capability. And that is the best deterrence."[10] Based on this line of thinking, nuclear latency can be a substitute for building nuclear weapons. In the words of historian Juan Cole, it is "almost as good as having a bomb."[11]

Other world leaders, by contrast, see the pursuit of latent nuclear capabilities as a recipe for inviting insecurity. As the US intelligence community concluded back in April 1981, the emergence of latent nuclear powers "could initiate a process of destabilizing counter-actions."[12]

---

[5] South Africa dismantled its nuclear arsenal roughly thirty years ago, so only nine countries are nuclear-armed today.

[6] The term nuclear latency is used in other international relations scholarship. See, for example, Sagan (2010), Fuhrmann and Tkach (2015), Mehta and Whitlark (2017a), Volpe (2017), and Saunders (2019).

[7] See, for example, Fisher (2017). This is an exaggeration, as it would take at least a few months for Japan to build a nuclear weapon.

[8] Some scholars and journalists refer to this as "weaponless deterrence." See, for example, Schell (1984).

[9] For example, US Department of State (1979) discusses Pakistan pursuing this strategy.

[10] Quoted in Sanger (2004).

[11] Quoted in NPR (2009).

[12] US Central Intelligence Agency (1981a).

In this view, the spread of nuclear technology raises the risk of nuclear weapons proliferation, fuels arms races, precipitates diplomatic crises, and encourages preventive wars.[13] Consider Iran's development of nuclear technology. Revelations that Tehran possessed nuclear plants that *could* be used to make nuclear bombs in 2002 incited a serious crisis and led to calls for preventive military strikes in Israel, the United States, and elsewhere.

Whether the political effects of nuclear latency are destabilizing or security-enhancing, its emergence can change the international landscape. Despite this, nuclear latency remains poorly understood in scholarship. Many books have been written about the political effects of nuclear weapons.[14] They often seek to explain how the development and deployment of nuclear forces, especially by the Soviet Union and the United States during the Cold War, influenced international security. Far fewer books have focused on the latent nuclear powers – the countries that come close to building nuclear weapons but do not go all the way.[15] As a result, we do not fully understand how the international spread of dual-use nuclear technology affects peace and security.

This book comprehensively assesses this issue. It addresses the big questions about the role of nuclear latency in world politics. Which countries have developed the capacity to build nuclear bombs, and why did they do so? Does having nuclear latency confer greater political influence? If so, how is it possible to gain leverage without assembled bombs? Why does nuclear latency sometimes generate crises and preventive wars? Does nuclear latency fuel arms races, or can having bomb-making potential dissuade others from arming?

Real World Stakes

Answering these questions matters for contemporary international relations and American foreign policy. This is partially because of global trends. The technological building blocks for nuclear weapons have spread internationally since the US bombings of Hiroshima and Nagasaki.

The most difficult step in making a bomb is obtaining fissile material – weapons-grade highly enriched uranium (HEU) or plutonium. As former US Secretary of State Henry Kissinger put it, "Once the requisite

---

[13] A similar argument is made by nuclear pessimists, who argue international spread of nuclear weapons is destabilizing. See, most notably, Sagan and Waltz (2003).

[14] Examples include Schelling (1966), Brodie (1946), Allison et al. (1985), Jervis (1989), and Powell (1990).

[15] A recent exception is Volpe (2023).

amount of fissile material has been produced, constructing and equipping a warhead is a relatively short and technologically straightforward process."[16] To produce fissile material, countries need uranium enrichment or plutonium reprocessing (ENR) facilities. These ENR plants are widely considered to be the most sensitive nuclear technology due to their bomb-making potential.[17] However, they could also be used in commercial applications such as making fuel for a nuclear power plant or managing nuclear waste.

This book classifies latent nuclear powers based on their ability to produce HEU or plutonium. States have nuclear latency when they operate uranium enrichment or plutonium reprocessing facilities capable of making fissile material. Throughout the book, I analyze two stages of nuclear latency: partial and full. Partially latent states are those with laboratory-scale ENR programs. Countries in this category did experimental ENR work and may have produced a few grams of plutonium or enriched uranium but not nearly enough for a single bomb. By contrast, those with full latency have pilot or commercial-scale ENR plants are are theoretically capable of producing enough fissile material for at least one bomb.

Table 0.1 lists the countries that achieved partial and full nuclear latency from 1939 to 2012, along with those that obtained nuclear weapons. The ten countries that ultimately built nuclear weapons were latent nuclear powers before arming. Since fissile material is necessary to make a bomb, any nuclear-armed country must first pass through a state of nuclear latency. Thirteen countries had full nuclear latency at some point during this time span, while ten were partially latent. In total, thirty-three countries have had ENR programs since the 1930s, achieving at least partial nuclear latency.

Figure 0.1 shows the number of countries with at least partial latency compared to the number of nuclear weapons states that existed each year from 1939 to 2012. The number of latent nuclear powers began to increase sharply in the 1950s, reaching fifteen by 1968. The trend then declined before leveling off between nine and eleven countries in the post–Cold War period (1992–2012). In virtually ever year from 1939 to 2012, the number of latent nuclear powers exceeded the number of states armed with nuclear warheads.

Sensitive nuclear technology continues to spread around the globe today. Saudi Arabia and others in the Middle East have expressed

[16] Kissinger (2012).
[17] Throughout the book I use "sensitive nuclear technology" and "ENR technology" interchangably.

Table 0.1 *Latent nuclear powers and nuclear weapons states, 1939–2012.*

Large-scale ENR program		Small-scale ENR program
Nuclear weapons	Full latency	Partial latency
China	Argentina	Algeria
France	Belgium	Australia
India	Brazil	Czechoslovakia
Israel	Canada	East Germany
North Korea	Germany	Egypt
Pakistan	Iran	Libya
Russia	Iraq	Romania
South Africa	Italy	South Korea
United Kingdom	Japan	Sweden
United States	Netherlands	Taiwan
	Norway	
	Spain	
	Yugoslavia	

interest in obtaining a uranium enrichment capacity to match Iran's bomb-making potential. South Korea also wants to expand its ENR program, shortening the time needed to build nuclear weapons, if necessary.

In light of the historical and contemporary spread of sensitive nuclear technology, it is important to understand the political implications of nuclear latency. On top of this, the issue of nuclear latency carries implications for two big issues facing policymakers today.

The Prospects for Nuclear Disarmament

For as long as nuclear weapons have existed, people have considered whether they should be eliminated. In June 1946, the United States introduced the Baruch Plan. This plan called for the United States to dismantle its nuclear arsenal after the creation of an international body to manage and inspect any site that could make material for bombs. The Baruch Plan was never implemented, but this did not stop scholars and government officials from thinking about nuclear disarmament. Even as the Cold War continued, Ronald Reagan and Mikhail Gorbachev discussed scrapping their nuclear forces during a historic October 1986 summit in Reykjavik, Iceland.

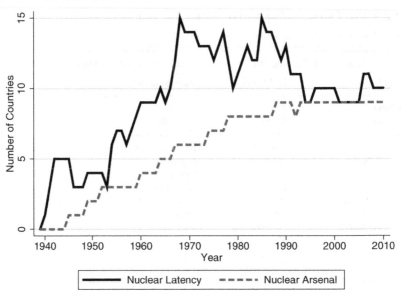

Figure 0.1 Number of countries with nuclear latency and nuclear arsenals, 1939–2012.

More recently, calls for the eventual elimination of nuclear weapons have received growing attention. In 2007, four former US senior officials – Henry Kissinger, Sam Nunn, William Perry, and George Schultz – wrote a widely discussed op-ed in the *Wall Street Journal* that advocated for a nuclear weapons-free world.[18] Shortly thereafter, during one of his first major speeches as president, Barack Obama echoed this vision: "I state clearly and with conviction America's commitment to seek the peace and security of a world without nuclear weapons."[19] Momentum on this front appears to continue, as the United Nations adopted a treaty in June 2017 that bans all nuclear bombs. Recent events – especially North Korea's development of long-range missiles that could hit the United States – may make the idea of nuclear disarmament seem like a misguided pipedream. There nonetheless remains a segment of the population, globally and in the United States, that continues to advocate for the elimination of nuclear weapons.

Would the world be safer or more unstable without nuclear weapons? Knowing whether latent nuclear deterrence works can help us answer

[18] Shultz et al. (2007).
[19] Obama (2009).

this question. Nuclear weapons cannot be totally uninvented because the knowledge required to make them would still exist in a disarmed world. If today's nuclear states dismantled their warheads, we would live in a world with nine additional latent nuclear powers. This would not be a purely nuclear-free world since formerly nuclear-armed countries could reassemble bombs quickly in the event of a crisis. A disarmed world, then, would be one in which weaponless nuclear deterrence operated.

The journalist Jonathan Schell made a serious case for latent nuclear deterrence in his 1984 book *The Abolition*.[20] Schell was a disarmament advocate, and he conceived of weaponless deterrence as an arms control measure. He called on nuclear powers such as the United States to dismantle their warheads but retain the capacity to reconstitute arsenals quickly if war came. In that case, they could rearm and potentially retaliate in a nuclear attack. This notion later became known in scholarship as a system of "virtual nuclear arsenals" (VNAs).[21] For Schell and other VNA advocates, this form of deterrence was better for peace and stability than a world in which countries maintained assembled warheads that were ready to launch on an moment's notice.[22]

Evidence that nuclear latency gives countries political leverage and bolsters deterrence would strengthen the case for eventual nuclear disarmament. In that case, we would have greater confidence that nuclear deterrence can function without assembled warheads. If latent nuclear powers such as Japan have been able to reduce their vulnerability to threats, a hypothetical nonnuclear United States should be able to do so as well. Having a locked-and-loaded nuclear arsenal, then, would appear less crucial for ensuring international security. If they recognize this, existing nuclear powers might be more willing to take steps toward the eventual elimination of their arsenals.

On the other hand, nuclear disarmament would seem like a less desirable policy goal if nuclear latency merely invites international instability. The case for disarmament rests in part on the notion that nuclear deterrence can still function in a disarmed world. If this claim is false, eliminating nuclear forces would seem far less attractive for the United States and other nuclear powers.

---

[20] The concept of latent deterrence is also discussed in Mazarr (1995a), Paul (2000, 59), and Mount (2014).

[21] See, for example, Mazarr (1995a, 1997b), Holdren (1997), Perkovich and Acton (2008), and Drell and Goodby (2009).

[22] This conception of deterrence is similar to what I call deterrence by delayed attack. In this body of work, however, only former nuclear powers engage in weaponless deterrence – not latent states that were never nuclear-armed.

The Pace of Nuclear Proliferation

The issue of nuclear latency is important for understanding the behavior of nonnuclear countries, not just nuclear-armed states that may one day disarm. Will the "club" of nuclear-armed countries gain new members in the future? How many nonnuclear states will join? The answers depend on how nuclear latency affects international peace and stability.

If nuclear latency cannot serve as a substitute for possessing a nuclear arsenal, we would expect a relatively high rate of nuclear weapons proliferation. A potential pathway to greater security – nuclear latency – would not be viable, strengthening the case for building nuclear weapons.

Many observers have made this argument in the context of Iran's nuclear future. As political scientist Kenneth Waltz put it: Tehran will "conclude that a breakout capability is an insufficient deterrent, after all, and that only weaponization can provide it with the security it seeks."[23] If this is correct, we should expect Iran to build nuclear weapons in the near future.[24] We might then expect to see an arms race in the Middle East. There are already signs that this might be happening. Saudi Crown Prince Mohammed bin Salman drew international attention in March 2018 when he proclaimed that if Iran "developed a nuclear bomb, we will follow suit as soon as possible."[25] This is a seemingly clear indication that Saudi Arabia sees a nuclear arsenal as necessary to counter a hypothetical nuclear-armed Iran's influence.

In a world where nuclear latency confers few political benefits and only brings insecurity, the picture in East Asia would be similar. North Korea's six nuclear tests from 2006 to 2017 heightened anxiety among officials in Seoul, Tokyo, and elsewhere. Japan and South Korea may be tempted to seek their own nuclear weapons if they believe that their latent nuclear forces are only a political liability, especially if they lose confidence in American security guarantees.

These predictions seem to be at odds with an enduring puzzle about nuclear proliferation: As noted earlier, just ten countries have built nuclear weapons, despite the fact that many more have the technical wherewithal to proliferate.[26] Evidence that nuclear latency enhances international influence would partially explain this puzzle. If countries can address their security concerns at least in part by developing the latent capacity to make the bomb, without going all the way, we would

[23] Waltz (2012, 3).
[24] One might argue that it should have already happened if Waltz's view is correct.
[25] Quoted in Sanger and Broad (2018).
[26] The puzzle has been addressed by Hymans (2006), Rublee (2009), and others.

expect nuclear weapons proliferation to occur at a slower clip.[27] In that case, building a nuclear arsenal would not be the only solution to international insecurity.

If true, this would help explain why a country like Japan – a strong candidate to have obtained a bomb over the past several decades – has remained nonnuclear even after North Korea's nuclear tests.[28] Similarly, Iran may eventually build a nuclear bomb, but there are good reasons to think that it will be content with latent nuclear forces, especially if no country threatens it militarily.[29]

Rethinking Nuclear Deterrence

Nuclear deterrence has attracted considerable attention in international relations scholarship. Nearly 50,000 books and articles address this subject.[30] The basic logic of nuclear deterrence is straightforward. Countries armed with nuclear weapons can inflict tremendous pain on their adversaries. For example, an airburst detonation of a single 1.2 Mt warhead – the size of the B-83, the largest weapon currently in the American arsenal – above New York City would kill an estimated 1.84 million people and leave more than three million others injured.[31] Given the destructive power of this military technology, war with a nuclear power is too costly for any sane leader to contemplate. Countries therefore avoid picking fights with nuclear-armed counterparts.

Scholars who study nuclear deterrence have many disagreements. They continue to debate, for example, how many warheads and what kind of force structure is necessary to achieve deterrence. Yet just about everyone assumes (at least implicitly) that nuclear technology has little value for deterrence unless countries can immediately retaliate with nuclear weapons. Nuclear deterrence works when countries have the capacity to destroy swiftly an opponent's dearest possessions, like cities. Countries without assembled warheads cannot inflict this kind of pain, rendering nonweaponized nuclear programs feeble for deterrence.

---

[27] Developing nuclear latency with the intent to shorten the time needed to build a bomb is known as *hedging*. On various hedging strategies, see Narang (2017).

[28] Levite (2002) also makes this argument. Of course, many factors (including the alliance with the United States) have contributed to Japan's nonnuclear policy.

[29] I made this argument in earlier writing (Fuhrmann, 2013).

[30] This is based on a Google Scholar search for "nuclear deterrence" carried out on January 11, 2023. See, for example, Brodie (1959), Kahn (1960), Schelling (1966), Miller (1984), Jervis (1989), Powell (1990), Gartzke and Jo (2009), Sagan and Waltz (2012), Narang (2009, 2014), and Bell and Miller (2015).

[31] I generated these estimates using the NUKEMAP software developed by Alex Wellerstein available at https://nuclearsecrecy.com/nukemap/.

However, as this book will show, many world leaders believe that nuclear latency brings greater international influence. We need an updated theory of nuclear deterrence that accounts for the latent nuclear powers. How is nuclear deterrence without bombs possible? Policymakers who seem to believe in latent nuclear deterrence do not provide a clear answer. Nor does existing academic research. I am not the first person to suggest that nuclear deterrence without arms might be possible.[32] Yet, based on existing scholarship, how exactly latent nuclear deterrence works remains unclear.

Gaining Influence without Arms: Deterrence by Proliferation, Delayed Attack, and Doubt

There are three ways through which latent nuclear powers can potentially gain influence over other countries. I call these means of influence deterrence by proliferation, delayed attack, and doubt.

Deterrence by proliferation is the threat to arm with nuclear weapons in order to gain international leverage. When states obtain nuclear latency they send a warning to others: "we have come this far and we can go further, if necessary." If a latent nuclear power perceives that its interests are threatened, it might begin a nuclear weapons program or accelerate an existing one. Indeed, it is widely understood that external security threats may compel a state to arm itself with an atomic arsenal. The prospect of fomenting nuclear proliferation may induce caution among adversaries, generating international influence for the latent nuclear power.

The threatened punishment here, which may be implicit, is to possess nuclear weapons in the future – not to use them in combat, like in traditional nuclear deterrence. Although this kind of punishment is nontraditional in the context of scholarship on nuclear deterrence, it can influence other countries as long as they find the latent nuclear power's development of the bomb undesirable. In that case, its mere possession of an arsenal can impose costs on the aggressor.

Take, for instance, US views of Iran's nuclear program today. Virtually all senior US policymakers – both Republicans and Democrats – have opposed an Iranian bomb. It is not that these officials think that Iran would launch a nuclear attack against US cities, though this is one potential danger. They instead tend to focus on other costs, like the possibility that an Iranian bomb would fuel an arms race in the Middle East. Donald Trump's national security adviser John Bolton,

---

[32] See especially Beaton (1966), Schell (1984), and Mazar (1995a).

for example, wrote in 2015 that the United States was on "the brink of catastrophe" because an Iranian bomb would cause Egypt, Turkey, and Saudi Arabia to follow suit.[33] Even if Iran never used nuclear weapons against the United States in war, then, Washington believes that it would suffer political costs as a result of Iranian proliferation. This might give Iran leverage over the United States since Tehran can (implicitly) threaten proliferation if the United States pursues policies that Tehran finds undesirable.

Countries routinely engage in deterrence by proliferation. A diverse set of world leaders, ranging from Egyptian strongman Gamal Abdel Nasser to Indian Prime Minister Rajiv Gandhi, have used threats to arm with nuclear weapons in an attempt to gain influence over other countries. At least some foreign officials believe that Iran is pursuing this strategy today. As Israeli diplomat Alon Pinkas wrote in August 2021, Iran is using "the threat of crossing the [nuclear weapons] threshold" as a "shield," making it more difficult for other countries to intervene, even if the latent nuclear power pursues aggressive policies.[34] Meanwhile, Saudi Crown Prince Mohammed bin Salman's assertion that his country will build nuclear weapons if Iran does is an attempt to keep Tehran nonnuclear.[35]

The second means of influence, deterrence by delayed attack, works like traditional nuclear deterrence with one key difference: There is a time gap between the challenge to the status quo and the nuclear response.[36] Latent nuclear powers, by definition, cannot immediately retaliate with nuclear forces. However, states with nuclear latency might be able to launch delayed nuclear strikes. After suffering an initial attack, a latent nuclear power could quickly assemble a nuclear device and use it against the aggressor. The prospect of suffering a devastating counterstrike might make a country think twice before attacking a latent nuclear power, especially in situations where fighting could persist for months or years.

Argentina's nuclear program illustrates how countries might gain influence over their adversaries via deterrence by delayed attack. As Argentina's nuclear program advanced, it experienced a crisis with Chile over disputed islands in the Beagle Channel. The International Court of Justice ruled in May 1977 that the islands rightfully belonged to Chile. However, Argentina rejected this ruling and threatened to use military

---

[33] Bolton (2015).
[34] Pinkas (2022).
[35] Sanger and Broad (2018).
[36] A similar form of deterrence is described in Schell (1984), Mazarr (1995a, 1997b).

force to seize the islands. Pope John Paul II mediated this dispute and the two sides ultimately committed to a peaceful settlement in January 1979.[37] Yet Chile accused Argentina of dragging its feet on implementing the Vatican-backed settlement. Chilean officials complained about this to the American Principal Deputy Assistant Secretary of State Harry Marshall during a meeting in Santiago on November 1, 1981.[38] Later that same day, representatives from the Chilean government expressed concerns about Argentina's ability to go nuclear. According to the US Embassy's account of the meeting, "[Director General Fernando] Zeggars talked in terms of Argentina having the capability to *suddenly* build a nuclear weapon."[39] This prompted a discussion about the details of Argentina's nuclear program – something that Zegers "expressed great interest in."[40] Given their perception of Argentina's nuclear potential, Chilean officials may have worried that pushing Argentina too hard over the Beagle Channel islands could make them vulnerable to an eventual nuclear attack.

Deterrence by doubt is the third mechanism by which nuclear latency confers leverage.[41] As a latent nuclear power gets close to a bomb, it may be difficult to know for sure whether or not it is in possession of nuclear weapons. This uncertainty can act as a deterrent. If a country thinks that a latent nuclear power *might* already be nuclear-armed, they may worry about suffering a near-immediate retaliatory strike, making them think twice before attacking. Deterrence by doubt therefore straddles deterrence by delayed attack and traditional nuclear deterrence. The latent nuclear power is not actually nuclear-armed (distinguishing it from traditional deterrence) but its adversaries might think that there would not be a time delay in the imposition of nuclear punishment (distinguishing it from deterrence by delayed attack).[42]

Nuclear dynamics in South Asia during the 1980s illustrate how deterrence by doubt might operate. During this decade, India and Pakistan moved closer to building a bomb – so close that it became difficult

---

[37] This discussion draws on the summary of the crisis in Brecher and Wilkenfeld (1997).

[38] US Department of State (1981).

[39] Ibid. Emphasis added. This perception was not necessarily accurate. The document cited above characterizes the Chilean assessment as "unrealistic." When it comes to deterrence, however, perceptions may be more important than reality.

[40] Ibid.

[41] The phrase deterrence by doubt comes from Baliga and Sjöström (2018, 1024, 1035) and Gordon and Trainor (2006, 65).

[42] Deterrence by doubt can potentially operate after a country has assembled one or more nuclear weapons but does not publicly declare its status, like in the case of Israel after 1967. However, if a country is already nuclear-armed, I classify them as a nuclear weapons state – not a latent nuclear power – even if they do not openly acknowledge their capability.

to conclude with certainty that they were not already nuclear-armed. Precisely when they assembled combat-ready weapons remains unclear – it may have been as late as the mid-1990s.[43] Well before this point, however, nuclear deterrence operated in South Asia. As Pakistani leader Muhammad Zia-ul-Haq put it in 1988, his country's nuclear program has achieved a level that is "good enough to create an impression of deterrence."[44] Indian leaders hold a similar view.[45] Each country knew that the other side might already have a bomb, and this fear made them think twice about pushing the other country too hard.

Latent Nuclear Deterrence Theory

Most scholarship on nuclear deterrence does not seriously consider the possibility that countries can gain influence without arms. However, many of the analysts who have commented on this issue express skepticism about weaponless nuclear deterrence. For these scholars, deterrence by proliferation, delayed attack, or doubt does not work. As Waltz put it, "a latent nuclear force is at best a shaky deterrent."[46]

This perspective is partially correct. Under some conditions, weaponless deterrence is indeed ineffective and potentially destabilizing. But there are also circumstances under which countries can gain influence without arms. A complete theory of latent nuclear deterrence, which this book provides, should be able to explain this variation.

The theory unfolds in two parts. It first considers three major challenges that countries face when attempting to use nuclear latency for international influence. Next, it identifies some things countries can do to mitigate these challenges. The end result is a theory that helps us understand when nuclear latency promotes international stability and confers foreign policy influence – and when it incites insecurity.

Challenges

The first challenge in latent nuclear deterrence is that punishment is delayed. There is a time gap between an infraction and when the latent nuclear power can implement its threatened form of retaliation. Depending on how close a latent nuclear power is to a bomb, this time delay could be measured in hours, days, weeks, months, or years.

---

[43] Khan (2012, 233).
[44] Quoted in Levy and Scott-Clark (2007, 171).
[45] Perkovich (1999, 189).
[46] Waltz (1997, 155). See also Mehta and Whitlark (2017a).

For example, in the 1960s, Indian Prime Minister Lal Bahadur Shastri threatened to build nuclear weapons if China developed nuclear delivery systems.[47] Around this time, the CIA concluded that India could build a bomb in one to three years from a political decision.[48] From China's perspective, it might pay a price by obtaining deliverable nuclear weapons, but that cost would not be felt immediately.

The delay in punishment generates three specific problems for latent nuclear powers. First, it means that other countries must have keen foresight – they must be able to anticipate a form of punishment that the latent nuclear power does not presently have the capacity to implement. If leaders do not see the connection between their behavior and what their latent counterpart might do in response, weaponless deterrence is doomed to fail. Moreover, even if they recognize the threatened form of punishment, more immediate considerations could drown out longer-term consequences, especially in crisis situations. Second, the punishment delay may allow countries to believe that they could escape retaliation. In deterrence by proliferation, for example, the potential challenger might conclude that it would have ample time to stop the latent nuclear power's armament even if it begins racing toward a bomb. Third, countries might discount costs that are implemented in the future, decreasing the bite of punishment in weaponless deterrence.

A second major challenge is that implementing the threat is costly for the latent nuclear power. Building nuclear weapons generally prompts a swift international response, which could include crippling economic sanctions. Moreover, it requires a sustained financial investment that could detract from other domestic priorities. Actually carrying out a nuclear attack would be exceedingly consequential for the user, not just the country whose territory was destroyed. Scholars have long recognized this, which is why it is difficult to extract political leverage from a nuclear arsenal, in addition to latent nuclear forces.[49] In light of these costs, countries may dismiss threats from latent nuclear powers as not believable.

I have already previewed the third big challenge: Nuclear latency can invite instability. States that obtain sensitive dual-use nuclear technology create uncertainty about their intentions, and this can induce violent conflict.[50] Fearing eventual nuclear proliferation, a country may launch preventive attacks to destroy a latent nuclear power's nuclear facilities

---

[47] Simons (1965).
[48] US Central Intelligence Agency (1964).
[49] See Sechser and Fuhrmann (2017).
[50] See, for example, Mehta and Whitlark (2016, 52).

before it has an opportunity to weaponize. This is not merely a hypothetical concern: Israel carried out preventive strikes to eliminate nuclear plants in Iraq (1981) and Syria (2007). Latent nuclear powers can also provoke destabilizing arms races.[51] A state's development of nuclear latency may prompt its adversaries to arm themselves with nuclear weapons.

Solutions

The above challenges are daunting, but they are not necessarily insurmountable. Three factors can mitigate these problems to some degree, increasing the likelihood of success in latent nuclear deterrence. Implementing these solutions does not guarantee success, but it does put countries in a better position to succeed.

The first solution is for a country to develop the capability to produce fissile material, achieving nuclear latency as I define it. Having a viable ENR program lessens the problem of delayed punishment in two ways: shortening the time to a bomb and signaling resolve to foreign audiences. Countries that have an active program to produce fissile material, then, have both the means to make a bomb and the political will to take some steps in that direction. This makes threats in weaponless deterrence easier to observe and more credible. On top of this, countries with ENR capabilities generally have more survivable nuclear programs, meaning that they are most difficult to destroy in a preventive attack.

One might consider any industrialized country a latent nuclear power, even if they presently lack the means to make fissile material. Switzerland, for example, could undoubtedly build a nuclear bomb quickly if it made a political decision to do so. With considerable financial resources at its disposal, Saudi Arabia probably could too. This is where the signaling value of an active ENR program becomes important.

Producing fissile material is analogous to a shot across the bow. It is a means through which countries force their counterparts to consider the possibility that they might go nuclear. When a country is producing fissile material, its bomb-making potential is staring foreign observers right in the face, making it clearer that deterrence by proliferation, delayed attack, or doubt could be on the table. By contrast, without an ENR program, the forms of punishment in latent deterrence are far less obvious and might be missed altogether. The CIA, for example, thought a Belgian bomb was a possibility in the 1950s when the country had an active reprocessing facility, but this seemed far-fetched after Belgium

[51] See, for example, Kahn (1985, 156), Ford (2011), and Schelling (1962).

shuttered this plant in the 1970s.[52] Countries interacting with Belgium in the 1950s, therefore, might have worried that their behavior, if it were seen as too threatening to officials in Brussels, could induce nuclear armament. This fear is essentially absent today because Belgium has not interjected its bomb-making potential into world politics by operating an ENR facility.

High stakes are a second factor that can mitigate the challenges in latent nuclear deterrence – specifically the high costs of threat implementation for the latent nuclear power. Because building (or using) nuclear weapons is costly, countries do not embark down this path on a whim. Instead, it would likely take a major national security threat to push a latent nuclear power over the line into the metaphorical end zone. It is believable that Iran might quickly weaponize its program if Israel or the United States launched a large-scale aerial assault or attempted to topple the regime of Ali Khamenei, the country's second Supreme Leader. However, it is more difficult to imagine Tehran going down this path in response to lower-level military actions, like sending drones over Iranian airspace. Threats to develop or use nuclear weapons are most believable when states are trying to deter high stakes crises and conflict. These threats may lack credibility when it comes to deterring lower-level threats that would not severely harm a country's national security were they to materialize.

The third solution is to demonstrate nuclear restraint. Launching an unrestrained program – one that is unambiguously intended to produce weapons – exacerbates the third challenge in latent nuclear deterrence. If countries see a latent nuclear power's production of bombs as inevitable, they are much more likely to take destabilizing countermeasures, like preventive military attacks and getting their own nuclear weapons. Moreover, an unrestrained program takes deterrence by proliferation off the table. A threat to build nuclear weapons cannot influence a country who believes that armament will occur regardless of how it behaves. Latent nuclear powers with unrestrained programs must therefore rely only on deterrence by delayed attack or doubt. By contrast, those with restrained programs preserve all three means of influence and mitigate the problem of inciting instability to some degree.

Many foreign governments believed that Iraq was bent on obtaining a bomb after Saddam Hussein became president in 1979. Baghdad's pursuit of nuclear latency therefore prompted a serious international backlash. Three different countries – Iran, Israel, and the United States – bombed Iraqi nuclear facilities from 1980 to 1991. And the United

[52] US Central Intelligence Agency (1958, 14).

States launched a war to overthrow Saddam Hussein and his Baathist regime in March 2003, in part, because Washington believed – wrongly, as it turned out – that Iraq was on the cusp of obtaining a nuclear bomb. In this kind of situation, an ENR program offers serious potential for international instability. However, latent nuclear powers such as Argentina, Australia, Germany, and Spain were able to stave off a serious international backlash by showing some restraint, even if they flirted with getting nuclear weapons and took some moves in that direction.

Yet having an unrestrained program is not entirely bad for an ENR-capable country hoping to gain international influence. This comes with an advantage: It strengthens deterrence by doubt and may eliminate, rather than just reduce, the time delay for imposing punishment in the eyes of other countries. Awareness that a country is actively trying to arm – not just building up the capability to do so, if necessary – and has the means to produce fissile material should make others more inclined to worry that it might be already have a bomb, potentially bolstering deterrence.

Research Strategy: Getting to the Truth

How do we know if latent nuclear deterrence theory is correct? The theory generates predictions about what countries think and how they should behave. It expects that successfully gaining influence without arms depends on three key factors: active ENR capabilities, stakes, and the level of nuclear restraint. Countries with restrained nuclear programs should gain international influence when they obtain ENR capabilities if the stakes are high enough to credibly threaten sufficient punishment costs. By contrast, countries with unrestrained nuclear programs may not reliably enhance their international influence when they obtain ENR capabilities, regardless of the stakes. These countries may actually increase their vulnerability to serious forms of international blowback, like preventive military attacks.

If the theory is true, we should also find evidence that world leaders believe that nuclear latency confers international influence. They should covet this capability when facing potential nuclear threats, seeing latent nuclear forces as a partial solution to insecurity. Countries should also actually attempt to use deterrence by proliferation, delayed attack, and doubt to gain influence over others. When it is tried, we should find at least some "smoking gun" evidence that the target countries were deterred by proliferation, delayed attack, or doubt.

I evaluate these expectations in several contexts that are central to international relations: technology diffusion, military conflict, international crises, foreign policy preferences, preventive war, and arms racing. The book takes a comprehensive look at the evidence, analyzing an abundance of quantitative and qualitative data. Relying on both kinds of evidence increases my confidence in the book's conclusions.

Using quantitative analysis, I strive to assess whether nuclear latency *causes* changes in foreign policy outcomes, not just whether there is an association between the two things. This is a challenging task. Nuclear latency arises due to strategic decisions made by governments, not random change. It is therefore possible that correlations we observe result from the factors that give rise to nuclear latency rather than latency itself. I address this by taking a design-based approach to causal inference.[53] My research strategy brings us closer to identifying the causal effects of nuclear latency compared to other published research.[54] However, when analyzing preventive military attacks and arms races, I rely on qualitative analysis due to the small number of cases.

The quantitative tests use an updated version of the Nuclear Latency (NL) dataset. This database, which I compiled with collaborators over a multiyear period, identifies all publicly known ENR facilities built globally from 1939 to 2012.[55] Based on the NL dataset, I identify the thirty-three latent nuclear powers shown in Table 0.1.

I use qualitative analysis to directly assess latent nuclear deterrence theory's causal logic. The book presents twenty case studies that are designed to determine whether world leaders actually think along the lines the theory expects. I examined beliefs about latent nuclear deterrence in ten countries, focusing on the views of presidents, prime ministers, and other senior-level government officials. I also conducted an in depth study of decision-making in four cases where leaders considered preventive military attacks to stop nuclear proliferation. In addition, I probed views about nuclear weapons proliferation and arms racing in six countries. To get inside of leaders' heads, I combed through publicly available sources including memoirs, press reports, and declassified documents. I also relied on oral history interviews carried out by other scholars and my own conversation with a former US Secretary of Defense.

---

[53] I use a procedure recently developed by political scientists Kosuke Imai, In Song Kim, and Erik Wang: difference-in-differences (DiD) with matching or weighting (2023). This procedure allows me to identify how a latent nuclear power's fortune changed after it developed nuclear latency compared to a hypothetical world where it remained nonlatent. In technical terms, I identify the average treatment effect on the treated, or ATT.

[54] For example, Fuhrmann and Tkach (2015) and Mehta and Whitlark (2017a).

[55] An earlier version of this database is described in Fuhrmann and Tkach (2015).

Overall, a deep examination of the historical record yields supporting evidence for latent nuclear deterrence theory. The theory does not explain every country's attitude or behavior at all points in time, and some unexpected findings emerge. Yet much of the evidence is broadly consistent with the theory.

Roadmap

The chapters that follow take a deeper dive on the arguments and evidence described here. Chapter 1 unpacks the logic of latent nuclear deterrence. It begins by describing the logic of deterrence and explaining why many scholars and policymakers see nuclear weapons as a valuable tool of international influence. The chapter then goes into detail about the mechanisms of weaponless deterrence, providing examples of all three forms in action. It overviews existing views on these forms of influence in scholarship, focusing on VNAs and a more pessimistic perspective that I call the weaponless instability school. An in-depth discussion of the challenges in latent nuclear deterrence follows, along with an articulation of the potential solutions. This chapter also lays out the implications of the theory for international peace and stability.

Chapter 2 presents the results of case studies designed to assess what world leaders think about latent nuclear deterrence. It serves as a plausibility probe, allowing us to evaluate whether the theory's basic claim has any merit. The chapter will show that leaders in a diverse set of countries – Argentina, Egypt, Iran, South Africa, Spain, and others – believe that having nuclear latency enhances a country's international influence. They do not always explain why they hold this view. Yet these leaders express views that are in line with all three means of influence in weaponless deterrence. Of the cases I examined, support for deterrence by proliferation appears in 80 percent, deterrence by delayed attack in 60 percent, and deterrence by doubt in 30 percent. The case studies show that leaders see these mechanisms as mutually reinforcing rather than competing.

Chapter 3 describes the NL dataset, which I use to analyze the causes and political effects of nuclear latency throughout the book. This chapter explains other approaches to measuring nuclear latency and why I focus on ENR capabilities. It also identifies all of the latent nuclear powers.

In Chapter 4, I assess the causes of nuclear latency adoption. What accounts for the emergence of ENR programs in some countries and not others? Statistical models reveal that two variables are most reliably correlated with the adoption of ENR programs: military capabilities and having a rival that is already nuclear-armed. A survey of countries' motives shows that many states seek ENR programs to shorten the time to a bomb, a strategy known as nuclear hedging.[56] These states see national security value in having latent nuclear forces. Yet many other factors contribute to the global spread of ENR technology. This includes a desire for greater international status and prestige, energy security, and financial gain. About one-third of all ENR-capable countries pursue this capability because they are bent on building bombs. For these states, nuclear latency is merely incidental, a temporary stop along the way on the path toward a full-blown nuclear arsenal.

The next three chapters present evidence about the political effects of nuclear latency. Chapter 5 uses a design-based approach to causal inference to assess how nuclear latency influences several foreign-policy outcomes: international crises, military disputes that result in fatalities, foreign-policy preferences among adversaries, and US troop deployments. Three main findings emerge. First, countries that develop large-scale ENR programs and exercise nuclear restraint accrue benefits in some – but not all – of the years that follow full nuclear latency onset. These countries see a reduction in crises during five of the ten years that follow latency onset. They also change their adversaries' foreign policy preferences the year after obtaining full nuclear latency, resulting in greater preference alignment. This effect persists for several years before eventually fading away. Allies of the United States also see a greater number of American troops on their soil after obtaining full latency, but this benefit takes several years to kick in. There is some evidence of a modest reduction in fatal disputes for fully latent states with restrained programs but this finding is fragile, partially due to low variation in the outcome. Second, among states with unrestrained nuclear programs, obtaining an ENR capability results in fewer benefits and greater risks. Third, partial nuclear latency has little effect on international peace and conflict compared to full nuclear latency.

These results underscore that the political effects of nuclear latency are nuanced. To have any hope of success at weaponless deterrence, states must obtain a sizable fissile material production capacity and avoid racing to a bomb. Even doing this, however, generates foreign-policy benefits only sometimes. Leaders are correct to think that nuclear latency can be beneficial, but it is hardly a panacea to the problem of insecurity.

Chapter 6 analyzes cases where countries considered and actually used military force to stop or delay nuclear proliferation. It shows that ENR-capable countries with restrained nuclear programs are less susceptible to preventive military action because they can engage in

---

[56] Levite (2002) and Narang (2017).

latent nuclear deterrence. Moreover, once a country is ENR-capable, it is more difficult to effectively roll back a country's nuclear program using military force. Countries that pair an unrestrained program with an ENR capability are much more likely to trigger consideration of preventive military strikes, providing additional evidence that this combination is destabilizing. Considered attacks are most likely to be carried out when an unrestrained target is in a pre-ENR stage. This situation describes Israel's attacks against Iraq's nuclear program from 1977 to 1981, Israel's bombing of Syria's nuclear reactor in 2007, and the American and British joint actions against Iraq's nuclear program after the 1991 Persian Gulf War.[57] When an unrestrained target obtains a fissile material production capability, weaponless deterrence – particularly deterrence by doubt – can dissuade attacks, making them less likely in that situation. On top of this, as noted above, rolling back a nuclear program becomes more difficult once a country is ENR-capable.

Chapter 7 turns our attention to nuclear weapons proliferation and arms races. When a latent nuclear power has one or more rivals with an ENR capability and no rivals with unrestrained programs, my analysis shows that they are less likely to arm. In that case, the possibility of inducing a rival's weaponization deters armament. However, these conditions held for just one of the thirty-three latent nuclear powers: Brazil. Without an ENR capability, attempts at deterrence by proliferation fail. When a country has one or more rivals with unrestrained programs, having an ENR-capable rival does not reduce the likelihood of nuclear armament. Instead, it increases it, generating an arms race. Third parties often complicate latent nuclear deterrence in this context. Many countries face potential nuclear threats from more than one country. If any one of a country's rivals has an unrestrained nuclear program, weaponless deterrence may fail. India, for example, wanted to match China's nuclear weapons capabilities after Beijing conducted its first nuclear test in 1964.[58] Therefore, Pakistan's attempts at deterrence by proliferation may have failed even if Islamabad had a restrained program and was ENR-capable prior to India's 1974 test. The stakes for a potential proliferator matter, too. Threats to build nuclear weapons carry weight in the presence of an interstate rivalry, as the target would clearly find this outcome undesirable, but become more feeble as bilateral relations warm.

---

[57] Officials in Washington and London believed Iraq to have an active ENR program after 1991, but this turned out not to be the case.

[58] This was mostly for status and prestige reasons rather than concerns about a Chinese nuclear attack or blackmail.

Chapter 8, the book's final chapter, synthesizes what we learned and explains why the findings matter. It identifies ten lessons about nuclear politics that emerge from the book's arguments and evidence. Some of these lessons pertain to the two big issues highlighted above: the prospects for nuclear disarmament and the future spread of nuclear weapons.

1   The Logic of Latent Nuclear
       Deterrence

On March 11, 1977, General Ivan Kukoč, a senior military commander in the former Yugoslavia, sent a message to other countries. "Yugoslavia has succeeded in developing a powerful industrial–technological research capacity that can basically meet the requirements of Yugoslavia's armed forces," General Kukoč said.[1] Yugoslavia had indeed been developing dual-use technology that provided the foundation for a nuclear weapons program. By 1966, it had nuclear reactors and a small plutonium reprocessing facility operating at its nuclear research institute in Vinca, a suburb of Belgrade.[2] These capabilities provided the potential to produce fissile material: the most essential ingredient for making a bomb.

If anyone launched an armed attack against his country, General Kukoč warned, Yugoslavia would arm with nuclear weapons and World War III would ensue. He made it clear, however, that other countries could prevent Yugoslavia from arming with nuclear weapons by maintaining peace. As the general put it, "Whether Yugoslavia will be forced . . . to start production of an atomic bomb depends least of all on Yugoslavia."[3]

This was a clear attempt to gain international influence by raising the prospect of nuclear weapons proliferation. Yugoslavia is hardly alone in following this blueprint. Over the past 75 years, many nonnuclear countries – Argentina, Iran, Germany, Spain, Taiwan, and others – have used their bomb-making potential to deter military threats and enhance political leverage internationally. I refer to this strategy as "latent nuclear deterrence" or "weaponless deterrence." Does it work?

To find out, we must first develop the logical foundations of latent nuclear deterrence. This chapter does just that. It starts by returning to the fundamentals of deterrence in world politics, explaining how it works and what it takes to succeed. I then explain why nuclear weapons

---

[1] Browne (1977).
[2] Potter et al. (2000).
[3] Browne (1977).

are an effective deterrent. However, having assembled nuclear weapons is not the only way to gain political leverage from a nuclear program. This chapter explains how countries can gain political benefits from their nuclear programs despite being unarmed. There are three mechanisms through which latent nuclear deterrence can work: proliferation, delayed attack, and doubt.

Many scholars are skeptical that these means of influence offer a path to greater security. Others see latent nuclear forces as an effective substitute for having assembled weapons. The reality is somewhere in the middle.

Nuclear latency offers a path to greater security, but one that is rife with obstacles. I develop latent nuclear deterrence theory in two parts. First, I describe three major challenges that make latent nuclear deterrence difficult. Second, I articulate three solutions that help countries overcome these challenges, increasing the likelihood of success. The end result is a theory that helps us understand when nuclear latency enhances international influence, and when it incites instability. The chapter closes by describing the predictions about international relations that follow from the theory. It tells us something about a diverse array of topics in international relations: technology diffusion, military conflict, foreign policy preferences, preventive war, nuclear armament, and arms races.

The Logic of Deterrence

This book is about international influence. At the broadest level, it examines one country's ability to alter another's behavior. I focus here on a narrower concept: deterrence. Scholars and policymakers sometimes use this term colloquially as a proxy for influence, but it has a specific meaning.

Deterrence is an exercise in political power. As the political scientist Glenn Snyder put it more than 60 years ago, deterrence is broadly "a process of influencing the enemy's *intentions*."[4] In deterrence, one actor (the defender) attempts to dissuade another (the challenger) from taking an unwanted action. The defender's goal is to preserve the status quo by altering how the challenger views the costs and benefits of its choices. The theory developed in this chapter has implications for a broad array of foreign policy outcomes, including some that may be intended to change – not preserve – the status quo.[5]

[4] Snyder (1961, 11).
[5] Attempts to change the status quo – for example, by annexing territory from a neighboring state – is usually called "compellence." Some of the outcomes studied in the book – especially foreign policy alignment and US troop deployments – straddle

Regular people experience deterrence on a daily basis. Homeowners can deter break-ins by installing security systems on their property. A spouse might help their partner maintain a difficult-to-keep diet by eliminating all foods from the refrigerator that are off limits to the dieter. Companies include requirements in their job ads in part to limit applications from those who are clearly unqualified. Parents might proactively seek to avoid embarrassing public outbursts by telling their toddlers that temper tantrums will result in the loss of their postdinner dessert. Police forces hope to deter people from driving too fast by issuing fines to speeders. Employees tend to show up to work on time, even when they would prefer to sleep in, since their bosses might fire them for repeated tardiness.

Deterrence is an essential feature of international relations, too. World leaders routinely seek to prevent their counterparts from taking threatening actions. Although deterrence operates in the nonmilitary sphere of world politics, in international-relations scholarship, it usually involves military force.[6] Leaders issue threats of military retaliation in order to deter another country from employing force in a threatening way.[7] Leaders may practice deterrence by issuing explicit verbal threats. They may tell their rivals, "if you take that action, which I find undesirable, I will respond in the following way." Yet leaders often communicate their intentions implicitly through military maneuvers, like troop deployments.

Consider a few examples. In the 1930s, France built defensive fortifications along its border, known as the *Maginot Line*, to stymie a potential German invasion.[8] The United States installed metal detectors in airports beginning in 1973, partially to dissuade terrorists from bringing weapons on planes. Since 2011, Israel has deployed a missile defense system called *Iron Dome* to intercept rockets fired from Hamas-controlled Gaza and elsewhere. After an Iraqi troop buildup along the border with Kuwait in October 1994, four years after Saddam Hussein's first invasion of the country, US Secretary of State Warren Christopher asserted that Iraq would pay a "horrendous price" if it attempted a second land grab.[9] During a crisis between Afghanistan and Iran in September 1998, a spokesman for the Taliban issued a deterrent threat:

---

the line between deterrence and compellence. On compellence, see Schelling (1960), Sechser (2011), Sechser and Fuhrmann (2017), and Volpe (2023).

[6] See Snyder (1961, 11) and Huth (1999, 26).

[7] For examples of scholarship that conceives of deterrence in this way, see Zagare and Kilgour (2000), Danilovic (2002), Leeds (2003), Sartori (2005), and Narang (2014).

[8] The *Maginot Line* was names after André Maginot, the French war minister.

[9] Gordon (1994).

"Iran must know that if the soil of Afghanistan is attacked, we will target Iranian cities and the entire responsibility will rest with Iranian authorities."[10] In August 2012, Barack Obama threatened to intervene in Syria's civil war if Bashar al Assad used chemical weapons: "That's a red line for us ... there would be enormous consequences if we start seeing movement on the chemical weapons front or the use of chemical weapons."[11]

The preceding examples reveal two distinct strategies of deterrence. First, defenders can manipulate the likelihood that challengers will obtain the benefits they seek. This strategy, which is commonly called deterrence by denial, is designed to threaten adversaries with failure.[12] The first three aforementioned examples from everyday life follow this logic. So do the *Maginot Line* and *Iron Dome*. A second strategy, deterrence by punishment, is to make it more costly for the challenger to change the status quo. Rather than making it physically more difficult for an actor to carry out a certain action, as in the denial case, this approach relies on inflicting pain on those who make undesirable decisions. The latter three examples from everyday life fall into this category, along with the threats from Secretary Christopher, the Taliban spokesman, and President Obama.

Successful deterrence – whether by denial or punishment – depends on three main requirements. First, a defender must have the capability to deny benefits or impose costs on challengers.[13] Second, there must be a nonzero probability that the defender would carry out its threat.[14] The third requirement is implicit in deterrence theory but is often not made explicit in scholarship.[15] A challenger must believe that it will not pay the costs associated with an attack if it maintains the status quo. Behind every threat is a promise. As economist Thomas Schelling put it, "To say, 'One more step and I shoot,' can be a deterrent threat only if accompanied by the implicit assurance, 'And if you stop I won't.'"[16]

---

[10] Muir (1998).

[11] Obama (2012).

[12] See Snyder (1961), Mearsheimer (1983), and Pape (1996).

[13] Zagare and Kilgour (2000, 290) call this the only condition that is "absolutely necessary" for deterrence success.

[14] The first two requirements work in tandem to shape deterrence outcomes. Whether the defender's threat is sufficient to dissuade an attack depends on the costs of attacking discounted by the probability that those costs will be imposed. Thus, low-likelihood threats may deter if the potential costs are high.

[15] Kydd and McManus (2017) is one relevant exception. See also Pauly (2019).

[16] Schelling (1966, 74).

Deterrence with Nuclear Weapons

Countries frequently invoke nuclear weapons to influence the behavior of their adversaries. During the Cold War, the United States depended on its nuclear arsenal to deter aggression by its enemies. As President Ronald Reagan explained to the American people in a televised address on March 23, 1983, "Since the dawn of the atomic age, we've sought to reduce the risk of war by maintaining a strong [nuclear] deterrent."[17] Nuclear weapons figured prominently in many Cold War episodes. Early in the Cold War period, Washington deployed tactical nuclear weapons to several European allies – Belgium, the Netherlands, West Germany, and others – to dissuade the Soviets from invading Western Europe.[18] During two crises with China in the Taiwan Strait during the 1950s, US officials threatened to use nuclear weapons if China invaded Taiwan. In 1955, after the United States conducted a series of tactical nuclear tests designed to intimidate China, Dwight D. Eisenhower warned Beijing not to invade, saying that you can use nuclear weapons "as you would use a bullet or anything else."[19] During the 1971 Indo-Pakistani War, Richard Nixon deployed the USS *Enterprise*, an aircraft carrier that contained nuclear weapons, to the Bay of Bengal. Nixon clarified the aim of this implicit nuclear threat in his memoirs: It was "a display of old-fashioned gunboat diplomacy aimed at India and Russia" warning them "not to attack West Pakistan."[20]

The Soviet Union similarly relied on nuclear weapons to restrain its adversaries and prevent undesirable changes to the status quo. After the Americans carried out nuclear attacks against Hiroshima and Nagasaki in August 1945, Soviet dictator Josef Stalin reportedly told those in charge of Moscow's atom bomb project, "The equilibrium has been destroyed. Provide the bomb – it will remove a great danger from us."[21] The Soviet Union obtained nuclear weapons four years later, thereby reducing its perceived vulnerability to American aggression. In addition to protecting its homeland and the territorial integrity of its Warsaw Pact allies, Moscow used its nuclear arsenal as a means of influence in Cold War crises. Soviet leader Nikita Khrushchev placed nuclear forces in Cuba in 1962, for example, in part to deter a US invasion of the island, an action that precipitated the Cuban missile crisis. The Soviet Union also relied on its arsenal to limit military escalation in the 1969 border

---

[17] Reagan (1983).
[18] See Fuhrmann and Sechser (2014).
[19] Quoted in Betts (1987, 59). See also Sechser and Fuhrmann (2017, 190).
[20] Quoted in Black (2010, 21).
[21] Quoted in Holloway (1981, 183).

crisis with China. A Soviet official conveyed an ominous warning to his American counterpart: "[we] would not hesitate to use nuclear weapons against the Chinese if they attacked with major forces."[22] In addition, the Soviets increased the combat readiness of their nuclear rocket forces during the 1968 invasion of Czechoslovakia, the 1973 Yom Kippur War, and in moments of tension with the United States from 1982 to 1984.[23]

Nuclear deterrence remains a key feature of world politics thirty-plus years after the collapse of the Soviet Union. Since their reciprocal nuclear tests in May 1998, India and Pakistan have each issued nuclear threats in order to deter military aggression. A Pakistani official told the *Financial Times* in January 2017, for instance, "If ever our national security is threatened by advancing foreign forces, Pakistan will use all of its weapons – and I mean all of our weapons – to defend our country."[24] Russian President Vladimir Putin was prepared to put nuclear forces on alert in order to deter Western intervention following his annexation of Crimea – territory that had previously belonged to Ukraine – in March 2014.[25] Putin went further with his nuclear threat-making after Russia's full-scale invasion of Ukraine in February 2022. If anyone "stands in our way," he said, "they must know that Russia will respond immediately, and the consequences will be such as you have never seen in your entire history."[26] Donald Trump and Kim Jong Un exchanged nuclear threats prior to their June 2018 summit meeting in Singapore. In August 2017, Trump threatened to inflict "fire and fury like the world has never seen" on North Korea if it threatened the United States. Four months later, Kim warned Trump not to invade his country: "It's not a mere threat but a reality that I have a nuclear button on the desk in my office," adding, "All of the mainland United States is within the range of our nuclear strike."[27]

Why Nuclear Deterrence Is Effective

Nuclear weapons are widely viewed as effective deterrents. Many scholars have argued that nuclear weapons prevented major power war after 1945.[28] This view is pervasive among world leaders as well. Khrushchev

---

[22] US Department of State (2001). For a more complete discussion of Soviet nuclear signaling during this crisis, see Sechser and Fuhrmann (2017, 210–218).

[23] Blair (1993, 25–26).

[24] Stacey and Bokhari (2017).

[25] MacFarquhar (2015).

[26] Quoted in Cirincione (2023).

[27] Quoted in Sang-Hun (2017).

[28] See especially Gaddis (1986) and Jervis (1989).

believed that the Soviet Union's nuclear arsenal made a US-backed attack virtually impossible: "our enemies probably feared us as much as we feared them," he wrote in his memoirs, "they had to to respect our borders and our rights, and ... they couldn't get what they wanted by force or by blackmail."[29] Western leaders similarly believed that nuclear weapons prevented the Cold War from turning hot. This is exemplified by Winston Churchill's famous proclamation, in his last major speech before parliament in 1955, that we "have reached a stage in this story where safety will be the sturdy child of terror, and survival the twin brother of annihilation."[30] Belief in the deterrent value of nuclear weapons is hardly anachronistic. Obama, who called for the eventual elimination of nuclear weapons, also acknowledged the potential for nuclear weapons to bring peace and stability. His administration's *Nuclear Posture Review* stated that US nuclear weapons "will continue to play an essential role in deterring potential adversaries" as long as they exist.[31]

This military technology bolsters deterrence because it greatly enhances a state's capability to deny benefits or impose costs on aggressors. Nuclear weapons, particularly small tactical weapons, are potentially useful for military denial: They can blunt invasions by swiftly killing many advancing forces and rendering land impenetrable due to radioactive contamination.[32] The biggest feature of nuclear weapons from a deterrence standpoint, however, is their unique ability to inflict pain. With nuclear weapons, entire cities could be eviscerated in a matter of minutes. An airburst of a nuclear weapon the size of the *Little Boy* bomb the United States dropped on Hiroshima (15 kilotons) above Houston – the fourth largest US city – would kill an estimated 83,800 people and leave another 69,130 injured. The *Little Boy* bomb is small by today's standards. If we increase the yield to 1.2 megatons – the size of the B-83, the largest bomb currently in the US arsenal – the estimated number of people killed in Houston spikes dramatically to 355,890.[33] To put these figures in perspective, about 3,000 Americans died in the al

---

[29] Quoted in Holloway (1994, 343).

[30] Churchill (1955).

[31] US Department of Defense (2010).

[32] The United States deployed tactical nuclear weapons to Europe in large part for this reason. Weapon systems such as the *Davy Crockett*, which had a maximum firing range of about two-and-a-half miles and weighed less than 100 pounds, could be fired on advancing Soviet or Warsaw Pact troops if they attempted an invasion, while limiting the damage to civilians due to their relatively small explosive yield. The yield was 20 tons TNT, less powerful by a factor of 750 than the Hiroshima bomb.

[33] These calculations are based on the NUKEMAP simulator developed by the historian Alex Wellerstein, which is available at https://nuclearsecrecy.com/nukemap/.

Qaeda-orchestrated 9/11 attacks. Human casualties aside, large portions of the city would be destroyed and littered with radioactive fallout.

The ability of nuclear weapons swiftly to wipe cities off the map is unparalleled, giving them unique value for deterrence by punishment. The prospect of catastrophic retaliatory action forces potential aggressors to think twice before attacking nuclear powers. However, countries armed with nuclear arsenals are hardly invulnerable. In 1968, North Korea seized the USS *Pueblo* and its crew. Egyptian and Syrian forces mounted an attack against Israel in 1973, leading to the Yom Kippur War. Argentina attempted to wrest the Falkland Islands from the United Kingdom in 1982. And Pakistan instigated the 1999 Kargil War with India. How could nuclear deterrence fail, given the destructive power of atomic bombs?

The answer has to do with credibility. It is difficult for countries to make nuclear threats believable because carrying out a nuclear strike would be costly for the defender, in addition to the country that it attacks. If the challenger is also a nuclear power, launching a nuclear attack in response to conventional aggression could be suicidal. Using nuclear weapons would also invite substantial political blowback, lead to international isolation, set a dangerous precedent, and shatter the longstanding taboo against nuclear use.[34] Nuclear use, therefore, would be costly even against a nonnuclear state. As Newt Gingrich, the conservative Congressman from Georgia who would later become House speaker, put it in 1991 during a debate about the possible use of nuclear weapons against Iraq during the Persian Gulf War: If the United States were to "establish a pattern out there that it is legitimate to use those kinds of weapons, our children and grandchildren are going to rue the day."[35]

In light of these costs, countries will most likely resort to nuclear use only in dire circumstances. As President Kennedy put it when thinking about the dispute with the Soviet Union over the status of Berlin in 1961, "If I'm going to threaten Russia with a nuclear war, it will have to be for much bigger and more important reasons than that [access to Berlin]. Before I back Khrushchev against the wall and put him to a final test, the freedom of all Western Europe will have to be at stake."[36] Threats to carry out nuclear strikes in retaliation for the occupation of disputed islands located thousands of miles from the homeland or the seizure of a

---

[34] For an in depth discussion of the nuclear taboo, see Tannenwald (2007). Sechser and Fuhrmann (2017) provide a broad discussion about the costs of using nuclear weapons in pursuit of coercive goals.

[35] Quoted in Bundy (1991, 86).

[36] Quoted in Beschloss (1991).

small amount of land that the defender could live without, by contrast, would be easier to dismiss.

Defenders can manipulate how challengers view the credibility of their nuclear threats. A central question for deterrence theorists during the Cold War was how the United States or the Soviet Union could use their arsenals for political leverage in a world of mutually assured destruction (MAD), particularly when it came to defending peripheral interests.[37] This problem gave rise to brinkmanship theory – the idea that states can make seemingly incredible threats believable by taking dangerous actions that raise the risk of mutual disaster.[38] In brinkmanship, a leader's goal is to convince the adversary that nuclear weapons might be used even if the leader seemingly lacks the resolve (or the ability) to order an attack. A leader can do this by reducing their control over nuclear launch decisions. A nuclear alert, for instance, may give launch authority to pilots or local military commanders, increasing the odds of a launch due to an accident or miscalculation. The United States alerted its nuclear forces during the Cuban missile crisis, ultimately going to DEFCON 2 for the first and only time in its history. This contributed to a sense among both Kennedy and Khrushchev that they were losing control of events, which increased the believability of the US nuclear threat.[39]

In many deterrence contexts, successful reassurance can be difficult. This is not so when it comes to deterrence with nuclear weapons. It is unlikely that a country would suffer an unprovoked nuclear attack. A country may turn to nuclear use in extreme contingencies, especially if it has been invaded. Yet a nuclear strike is unlikely in peacetime. Russia might say to the United States "we will use nuclear weapons if you seize Kaliningrad" (a noncontiguous part of Russia that borders Poland and Lithuania). The United States is unlikely to fear that it will suffer a nuclear attack if it does not invade. Russia's hypothetical threat may still fail, but this probably would not be because Washington felt that it was going to incur the threatened punishment anyway. Accidental or unauthorized nuclear use may occur, raising the possibility of vulnerability to a peacetime strike. To be sure, as I will discuss momentarily, countries worry about this kind of thing. In traditional nuclear deterrence, though, the third requirement poses less of a challenge than the first two.

---

[37] See, for example, Powell (1990).

[38] Schelling (1966).

[39] History shows, however, that countries struggle to make nuclear threats credible when they pursue ambitious foreign policy goals beyond deterring major attacks – even when they engage in brinkmanship. See Sechser and Fuhrmann (2017).

How Latent Nuclear Deterrence Works: Unpacking the Mechanisms

The vast scholarship on nuclear deterrence typically leaves one with the impression that assembled warheads are necessary to reap political benefits. This may not be the case. There are three ways in which countries could use nonweaponized nuclear programs to reap political benefits. I call these means of influence deterrence by proliferation, deterrence by delayed attack, and deterrence by doubt. Although these mechanisms are analytically distinct, it can be difficult to separate them in practice. As we will see throughout this book, countries sometimes employ more than one of these strategies at the same time in order to advance their interests.

All three forms of influence involve nonnuclear countries using the possibility of future weaponization to gain international leverage. They are distinct from traditional nuclear deterrence because the defender is not already nuclear-armed. As shown in Table 1.1, these mechanisms vary along two dimensions: the means of inflicting pain and whether there is a delay in the imposition of punishment.

When it comes to punishment, defenders threaten to carry out retaliatory nuclear attacks in deterrence by delayed attack and doubt. In these two means of influence, then, the threatened punishment is the same as in traditional nuclear deterrence. The threat is a less severe one in deterrence by proliferation: to possess nuclear weapons without actually using them in an armed attack.

Delayed punishment is a certainty in deterrence by proliferation and delayed attack, meaning that countries will not be unable to inflict pain immediately after a challenge to the status quo. In deterrence by doubt, by contrast, potential challengers have uncertainty about whether there would be a delay. This is because defenders attempt to create the impression that they *might* have nuclear weapons even though they are, in fact, nonnuclear.[40]

Given these differences, the three means of influence vary in their capacity to meet the basic requirements for deterrence success. In deterrence by proliferation the threat is easier to make credible but carries less bite because the punishment costs are smaller. On top of this, reassurance can pose a major challenge. The punishment costs are greater in the other two means of influence but the threats are more difficult to make believable, and reassurance is a less thorny problem.

---

[40] Countries can also generate doubt about their capabilities when they have assembled one or more nuclear bombs, as Israel has done since 1967. As described shortly, however, I do not treat these cases as latent nuclear deterrence.

Table 1.1 *Comparing the mechanisms of latent nuclear deterrence.*

Mechanism	Punishment delay?	Means of punishment
Proliferation	Yes	Weapons possession
Delayed attack	Yes	Nuclear attack
Doubt	Maybe	Nuclear attack

However, all three mechanisms potentially offer countries a path to greater international influence.

Deterrence by Proliferation

In deterrence by proliferation, countries threaten to build nuclear weapons if another state challenges the status quo. This is a nontraditional form of punishment because it does not involve physical destruction. Yet policymakers and analysts think about the mere possession of nuclear weapons as a means of retaliation in international relations. For example, in January 2020, after the United States killed Iranian General Qasem Soleimani in a drone strike, some observers worried that Iran would punish the United States by marching toward a nuclear weapon. As US Senator Lindsey Graham said, Iran would probably retaliate by making "a dramatic escalation in their enrichment program." He added, "a race for a bomb is the most likely thing they will do," to punish Washington.[41]

Arming with nuclear weapons, or taking steps in that direction, can be a viable form of punishment because many countries find the international spread of nuclear weapons undesirable. For starters, one state's development of nuclear weapons can harm others' foreign policy interests. Nuclear weapons proliferation limits a state's freedom of action militarily.[42] For example, the United States might find it desirable to depose North Korean leader Kim Jong Un at some point in the future but the country's possession of a nuclear arsenal would make implementing this policy exceedingly risky. By contrast, when an adversary does not possess nuclear weapons, the United States has more flexibility when considering invasions, foreign imposed regime changes, or other offensive military operations, as the cases of Iraq (2003) and Libya (2011) illustrate. In addition, nuclear powers might

[41] Quoted in Rogin (2020).
[42] Kroenig (2010, 2014a).

be emboldened to take greater foreign policy risks after they obtain an arsenal, thereby making other states more susceptible to military conflict.[43]

Nuclear weapons proliferation also forces other countries to live in a state of vulnerability. The spread of nuclear weapons increases the possibility that they could be used as a result of accidents, unauthorized launches, or false alarms.[44] In addition, leaders may pay a domestic political price for an adversary's obtainment of nuclear weapons. Armament by a rival could cause the public to view their leader as inept in foreign policy, especially if he or she is responsible for stoking the adversary's nuclear program. At the very least, nuclear weapons proliferation is likely to generate criticism from domestic political opponents. For example, during the 2008 presidential campaign, then-candidate Barack Obama blamed the Bush administration for fueling North Korea's nuclear program. After highlighting Bush's aggressive actions toward Pyongyang, Obama said, "And you know what happened? They went – they quadrupled their nuclear capacity. They tested a nuke. They tested missiles. They pulled out of the nonproliferation agreement [the NPT]."[45]

Given these costs, it is not surprising that many world leaders have voiced strong opposition to other countries getting nuclear weapons.[46] For example, John F. Kennedy thought that China's acquisition of nuclear weapons was likely to be, as one of his advisers put it, "the most significant and worst event of the 1960s."[47] More recently, Donald Trump understood that Iranian weaponization would be politically costly for him. He went out of his way to assert that this would not happen: "As long as I am President of the United States," he said as his

---

[43] See Bell (2015) for a detailed discussion of emboldenment in the context of nuclear proliferation. If nuclear weapons increase a country's coercive bargaining power, states might be forced to make costly concessions following an adversary's acquisition of nuclear forces. Whether nuclear weapons are useful for coercion – as opposed to deterrence – is still debated in scholarship. See, for example, Beardsley and Asal (2009b), Sechser and Fuhrmann (2017), and Kroenig (2013). Regardless of the reality, policymakers worry about nuclear blackmail.

[44] Sagan (1993) provides a classic discussion of this issue.

[45] Obama's remarks, which were made during his first presidential debate with John McCain on September 26 (2008).

[46] The United States and the Soviet Union cooperated during the Cold War to create a nonproliferation regime backed by the 1970 nuclear Nonproliferation Treaty (NPT). See Coe and Vaynman (2015).

[47] The quotation is from Walt Rostow and is quoted in Burr and Richelson (2000/2001, 61).

opening remarks in an address to the nation on January 8, 2020, "Iran will never be allowed to have a nuclear weapon."[48]

The defender in deterrence by proliferation exploits international opposition to nuclear armament in hope of gaining international leverage. This strategy is commonplace in international relations. In 1974, for example, Mohammad Reza Pahlavi, the Shah of Iran, reportedly boasted that his country will have nuclear weapons "without any doubt, and sooner than one might think." This statement did not necessarily reveal the Shah's determination to build nuclear weapons as quickly as possible, although some Western press reports interpreted it in this way. Instead, his remarks were a threat aimed at other potential proliferators. As the Shah put it, if "each country attempts to arm itself with with [sic] atmic [sic] weapons, maybe the interest of each requires that it arm itself."[49] Richard Helms, then US ambassador to Iran, understood the Shah's strategy: "the Shah wished to signal his concern about further proliferation," Helms wrote in a then-confidential cable, "and indicate that Iran could not stand idly by if other nations like Israel of [sic] Egypt should go nuclear."[50]

Egypt's Gamal Abdel Nasser pursued a similar strategy. In 1961, he declared, "we will secure atomic weapons at any costs" if Israel builds nuclear weapons.[51] Nasser, like the Shah, hoped to keep a rival nonnuclear by threatening to follow suit if the rival armed. There was an implicit promise behind each of these threats: "if you don't build nuclear weapons, neither will I."

In the preceding examples, the defenders made verbal threats. Yet deterrence by proliferation can operate in the absence of explicit rhetoric. Leaders may prefer to be subtle when making proliferation threats, since raising the specter of nuclear proliferation can be politically and diplomatically costly. Deeds can convey deterrent threats without words, as noted earlier. Mobilizing troops or deploying naval assets can communicate a willingness to fight even if a leader never says anything like "if you threaten me, I will attack you." Similarly, developing certain nuclear technologies can be sufficient to convey a proliferation threat, as I will discuss in more detail later in the chapter.

---

[48] The full text of Trump's address is available at www.whitehouse.gov/briefings-statements/remarks-president-trump-iran/.
[49] The Shah is quoted in a telegram written by Helms (1974a).
[50] Helms (1974b).
[51] Quoted in Solingen (2007, 239).

Deterrence by Delayed Attack

In the first means of influence, deterrence by proliferation, countries attempt to gain leverage over their adversaries by threatening to obtain nuclear weapons if they experience threats. Deterrence by delayed attack takes things one step further: A defender threatens to quickly assemble at least one nuclear bomb and then use it in a counterattack against the challenger. This type of latent nuclear deterrence works like traditional deterrence, except there is a delay between the challenger's action and the defender's response. The defender must convert its nonweaponized nuclear program into at least one deliverable bomb. Once it has a bomb, the defender can use it in a military attack against the challenger to deny benefits or inflict pain. The ultimate response – a nuclear retaliatory attack – could come days, months, or even a few years after the initial act of aggression.

Nuclear weapons are generally seen as a weapon of last resort. They are most likely to enter the picture if a nuclear power becomes embroiled in a long slog and realizes that its conventional capabilities alone are insufficient to prevent a crushing defeat. In this kind of situation, there is a time gap between the opening salvo of a conflict and the moment in which countries seriously consider nuclear use.[52] The first real US attempt to invoke nuclear weapons during the Vietnam War – President Nixon's October 1969 nuclear alert – occurred about four years after the first American combat forces entered the fray. A time gap such as this creates an opportunity for a nonnuclear defender to weaponize its previously latent nuclear capabilities.

According to the logic of deterrence by delayed attack, potential challengers anticipate this possibility and may exercise restraint as a result. As far as the challenger is concerned, nuclear retaliation does not have to be immediate in order to be effective. As long as it believes that it will – or *could* – suffer a nuclear attack in response to its aggression, it may think twice about provoking war. Given the severity of the consequences, potential attackers are likely to find little solace in the nonimmediacy of the nuclear response. Like in deterrence by proliferation, explicit threats are not necessary to threaten delayed nuclear retaliation.[53] Having the underlying technological capacity to make a bomb sends an implicit warning to potential aggressors. Explicit threats do occur, as the following discussion will make clear, but they are rare since raising the possibility of a nuclear attack could invite blowback for the threat-maker.

[52] Paul (2000, 59) makes a similar argument.
[53] Hagerty (1995, 90) makes a similar argument.

The case of Japan provides a fitting illustration of deterrence by delayed attack in action. Japan has ratified the nuclear Nonproliferation Treaty (NPT) and subjects its nuclear facilities to inspections by the International Atomic Energy Agency (IAEA). No credible analyst believes that Japan currently possesses (or might possess) nuclear weapons. Everyone understands, though, that Tokyo could obtain at least a crude nuclear explosive device quickly – within one year, according to a 1999 assessment by the US Defense Intelligence Agency.[54] If Japan experienced a serious crisis with a country such as China or North Korea, Tokyo could weaponize its nuclear program in relatively short order. Once it is in possession of a bomb, assuming that the conflict escalates, Japan could deliver a nuclear blow. The risk of inviting a nuclear retaliatory strike, albeit a delayed one, might induce caution among Japan's rivals. It may be prudent, therefore, for China and North Korea to treat Japan as if it were a nuclear-armed country, even though Tokyo's program is currently nonweaponized.

Deterrence by Doubt

The perception that a country might already have a crude nuclear arsenal – not just the means to obtain one quickly – may also bolster deterrence. Obtaining a complete picture of another country's nuclear activities is difficult because states often shroud their nuclear programs in secrecy. The dual-use nature of nuclear technology also makes it hard to decipher a country's intentions, since the same plants could be used to produce energy or make bombs. As a result, when a nonnuclear country gets close to a bomb (but does not actually build one), others might fear that it could be nuclear-armed. This fear could induce restraint, as a military challenge could prompt near-immediate nuclear retaliation. Economists Sandeep Baliga and Tomas Sjöström call this strategy "deterrence by doubt."[55]

The distinguishing feature of deterrence by doubt is that potential challengers have uncertainty about the country's existing nuclear capabilities. When it comes to deterrence by delayed attack, challengers know that a country is nonnuclear but could arm itself at some point in the

---

[54] Quoted in Fitzpatrick (2016). Some analysts think that two years might be a more reasonable estimate. Others suggest that the time frame is less than six months.

[55] Baliga and Sjöström (2018, 1024, 1035). The phrase "deterrence by doubt" originally appeared in Gordon and Trainor (2006, 65). Their game theoretic model shows that unarmed countries have incentives to maintain ambiguity about their capabilities in order to deter attacks. Armed states also have incentives to maintain ambiguity, according to their model.

future. In traditional nuclear deterrence, everyone knows that a country is already equipped with nuclear weapons. Potential challengers could perceive either outcome in deterrence by doubt; they could conceivably think that their counterpart is nuclear-armed *or* nonnuclear.

The Persian Gulf War illustrates how deterrence by doubt may work in practice. On August 2, 1990, Iraq invaded Kuwait. Within one week, Saddam Hussein fully controlled his oil-rich neighbor. Not long after, President George H. W. Bush made it clear that Iraq must reverse its land grab or face war with the United States: "The message is steady, strong, and certain," he said in a speech on September 18, "Iraq's act of aggression will not stand."[56] Despite Bush's warning, the Iraqi dictator refused to back down. As a result, on January 17, 1991, the United States, backed by a broad international coalition, began airstrikes against Iraq. After pummeling Iraqi targets from the air for five weeks, the US-backed coalition prepared to launch a ground war to expel Iraqi forces from Kuwait.

As the ground campaign approached, Iraq's nuclear program weighed on the mind of US officials. General Norman Schwarzkopf, the head of US Central Command who was then leading all coalition forces, feared that Baghdad might be in possession of a nuclear bomb. Schwarzkopf wondered: Might Iraq be planning to use a nuclear device against his forces as they marched across the desert?[57] Colin Powell, then Chairman of the Joint Chiefs of Staff, also pondered Iraq's nuclear potential during the crisis. He later wrote that "Saddam's feverish drive for nuclear capability" was "hanging like a specter over the desert" as the United States prepared for war.[58]

These concerns were justified. Saddam launched a crash program in August 1990, immediately after invading Kuwait, to obtain a crude nuclear device as quickly as possible. Baghdad hoped to have its first weapon by April 1991.[59] This was an ambitious timeline but not an inconceivable one given that Iraq had spent much of the previous decade building up its nuclear infrastructure. The possibility of Iraqi nuclear use, then, was not necessarily off the table even though Baghdad was nonnuclear at the start of the Persian Gulf crisis. The crash program ultimately failed. The American-backed coalition launched a ground war on February 24 and Bush declared Kuwait fully liberated four days

---

[56] Bush (1991, 1253).
[57] Gordon and Trainor (1995, 337).
[58] Powell (1995, 480).
[59] Crossette (1995).

later.[60] Nevertheless, Iraq was able to insert its nuclear capabilities into world politics despite never possessing a bomb.

Countries can also generate doubt about their capabilities after they have assembled one or more nuclear weapons. The most prominent example is Israel; the country has maintained a policy of "opacity," meaning that it refuses to confirm that it has a bomb but does not deny this possibility either.[61] Virtually everyone knows, however, that Israel is a nuclear power and countries have treated it as such for decades. Israel therefore more closely resembles a traditional nuclear weapons state after 1967, when it was widely believed to have assembled its first bomb, than it does a latent nuclear power. When I refer to deterrence by doubt, then, my focus is exclusively on countries that have not assembled a bomb.[62]

Existing Views

Does deterrence by proliferation, delayed attack, or doubt work? Most scholarship on nuclear deterrence does not seriously consider the possibility that nonweaponized programs could provide countries with strategic benefits.[63] However, some scholars, policymakers, and journalists have previously commented on the efficacy of latent nuclear deterrence. I divide existing perspectives into two camps: One suggests that a breakout nuclear capability can deter aggression, while the other is much more skeptical.

Virtual Nuclear Arsenals

In his 1984 book *The Abolition*, the disarmament advocate Jonathan Schell made a forceful argument in favor of weaponless deterrence.[64] Schell was a strong critic of nuclear weapons: "[they] are truly an evil obsession," he wrote, "They degrade us. They soil us."[65] He sought a world in which atomic arsenals were a less salient feature of world politics. His idea for achieving this vision – weaponless deterrence –

---

[60] Iraq was therefore defeated several weeks prior to its target date for a bomb. Even if the war had persisted for several more months, though, it is unclear whether Iraq would have obtained a nuclear weapon.

[61] Cohen (1998).

[62] In addition to being more theoretically appropriate, this offers an empirical advantage as well by providing a more accurate estimate of the political effects of latent nuclear forces. Treating a case like Israel after 1967 as "latent" would probably make it easier to find evidence in favor of weaponless deterrence.

[63] See, for example, Jervis (1989), Powell (1990), Glaser (1990), and Narang (2014).

[64] Schell (1984).

[65] Schell (1984, 163).

was an arms control proposal: Nuclear powers would dismantle their warheads but retain the capacity to reconstitute their arsenals. In the event of war, countries such as the United States could quickly rearm, putting themselves in a position to retaliate with nuclear strikes. This was an early articulation of what I call deterrence by delayed attack.

For Schell, weaponless deterrence was akin to having your cake and eating it too: The risk of nuclear war due to miscalculation or an accident would decline, since no state would possess operational warheads, but countries could still reap the benefits of nuclear deterrence by rearming quickly in the event of aggression. Indeed, he believed that weaponless deterrence could effectively substitute for traditional nuclear deterrence:

The difference between our present world and a nuclear-weapon-free world would be only that people had all learned to see a few steps farther ahead than they do now – as though the chess players, having gained in experience, were to call of their game four moves before checkmate rather than two. Every statesman would see, just as he does today, that aggression leads inevitably to annihilation, and would feel no need to test the proposition in action.[66]

Subsequent writing characterized this form of deterrence as a system of virtual nuclear arsenals (VNAs).[67] The idea of VNAs gained traction after the collapse of the Soviet Union, when people began to rethink the role of nuclear weapons in world politics. In a 1997 book that built on Schell's initial concept, Michael Mazarr concluded that a system of VNAs "offers enormous potential" in part because it provides "a promising means of dramatically reducing the danger to humanity posed by nuclear weapons."[68]

The Weaponless Instability School

Many scholars who have taken up the notion of latent nuclear deterrence are skeptical that it is effective. Kenneth Waltz, one of the leading international relations theorists of his generation, was a prominent critic of weaponless deterrence.[69] He did not believe that countries could deter security threats with mere latent nuclear capabilities, and he argued that breakout capacity alone would simply invite instability. The strategist Colin Gray echoes this view, calling the idea of a latent deterrent "appallingly poor." "The idea of virtual nuclear arsenals,"

[66] Schell (1984, 124–125).
[67] Mazarr (1995a, 1997b), Holdren (1997), Perkovich and Acton (2008), and Drell and Goodby (2009).
[68] Mazarr (1997b, 390).
[69] Waltz (1997).

he wrote, "is such a bad one that even many among the Western opinion leaders who routinely will endorse propositions for policy that staple together disarmament, anti-nuclear action, and clever-sounding theory are unlikely to be seduced."[70] The political scientists Rupal Mehta and Rachel Whitlark, who have conducted some of the most recent analyses on latent nuclear deterrence, reached broadly similar conclusions. "[Nuclear] latency does not broadly function as a substitute for the deterrent effects of an operational nuclear arsenal," they wrote, adding that "latency by itself provides few security benefits."[71]

Skeptical views such as these represent a line of thinking that I call the weaponless instability school. Scholars in this camp often argue that latent nuclear capabilities pale in comparison to full-blown nuclear arsenals when it comes to deterrence.[72] The lion's share of commentary on latent nuclear deterrence in scholarship has occurred in the context of the debate over VNAs. Weaponless deterrence, therefore, has become intimately associated with nuclear disarmament. Pushback against latent nuclear deterrence often comes from people who oppose the elimination of nuclear weapons. In their view, nuclear weapons have brought substantial stability to the international system and latent nuclear capabilities cannot serve as effective substitutes for ready-to-launch missiles. Christopher Ford, who served as US Assistant Secretary of State for International Security and Non-Proliferation, aptly characterized this perspective in a 2010 essay: "When it comes to nuclear sabre-rattling, after all, weapons-in-being surely must be considered to trump merely potential weapons."[73]

What's Missing?

On the question of whether latent nuclear deterrence works, the jury is still out. Fortunately, our understanding of how nuclear energy programs influence armed conflict and international bargaining is growing.[74] Yet three factors have stymied our ability to fully assess the virtues and limitations of latent nuclear deterrence.

---

[70] Gray (1999, 117).

[71] Mehta and Whitlark (2017a, 526).

[72] The weaponless instability school also suggests that latent nuclear forces can encourage military conflict and catalyze arms races. To be sure, the potential to incite instability is one of the fundamental problems of latent nuclear deterrence, which I will address in detail later in this chapter.

[73] Ford (2011, 19).

[74] See Horowitz (2013), Fuhrmann and Tkach (2015), and Mehta and Whitlark (2017a), and Volpe (2017).

First, as noted previously, few scholars have taken the notion of latent nuclear deterrence seriously. Scholars and policymakers have obsessed about the requirements of nuclear deterrence for more than seventy years. Yet most people have ignored the possibility that states could engage in nuclear deterrence without possessing intact weapons. As Brad Roberts, who served as the Obama administration's Policy Director for its Nuclear Posture Review, put it, "The existence of a tier of states technically capable of making weapons offering them significant military options in war and political leverage in peace is hardly noticed by political scientists or policymakers."[75]

We therefore lack a clear sense of what it takes to gain influence from nuclear latency.[76] Mazarr, a leading proponent of VNAs, acknowledged this point in a 1997 essay: "the concept [of a VNA] remains at such a rudimentary stage of analytical development," he argued, "that no final case for it can yet be made."[77] Although this statement was written more than twenty-five years ago, it still rings true today.

Two of the most recent attempts to spell out the logic of latent nuclear deterrence each devote fewer than 500 words to explaining how and why weaponless deterrence might work.[78] These studies, along with others assessing whether latent nuclear deterrence works, assume that the answer is yes or no. In fact, however, the answer is more complicated: Sometimes latent nuclear deterrence works while it clearly fails on other occasions. There is undoubtedly some truth to the claims made by the weaponless instability school. It is also likely that countries benefit in some ways from having a nonweaponized nuclear program. We are missing a comprehensive account of the conditions under which latent nuclear deterrence is successful.

Second, much of the thinking about this subject addresses one specific context: where all countries have disassembled their nuclear weapons but could rebuild warheads quickly. Latent nuclear deterrence has therefore become closely associated with nuclear disarmament. Few scholars have seriously considered the possibility that nuclear latency could provide deterrence benefits when nuclear weapons are operationally deployed by some countries. The framing of the debate up to this point has allowed critics to dismiss VNAs on the grounds that latent nuclear deterrence does not work as well as deterrence with bombs. Even if this claim

[75] Roberts (1997, 264).
[76] The literature discusses several key challenges of weaponless deterrence, including verification and the survivability of latent nuclear forces (Mazarr, 1997c). But a complete theory is missing.
[77] Mazarr (1997b, 369).
[78] Fuhrmann and Tkach (2015) and Mehta and Whitlark (2017a).

is true, it does not mean that nuclear latency carries no deterrence benefits at all. In the world today – where nine countries possess nuclear arms – countries such as Iran and Japan seem to believe that their nuclear programs confer deterrence benefits, even though they have not assembled bombs. We know very little about whether these beliefs have merit.

Third, the debate about latent nuclear deterrence is largely devoid of evidence. Weaponless deterrence, as it is discussed by Schell and others, is fundamentally about a hypothetical world in which nuclear weapons are not assembled or deployed. It is therefore impossible – or, at the very least, exceedingly difficult – to design an empirical study to assess which view is correct. We must rely heavily on logic – not evidence – to adjudicate this debate. It is possible to empirically assess whether nuclear latency provides deterrence benefits in a world with nuclear weapons by using historical data, as some studies have done.[79] However, these studies do not identify the conditions under which nuclear latency deters military conflict. They therefore may not provide a fair test of latent nuclear deterrence theory. It is also not clear that we can reasonably infer a causal relationship from existing studies. At this point, we lack sufficient evidence to assess the viability of latent nuclear deterrence.

This book addresses these limitations. Recognizing that nuclear latency and nuclear arsenals can coexist, it assesses whether latent nuclear powers have derived any deterrence benefits since 1945. The book develops a complete theory of latent nuclear deterrence. Instead of arguing that latent nuclear deterrence "works" or "does not work," it identifies the conditions that have to be present for countries to derive deterrence benefits from latent nuclear capacity. The book presents and analyzes a large body of new quantitative and qualitative evidence. Drawing on a comprehensive database of global latent nuclear capabilities, it will evaluate whether countries have historically been able to gain international influence with latent nuclear capabilities. Taking a design-based approach to causal inference, I bring us closer to identifying the true relationship between nuclear latency and various foreign policy outcomes.[80] I also carry out twenty case studies to show what world leaders think about latent nuclear deterrence.[81]

---

[79] Fuhrmann and Tkach (2015) and Mehta and Whitlark (2017a).
[80] I describe this approach in Chapter 5.
[81] These are spread out over Chapters 2, 6, and 7.

Latent Nuclear Deterrence Theory

Recall that successful deterrence requires a minimum of three things: the capacity to inflict punishment on the challenger, the belief that the defender will use that capacity if its interests are threatened, and credible promises of restraint if the status quo persists. The first step in developing a complete theory of latent nuclear deterrence is to identify the problems that make it difficult for countries to meet these basic requirements. Next, I will consider if (and how) these problems could be overcome. This process will allow me to identify the conditions under which latent nuclear deterrence might succeed, as well as when it is doomed to fail or incite instability.

Challenges in Weaponless Deterrence

When it comes to latent nuclear deterrence, three major challenges may prevent countries from meeting the requirements for success: (1) delayed punishment, (2) high breakout costs, and (3) the potential to incite instability.[82] These challenges exist for all three mechanisms of weaponless deterrence, but they can vary in their severity. The first challenge is particularly thorny in deterrence by proliferation and delayed attack, while the third problem is more acute in deterrence by doubt. If left unaddressed, all three challenges can complicate a country's efforts to use their nuclear programs to gain leverage, and in some cases can render such attempts wholly ineffective.

Challenge #1: Delayed Punishment

A time-gap between a transgression and the imposition of punishment makes latent nuclear deterrence unique. In traditional deterrence, a country can retaliate immediately after suffering a military attack. By contrast, it takes time – days, weeks, or even a couple of years – to inflict pain in weaponless deterrence. This delay in punishment can have serious consequences for countries hoping to gain leverage from their nonweaponized nuclear programs. Three particular problems stem from a delay in the implementation of punishment.

Keen Foresight

Deterrence requires leaders to think strategically. Before making a policy decision, government officials must anticipate how an adversary would respond to possible actions they might take. A leader's expectations

---

[82] These challenges are sometimes anticipated by the weaponless instability school.

about the consequences of their behavior ultimately shape the choices they make. They imagine how the game will end before deciding whether to play. All else equal, policy options will be less attractive when officials expect that they will trigger damaging responses by other countries.

Latent nuclear deterrence requires particularly keen foresight. It is straightforward to anticipate that bombing a nuclear power's capital city might trigger a nuclear response. Any American official knows that attacking North Korea, for example, could lead to nuclear war.[83] Anticipating costly responses in weaponless deterrence requires greater analytic depth.

Shortsightedness is a potential problem in deterrence by proliferation. For some officials, the possibility of inducing armament after a crisis or armed conflict ends may not be an obvious form of punishment. The aggressor might instead focus initially on the defender's kinetic military responses. A natural question any responsible state would ask itself is, "if I take this action, will it lead to a big war?" But the aggressor must go beyond thinking about just traditional military retaliation in order for defenders to have any hope of deterring by proliferation. It must take a longer view and consider the downstream consequences of its actions. If they do not, potential aggressors would totally miss the possibility that their actions could trigger nuclear armament, and deterrence by proliferation would fail.

The challenger must also work through an extra step in the causal chain when the threatened punishment is delayed nuclear retaliation. It must realize that once fighting or a serious crisis starts, the defender could obtain a capability that it currently lacks and ultimately use it to carry out a devastating retaliatory strike. However, a leader may fail to incorporate this additional step into his or her thought process. They may think of threshold states as strictly "nonnuclear," so the possibility of nuclear retaliation during a conflict with such a state may never occur to them. At least one member of the weaponless instability school points to this as a reason to question the viability of deterrence by delayed attack. Sir Michael Quinlan, a strategist and former official in the British Ministry of Defence, wrote in 2007, "[I]t is sometimes suggested that the very fact of this reconstitution risk would serve as a deterrent to war – weaponless deterrence, it has been called, a sort of deterrence at one remove. But this implies a world-wide and long-sighted wisdom on which it would surely be imprudent to count."[84]

---

[83] This assumes, of course, that the United States could not wipe out North Korea's nuclear capabilities in a disarming first strike.

[84] Quinlan (2007–08, 12). Quoted in Sagan (2009, 166).

Deterrence by doubt requires less foresight than the other two mechanisms of weaponless influence. If a challenger believes that a defender might already be in possession of an assembled warhead – even when it is unarmed – it does not take too much imagination to anticipate that an armed attack could prompt nuclear retaliation, just like in traditional deterrence. Because this approach hinges on ambiguity, however, challengers may still perceive defenders as nonnuclear. In that case, the depth of strategic anticipation required for maintaining the status quo increases. When it comes to the level of foresight required for success, deterrence by doubt would resemble deterrence by delayed attack.

Escaping Retaliation

Awareness that punishment is possible hardly guarantees success in deterrence. A bank robber knows that, in theory, his actions could lead to a lengthy prison sentence. Yet he may have confidence that he can elude law enforcement, in which case the prospect of incarceration may not deter him. Similarly, the prospect of weaponization or a nuclear attack will not deter the challenger if it believes that the defender will be unable to inflict the threatened punishment.

Latent nuclear deterrence requires a defender to obtain something that it does not presently have: at least one nuclear weapon. A time delay between the infraction and the punishment delay could allow the challenger to stop the defender from obtaining weapons, thereby escaping retaliation.[85] The longer the time to armament, the more opportunities the aggressor has to stop its adversary from getting a bomb.

Nonproliferators such as the United States have a variety of foreign policy tools that could prevent nuclear proliferation. Economic sanctions can discourage a state from building nuclear weapons.[86] So can positive inducements such as economic aid, military assistance, or security assurances.[87] For example, economic pressure paired with sanctions relief may have (temporarily) motivated Tehran to curtail its nuclear ambitions and agree to the Joint Comprehensive Plan of Action (JCPOA) in 2015. If peaceful solutions fail, a potential aggressor might be able to erode the latent nuclear power's ability to retaliate by destroying its nuclear infrastructure. Even if the aggressor takes actions that initially harden the latent nuclear power's resolve to weaponize, it may believe that some combination of carrots and sticks will ultimately stop proliferation.

[85] I thank Vipin Narang for this insight.
[86] Miller (2018).
[87] Bleek and Lorber (2014), Reiter (2014), and Mehta (2020).

Delayed punishment becomes especially problematic for defenders when challengers are bent on territorial conquest or regime change. A country could suffer a devastating defeat before it has an opportunity to arm. In 1939, Nazi Germany and the Soviet Union annexed Poland in a little more than one month. Quick conquests pose an especially difficult problem for states hoping to engage in weaponless deterrence.[88] Defenders would need to assemble a bomb in a matter of days to have any hope of deterring challengers – something that is probably impossible for any nonnuclear country in the world today.

Yet military operations do not have to be historically quick to pose a problem for defenders. When a challenger's objective is occupation or leader decapitation, latent nuclear deterrence depends on the capacity to build nuclear weapons before the operation is complete.[89] If the defender is five years away from a bomb, for instance, the challenger would have ample opportunity to achieve victory before facing the prospect of nuclear punishment. In this hypothetical scenario, even a fairly lengthy timetable for success – say four years – would take weaponless deterrence off the table, enabling challengers to attack without risking delayed nuclear punishment.

As with the problem of keen foresight, creating the impression that it might already be nuclear-armed could cause challengers to question whether they could escape punishment. Even in deterrence by doubt, however, countries may believe that they could achieve victory before incurring nuclear punishment, possibly by eliminating nuclear infrastructure in a disarming first strike.

Discounted Costs

A potential aggressor may believe that it will ultimately pay a price for its actions. Even in that case, though, the time delay generates bad news for latent nuclear powers: Delayed consequences are likely to be discounted, even if they are certain to materialize.

According to standard economic theory, people calculate future costs based on a discount rate. The discount rate is usually less than one, meaning that individuals perceive the same penalty as less costly in the future compared to the present. When given a choice between paying $100 today or $100 in one week, for instance, people usually prefer the latter. By waiting, a person can use the money for investments or other purchases during the ensuing week, whereas they lose this

---

[88] This is partially why some members of the weaponless instability school believe that latent nuclear deterrence does not work. See Waltz (1997).

[89] A similar point is made in Mount (2014).

option by expending it immediately. In economic parlance, spending the money right away generates opportunity costs. Discount rates help explain human behavior outside the realm of money, such as why some people smoke cigarettes even when they know that doing so is bad for their health in the long run.[90] In the area of international relations, some of my earlier research shows that countries are often willing to share nuclear technology and know-how – even in cases where doing so ultimately facilitated unwanted nuclear weapons proliferation – because the benefits of nuclear assistance are immediate and the costs are longer term.[91] The United States, for instance, was enthusiastic about assisting Iran's nuclear program from the 1950s until the Islamic Revolution in 1979 even though officials in Washington recognized the possible long-term security risks of doing so. The propensity of people to discount future costs carries implications for deterrence, too.

Criminologists have long recognized that celerity – the immediacy of punishment – affects deterrence.[92] The eighteenth-century Italian philosopher Cesare Beccaria, who is known as the father of criminal justice, wrote in the 1764 book *On Crimes and Punishment*, "The more immediately after the commission of a crime a punishment is inflicted, the more just and useful it will be."[93] Consistent with this view, modern research has found that punishment is less likely to deter crime when there is a long delay in the imposition of a sanction.[94] Imagine that the hypothetical bank robber mentioned earlier knows for certain that he will be caught, but he will not begin a prison sentence until five years after he committed the crime. This punishment, while still consequential, has less deterrent value than a prison sentence of the same duration that would begin immediately. The bank robber discounts future costs to some degree because he can live a consequence-free happy life for five years, during which time he can enjoy whatever benefits resulted from his crime. He would surely prefer to escape punishment entirely, but the five-year delay is preferable to an immediate prison sentence.

Celerity matters for latent nuclear deterrence as well, especially when the threatened punishment is proliferation rather than delayed attack. Inducing an adversary to obtain nuclear weapons becomes less costly for the aggressor as the amount of time since its hostile act increases.

---

[90] Torgerson and Raftery (1999)

[91] Fuhrmann (2012a).

[92] See, for example, Nagin and Pogarsky (2001). I thank Phillip Bleek and Jeffrey Knopf for bringing the literature on celerity to my attention.

[93] Beccaria (2009, 54).

[94] For an alternative view that celerity is irrelevant for general deterrence, see Gibbs (1975).

A long time delay allows the leader in the attacking country to advance his or her domestic and international agenda and score political points, which may bolster his or her domestic political future, before having to deal with any fallout from their actions toward the latent nuclear power. In some situations, the leader that induced proliferation may no longer be in office once the costs of his or her actions fully materialize. Moroever, delayed punishment weakens the causal connection between the aggressor's actions and armament by the latent nuclear power. This may allow a leader to deflect some of the blame for the adversary's armament, thereby reducing the costs of their aggression.

In deterrence by proliferation, a reduction in the expected punishment costs can be quite significant. The costs for the aggressor are modest to begin with, compared to provoking a military attack that leads to the immediate loss of life and infrastructure. Reducing these costs generates additional situations where the benefits of aggression exceeded the costs.

The situation is different in deterrence by delayed attack or doubt. The costs of a nuclear attack are extreme, even with a time delay. A country that experiences a nuclear strike today would suffer terrible consequences. Those costs would still be horrific if the attack happened in six months, one year, or eighteen months. Even if they are discounted to some degree, the costs imposed after a time delay may still be sufficient to deter military aggression – unless the stakes for the aggressor were exceedingly high. In this case, any cost-discounting stemming from the delay in punishment provides little solace to a leader who may be contemplating aggression.

Challenge #2: High Breakout Costs

States thinking about challenging the status quo consider the likelihood of costs being imposed, not just their magnitude. Even threats that would be extremely costly if implemented can fail to deter if the aggressor sees them as unbelievable. One key factor that influences threat credibility is the costs of implementation for the defender.[95] When those costs are high, challengers are more likely to dismiss the threat.

In latent nuclear deterrence, carrying out a threat can be costly for the threshold state, not just the potential aggressor, causing challengers to dismiss threats as unbelievable. Attempting to build nuclear weapons can be consequential, even if a bomb is never detonated in combat. The financial costs of obtaining a nuclear arsenal are substantial. According to an analysis by the Brookings Institution, the United States spent

---

[95] Sechser and Fuhrmann (2017) make this argument in the context of nuclear coercion.

$5.5 trillion on its nuclear forces from 1940 to 1996.[96] This kind of price tag requires states to make tradeoffs, often sacrificing programs that are necessary for social welfare or economic development in order to build bombs. On top of this, there is a longstanding international norm against pursuing nuclear weapons that is backed by treaties, international organizations, and powerful countries such as the United States. Violating this norm can result in economic or political sanctions, as well as strained relationships with countries that may be important for the state's security.[97]

Nuclear breakout can be a powerful card for a country to hold, but it can be played only once.[98] A country that obtains nuclear weapons is unlikely to give them up; only one country, South Africa, has fully dismantled indigenously built nuclear bombs.[99] Once a country implements a threat in latent nuclear deterrence, then, it has crossed the proverbial Rubicon. The gravity of such a move for the defender further increases the costs of nuclear breakout.

Implementing the threat in deterrence by delayed attack or doubt requires an actual nuclear strike, not just assembling bombs. It is well understood that the use of nuclear weapons in war would be a cataclysmic event – something that has not happened since 1945. As discussed earlier, a nuclear attack could invite considerable political, military, and economic blowback for the user.

Challenge #3: Inciting Instability

Merely attempting to engage in latent nuclear deterrence can be dangerous for defenders of the status quo. Raising the prospect of future nuclear proliferation or use may inadvertently invite military threats rather than prevent them. Recall that this is a central claim made by the weaponless instability school. The potential for instability is particularly worrisome in deterrence by doubt. This approach requires countries to raise the possibility that they might already be in possession of a bomb, which is especially likely to prompt political or military blowback. Engaging in weaponless deterrence can induce international volatility in two main ways.

---

[96] Schwartz (1998).

[97] A mad dash toward the bomb could also prompt the destabilizing events described later that form the basis of challenge #3.

[98] I credit a participant in a research seminar at Stanford University on November 17, 2016, whose name I regrettably cannot recall, for sharing this idea with me.

[99] Belarus, Kazakhstan, and Ukraine returned nuclear weapons to Moscow in the 1990s that were left on their soil when the Soviet Union collapsed.

First, it may generate incentives for preventive war. One state's development of dual-use nuclear technology, the argument goes, causes a rival to fear that the developer intends to build bombs, leading the rival to take military action before it is too late. Schelling voiced this concern long ago: "Even without possessing complex weapons, a nation might consider initiating war with whatever resources it had, on grounds that delay would allow an enemy to strike or mobilize first. If a nation believed its opponent might rush to rearm to achieve military preponderance, it might consider 'preventive war' to forestall its opponent's dominance."[100] In the decades that followed, scholars continued to draw a connection between nonweaponized nuclear programs and preventive war.[101]

There is some historical basis for the fear that latent nuclear capabilities may incite violent conflict. According to a database I compiled with political scientist Sarah Kreps, countries seriously considered launching preventive attacks that targeted an adversary's nuclear plants in eighteen cases from 1942 to 2000.[102] In more recent years, the nuclear programs of Iran, Iraq, North Korea, and Syria brought nonproliferation-based preventive wars to the forefront of public attention.

Concerns about nuclear proliferation can also catalyze disputes that are seemingly unrelated to the target state's nuclear program. Nuclear proliferation has the potential to result in large shifts in the balance of power. Countries may worry that their bargaining power will weaken once an adversary obtains nuclear weapons. If states have unresolved disputes with latent nuclear powers, then, they may use military force to resolve those conflicts on favorable terms before the expected increase in the opponents' military capabilities.[103]

Second, nonweaponized nuclear programs could lead to destabilizing arms races. Imagine that two rivals have latent nuclear capabilities but lack atomic warheads. Each will fear that the other might arm first, potentially providing it with a decisive military advantage. The fear of being vulnerable to nuclear blackmail or a devastating attack if it fails to act, based on this reasoning, will compel the latent nuclear powers

---

[100] Schelling (1962, 393).

[101] See, for example, Fuhrmann and Kreps (2010), Debs and Monteiro (2014), and Whitlark (2017).

[102] Fuhrmann and Kreps (2010).

[103] An attacker would not perceive that it is causing nuclear proliferation in this case, since it expects that the adversary will build nuclear bombs anyway. The use of force could, however, accelerate the rival's nuclear weapons program. Instigating military conflict could produce a negative outcome sooner than it would happen in the absence of an attack. Despite this risk, states might jump at an opportunity to settle disputes in their favor when they expect that their counterpart will ultimately build bombs.

to build weapons before its too late. Herman Kahn, a leading nuclear strategist of his generation, referred to this as a "mobilization war." "The side that mobilizes most effectively within a relatively brief period of time," he wrote, "can achieve a militarily dominant position, enabling it to inhibit the diplomatic or military initiatives of its opponent."[104] Waltz similarly worried about latent nuclear powers exploiting windows of opportunity: "States would hasten to equip themselves with nuclear weapons, lest a newly rearmed state somehow gain an advantage from its moment of superiority."[105]

Strategists sometimes draw a connection between these two forms of instability. In a world with latent nuclear powers only, they argue, one actor would quickly build nuclear bombs and then launch preventive wars against its adversaries – or at least dangle the threat of war – to ensure that they could not match its capabilities.[106] In this way, one state can dominate its rivals by making the first move. Indeed, the notion that latent nuclear programs generate first-mover advantages is central to the weaponless instability school.[107]

Addressing the Challenges

The challenges in latent nuclear deterrence can be daunting for a state hoping to gain leverage from its nonweaponized nuclear program. The weaponless instability school suggests that these problems render weaponless nuclear deterrence entirely ineffective. There is some truth to this claim, since these challenges can make success difficult, even impossible. But the weaponless instability school is too pessimistic about the viability of latent nuclear deterrence. Instead of totally writing off this form of influence, I consider whether and how the previously described problems can be mitigated.

There are three solutions to the challenges in weaponless deterrence: (1) possessing known sensitive nuclear capabilities, (2) high stakes, and (3) nuclear restraint. The first two solutions are necessary for success in all three forms of weaponless deterrence. The third is essential in deterrence by proliferation only, but can also mitigate risks for states relying on deterrence by delayed attack or doubt.

Figure 1.1 summarizes how these three factors combine to influence whether latent nuclear deterrence is successful. Implementing these solutions does not guarantee that latent nuclear deterrence will work, but doing so increases the odds of success. After describing these solutions, I will describe the theory's predictions for international relations.

---

[104] Kahn (1985, 156). This statement is quoted in Ford (2011, 17).
[105] Waltz (1997, 157).
[106] See Schelling (1962, 393–394).
[107] Waltz (1997).

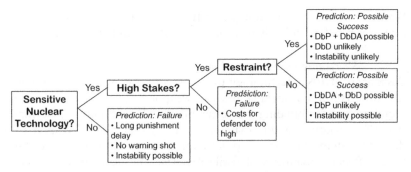

Figure 1.1 Pathways to success in latent nuclear deterrence theory. *Notes*: DbP = deterrence by proliferation; DbDA = deterrence by delayed attack; DbD = deterrence by doubt.

Solution #1: Sensitive Nuclear Technology

A state's nuclear capabilities play a critical role in shaping the efficacy of latent nuclear deterrence. One kind of technology reigns supreme: uranium enrichment or plutonium reprocessing (ENR) plants. Possessing ENR capabilities reduces all three of the problems stemming from delayed punishment in weaponless deterrence (challenge #1). It does so by shortening the time to a bomb and signaling resolve. In addition, having sensitive nuclear technology can make preventive military action less attractive for potential challengers.

In order to reap these benefits, however, a country's nuclear capabilities must be known to potential challengers. Otherwise, the defender's nuclear program cannot influence the challenger's decision-making. There are two ways that countries can learn about others' nuclear capabilities. First, a state could publicly reveal that it is in possession of sensitive nuclear technology. The IAEA requires countries to notify the agency when they build new nuclear facilities. Government officials can also announce technological breakthroughs outside of IAEA channels by holding press conferences or leaking information to journalists. For example, on November 18, 1983, Carlos Castro Madero, the Chairman of Argentina's National Atomic Energy Commission, announced to the world that Argentina had successfully enriched uranium on a pilot scale at a plant located in Pilcaniyeu.[108] Second, foreign intelligence services can discover covert nuclear sites. The United States and other countries with modern intelligence capabilities can monitor their adversaries using satellites or drones,or recruit human sources to provide information.

---

[108] Benjamin (1983).

Washington knew about Iran's enrichment plant in Qom, for instance, three years before publicly revealing its existence in September 2009.[109]

Shortening the Time to a Bomb

Possession of ENR technology provides countries with the technological foundation for making nuclear weapons. There are three main requirements for building a nuclear bomb: (1) obtaining fissile material, (2) weaponizing this material, and (3) mating the weapon to a delivery system. The first step is by far the most difficult. Once states have sufficient quantities of fissile material, they can make at least a rudimentary bomb similar to the one the United States dropped on Hiroshima with relative ease. As Matthew Bunn and Anthony Weir of the Harvard Kennedy School's project on *Managing the Atom* put it, "while it is not easy to make a nuclear bomb, it is not as difficult as many believe, once those essential ingredients [fissile materials] are in hand."[110]

Countries have used two fissile materials for bomb-making: plutonium and weapons-grade highly enriched uranium (HEU). It is theoretically possible for a state to purchase or steal enough HEU or plutonium for a bomb. In practice, though, nuclear powers generally produce it indigenously using reprocessing plants (to separate plutonium from fuel that is "burned" in a nuclear reactor) or enrichment facilities (to "enrich" uranium by increasing the composition of the the isotope U-235).

There is widespread recognition among policymakers and scholars that successful ENR programs allow countries to build nuclear weapons relatively quickly. As the International Panel on Fissile Materials (IPFM) put it, "If countries are allowed to separate plutonium from spent power-reactor fuel . . . they could use this plutonium to make nuclear weapons within weeks. Countries with large national enrichment plants could similarly quickly begin to make large quantities of HEU for weapons."[111] These ENR facilities have special significance due to the capacity they provide. The United States has worked hard to restrict the spread of ENR technology, even while allowing – and often encouraging – the international development of nuclear reactors for research or electricity production.[112] Dan Brouillette, the US Deputy Secretary of Energy, aptly characterized the sentiment about ENR plants in 2019 remarks: "this technology has a dual use and in the wrong hands it becomes a dangerous, dangerous world."[113]

---

[109] Ghosh (2009) and Sanger and Broad (2009).
[110] Bunn and Wier (2006, 134).
[111] Quoted in Pifer and O'Hanlon (2012, 171).
[112] On the distinction between exports of ENR technology and nuclear reactors, see Fuhrmann (2012a) and Kroenig (2010).
[113] Quoted in Reid (2019).

Countries have taken an average of about six years to demonstrate the feasibility of ENR technologies and ten years to produce significant quantities of HEU or plutonium.[114] A popular path to fissile-material production in recent years, especially among states suspected of harboring bomb-related ambitions, is uranium enrichment using centrifuge technology. Eighteen countries have pursued this technology, and only seven of them (39 percent) successfully developed it.[115] Among those that were successful, the average time to the first demonstration facility was ten years. These same countries took an average of fifteen years to produce a large-scale enrichment plant.[116] Iran took twenty-one years to get to this stage. Thus, a state with a successful ENR program would have a substantial head start – possibly more than two decades – over a counterpart that was attempting to build a bomb from scratch.

The shorter proliferation timeline that results from having sensitive nuclear technology mitigates two of the three problems related to delayed punishment. First, a challenger has fewer opportunities to stop a state in possession of sensitive nuclear technology from obtaining nuclear weapons. It may still be able to prevent proliferation, but the odds of doing so decline precipitously as the amount of time it has decreases. Second, challengers will discount the costs of aggression less than they would when facing a state without ENR technology, making the expected punishment more meaningful.

Having ENR technology is not always required to produce a bomb quickly. At the time of the attack on Pearl Harbor, the United States had made little progress on enrichment or reprocessing. By July 1945 – less than four years later – it had a deliverable nuclear weapon. Today, a highly industrialized state without an ENR program might be able to build a nuclear weapon even quicker, perhaps in less than a year, if it made the bomb program *the* top national priority. But this brings me to the next reason sensitive nuclear technology helps states address the problem of delayed punishment.

Signaling Resolve

Launching an ENR program conveys information to a country's adversaries. Obtaining the means to produce fissile material implicitly tells others something like, "we have the ability to build a bomb – if you give us a reason to need one." In sending this warning shot, a country inserts its nuclear capabilities into international relations, forcing its

[114] Zentner et al. (2005, 102).
[115] Zentner et al. (2005, 20).
[116] These figures are based on Zentner et al. (2005, 20) with my own updates for Iran.

adversaries to think about the prospect of nuclear proliferation. Without this message, a potential aggressor may never think about armament or a nuclear attack as potential forms of punishment. But by producing fissile material, a state forces its adversaries to consider the downsteam nuclear-related consequences of aggression.

Hence, ENR programs are a focal point for governments evaluating a foreign country's bomb-making capacity. Reports on nuclear proliferation prepared by the US intelligence community put a country's ENR capabilities front and center. For example, a June 1958 CIA assessment concluded that only three nonnuclear countries could obtain the bomb within five years: France, Canada, and Sweden.[117] The reason, according to the formerly secret document, is that all three had, or could quickly obtain, sufficient fissile material – not the broader industrial capacity that they possessed.[118]

The signaling value of ENR capabilities comes from having an *active* fissile material production program, not just previously demonstrating this capacity. Consider the comparison between Argentina and Belgium in the early 1980s. If both states began a sprint to build a bomb at that time, the race would have been close and Belgium could have plausibly finished first. Despite having similar proliferation timelines, however, there was a key difference: Argentina had an active ENR program in the early 1980s and Belgium did not. This difference affected the viability of latent nuclear deterrence by shaping the degree to which foreign counterparts thought about delayed nuclear responses as forms of punishment. Argentina's work on fissile material production caused other states to worry about nuclear proliferation.[119] By contrast, there is no indication that the prospect of a Belgian bomb loomed in the background of its interstate interactions during the early 1980s.

Yet this was not always the case. In the late 1950s, Belgium announced that it would host a pilot-scale reprocessing facility. After carrying out laboratory-scale activities for several years, the reprocessing plant operated from 1966 to 1974. During the years in which Belgium had active ENR ambitions and activities, foreign governments considered the possibility of nuclear proliferation. A 1958 CIA assessment, for instance, concluded that there would be "strong pressures in Belgium" to build nuclear weapons if France and West Germany went nuclear.[120] Foreign leaders at that time would have been more likely to consider

---

[117] US Central Intelligence Agency (1961b).
[118] US Central Intelligence Agency (1961b, 3).
[119] I provide evidence for this in Chapters 2 and 6.
[120] US Central Intelligence Agency (1958, 14).

the possibility of inducing proliferation if they behaved too aggressively toward Belgium.

Developing sensitive technology is not the only way a state could force its adversaries to consider the downsteam consequences of aggression. A country could make a public declaration that they will build (and perhaps eventually use) nuclear weapons if they are threatened. Leaders have certainly said things along these lines, and I provided examples earlier in this chapter. However, developing sensitive nuclear technology is a more effective way to communicate a credible threat to potential aggressors.

Signals are most effective in communicating resolve when they are costly for the sender.[121] Taking a costly action allows a country to distinguish itself from a less resolved type. When signals are costless to convey, by contrast, they may be dismissed as "cheap talk." Consider the case of military alliances.[122] One might reasonably question whether the United States would go to war to defend another country in a faraway land. Washington can signal that it would, in fact, fight on this state's behalf by establishing a formal defense treaty, like NATO. Creating and maintaining such a treaty is costly for the United States. The president would have to spend political capital to negotiate the agreement and get Congressional approval. The United States might then establish an overseas base on the ally's territory with forward-deployed troops and equipment, which can be pricey. Forging the treaty also risks reputation damage if a promise of military support goes unfulfilled. All of these costs make a US defense commitment more believable since a less resolved country would not incur them.

A similar logic applies to sensitive nuclear technology. Developing ENR plants is costly, in part, because it requires considerable financial investment. Also, ENR development could invite international wrath. During the 1970s, for instance, South Korea sought assistance from France in building a plutonium reprocessing plant. This plant was intended strictly for civilian use, but it would have made it easier for Seoul to build a bomb if it so desired. The United States strongly opposed the transfer and applied substantial political pressure. Richard Sneider, the American ambassador to South Korea, wrote in a cable, "I believe we must make it indelibly clear that far more than our nuclear support is at stake here, that if ROKG proceeds as they have indicated to date [by completing a deal on reprocessing with France] [the] whole range of security and political relationships between US and ROK will be

[121] Fearon (1997).
[122] Leeds (2003) and Fuhrmann and Sechser (2014) make this argument in greater detail.

affected, including potential for adverse congressional action on security assistance for Korea."[123] A state is unlikely to take on the economic and political costs of developing ENR technology unless it is serious about keeping its nuclear options open. Others know this, causing them to take proliferation threats more seriously when the state is ENR-capable.

Verbal threats to proliferate are hardly costless and they can contribute to latent nuclear deterrence in some situations. Yet investments in ENR technology convey more meaningful information to other countries because they are more costly. Moreover, a public threat in the absence of a successful ENR program would not necessarily shorten a state's proliferation timeline, rendering this approach ineffective.

Making Preventive Strikes Less Attractive: Survivability and Radioactive Contamination

The possibility of preventive military action presents a major challenge to defenders in latent nuclear deterrence (challenge #3).[124] A non-weaponized nuclear program may not bolster deterrence if the challenger believes that it can eliminate, or at least erode, the defender's capacity in a preventive strike. Countries that possess ENR technology typically have more survivable nuclear programs, meaning that their capabilities are less vulnerable to destruction by an adversary. Since countries are unlikely to launch preventive attacks if they expect failure, the possession of sensitive nuclear technology can reduce a country's vulnerability to such action.

One way to enhance the survivability of a nuclear program is to disperse key infrastructure. When nuclear programs are relatively under-developed, an attacker might be able to eliminate a state's bomb-making capacity by destroying a single plant, as in the Osiraq case. But this is not true for states that possess sensitive nuclear technology. By the time a program has evolved to the point where a country is operating one or more ENR plants, it is likely to have a large number of facilities that are geographically spread out. Brazil, for example, currently has nine sensitive nuclear fuel cycle facilities in operation, in addition to six reactors – two for generating electricity and four for research.[125] These facilities are located in four different states: Bahia, Minas Gerais, Rio de Janeiro, and Sao Paulo. To be successful, a preventive strike would need to eliminate or erode *all* of a country's critical infrastructure; taking

---

[123] US Department of State (1975b). Part of this telegram is quoted in Hong (2011, 500–501).

[124] This section draws on some of the ideas in Fuhrmann (2018).

[125] This is according to databases produced by the IAEA.

out three facilities, for instance, does little good if a country possesses a fourth plant that could provide material for a bomb. It may still be possible for a country with a robust military, like the United States, to locate and destroy multiple dispersed facilities. However, the probability of success declines as the number of targets that would need to be destroyed increases.

Uncertainty about the full scope of a state's program may also increase as it masters sensitive nuclear technology. In particular, once a country demonstrates the ability to develop ENR technology indigenously, it becomes harder for others to rule out the possibility of secret facilities. Iran has at least five publicly known facilities that an adversary may wish to destroy in a preventive attack: the Fordow and Natanz enrichment sites, a uranium conversation facility in Isfahan, a heavy water production plant at Arak, and the Bushehr nuclear power plant. On top of these sites, however, Iran may have other facilities about which the public or foreign governments do not know. It is impossible to know for sure, but leaders might reasonably worry about this possibility given the advanced state of Iran's nuclear program; Tehran possesses the technological wherewithal and has had sufficient time to conceivably build facilities at other sites. By contrast, because Syria's nuclear program was relatively underdeveloped in the lead up to the 2007 al Kibar raid, Israeli officials were confident that a single site represented the entirety of Syria's bomb-relevant capabilities.

The ability to make nuclear programs mobile further increases the survivability of latent nuclear forces. Technology or materials – particularly things like centrifuges, which are used to enrich uranium – can be moved on relatively short notice. For example, Libya initially installed centrifuges for enriching uranium in Al Hashan but quickly moved them to another site two years later, in 2002, due to concerns about a preventive strike.[126] Iraq did something similar on the eve of the Persian Gulf War. On orders from Qusay Hussein (Saddam's son) and Hussein Kamel (Saddam's son-in-law), Iraqi scientist Mahdi Obeidi buried components related to a gas centrifuge enrichment system under a rose bush in his garden.[127] Obeidi later wrote a book about his experiences working on Iraq's nuclear program fittingly titled *The Bomb in My Garden*.[128]

---

[126] Braut-Heggehammer (2016, 202, 207) and Fuhrmann (2018, 118).

[127] CNN (2003b).

[128] It is much more difficult to move a nuclear reactor, whether it is meant for research or electricity production. The benefits stemming from mobility, then, do not necessarily extend to countries that lack enrichment technology – including those that pursue the plutonium path to bomb-making.

On top of this, nuclear-related knowledge is inherently survivable. Short of rounding up hundreds if not thousands of scientists and assassinating them – an obviously reprehensible policy that no reasonable leader would pursue – expertise in nuclear matters cannot be eliminated. Targets can therefore reconstitute their nuclear programs following a successful attack. Once a country possesses the indigenous knowledge required to develop nuclear technology, they can rebuild nuclear sites in a few years. A one-off attack, therefore, may be insufficient to lower the likelihood of proliferation in the medium term, even if it delays progress in the short term.

There may be cases in which a potential attacker knows about all of a state's nuclear facilities and believes it can successfully destroy them. But once nuclear sites, especially reactors, are operational bombing them could disperse radioactive materials, leading to large-scale environmental contamination. A military attack could replicate the consequences of the nuclear disasters in Chernobyl (1986) and Fukushima (2011).[129] Concerns about radiation make countries think twice about bombing operational nuclear plants. It is not coincidental that preventive attacks, when they occur, tend to happen before nuclear sites become "hot." By the time that a state has operational ENR plants, it may be too late to target nuclear facilities at a cost that is acceptable to the attacker. Latent nuclear powers can use this to their advantage, further increasing the odds that their infrastructure will not be destroyed.

Countries can "harden" sites that house nuclear technology by locating them underground or surrounding them in protective shielding. Nuclear reactors are typically enclosed by 1.5-meter-thick concrete walls lined with steel.[130] These walls might be able to withstand impact from flying projectiles, including rockets or civilian airliners. Iran's nuclear enrichment plant at Fordo is located 300 feet below a mountain. These protective measures reduce but do not eliminate the possibility that bombing operational nuclear plants could lead to an environmental disaster. This is partially why the targeting of active nuclear facilities is prohibited under international law. Article 56 of Protocol I Additional to the Geneva Conventions (1977) states, "works or installations containing dangerous forces, [including] nuclear electrical generating stations, shall not be made the object of attack, even where these objects are military objectives, if such attack may cause the release of dangerous forces and consequent severe losses among the civilian population."[131]

---

[129] Ramberg (2017).
[130] Wald (2002).
[131] Quoted in Goldblat (2002, 164–165).

Solution #2: High Stakes

Carrying out threats is costly for the defender in latent nuclear deterrence, but this does not automatically make them unbelievable. Challengers judge credibility by considering the costs of threat implementation relative to the benefits. When the defender's gains from developing or using nuclear weapons exceed the costs, challengers will take this possibility more seriously.

Major security threats can provide defenders with a justification for possessing and perhaps using nuclear weapons, changing how challengers perceive the likelihood of nuclear proliferation as a form of punishment. Indeed, history shows that states often launch nuclear weapons programs shortly after experiencing major international threats. Chinese leader Mao Zedong made a strong push to build nuclear forces after being pushed around by the United States during the 1954–55 crisis in the Taiwan Strait. Indian Prime Minister Lal Bahadur Shastri acquiesced, albeit reluctantly, to a nuclear explosives project following the 1962 border war with China and Beijing's first nuclear test two years later. South Korea's nuclear weapons program followed numerous military provocations from North Korea, including an assassination attempt against President Park Chung Hee. And Iran's campaign to militarize its nuclear program began during the Iran–Iraq War (1980–88).

Policymakers recognize the connection between the instigation of serious military conflict and nuclear proliferation. During the crisis over the Falkland Islands, for instance, US officials concluded that a humiliating British defeat of Argentina could produce an Argentine bomb. As a May 28, 1982, memorandum from the National Security Council Staff to Robert McFarlane, who was then President Ronald Reagan's deputy national security adviser, put it: "A nuclear weapons capability would be virtually guaranteed, as both Brazil and Argentina would seek ultimate security in nuclear arsenals."[132]

Serious military threats can harden a defender's resolve to get nuclear weapons in at least three ways. First, military challenges may compel a state to take actions that lower the risk of suffering a similar fate in the future, even if seeking new capabilities is costly. A person living in an apparently safe neighborhood may refrain from purchasing an expensive home security system – until they experience an armed break-in. So it is with nuclear weapons. Second, external aggression may provoke nationalistic fervor among the public, potentially lowering domestic barriers to proliferation. Third, a latent nuclear power might withdraw

---

[132] US Department of State (1982).

from international nonproliferation commitments in retaliation for an attack, weakening external oversight over its nuclear program.[133]

However, the costs of threat implementation will probably be unacceptably high when the issues at stake are minor for the defender. In January 2006, for instance, Russian military planes briefly violated Japanese airspace. This troubled Japan to some degree – it scrambled its own fighters in response – but it would be hard to argue that this event produced a threat sufficient to raise the probability of Japanese proliferation.[134] The (implicit) threat to go nuclear lacks credibility in this episode and others like it, so there is little reason to expect that proliferation threats would deter this kind of military encounter.

Deterrence by delayed attack likewise depends on high stakes for the state seeking to preserve the status quo, as discussed in the preceding discussion of traditional nuclear deterrence. Actually using nuclear weapons in an attack would be even costlier than building them. For a nuclear use threat to be credible – whether an attack would be carried out immediately or with a delay – a defender must believe that vital national interests are at stake.[135]

Solution #3: Nuclear Restraint

Obtaining sensitive nuclear technology naturally generates concerns about a country's intentions, since the same plants could be used for generating electricity or bomb-making. A country may wish to quell fears about its nuclear program by convincing others that nuclear proliferation is not inevitable. States pursuing this path want their adversaries to know that they could build nuclear weapons if they so desired, but will not do so in the absence of a military challenge. Countries following this playbook have what I call a restrained nuclear program.[136]

Pursuing this solution has the flavor of a nuclear hedging strategy. Nuclear hedging occurs when a state develops nuclear technology to shorten the time needed to build nuclear bombs, recognizing that the security environment might quickly deteriorate in the future.[137] Countries such as Brazil, Germany, Japan, and Spain have embraced this strategy. Hedgers have not made a final decision to arm with nuclear weapons. But they seek the technological capability to do so. And, when they get it, they usually want their adversaries to know.

---

[133] Broad (2012) highlights these points in the context of Iran.
[134] This is case number 4,475 in the Correlates of War's Militarized Interstate Dispute (MID) dataset. See Palmer et al. (2015).
[135] This is also a point made in Sechser and Fuhrmann (2017).
[136] I provide an operational definition of this concept in Chapter 5.
[137] Studies on nuclear hedging include Levite (2002) and Narang (2017).

Countries following this path may explicitly try to reassure other countries that they are not racing to a bomb. This is not always an easy task, especially for states in possession of sensitive nuclear technology. Political scientist Tristan Volpe has argued that countries struggle to use nuclear programs for coercive leverage once they "can produce and weaponize fissile material," because others see armament as inevitable at that stage.[138] However, states have tools at their disposal to signal benign intentions – and these instruments can be effective. For example, they could ratify and comply with international nonproliferation commitments, like the NPT.[139] They can also refrain from doing single-use work on explosives, preparing a nuclear test site, or making other overt moves toward weaponization.

Showing nuclear restraint provides two main benefits. The first is that it can mitigate the problem of instability (challenge #3) to some degree. Political and military blowback are more likely when others think that a country will inevitably build nuclear weapons. This belief increases incentives for preventive strikes, as military force may become necessary to stop an imminent national security threat. For example, Israeli Prime Minister Menachem Begin seemingly believed that Iraq would have obtained nuclear forces imminently if his government had not destroyed Iraq's nuclear reactor in 1981: "we would have had to sit by passively from afar," he argued, "knowing that the Iraqis were creating atomic bombs of the type dropped on Hiroshima in the Second World War, and three, four or five such atomic bombs in the hands of such an evil person as Saddam Hussein."[140] Perceptions of proliferation inevitability could also compel the challenger to seek its own nuclear arsenal as a means to protect itself against a loss in future bargaining power, thereby fueling an arms race. Pakistan became more determined to arm, for example, once it perceived that India had introduced nuclear weapons into South Asia.

Nuclear restraint lowers the threat posed by a country's nuclear program and reduces the need for preventive military attacks and reactive nuclear proliferation. The argument for attacking Iran to erode its nuclear capabilities weakens considerably if Tehran is not planning to obtain a bomb in the absence of a strike. At the same time, the pressures for Egypt, Turkey, and Saudi Arabia to arm themselves with nuclear

---

[138] Volpe (2017, 529).

[139] Volpe (2017, 526) acknowledges that nonproliferation deals could signal restraint but contends that the costs of sending a credible signal are too great once a state has produced fissile material. Nonproliferation agreements are an imperfect indicator of a state's intentions. See Fuhrmann and Berejikian (2012).

[140] Quoted in Shipler (1981).

weapons decline if officials in those countries believe that Iran is content to remain nonnuclear.

The second advantage of restraint is that it preserves the viability of deterrence by proliferation. Proliferation threats have deterrence value only if challengers believe that the defender is content to remain nonnuclear in the absence of a change to the status quo.[141] There is little reason for a challenger to hold back if it believes that it is going to suffer a threatened punishment anyways. Credibly signaling restraint, then, is essential to keep deterrence by proliferation on the table.

This is especially critical for states hoping to deter arms-racing with their latent nuclear forces. Dissuading a rival's armament depends on deterrence by proliferation. Deterrence by delayed attack or doubt are ineffective in this context because threats to punish an opponent for arming by launching a nuclear attack lack credibility. Effectively communicating peaceful intentions, then, is crucial for a country hoping to stave off an arms race. Eliminating deterrence by proliferation is less problematic in the context of military conflict because the other two mechanisms can operate effectively.

Pursuing a strategy of restraint comes with a downside: It weakens deterrence by doubt. When a defender sends a credible message that its intentions are peaceful, its adversaries are less likely to suspect that the defender may already be in possession of a nuclear bomb. Challengers who know for certain that their adversary is not in possession of a bomb may see a window of opportunity to attack due to the delay in punishment (challenge #1). Developing sensitive nuclear technology shortens the time delay but does not eliminate it.

Reassurance also has a limitation when it comes to stopping an arms race. Effective reassurance by the defender may not dampen the challenger's resolve to seek an arsenal if the challenger faces a third-party nuclear threat. In that case, the challenger's motivation to arm could remain high even if it knows that the defender will remain nonnuclear. Consider the role of deterrence by proliferation on the Korean Peninsula. North Korea likely anticipated that testing a nuclear weapon for the first time in 2006 would increase South Korea's resolve to obtain the same capability – and that refraining from testing would dampen these ambitions in Seoul. Effective reassurance by South Korea was largely irrelevant for officials in Pyongyang, however, because they were more worried about perceived nuclear threats from the United States. Proliferation threats may fail when the challenger already has a third-party rival that possesses, or will soon obtain, nuclear forces.

---

[141] Volpe (2017) raises this point in the context of using nuclear latency for coercive diplomacy. See also Volpe (2015).

Unrestrained Programs: Racing to a Bomb

An alternative approach is to push hard to weaponize a latent nuclear capability. Instead of attempting to reassure others that its intentions are peaceful, a country could make a dash to a bomb. States that follow this path have what I call unrestrained nuclear programs. They have little interest in nuclear latency, seeing it merely as a necessary step along the way to something bigger. In this situation, leaders have made firm political decisions to arm. The US Manhattan Project fits this model, as does Iraq's nuclear program under Saddam Hussein in the 1980s.

Despite its clear military aims, this approach may yield political benefits during the period of latency. It could strengthen deterrence by doubt by creating uncertainty about whether a state is already nuclear-armed. Seeing that the "latent" nuclear power has taken steps toward assembling bombs, not just producing the requisite fissile material, others may think that it could possess a bomb. This pathway therefore has the potential to eliminate the punishment-related time delay (challenge #1) in the eyes of potential challengers.

An unrestrained nuclear program comes with two clear downsides, which can be avoided by adopting a restrained program. First, cultivating ambiguity is more likely to incite instability (challenge #3). Second, it virtually eliminates the viability of deterrence by proliferation. These problems carry significant implications for military conflict and arms-racing. When it comes to conflict, unrestrained programs are high-risk, high-reward propositions: They create a window of opportunity for preventive strikes (if the challenger is confident that the defender is nonnuclear) but can also bolster deterrence (if the challenger thinks the defender might be in possession of at least one bomb). Unrestrained programs offer countries a double whammy for arms-racing: They give adversaries incentives to arm while simultaneously stripping countries of deterrence value they could otherwise derive from their latent capacity.

Predictions about International Peace and Stability

Latent nuclear deterrence theory generates six main predictions about international relations. These are the things we would expect to see in the real world if the theory is correct.

- *Prediction #1: World leaders believe in latent nuclear deterrence.* Officials from around the globe should express the view that nuclear latency confers political influence. What goes on inside their heads should match how the theory expects leaders to think.
- *Prediction #2: Countries obtain nuclear latency for greater international influence.* Although the book's focus is on the political effects of nuclear

latency, the theory also carries implications for the causes of ENR technology adoption. Countries should covet nuclear latency, in part, because they believe that it provides political benefits – even if they do not go all the way to a full-blown nuclear arsenal.

- *Prediction #3: For countries with restrained nuclear programs, obtaining ENR technology increases international influence in high-stakes situations.* Becoming ENR-capable shortens a country's time to a bomb, putting it on the technological cusp of building nuclear bombs. This increases the expected punishment costs for challengers. When the stakes are small, however, ENR-capable defenders face a credibility problem: The costs of carrying out a threat will probably exceed what they stand to gain. Threats become more believable if a challenger's action would pose a major national security threat for the defender. Embracing nuclear restraint makes ENR possession less threatening to others, resulting in fewer countermeasures. And going this route preserves deterrence by proliferation, although deterrence by doubt becomes less viable.

- *Prediction #4: Being closer to a bomb confers more influence.* Latent nuclear deterrence theory holds that having ENR technology is crucial for gaining international influence. Yet ENR programs vary in their scale. I distinguish between two stages of latency based on a state's capabilities: partial and full. Partially latent states conduct small-scale fissile material production in a laboratory but do not come close to making enough plutonium or HEU for a single bomb. Fully latent states, by contrast, have pilot- or commercial-scale plants that give them the ability to to produce fissile material for one or more nuclear weapons. The theory expects that, in general, full nuclear latency will be more consequential for international peace and stability than partial latency. By shortening their proliferation timelines, fully latent states should be able to mitigate the three problems in latent deterrence more effectively.

- *Prediction #5: The political benefits from nuclear latency may be small and inconsistently obtained.* Even under ideal circumstances, latent nuclear deterrence may fail: ENR capabilities, high stakes for the defender, and nuclear restraint alleviate – but do not eliminate – the major challenges in weaponless deterrence. The anticipated delay in punishment could stymie success even when the defender substantially shortens its time to a bomb by producing fissile material, especially if the challenger is impulsive or risk-acceptant. Misperceiving the defender's capabilities or intentions also opens the door to failed deterrence. Moreover, the theory focuses on the costs the challenger might incur from taking a particular foreign policy action, but the benefits matter as well.

If the challenger is highly revisionist, the expected benefits of changing the status quo may exceed the costs. This is especially true in deterrence by proliferation, where the punishment costs are significant but not necessarily devastating. Many scholars and policymakers believe that nuclear weapons revolutionized international relations.[142] Latent nuclear forces, at least the kind that countries have typically wielded over the past seventy-five years, influence world politics in discernible ways but are probably less transformative.

- *Prediction #6: In the presence of an unrestrained nuclear program, getting an ENR capability does not reliably increase a country's international influence, and may invite instability.* Launching an unrestrained weapons program puts countries on a riskier and more uncertain path. It makes others more threatened by a country's nuclear ambitions, potentially triggering destabilizing countermeasures. Moreover, initiating an unrestrained weapons program takes deterrence by proliferation off the table, forcing countries to rely on deterrence by delayed attack and doubt to gain influence. On the plus side, pursuing this path increases the expected punishment costs by making sudden or slightly delayed nuclear retaliation more conceivable.

The book will evaluate the first two predictions by determining what world leaders think about the viability of weaponless deterrence (Chapter 2) and evaluating why they covet latent nuclear forces (Chapter 4). It will explore predictions 3–6 in several foreign policy contexts, providing a comprehensive test of the theory. I will determine how nuclear latency affects the onset of international crises and serious military disputes, foreign policy preferences among adversaries, and leverage within military alliances (Chapter 5). Then, I will take a close look at how nuclear latency influences the consideration and use preventive military force (Chapter 6) and nuclear armament (Chapter 7).

Conclusion

This chapter developed the logical foundations of latent nuclear deterrence theory. It began by describing the nuts and bolts of deterrence and explaining why many policymakers and scholars see nuclear weapons as an effective deterrent. The chapter argued, however, that having assembled warheads is not the only way to gain influence from a nuclear program. It introduced three mechanisms by which latent nuclear

---

[142] Jervis (1989) exemplifies this view.

powers can conceivably gain political leverage: threatening to build nuclear weapons (deterrence by proliferation), quickly assembling and using a bomb upon the onset of hostilities (deterrence by delayed attack), or cultivating the impression that they might already possess a bomb (deterrence by doubt).

Three challenges make it difficult to succeed when using these three means of influence in world politics. First, there is a time delay between a challenge to the status quo and the imposition of punishment. Second, nuclear breakout and use is costly for the defender, not just the challenger. Third, attempting to use latent nuclear forces to gain leverage can incite instability. Latent nuclear deterrence theory suggests three solutions to alleviate these problems: ENR technology, high stakes for the defender, and nuclear restraint. According to the theory, states that are not bent on building nuclear weapons can deter serious national security threats by obtaining the ability to produce fissile material. However, an ENR capability brings fewer political benefits when states have unrestrained nuclear weapons programs. The potential for instability in that situation is high too, as consideration of preventive military strikes and reactive nuclear armament are more likely.

Ultimately, the theory offers a mixed bag for states hoping to gain leverage from latent nuclear forces. On one hand, countries do not need assembled bombs for their nuclear programs to deter undesirable outcomes. On the other, meeting the requirements for success is difficult and there is potential to incite instability. Countries that are able to do so may succeed, while those that cannot will fail and possibly destabilize world politics.

Logic alone can only take us so far. To determine if latent nuclear deterrence theory is correct, we need to examine the evidence. The following chapters evaluate the theory's predictions based on a comprehensive assessment of seventy years' worth of history.

2 What Leaders Think: Beliefs about Latent Deterrence

The previous chapter established the logical foundations of latent nuclear deterrence. It showed that dual-use nuclear capabilities can, in theory, bring greater international influence. But do any government officials actually believe that nuclear latency can bolster deterrence?

In a word: yes. Latent nuclear deterrence is not merely an abstract concept – the theory translates to the real world. Throughout the nuclear age, government officials from Tehran to Tokyo have expressed confidence that they can gain influence over their foreign counterparts by possessing bomb-making capabilities without actually arming.

This chapter examines policymakers' views about nuclear technology in ten countries. This serves as a plausibility probe of the theory.[1] Before moving on to a more in-depth test, it is useful to know whether they theory passes an initial "sniff test." Evidence from inside leaders' heads showing that they believe in latent deterrence would suggest that a deeper investigation is worthwhile. By contrast, if we cannot find supporting evidence from any cases, the theory is probably off the mark – and any statistical patterns that we might find become less believable. In addition to assessing plausibility, the case studies that follow will illustrate the theory and unpack the mechanisms of latent deterrence.

The evidence will show that at least some officials in all ten countries think that nonweaponized nuclear programs confer influence. Leaders are sometimes reluctant to vocally embrace weaponless deterrence in public. A deep examination into these cases shows, however, that a broad swath of officials think that having latent nuclear forces benefits a country politically. Leaders believe they can gain leverage through all three mechanisms of weaponless deterrence, sometimes at the same time. That there are believers in latent deterrence across a diverse set of countries justifies a deeper look at the evidence and a more complete test of the theory's predictions, a task that I take up in subsequent chapters.

---

[1] On the role of plausibility probes in international relations research, see Levy (2008).

Cases and Mechanisms

Table 2.1 lists the ten countries investigated in this chapter. They have something in common: They developed dual-use nuclear technology that provided the potential foundation for a bomb program. These cases provide variation along four main dimensions: (1) the nuclear program's scale, (2) the level of militarization within the program, (3) the region, and (4) the country's geopolitical position.

Two of the countries I examined – Egypt and South Korea – had laboratory-scale enrichment or reprocessing (ENR) programs but never produced sufficient fissile material for a bomb. Of these cases, Egypt never successful built a nuclear power plant while South Korea is highly reliant on nuclear energy for electricity production. The other eight countries listed in Table 2.1 had larger-scale ENR plants in operation and possessed the ability to make enough fissile material for a bomb, at least in theory. Seven of the ten countries did not build nuclear weapons while the other three (India, Pakistan, and South Africa) eventually armed after a period of latency. Among the states that never weaponized, some of them at one point had a concerted program to seek a bomb (Iran and South Korea) while others engaged in suspicious activities but only halfheartedly attempted to build nuclear weapons (Argentina, Brazil, Egypt, and Spain). Still others thought about building a bomb but never really had a program that went beyond flirtation (Japan).

The countries are situated in six different regions: Africa, East Asia, Europe, Latin America, the Middle East, and South Asia. In terms of

Table 2.1 *Beliefs about latent nuclear deterrence in ten countries.*

Country	Mechanism		
	Deterrence by proliferation	Deterrence by delayed attack	Deterrence by doubt
Argentina	✓	✓	
Brazil	✓	✓	
Egypt	✓		
India		✓	✓
Iran	✓	✓	
Japan	✓		
Pakistan		✓	✓
South Africa	✓	✓	✓
South Korea	✓		
Spain	✓		

geopolitics, there are countries that had US treaty-backed protection and a large number of American forces on their soil (Japan, Spain, and South Korea), formal treaty allies with only a small US military presence (Argentina, Brazil, and Pakistan), nonenemies that lack formal security guarantees (India and South Africa), and clear adversaries of Washington today (Iran). Some countries moved through these categories over time. Spain had a policy of neutrality during World War II and eventually received formal security guarantees from the United States. Iran was a US ally prior to the Islamic Revolution in 1979.

Latent nuclear deterrence theory, which I presented in Chapter 1, expects that bomb-making capabilities have nuanced effects on international peace and stability. This chapter does not evaluate the conditions under which latent nuclear forces might bring political leverage – I will take up that task in Chapters 5–7. Instead, it assesses how government officials in the ten countries perceived their country's latent capacity to build nuclear weapons. Did they think that possessing the mere technological foundations for a bomb gave them international influence? If so, why exactly did they believe this capability conferred political benefits?

Answering these questions is challenging because leaders' views on weaponless deterrence are often hidden from plain view. Officials do not always say what they think in public, making it difficult for an analyst to get inside their heads. A thorough examination of these cases nonetheless turns up considerable evidence that officials in these countries believe in latent nuclear deterrence. When policymakers express confidence in weaponless deterrence, however, they do not always explain their reasoning. Leaders sometimes convey a vague sense that having the potential foundation for a bomb program can bring political influence without walking others through their causal logic.

In these situations we can fill in the blanks by answering two questions. First, do officials seem to view a nuclear strike or just arming as the means of punishment? When the anticipated punishment comes in the form of militarizing a previously latent capability, the means of influence is deterrence by proliferation. If elites view a nuclear attack as the threatened pain we must answer a second question: Does the country attempt to reassure others that it is nonnuclear, or does it create ambiguity about whether it might already be nuclear-armed? The former is suggestive of deterrence by delayed attack; the latter indicates doubt.

Table 2.1 also shows the mechanisms that appear in the ten cases. The lines between the three means of influence are fuzzy in practice, as countries may employ more than one simultaneously. Yet some clear patterns emerge. Deterrence by proliferation is the sole mechanism leaders emphasize in Japan and South Korea. Spanish leaders seemed to view armament as the primary form of punishment, but the other two mechanisms could have been in play as well. Three countries – Argentina, Brazil, and Iran – feature the logic of deterrence by proliferation and delayed attack, although armament is the dominant form of punishment. Deterrence by doubt is the main mechanism in India and Pakistan, but deterrence by delayed attack was also viable in these cases. The South African case is the only one where leaders expressed confidence in all three mechanisms. Deterrence by doubt is the most salient, though, as ambiguity played a key role in this case.

This evidence underscores a point from the previous chapter: We should not think about the mechanisms as competing, where one is "right" and the others are "wrong." They are all viable forms of influence that work together to enhance a latent nuclear power's political influence. Some of them are more compatible than others, however. It is difficult to pair deterrence by proliferation and doubt. Generating ambiguity can undermine threats to gain influence by militarizing a latent capability, since adversaries may think that a country is already nuclear-armed. Two combinations are therefore most likely: (1) deterrence by proliferation working alongside delayed attack and (2) deterrence by delayed attack operating in tandem with doubt.

I start by discussing the cases where deterrence by proliferation was the primary means of influence, according to statements made by government officials. I then turn to the cases where leaders articulated the logic of deterrence by proliferation and delayed attack. Finally, I present the evidence from cases where deterrence by doubt was salient.

Breakout Capabilities in East Asia

East Asia has been a hotbed for concerns about nuclear weapons proliferation, particularly since China's first nuclear test in 1964. Today the region is home to two prominent latent nuclear powers: Japan and South Korea.[2] Both countries pursued ENR technology for decades, with varying degrees of success, and continue to nurture this capability with vigor. Officials in Tokyo and Seoul believe that having the foundation for a bomb program gives their countries political influence, even if they do not go all the way to a bomb.

Japan possesses a sprawling nuclear infrastructure that includes an industrial-scale plutonium reprocessing plant in the village of Rakkasho

---

[2] Taiwan, another county located in the region, also had an ENR program in the past. For more on Taiwan, see Fitzpatrick (2016).

at the northern tip of Honshu, the country's largest island. Japan's dual-use capabilities give it the capacity to build nuclear weapons on short notice, possibly within six months of a political decision. At the same time, Tokyo has long maintained that it has no intent to arm in the absence of a major national security threat. A formerly secret Japanese government document from 1969 concluded that Tokyo did not currently need nuclear weapons but that it should "keep the economic and technical potential for the production of nuclear weapons, while seeing to it that Japan will not be interfered with in this regard."[3] Literary scholar Norihiro Kato describes Japan's approach as one of "technological deterrence," which "relies not on any overt threat, but the mere suggestion of a latent possibility."[4]

There is a widespread feeling in Japan that the country's breakout potential provides political benefits – but policymakers have historically kept this view close to their chests. As former Prime Minister Naoto Kan said, officials value the capacity to make a bomb but "they do not say it in public."[5] Increasingly, however, Japanese politicians are willing to trumpet the benefits of nuclear latency in public. In recent years, numerous Japanese officials have openly expressed the view that the country's ENR program bolsters deterrence.

In 2011, Shigeru Ishiba, a former Japanese Defense Minister, said, "I don't think Japan needs to possess nuclear weapons, but it's important to maintain our commercial reactors because it would allow us to produce a nuclear warhead in a short amount of time." The civilian nuclear program, he added, serves as "a tacit nuclear deterrent."[6] Ishiba told the *Associated Press* a year later, "Having nuclear plants shows to other nations that Japan can make nuclear weapons."[7] Another former Defense Minister, Satoshi Morimoto, similarly claimed that Japan's nuclear capabilities provide "very great defensive deterrent functions."[8] These two former defense ministers represent different political ideologies: Ishiba is a member of the conservative *LDP* while Morimoto is an independent academic – the first nonpolitician to serve in this role since World War II. This underscores that views about latent nuclear deterrence in Japan extend across the political spectrum.

Another official, speaking to a reporter in 2014 on the condition of anonymity, agreed with Ishiba and Morimoto, saying that once

[3] Quoted in Kato (2014).
[4] Kato (2014).
[5] Smith (2016).
[6] Quoted in Dawson (2011). See also Hoey (2016, 485).
[7] Nuclear Threat Initiative (2012).
[8] Quoted in Adelstein (2018).

Japan possessed enough plutonium for a bomb it had "already gone over the threshold" and possessed a nuclear deterrent.[9] Along similar lines, the prominent Japanese newspaper *Yomiuri Shimbun* published an editorial in 2011 stating that Japan's latent nuclear potential "functioned diplomatically as a potential nuclear deterrent."[10] Expressing apparent satisfaction with the benefits Japan reaps from its ENR capabilities, a Japanese defense official told Mark Fitzpatrick, a former US foreign service officer, "if China thinks the reprocessing is a deterrent, fine."[11]

Tokyo has exploited the ease with which it could build nuclear weapons to influence the behavior of its adversaries, particularly China and North Korea. For example, an unnamed Japanese official in the Ministry of Defense stated in a February 2018 interview: "If a North Korean missile, even one with no nuclear component, hits Japanese soil, I think the process [of building nuclear weapons] will begin. That's all that's needed. If someone is actually hurt or killed by North Korean missiles, the wheels will turn quickly."[12] The United States has issued similar threats on behalf of its ally. In an apparent attempt to motivate China to rein in North Korea, then-US Vice President Joe Biden told Xi Jinping, the Chinese leader, that Japan could go nuclear "virtually overnight."[13]

South Korea pursued nuclear weapons during the tenure of Park Chung Hee in the 1970s. In support of this effort, Seoul planned to buy a large-scale reprocessing plant from France in the mid-1970s. As a result of US pressure, however, this deal was never consummated.[14] South Korea officially terminated its bomb program following Park's assassination in October 1979, but continued to seek and develop dual-use capabilities.

Unlike Japan, South Korea has yet to obtain a commercial-scale ENR facility. As part of a formal agreement with North Korea in January 1992, the south pledged not to possess enrichment or reprocessing plants or build nuclear weapons.[15] Yet Seoul has an expansive civilian nuclear infrastructure that includes twenty-three nuclear reactors that produce electricity. It has also done considerable laboratory-scale ENR work, including chemical enrichment experiments from 1979 to 1981, some plutonium separation in the early 1980s, and work on laser enrichment

---

[9] Windrem (2014).
[10] Quoted in Fitzpatrick (2016, 82).
[11] Fitzpatrick (2016).
[12] Quoted in Adelstein (2018).
[13] Quoted in ibid.
[14] See Burr (2019).
[15] Fitzpatrick (2016, 23).

beginning in 1990. South Korea also developed pyroprocessing technology, which could be used to make weapons-grade plutonium, beginning in the late 1990s.[16]

Weaponless deterrence is politically sensitive in South Korea, like in Japan. For more than forty years, the United States has attempted to restrain Seoul's ENR capabilities, fearing the weapons proliferation implications of this dual-use technology. Public discussions that link sensitive nuclear technology and national security typically incite concerns in Washington, even if Seoul's ambitions are for a nonweaponized capability. South Korean officials are therefore sometimes reluctant to speak openly about weaponless deterrence. It is clear, though, that at least some South Korean elites understand the potential political benefits of nuclear latency, perhaps more so than their counterparts in Japan. As Thomas Countryman, a former US Assistant Secretary of State, indicated, "the 'latent deterrent' argument heard in Tokyo is voiced more openly and frequently in Seoul."[17]

A former South Korean cabinet-level official said that the first signs of a North Korean test in 1989 catalyzed the south's interest in ENR technology.[18] Years later, in 2014, Moon Chang-keuk, who was a nominee for prime minister, argued that South Korea should be a "nuclear technology" power – a state that does not build bombs but has the capacity to do so – because it lives next to nuclear-armed China and North Korea.[19] Further developing the capacity to make fissile material, according to this line of thinking, would enhance the country's leverage vis-à-vis its regional rivals, especially North Korea. Kim Tae-woo, who worked as an adviser to President Myungbak Lee, made this argument explicitly. "One can readily achieve the potential for nuclear armament without leaving the Nuclear Non-Proliferation Treaty (NPT)," Kim said, and "such discussion itself will have a deterrence effect against North Korea's nuclear weapons."[20] Echoing this view, a member of the South Korean business community told Robert Einhorn and Duyeon Kim "that possessing a latent nuclear capability would be a sufficient deterrent."[21]

South Korea has attempted to engage in deterrence by proliferation. In April 2014, President Park Geun-hye told Chinese leader Xi Jinping that another North Korean nuclear test would dramatically alter the

[16] On the proliferation risks of pyroprocessing, see Woo et al. (2020).
[17] Squassoni (2018).
[18] Fitzpatrick (2016, 32).
[19] Fitzpatrick (2016, 31).
[20] Quoted in Oh (2019). Translated from Korean by Hankyeul Yang.
[21] Einhorn and Kim (2016).

security situation in the region and lead to a "nuclear domino" effect.[22] Her apparent intent was to send a message: South Korea might build nuclear weapons if the north's program continued to advance. Park wanted help from China in reining in North Korea's nuclear arsenal. Chung Mong-joon, a longtime member of the National Assembly, has similarly indicated that proliferation threats enhance political leverage. Summarizing Chung's views on public armament discussions, one of his colleagues said, "The purpose is not for the ROK to have nuclear weapons. Chung wants others – China and the US – to pay attention and do something about [North Korea's] nuclear program."[23]

Nuclear Energy and Influence in Egypt

In 1958, the Soviet Union exported an experimental research reactor to Egypt, allowing Cairo to get its nuclear program off the ground. The reactor was housed at Egypt's nuclear research center in Inshas, which would become the hub of the country's program. During the ensuing decades, Egyptian officials sought to ramp up their country's dual-use nuclear capabilities. Egypt pursued an ambitious plan to build several nuclear power plants. It also established a laboratory-scale reprocessing capability at Inshas during the 1980s. According to the CIA, this provided the Egyptians with "valuable research and training with radioactive materials that would prove useful in the future should a weapons program be undertaken."[24] The planned nuclear energy expansion did not materialize, but officials have revived this effort at various points over the past fifteen years. Egypt is currently planning to bring its first nuclear power plant online in 2030, with Russian assistance.[25]

Egyptian attempts to gain influence without arms date back to the tenure of Gamal Abdel Nasser, who ruled the country from 1956 to 1970. Nasser repeatedly threatened to build nuclear weapons in public. During a television interview with the BBC on May 8, 1966, for example, the Egyptian leader said that his country was considering developing the bomb because "Israel is working in this field."[26] These statements were at least partially (and probably mostly) an attempt to send a message to officials in Israel: If you arm with nuclear weapons, we will too. As a senior nuclear expert working in the Egyptian government

[22] Chang (2014).
[23] Quoted in Fitzpatrick (2016, 40)
[24] US Central Intelligence Agency (1981b).
[25] Mikhail (2021).
[26] *The New York Times* (1966).

said in March 2004, "Nasser's statements [about nuclear weapons] did not reflect his real intentions. They were intended to convey political messages to different audiences – Egyptians, the Arab world, Israel. They were a form of political deterrence."[27]

Egypt's nuclear capabilities during Nasser's time in office were nascent, which weakened the country's attempts at weaponless deterrence. Advocates of the planned nuclear energy expansion during the 1980s seemingly understood this. They argued that having the capacity to make a bomb would enhance Egypt's political leverage, even if the country did not ultimately arm itself with nuclear weapons. As one official put it, "A peaceful nuclear program could be a deterrent against Israel, just in that it would have given Egypt deterrence by having advanced technology."[28] Another governmental expert reinforced this view, saying that Egypt's nuclear behavior was a way to tell other countries and the Egyptian public, "Don't force us to go that way."[29] Ibrahim Nafi, the editor of the government-run newspaper *Al-Ahram*, also expressed confidence in weaponless deterrence. He wrote in a February 1981 editorial that if Egypt were to enhance its nuclear energy program, it would gain influence over Israel: "becoming open to nuclear technology on the largest scale will prompt Israel and others to think deeply of the futility of starting a nuclear race in the area."[30] Nafi went on to write that his country's "inclination toward the use of nuclear power for peaceful purposes will strengthen Egypt's nuclear option in the future."[31]

United States intelligence recognized this line of thinking. A formerly top secret assessment from September 1981, written as Egypt was seeking to ramp up its nuclear energy program, concluded, "Egypt probably believes that an expanded nuclear power program eventually will give it the technical capability to develop nuclear weapons and that such a capability would provide leverage in future dealings with Israel, Iraq, and Libya."[32] By this time, Egyptian policymakers were well aware that Israel possessed nuclear weapons. They also knew that Libyan leader Muammar Qadaffi and Iraqi strongman Saddam Hussein coveted the bomb. According to the CIA, Egyptian president Anwar Sadat believed that ratifying the NPT, a move Egypt took in 1981, thereby gaining greater access to peaceful nuclear technology would "put more pressure

---

[27] Author's email communication with Maria Rost Rublee, January 13, 2020.
[28] Rublee (2009, 122–123).
[29] Author's email communication with Maria Rost Rublee, January 13, 2020.
[30] This is from an editorial quoted in US Central Intelligence Agency (1981c).
[31] US Central Intelligence Agency (1981c).
[32] US Central Intelligence Agency (1981b).

on Israel to do the same." It would also give Sadat "more options in the future for dealing with Libya and Iraq."[33] Those options included using the prospect of an Egyptian bomb to deter Iraqi or Libyan armament and, if that did not work, being in a position to follow suit.

Spain: Europe's Forgotten Latent Nuclear Power

In 1958, Spain established the Juan Vigón National Center for Nuclear Energy in Madrid. That same year, the country received its first research reactor via the US "Atoms for Peace" program.[34] Spain quickly ramped up its nuclear capabilities over the next decade, obtaining one of the most advanced nuclear programs in Europe by the early 1970s. The United States supplied Spain with its initial nuclear power plants. *Zorita* came online in 1968, followed by *Garoña* three years later.[35] Spain also received a gas-cooled reactor from France in 1972, known as *Vandellós*, which was ideal for plutonium production. Over the preceding decade, Madrid had invested in a significant reprocessing capability. Spain began building a pilot-scale plant for plutonium reprocessing at Juan Vigón in 1964. This facility separated plutonium from spent nuclear fuel between 1967 and 1971.[36] These dual-use capabilities gave Spain the technological capacity to produce fissile material for a bomb. Spain planned to build a second, larger research center in Soria, located about 150 miles northeast of Madrid, during the 1970s. The goal was to have a second reprocessing plant at Soria, but these plans were ultimately scrapped.[37] In the 1980s, Spain pared back its nuclear development and ceased constructing new atomic facilities, while continuing to operate previously constructed nuclear power plants.

Spanish leaders understood the political and military significance of its nuclear program. In the immediate aftermath of World War II, Spain considered research on nuclear energy a military matter.[38] In 1946, Spanish officials said, "at the moment, the atomic bomb is not being produced in Spain," while suggesting that the country might need this new military technology in the future to protect itself.[39] As Spain's nuclear capabilities advanced, in 1963, José María Otero Navascués, the

---

[33] US Central Intelligence Agency (1981b).
[34] Puig (2005, 212).
[35] IAEA (2013).
[36] IAEA (1976b) and IAEA (1976a), respectively.
[37] Sánchez-Sánchez (2017b).
[38] Puig (2005, 200–201). This was true of most countries doing nuclear research during this period.
[39] Quoted in Puig (2005, 201–202).

head of the nuclear energy board, carried out a secret study to assess the feasibility of building a Spanish bomb.[40] This study represented the beginning of Project Islero – a Spanish effort to seek nuclear weapons. According to General Guillermo Velarde, who directed the program, Project Islero was active during two periods: 1963–66 and 1974–81.[41] The Center for National Defense Studies (CESEDEN) conducted a more detailed study in the early 1970s. It concluded that Spain now had the capacity to make a bomb at an estimated cost of 8.7 billion pesetas (around 1.3 billion US dollars today) and even suggested the best place to conduct a nuclear explosives test: the Sahara.[42]

The degree to which Project Islero represented a concerted nuclear weapons program – as opposed to a campaign to give Spain a nuclear option – is unclear based on information presently in the public record. This program did not seem to resemble a mad dash to a bomb, à la the US Manhattan Project. There were influential voices within the country calling for an arsenal, but there were also domestic forces pushing in the other direction. Francisco Franco, the Spanish dictator from 1939 to 1975, was an early proponent of the project. But he grew weary of it and ordered Velarde to shut it down in 1966, while allowing some theoretical work to continue.[43] Resistance to all out weaponization continued in some circles even after Spain restarted Project Islero. During a 1975 meeting, for example, members of the military said they wanted to be equipped with nuclear weapons. An official in the Ministry of Foreign Affairs vehemently pushed back, saying that dropping a bomb on Rabat, the Moroccan capital, would contaminate the Ebro River in Spain, essentially rendering such a weapon unusable.[44] Years later, one Spanish official said plainly, "No bomb was going to be built in Soria," the larger nuclear center that aroused considerable suspicions of Spain's intentions in the United States.[45]

There was general consensus about one thing, even among critics of Project Islero: Spain should have the means to build a bomb in short order. Spanish government documents show, according to economic historian Esther Sánchez-Sánchez, that "Spanish military leaders repeatedly admitted that Spain had the technological capability to manufacture

---

[40] Bolaños (2014).
[41] Figueredo (2017).
[42] El País (1987).
[43] Berrojo (2015, 105) and Bolaños (2014). Franco felt that it would be difficult to keep the project secret. He also worried about blowback from the United States when Washington inevitably found out.
[44] El País (1987).
[45] El País (1987).

bombs and did not want to renounce it in advance in order to leave the possibility open to having someday its own nuclear arsenal."[46] This view persisted at least until the 1980s. A February 1987 story in the Spanish newspaper *El País* reported that the country's leaders have not closed the door on one day building a bomb. This included the socialist government of Felipe González, which was then in power. "The bomb has not been manufactured, but the way remains open," and numerous cabinet-level officials acknowledged this.[47] To support this policy of fence-sitting, Spain refrained from joining the NPT until November 1987.

Spain had political incentives to maintain bomb-making capabilities. Latent nuclear forces, Spanish officials believed, strengthened Spain's influence on the international stage. Franco knew, according to a report in the Spanish newspaper *El Mundo*, that nuclear latency gave Spain "special status."[48] That special status brought greater leverage via deterrence in the eyes of some Spanish elites. A well-sourced story in *El País* offered an explicit endorsement of weaponless deterrence: "The simple existence of Vandellós and other facilities, which opened the possibility of manufacturing atomic weapons, constituted a powerful deterrent against the North African countries."[49]

During the period of its nuclear buildup, Spain worried about threats emanating from two main states: Morocco and Algeria. In October 1957, one year after Morocco's independence, insurgents infiltrated Spanish West Africa, leading to the eight-month Ifni War. After the war, officials in Madrid worried about additional Moroccan attacks on Spanish territory, possibly with Algerian assistance.[50] As a former Spanish foreign minister put it, "For the military, the greatest danger came from a possible agreement between Rabat and Algiers, which was talked about a lot in those years. It would have posed a huge risk for Ceuta, Melilla and the Sahara."[51] Spain and the United States formalized a defense relationship in 1953 but Washington did not provide strong bilateral security guarantees until 1976 (Spain would go on to join NATO in 1982).[52] Some in Madrid felt that they could not rely on US support in the event of military conflict in Northern Africa. Morocco, after all, was a key US partner and was the first foreign country

---

[46] Sánchez-Sánchez (2017a).
[47] *El País* (1987).
[48] De la Cal and Garrido (2001).
[49] *El País* (1987).
[50] Bolaños (2014).
[51] *El País* (1987).
[52] Kim (2010).

to host American nuclear weapons on its soil beginning in 1954.[53] In this view, Spain needed nuclear weapons to address these challenges and bolster the country's position internationally.[54] Others came to adopt a different view: that Spain could counter these threats by developing and maintaining the capacity to make a bomb without actually arming.

The behavior of Spanish officials underscores the political value they saw in a latent deterrent. They routinely told their foreign counterparts that Madrid could build a bomb if it wanted to, in apparent attempts to gain leverage.[55] Spanish sources refer to these overtures as bluffs, indicating that they were meant to garner influence and did not imply that the government was in the midst of an unrestrained race to a bomb.[56]

A remarkable illustration comes from a meeting between Spanish Prime Minister Luis Carrero Blanco and US Secretary of State Henry Kissinger in Madrid on December 19, 1973. A few days earlier, Velarde had told Lieutenant General Manuel Díez-Alegría, the head of Defense High Command, that Spain now had the capacity to build three bombs per year using the Vandellós reactor and the indigenously built reprocessing plant. The general ordered Velarde to prepare a two-page report for Carrero Blanco laying out this conclusion. During the meeting with Kissinger, Carrero Blanco sought ironclad assurances that the United States would have Spain's back in the event of armed conflict. When Kissinger refused, the Spanish leader showed him Velarde's report.[57] The message was clear: Help us feel more secure or we will take matters into our own hands by arming with nuclear weapons – something that we now have the technological capacity to do. Episodes such as this suggest that Spanish officials saw the country's latent nuclear capacity as useful for gaining influence over the United States, in addition to deterring adversaries.

Views from Latin America

Two countries in Latin America developed the capacity to make nuclear bombs without actually arming: Argentina and Brazil.[58] Analysts in the United States have long suspected that both countries coveted nuclear weapons prior to the mid-1980s, when they transitioned from military

[53] Fuhrmann and Sechser (2014).
[54] Bolaños (2014).
[55] Sánchez-Sánchez (2017b).
[56] Cervera (2014).
[57] My summary of this meeting is based on Bolaños (2014).
[58] I discuss this case in greater detail in Chapter 7.

regimes to democracies.[59] However, neither Argentina nor Brazil had a concerted nuclear weapons program that resembled the US Manhattan Project. They launched dual-use ENR programs that gave them the capacity to build a bomb in the future, if necessary, but were not racing to build one. Argentina was doing laboratory-scale reprocessing work as early as the late 1960s and mastered enrichment technology during the 1980s. Brazil got a later start but had a pilot-scale enrichment plant operating by 1987. Today, both countries operate commercial enrichment plants. Officials in Brasilia and Buenos Aires acknowledge that having ENR capabilities gives them political influence.

Brazil understood the value of an indigenous ENR program from an early stage. A 1978 document prepared by Brazil's National Security Council noted that ENR capacity "Increases the [country's] political–economic bargaining power."[60] A policy analyst working in Brazil's foreign minister conveyed this sentiment: "dual-use technologies are valuable in themselves for the demonstration-effect of national competence, even if this competence is not necessarily translated into equipment of possible bellicose use." Latent capabilities can bolster deterrence, he added, "by filling the absence of effective military power with the certainty that there exists capacity for rapid mobilization."[61] Along similar lines, Pires Goncalves, Brazil's Army Minister, argued in the late 1980s that Brazil needed to develop nuclear technology to become "strong and respected." "This is deterrence by greatness," he added.[62]

Brazilian politicians did more than just speak about the deterrence benefits of nuclear latency in broad strokes – they explicitly argued that having this capability could dissuade Argentina from arming. According to Michael Barletta, who is now an analyst with the International Atomic Energy Agency, Brazilian officials perceived nuclear latency as a "species of deterrent," meaning that "the mere capacity to match a potential Argentine bomb was presumed sufficient to deter its construction."[63] An unnamed Brazilian official stated with a surprising degree of candor that Brazil's efforts on this front were intended to send a message: "watch your step; I can do it too, and I'm bigger than you are."[64]

---

[59] Databases used by political scientists classify Argentina and Brazil as "pursuing" nuclear weapons. See Singh and Way (2004) and Jo and Gartzke (2007).
[60] Venturini (1979).
[61] Barletta (1997, 16).
[62] Barletta (1997, 16).
[63] Barletta (1997, 15).
[64] Barletta (1997, 15).

Argentine officials similarly recognized that latent nuclear forces could give the country political leverage. A May 1974 memo prepared for President Ernesto Geisel by the Foreign Ministry states "that the acquisition of nuclear status does not necessarily require the existence of a nuclear arsenal."[65] All you needed, according to General Osiris Villegas, was to "master adequately the techniques for the peaceful uses of nuclear energy – including explosions for peaceful purposes – technological capability and infrastructure to provide sufficient assurances of convertibility and the objectives of national defense."[66] General Juan Guglialmelli similarly emphasized the value of nuclear latency: "For some, manufacturing the atomic bomb is a question of prestige. We believe that there is equal prestige in the international recognition of the scientific and technical capacity to manufacture it."[67]

The CIA seemed to pick up on Argentina's strategy. A 1982 assessment concluded that as Argentina's ENR program advanced "other nations will almost certainly believe that Argentina has the material available to build nuclear weapons on short notice, and we believe that Buenos Aires would exploit this perception for whatever diplomatic and national prestige benefits it may offer."[68] Edward S. Milenky, a former CIA analyst, made a similar argument in a 1978 book: "[B]y carefully cultivating the impression that it can explode a bomb easily Argentina reaps the prestige of near nuclear status and maintains a potential means of exerting pressure on its neighbors or even the U.S, which would not like to see such a radical revision in the South American balance of power."[69]

Argentina attempted to use the specter of nuclear armament to gain influence over other countries. Carlos Castro Madero, the Chairman of Argentina's National Atomic Energy Commission, made a thinly veiled proliferation threat on January 11, 1982. He declared, "We have the degree of scientific and technical development which would enable Argentina to manufacture an atomic bomb." When asked by the Brazilian reporter Rosental Calmon Alves whether the capacity to make nuclear weapons increases the likelihood of nuclear weapons proliferation in Latin America, Castro Madero replied, "No, I do not believe so because proliferation must have a stimulus behind it, a need to have an atomic bomb. Fortunately, on our continent there are no geopolitical conditions to force a country" down this path. When reminded that

---

[65] Silveira (1974a).
[66] Silveira (1974a).
[67] Quoted in FBIS (1982b).
[68] US Central Intelligence Agency (1961a).
[69] Milenky (1978, 36).

there are many unresolved international disputes in South America, the chairman asserted, "But these conflicts can be solved by peaceful means."[70] The implication of Castro Madero's remarks seems clear: Argentina could build nuclear weapons if threats against it necessitated that action, so other countries would do well not to threaten it. However, he also underscored that Buenos Aires does not intend to proliferate if others showed restraint.

A specific aim of this kind of threat was to influence the course of Brazil's nuclear program. Argentina raised the specter of nuclear armament in order to deter Brazil from building a bomb. Buenos Aires made it clear that its nuclear program could advance while simultaneously signaling openness to stopping – if Brazil placed restrictions on its capabilities. A 1977 US assessment that US Secretary of State Cyrus Vance left behind after meeting with Brazilian President Geisel underscored this approach. The document stated, "Argentina can and will otherwise proceed rapidly to a sizeable, autonomous, and unsafeguarded reprocessing capability, putting them way ahead of Brazil." Importantly, however, the document added, "This outcome can be avoided: the Argentine's are specifically interested in the possibility of an arrangement which would maintain 'regional equilibrium.'"[71]

Iran's Virtual Nuclear Arsenal

Iran began to covet nuclear weapons during its protracted war with Saddam Hussein's Iraq that began in 1980 and lasted until 1988. With assistance from the Pakistani-based A. Q. Khan Network, Iran began developing the capacity to enrich uranium in the late 1980s. By the early 2000s, Tehran was on its way to mastering the nuclear fuel cycle. Following public revelations of previously secret nuclear facilities in 2002, however, Iranian leaders appeared less determined to obtain a bomb. Prominent officials began expressing the view that Iran's latent nuclear capacity could provide political benefits.

Akbar Hashemi Rafsanjani, who served as president of Iran from 1989 to 1997, said in 2005, "once we have mastery of the fuel cycle, all our neighbors will draw the proper conclusion."[72] That conclusion, Rafsanjani went on, is as follows: "no one else in the region has these

---

[70] FBIS (1982b). I first became aware of this exchange while reading Thornton (1998, 81–82).

[71] Vance (1977).

[72] Quoted in Fukushima (2021). I thank George Perkovich, who attended the conference in Tehran where Rafsanjani made this statement, for bringing this evidence to my attention.

capabilities and that to dare to attack Iran would be foolhardy."[73] Seyed Hossein Mousavian, a senior negotiator on the nuclear issue from 2003 to 2005, also held this view. Peaceful enrichment technology "is extremely important for Iran," he wrote, "not only for industrial development, but also as a 'virtual deterrent.'" He went on to articulate the logic of weaponless deterrence: "A military attack might change Iran's objective from a virtual to a real nuclear deterrent."[74]

Outside observers understood how Iranian leaders thought and agreed that nuclear latency provided Iran with political benefits. Mohamed ElBaradei, the former Director General of the International Atomic Energy Agency, put it best. Referring to Iran's uranium enrichment program, he said, "they know it's a deterrent, they don't need a weapon, it sends a message." "If you have an enrichment program or a reprocessing program," he explained, "you are really sending a message that we know how to do it, should we decide to make a weapon."[75] Henry Kissinger, a former US Secretary of State and national security adviser, similarly believed that Iran's possession of "a military nuclear program at the very edge of going operational" would cause other countries to "reorient their political alignment toward Iran."[76] Journalist Brian Fung laid out how Iran's enrichment program allows it to engage in deterrence by delayed attack in *The Atlantic*: "They would be close enough to a bomb to feel secure in their deterrent – if they fear an imminent foreign invasion, as Tehran sometimes does, they could always 'break out' and put together a bomb."[77]

Some proponents of latent deterrence in Iran believe that the country's nuclear capacity has helped deter Israel or the United States from carrying out a preventive strike against Tehran's nuclear facilities. Mousavian, for example, argued that such an attack "would unify Iranians around the necessity of having nuclear weapons to deter attacks and threats to their land, integrity, identity, and rights."[78] Because Iran has the ability to make the most critical ingredient for a bomb, fissile material, it could convert this increased demand into a bomb more easily than its nonlatent counterparts, making the threat to arm following a preventive strike more credible. As we will see in Chapter 6, Iran's leaders were not the only ones to have this view. Key US officials believed that attacking Iran would

---

[73] Perkovich (2008).
[74] Mousavian (2012, 14).
[75] Warner and Elbaradei (2004).
[76] Kissinger (2012).
[77] Fung (2012).
[78] Mousavian (2012, 14).

be counterproductive, as it would merely fuel the very thing Washington was trying to stop: Iranian nuclear armament.

Iranian elites have used proliferation threats to enhance their political influence in negotiations with Washington. In 2015, the United States and its allies concluded an agreement with Tehran, known as the Joint Comprehensive Plan of Action (JCPOA), that curtailed some sensitive nuclear activities in exchange for lifting economic sanctions. In 2018, US President Donald Trump unilaterally withdrew from this agreement. In response, Iran gradually rolled back restrictions on its nuclear capabilities, reducing its breakout time – the time needed to obtain enough fissile material for at least one bomb – from one year to a handful of weeks and then days. Hoping to resuscitate the nuclear deal, or something like it, Iranian officials have raised the specter of nuclear armament. In February 2021, Mahmoud Alavi, Iran's intelligence minister, said, "Our nuclear program is peaceful ... but if they push Iran in that direction, then it wouldn't be Iran's fault but those who pushed it." He added, "If a cat is cornered, it may show a kind of behavior that a free cat would not."[79] Mohammad Baqer Qalibaf explicitly referred to the expansion of Iran's enrichment capabilities in March 2021 as a "bargaining chip" to dissuade the United States from taking a hard-line stance and reach a new political settlement.[80] These statements underscore that Iran has tried to use its latent nuclear capacity, particularly deterrence by proliferation, to enhance its international influence.

South Africa's Latent Nuclear Forces

South Africa initiated a peaceful nuclear program in the late 1940s. The program gained steam in 1965 when the country received its first research reactor from the United States, along with highly enriched uranium to fuel it. During the ensuing years, South Africa began to master ENR technology. By the late 1960s, it was enriching uranium on a laboratory scale and a larger facility, known as the *Y-Plant*, came online at the Valindaba nuclear complex in 1975. During the 1980s South Africa weaponized its nuclear capabilities, assembling a total of six nuclear bombs.[81] However, on March 24, 1993, President President F. W. de Klerk announced to the world that South Africa had dismantled its small

---

[79] Karami (2021).
[80] Brennan (2021).
[81] President F. W. de Klerk indicated that the weapons were "in the making" when he became minister of mineral and energy affairs during the early 1980s. See Friedman (2017).

nuclear arsenal. It remains the only country to give up indigenously built nuclear weapons.

In the late 1970s – after South Africa gained the capacity to produce HEU but before it assembled a bomb – the country attempted to gain leverage from its latent nuclear forces. It sought, in particular, to use deterrence by doubt and/or delayed attack as a form of international influence. As a formerly top secret CIA assessment put it, "Since 1977 South Africa has followed a policy of calculated ambiguity with respect to the nuclear option by intimating that it has the capability to produce nuclear weapons while disavowing any interest in doing so."[82]

Connie Mulder, South Africa's Information and Interior Minister, exemplified this approach with a thinly veiled warning in February 1977: "Let me just say that if we are attacked, no rules apply at all if it comes to a question of our existence. We will use all means at our disposal, whatever they may be. It is true that we have just completed our own pilot plant that uses very advanced technology, and that we have major uranium resources."[83] Prime Minister John Vorster similarly put the spotlight on South Africa's ENR capabilities. In 1976, he said, "we are only interested in the peaceful applications of nuclear power," but added that his country "can enrich uranium and we have the capability" to build a bomb.[84]

Officials in Pretoria and elsewhere believed that this approach bolstered deterrence. As a story in the *Washington Post* plainly stated, "South African officials indicate that they see the high level of nuclear technology they have developed as giving them both strategic bargaining power with the United States and the Soviet Union."[85] According to J. D. L. Moore, members of the South African publicly similarly viewed the country's uranium enrichment program as giving the "appearance of invulnerability in the eyes of the outside world."[86]

The US intelligence community agreed with this assessment. In July 1982, the CIA concluded that nuclear latency brought South Africa political benefits: "In our view, the perception of a South African *potential* to build nuclear weapons now has greater value to Pretoria than nuclear weapons testing could have."[87] Two years later, the agency prepared a thirty-one-page assessment dedicated to South Africa's nuclear program that amplified the value of nuclear latency for deterrence. "The assumption on the part of its adversaries that South Africa has

---

[82] US Central Intelligence Agency (1984b).
[83] Hoag (1977).
[84] Hoag (1977).
[85] Hoag (1977).
[86] Moore (1987, 66).
[87] US Central Intelligence Agency (1982b, 24). Emphasis added.

a nuclear weapons capability also gives Pretoria a deterrent credibility," the CIA concluded, "while allowing it to avoid the stigma of being the first to introduce nuclear weapons on the African continent." South Africa's latent nuclear capacity, the document added, "forces Pretoria's adversaries to assume that South Africa has a weapons capability and to factor that assumption into their policy formulation." Citing a specific example, the CIA stated, "even though Moscow need have no fear of South Africa's ability to launch a nuclear strike against the Soviet Union, it must take into consideration the damage South Africa could inflict on the Soviet Union's African clients, as well as on Soviet and Cuban garrisons in Africa."[88]

There are also indications that South African leaders bought into deterrence by proliferation during the late 1970s, before it assembled its first bomb. According to media reports at the time, South Africa's nuclear latency may have been "intended more as a diplomatic weapon than a battlefield one."[89] In this view, Pretoria could use the prospect of arming – but not actually launching a nuclear attack – to dissuade the United States from attempting to alter the government's policy of apartheid, which racially segregated the population.

South Africa entered a second phase of nuclear latency after dismantling its warheads.[90] The country shuttered its enrichment plants by the mid-1990s but retained nearly 500 pounds of HEU, enough for six nuclear weapons. Moreover, South Africa still had all of the knowledge needed to make a bomb. Officials recognize the political value that comes with the means to rearm quickly, which is partially why they have repeatedly resisted US pressure to eliminate its stockpile of weapons-usable fissile material. South Africans argue that its latent nuclear forces give the country "higher political and scientific stature."[91] In 2009, as South Africa was seeking to enhance its plutonium production capabilities, one nuclear official called reprocessing, "an element of contemporary power relations," further underscoring the perceived political benefits that come from an ENR program.[92]

Nuclear Ambiguity in South Asia

In May 1998, India carried out five nuclear tests, prompting Pakistan to detonate nuclear explosives two weeks later. Prior to openly declaring

---

[88] US Central Intelligence Agency (1984b).
[89] Hoag (1977).
[90] On South Africa's nuclear strategy during the period where it possessed assembled warheads, see Narang (2014).
[91] Birch and Smith (2015).
[92] von Hippel (2010).

their status as nuclear powers, ambiguity played a role in South Asian nuclear dynamics.[93] Both countries began to seek dual-use nuclear capabilities in the early days of the nuclear age. India obtained the capacity to reprocess plutonium in 1964, in part, because of peaceful nuclear assistance provided by Canada and the United States. Following closely behind, Pakistan carried out key enrichment and reprocessing activities in the 1970s. By the 1980s, both countries had the capacity to build a bomb quickly. Their proximity to a bomb fueled the perception that they might already be nuclear-armed. This belief, officials believed, bolstered deterrence. As Pakistani leader Muhammad Zia-ul-Haq acknowledged, the Indian and Pakistani nuclear programs served as a deterrent by the late 1980s in part because they had "a lot of ambiguities."[94]

Pakistan obtained all of the necessary components for making nuclear bombs at some point during the 1980s, but it probably did not deploy ready-to-fire nuclear weapons at this time. Islamabad had all of the ingredients in the kitchen but had not prepared the meal. In March 1987, Zia underscored the state of his country's program: "Pakistan can build a [nuclear] bomb whenever it wishes," implying that it had not yet done so.[95] Foreign assessments reached a similar conclusion. A story published in the *Washington Post* shortly after Zia's statement, stated that US officials "do not believe Pakistan has a nuclear device" but the country had the technological capacity to build one in short order.[96] According to Ashley Tellis, who later served as a special assistant on the National Security Council staff, most Indian scientists concluded that "Pakistan had no nuclear capabilities worth the name" at this time.[97]

Estimates vary as to how long it would have taken Pakistan to build a bomb during this period. In 1987, a Belgian scientist thought it would take one month from the moment of a political decision.[98] However, US officials thought it could be done quicker: One said that Pakistan could assemble a bomb within two weeks, while another claimed that Pakistan was just "two screwdriver turns" from having an intact, usable

---

[93] Hagerty (1993, 1995) also makes this point, focusing especially on the 1990 Kashmir crisis.

[94] Quoted in Hagerty (1995, 95).

[95] Weintraub (1987).

[96] Weintraub (1987).

[97] Tellis (2001, 191). Samar Mubarakmand, a nuclear physicist who led the team that carried out Pakistan's nuclear tests in 1998, has said that Islamabad did not have the means reliably to deliver a nuclear warhead until 1995. Quoted in Khan (2012, 232–233).

[98] A journalist asked Zia about this assessment, which was based on the Belgian's conversation with Pakistani scientists, prompting Zia's March 1987 comment about Pakistan's nuclear potential. "For that you don't have to quote a scientist from Belgium," Zia said. See Weintraub (1987).

bomb. In any case, the available evidence suggests that Pakistan was close to making a nuclear bomb by the late 1980s but had not yet gone all the way.[99]

Despite the apparent latent state of its nuclear capabilities, Pakistan raised the possibility of a nuclear strike in the 1980s. In 1987, during the Brasstacks crisis with India, A. Q. Khan, the so-called father of the Pakistani bomb, boasted to an Indian journalist, "we are here to stay and let it be clear that we shall use the bomb if our existence is threatened."[100] In May 1986, India began a military exercise called *Brasstacks* that was as big as the largest NATO exercises at the time. Designed to test military readiness, the exercise included 250,000 troops, 1,300 tanks, and cost one billion dollars.[101] Pakistan viewed the operation as a potential prelude to war and mobilized its forces along the border with India.[102] Khan's nuclear threat came at the height of the crisis, as 340,000 troops from both sides faced each other along the border. Many analysts believe that Khan issued the threat deter Indian aggression.[103] Both countries ultimately stood down and the crisis came to an end in March 1987.

At least some Pakistanis believe that its ambiguous nuclear capabilities bolstered deterrence. Officials in the Army reportedly hold an "enduring belief" that the country's latent nuclear capabilities deterred military conflict in the 1980s.[104] During this period, Pakistan could not have launched an immediate nuclear strike in retaliation for Indian aggression. Yet, in the event of war, Pakistan may have had time to assemble a nuclear bomb and potentially use it to attack Indian territory. Moreover, its close proximity to the bomb forced officials in New Delhi to grapple with the possibility that Pakistan might already be nuclear armed.[105]

India similarly engaged in deterrence by doubt. A February 1965 CIA assessment concluded that India "can proceed with a number of the steps which are prerequisites to a weapons program without making a firm decision to develop nuclear weapons," adding that it could have

---

[99] I cannot rule out the possibility that Pakistan assembled a bomb during this period. Pakistan conducted a successful cold test in March 1984, making it plausible that it had an assembled, workable bomb by the late 1980s. See Khan (2012, 189) and Fair (2017, 132).

[100] Quoted in Hagerty (1998, 103).

[101] Chari et al. (2007, 44).

[102] Weisman (1987).

[103] See, for example, Hagerty (1998, 111).

[104] Fair (2014, 223).

[105] Despite Pakistan's beliefs, no Indian official, to my knowledge, has admitted that they were deterred by doubt or delayed attack. See Narang (2017, 52).

a bomb within a year of a political decision to go for it.[106] Nine years later, New Delhi detonated a nuclear explosive device underground in the Rajasthan desert. One might expect that such an event would bring a country into the club of nuclear-armed nations, just like when the United States carried out its first test in July 1945. Things worked differently in this instance. India characterized its first test as a peaceful nuclear explosion and it did not immediately build and deploy nuclear bombs.[107] As a September 1985 CIA memorandum stated, India "has not proceeded with weaponization ... most analysts believe that India is not likely to develop nuclear weapons unless it becomes convinced that Pakistan" has assembled and stockpiled warheads.[108] India ultimately built nuclear forces, achieving the ability to reliably deliver them by the mid-1990s.[109] However, for a period that spanned at least three decades, India possessed a nonweaponized nuclear program that provided it with the means to assemble a bomb quickly.

During this time, India exploited its latent nuclear capability to induce restraint among its adversaries. George Perkovich, who has written a definitive history of India's nuclear program, refers to this as "the 'nuclear option' strategy."[110] In his words, this approach gave India "enough military potential to give adversaries pause."[111] It allowed India to potentially deter international aggression by (implicitly) threatening to launch a delayed nuclear attack in the event of war, and/or raising the possibility that it might already be in possession of a bomb.

Conclusion

The preceding discussion shows that officials in ten countries believe that latent nuclear forces enhance political influence. This evidence usefully illustrates the theory, showing that policymakers think it is possible to gain leverage through all three mechanisms of weaponless deterrence: proliferation, delayed attack, and doubt. In doing so, it adds to the plausibility of latent nuclear deterrence theory. The evidence offered in this chapter, while consistent with the theory, is subject to three caveats.

---

[106] US Central Intelligence Agency (1965).
[107] Although the phrase *peaceful nuclear explosion* might sound inherently contradictory, in the early years of the nuclear age officials envisioned civilian uses for nuclear explosions, like making canals or tunnels.
[108] US Central Intelligence Agency (1985b, 8).
[109] Kampani (2014).
[110] Perkovich (1999, 189). See also Narang (2014, 96).
[111] Perkovich (1999, 189).

First, there may be a disconnect between leaders' beliefs and the reality of world politics. Consider, for example, that US President Harry Truman was convinced that he compelled the Soviet Union to withdraw its forces from Iran in 1946 by issuing a nuclear threat. In fact, however, Truman never conveyed a threat to use nuclear weapons.[112] Just because leaders believe that they gain influence from having bomb-making potential does not make it true. Potential adversaries may not ultimately be deterred by mere latent nuclear forces.

Second, I have examined a significant subset of the latent nuclear powers – about 30 percent of the cases – but many others have not yet been analyzed. Although we can reasonably conclude that belief in weaponless deterrence is not limited to just a handful of countries, the pervasiveness of this view across the full universe of cases remains unclear.

Third, within the countries examined here, the beliefs of governmental officials varied. Some were enthusiastic about the value of a latent force while others were more skeptical. This is hardly unique to weaponless deterrence. In the United States today, for example, there is some disagreement among US officials about virtually every foreign policy issue: the withdrawal of forces from Afghanistan, how to respond to Iran's nuclear program, whether continuing to maintain military alliances serves American interests, and what to do about China's growing military and economic power. The cases in this chapter show that multiple officials in these countries, as well as outside observers, see political value in having dual-use nuclear technology. Confidence in the ability to gain influence without arms, then, is not limited to a single minority voice – but this does not necessarily imply that every official in the country accepted this view.

We still do not know, on the basis of the evidence presented so far, whether the theory is correct. What I can say is that an initial survey of views worldwide give us reason to believe that latent nuclear forces are an important and under appreciated form of international influence. Given the pervasiveness of this view among political leaders, this issue is worthy of further examination, a task that I take up in the following chapters.

---

[112] Sechser and Fuhrmann (2017, 173).

3   Almost Nuclear: Identifying Latent Nuclear Powers*

On November 15, 1964, Indonesian Brigadier General Hartono Rekso Dharsono, the Director of the Army Arsenal, asserted that his country could explode a nuclear bomb during the following year.[1] This claim was dubious. At the time, Indonesia possessed only one relevant nuclear facility: a US-supplied research reactor in Bandung, about ninety miles from Jakarta. It was far from the point of having the capacity to produce fissile material – the most essential ingredient for a bomb. United States officials understood this and called the general's claim "absurd."[2] Indonesia was probably at least a decade away from a bomb in late 1964. But this reality did not stop Hartono from boasting that his country would have a bomb within fourteen months.

Countries may claim to have bomb-making capabilities when they cannot actually arm in short order. How, then, do we know which countries possess genuine latent nuclear potential? Answering this question is essential for analyzing the causes and political effects of nuclear latency. Knowing which countries are nuclear-weapons-capable, and when they achieved the capacity to arm, allows us to determine how a country's fortune changes once it achieves nuclear latency. Without this information, a systematic test of latent nuclear deterrence theory is impossible.

At this point in the book, it is clear that some government officials around the world believe that latent nuclear forces bring greater international influence. What we want to know now is whether they are justified in holding this view, or if their beliefs in weaponless deterrence are misguided. An important first step in finding out is to identify the states that could make a bomb with relative ease.

---

* An earlier version of the database described in this chapter was introduced in Fuhrmann and Tkach (2015). I am grateful to Benjamin Tkach for his work on the initial iteration of the database.

[1] *The New York Times* (1964).

[2] Cornejo (2000, 33).

This chapter introduces the latent nuclear powers and provides information about their capabilities. It describes the concept of nuclear latency and the strategies that scholars have taken to measure it. I then explain my approach to measuring nuclear latency, which is based on enrichment and reprocessing (ENR) capabilities, and why it is well suited for analyzing weaponless deterrence. This book relies on the Nuclear Latency (NL) dataset, which contains information on more than 250 ENR facilities or laboratories in thirty-three countries, to identify latent nuclear powers across countries and over time. Chapters 4–7 will draw on this database to test various aspects of latent nuclear deterrence theory.

Nuclear Latency: Concept and Measurement Strategies

Nuclear latency is the underlying capacity to make nuclear weapons without actually arming. It sometimes refers to a timetable: how long it would take a country to build nuclear weapons following a political decision.[3] Scholars also conceive of this concept in binary terms, whereby countries achieve latency once they surpass a particular threshold.[4] Researchers in fields ranging from political science to nuclear engineering have measured latency based on a variety of indicators.

Nuclear technology is dual-use in nature, meaning that it can serve both commercial and military purposes. Even peaceful nuclear programs, then, augment a state's capacity to make a bomb to some degree.[5] Some scholars imply that any country in possession of dual-use nuclear technology is weapons-capable. Nuclear physicist Frank Barnaby, for example, argues that "a country with a civil nuclear program will have little difficulty in designing, developing and fabricating nuclear weapons."[6] By this standard, there are nearly seventy latent nuclear powers in the world today. However, most research raises the technological bar for what constitutes nuclear latency or incorporates additional indicators beyond just research or power reactors.

Stephen Meyer pioneered an index-based approach to nuclear latency within political science during the 1980s.[7] His measure of latent nuclear capabilities includes fourteen "surrogate indicators": mining activities, known uranium deposits, steel production, cement production, nitric acid production, sulfuric acid production, production of nonorganic

---

[3] Sagan (2010, 80).
[4] See, for example, Mehta and Whitlark (2017a).
[5] On the dual-use dilemma in nuclear politics, see Fuhrmann (2012a).
[6] Barnaby (2004, 68).
[7] Meyer (1984).

nitrogenous fertilizers, electrical production capacity, operation of research reactors, petroleum distillation, coal coking, the manufacture or assembly of motor vehicles, and radio production.[8] Meyer considers a country to be latent once it meets relevant thresholds in these areas. According to his approach, thirty-four countries were latent nuclear powers by 1982.[9] Political scientist Richard Stoll extended this database through 1992.[10] He dropped the uranium deposit requirement, arguing that states had open access to this resource on the market after 1970. Fourth-eight countries had the latent capacity to build nuclear bombs in the early 1990s, according to Stoll's updated database.

Political scientists Dong-Joon Jo and Erik Gartzke produced a seven-point indicator of latency based on the Meyer-Stoll approach.[11] They dropped some of Meyer's original indicators – mining activities, cement production, petroleum distillation, and coal cocking – on the grounds that they were "too easily available to be thresholds."[12] Jo and Gartzke sum the number of other thresholds that each country crosses in a given year, producing a variable that ranges from 0 to 7. Higher scores on their composite index indicate greater capacity. Countries that score 7 have all the domestic resources and skills needed to make a bomb, according to their approach, and should be able to do so with relative ease. According to their database, forty-five countries met this threshold in 2001 – the most recent year of data availability.

Political scientists Bradley Smith and William Spaniel built on this work by developing an updated measure of nuclear proficiency called ν-CLEAR (the Greek letter is "nu").[13] They used an item-response approach, rather than an additive index, to estimate the capacity to make a bomb based on twelve indicators. Their measure includes the seven variables from the Jo and Gartzke database along with the possession of heavy water reactors, other nuclear power plants, uranium enrichment facilities, plutonium reprocessing centers, and submarines.[14] ν-CLEAR weights these variables according to their relative importance and

---

[8] See Appendix B in Meyer (1984, 173–193).
[9] Meyer (1984, 41).
[10] Stoll (1996). For further discussion, see Sagan (2010). and Fuhrmann and Tkach (2015).
[11] Jo and Gartzke (2007).
[12] Jo and Gartzke (2006).
[13] Smith and Spaniel (2020).
[14] They also include a broader measure with four weapon-related indicators: exploring nuclear weapons, having a concerted bomb program, conducting a nuclear test, and successfully assembling a nuclear bomb. Because this inclusive measure captures actual weapons possession along with other capabilities that influence bomb-making capacity, however, it is not a pure measure of latency.

accounts for the uncertainty that arises in measuring nuclear proficiency, a concept that is not directly observable.

Nuclear engineer David Sweeney developed an alternative approach that can identify the number of days it would take a country to build a bomb based on its existing capabilities.[15] Sweeney's Nuclear Weapon Latency (NWL) tool accounts for the three main stages in weapons development: obtaining fissile material, weaponizing that material, and delivering the weapon with bombers, missiles, or submarines. This tool permits sensitivity analysis to assess the nonproliferation implications of changes in capabilities. Using the NWL tool, for example, nuclear engineer Mary Johansen analyzed how the 2015 Joint Comprehensive Plan of Action (JCPOA) increased Iran's latency time by placing limits on its enrichment activities.[16] Unlike the approaches described previously, however, the NWL tool does not come with precanned estimates for each country's latency values across many years. The tool's user must determine whether a country has completed a subtask at a given point in time and, if not, how long it would take to finish.

All of these approaches to measuring nuclear latency have value for scholars and policymakers. Depending on a researcher's aims, one of these databases or tools may provide the best indicator of latent nuclear capacity. When it comes to analyzing weaponless deterrence, though, an alternative approach is more appropriate.

Making Fissile Material: Enrichment and Reprocessing Programs

This book measures nuclear latency based on a country's ability to produce fissile material – plutonium or weapons-grade HEU. I classify countries as latent nuclear powers if they meet two criteria: (1) having one or more *operational* ENR facilities on their national territory and (2) the absence of one or more assembled nuclear weapons. Nations can move in and out of latency over time. A previously ENR-capable country would no longer be classified as latent if it shuttered all its facilities, as was the case in Belgium after 1974. Countries can also move out of latency if they go on to build one or more bombs, a path followed by ten countries.

The book focuses on ENR capabilities because they provide the most appropriate test of latent nuclear deterrence theory. As I explained in Chapter 1, two factors give sensitive nuclear technology value in weapon-

---

[15] Sweeney (2014).
[16] Johansen (2016).

less deterrence. First, having an ENR program shortens a country's time to a bomb. It is well known that producing (or otherwise obtaining) sufficient quantities of plutonium or weapons-grade HEU is the most difficult step in making a bomb. Possessing ENR technology, therefore, is perhaps the most essential feature of nuclear latency. As political scientist Scott Sagan put it, whether a country could separate plutonium or enrich uranium "should be at the core of any assessment of a state's latent nuclear weapons capability."[17] Second, given the tight and widely recognized connection between ENR capabilties and bomb-making potential, developing the capacity to make fissile material has important signaling value. It is a key means by which countries convey threats in latent deterrence. Without an adversary's bomb-making potential starring them in the face, policymakers may fail to consider it, making latent deterrence impossible.

Alternative measures of latency have less desirable features – at least when it comes to testing latent nuclear deterrence theory. Adopting a technological threshold below ENR programs – for example, simply having a nuclear power plant – would result in Armenia, Ukraine, and the United Arab Emirates being labeled latent nuclear powers. These countries probably could not arm as quickly as an ENR-capable state. Because Jo and Gartzke's index does not directly distinguish states based on their present ability to make plutonium or HEU, it produces some surprising results.[18] Uzbekistan and Japan both received the maximum score in 2001, for example.[19] While Japan is widely seen as having the capability to build a bomb quickly, to my knowledge, no officials in Washington have called Uzbekistan a latent nuclear power due to its relatively rudimentary capabilities in this domain.

In addition, other measures of latency include some capabilities that attract little attention from policymakers. Expertise in metallurgy, for example, is relevant for building nuclear reactors and other fuel-cycle facilities. But this is not something on which world leaders or other senior government officials fixate when they are thinking about proliferation risks. After seeing a foreign country build up expertise in metallurgy, a government official probably would not think, "this shows they have bomb-making potential, so I'd better not back them into a corner." Even if other indicators of latency provide more precise proliferation timelines – and they sometimes do – ENR capabilities have stronger

---

[17] Sagan (2010, 90).
[18] However, their index does account for the skills and resources that are needed to build an ENR plant.
[19] For a related discussion, see Sagan (2010, 85–89).

signaling value, making them better in the context of latent nuclear deterrence theory.

Stages of Latency: Partial and Full

I distinguish between two stages of nuclear latency: partial and full. Table 3.1 summarizes the differences between these two stages. Fully latent states have pilot or commercial scale ENR plants in operation during a given year. Countries that get to the point of having at least one operational pilot plant can credibly make sufficient fissile material for one or more bombs. A relevant example is India's reprocessing plant at Trombay, which began operating in 1964 and separated the plutonium used in the country's first nuclear explosive test ten years later. This does not necessarily mean that they are already in possession of sufficient weapons-grade HEU or plutonium, just that they have facilities capable of meeting this technological threshold. Countries are partially latent if they have laboratory-scale ENR programs without pilot/commercial plants. These states may have produced small amounts of fissile material in an experimental setting but have not (yet) made enough for a bomb, nor could their small-scale facilities reasonably do so. Australia, for instance, enriched a small amount of uranium – not nearly enough for a single bomb – at its Lucas Heights laboratory after launching a centrifuge program in the mid-1960s.

How many days, months, or years would it take partially or fully latent states to build nuclear weapons? Once states possess fissile material, they must complete two additional steps: weaponizing this material and mating the weapon to a delivery system. How quickly a state could complete these other requirements depends partially on the sophistication of the weapon. Producing a gun-type fission weapon like the *Little Boy* bomb the United States dropped on Hiroshima would be relatively straightforward for most countries in possession of weapons-grade HEU. An implosion-type bomb is another kind of fission weapon – one that is

Table 3.1 *Stages of nuclear latency.*

Latency stage	ENR capability	Enough fissile material for a bomb	Likely time to a bomb	Signaling value
Full	Pilot/commercial plant	Yes	Days–2 years	Strong
Partial	Laboratory-scale	No	3–10 years	Weak

Note: ENR = enrichment and reprocessing.

more common in the world today. This design, which the United States used for the *Fat Man* bomb dropped on Nagasaki, can use weapons-grade HEU or plutonium. Gun- and implosion-type fission weapons could be dropped from an airplane; the United States used a B-29 to deliver these weapons to Japanese targets. Using a long-range missile, however, requires countries to produce small and light nuclear weapons, a more time-consuming process known as miniaturization. For example, North Korea conducted its first nuclear test in 2006 but probably did not have miniaturized warheads that could be mated to intercontinental ballistic missiles (ICBMs) until around 2017 – eleven years after the first test.[20] Producing more-powerful thermonuclear weapons, which use both fission and fusion, also takes more time than making a much simpler fission bomb. The United States tested its first thermonuclear weapon in 1952, seven years after its use of fission weapons in World War II.

Table 3.1 estimates how long it would take partially and fully latent states to obtain a first-generation fission bomb. Most states with full nuclear latency should be able to build a crude nuclear device within two years of a political decision. To generate this timeline, I identified countries that were sprinting to build a bomb as quickly as possible before reaching each stage of nuclear latency.[21] Four countries fit this profile: China, the Soviet Union, the United Kingdom, and the United States. Then, I calculated how long it took these states to assemble weapons once they crossed the latency threshold. Technological capacity was the main constraint for these states, making them useful for estimating the time it would take a politically determined country with full latency to get a bomb. Three of the countries that were sprinting to a bomb before their first pilot-scale ENR plant came online had built a weapon by the next year (China, the Soviet Union, and the United Kingdom) and the fourth (the United States) did so within two years. The estimate of less than two years should be interpreted cautiously because it emerges from a small number of cases, and future proliferators might not resemble those from the past.

Some fully latent states in the world today could build a fission bomb in a matter of months. Journalists and experts report that Japan, for instance, could have a weapon in six to twelve months if it used stockpiled civilian plutonium.[22] Iran could have a "crude" nuclear

---

[20] Warrick et al. (2017).

[21] Data on nuclear sprinting come from Narang (2017).

[22] Estimating a precise timeline for Japan (or any other country) is difficult and requires making assumptions that may or may not turn out to be true. On some of the

weapon in a few months, according to one recent report, and be able to deliver such a weapon on a ballistic missile within two years.[23] In theory, a state that already had sufficient fissile material could build a bomb in a matter of days, if it had mastered the other requisite steps.

The proliferation timeline for a partially latent state is longer and more uncertain. The likely range for most states in this category is three to ten years. To generate this timeline, I started by repeating the procedure described above but for states with laboratory-scale ENR programs. However, only one country, China, was sprinting to a bomb at least one year before becoming partially latent. Beijing had a nuclear weapon six years after first obtaining partially latency. This is instructive, but it does not provide a sense of what the range might look like. Looking to other cases can provide further guidance. Argentina gives a helpful baseline. In 1982, the CIA estimated that Buenos Aires would take three years to build a bomb.[24] At this time, Argentina had done significant laboratory-scale work on both reprocessing and enrichment. It was one year away from announcing the opening of its pilot-scale enrichment plant in Pilcaniyeu.[25] Argentina's capabilities were advanced for a partially latent state in 1982, making three years a reasonable lower-bound estimate for the time it would take a country in this category to obtain a bomb. To determine the upper-bound estimate, I returned to the average amount of time it has taken countries to produce significant quantities of fissile material historically, which is about ten years from the start of a program (see Chapter 1). Partially latent countries have already made some progress toward mastering the most difficult part of making a bomb. They should therefore be able to make enough fissile material quicker than the average historical time for states starting from scratch. It is difficult to know exactly how much quicker; I assume 20 percent.[26] I further assume that it would take another two years to complete weaponization and delivery, giving an upper-bound estimate of ten years.

Some fully or partially latent countries could have proliferation time-lines that fall outside of the ranges reported in Table 3.1. The point here is not to provide precise estimates. It is instead to give a rough sense of how long it would likely take a state with partial or full latency to get a simple fission bomb following a political decision. For a fully latent

controversies associated with estimating Japan's proliferation timeline, see Lewis (2014).

[23] See Bob (2022).
[24] Anderson (1982).
[25] Benjamin (1983).
[26] This is admittedly an arbitrary threshold.

state, the timeline would probably be measured in months or a couple years, and possibly days. Partially latent states would take several years longer, but they could get there quicker than a totally ENR-free country in most circumstances. The timelines for building more-sophisticated weapons, including those that could be miniaturized and mated to long-range missles, would be longer than those shown in the table.

The signaling value of an ENR program will vary based on its scale, as shown in Table 3.1. Having a large-scale ENR program capable of producing enough fissile material for a bomb, giving a state full nuclear latency, sends a much stronger signal. Laboratory-scale activities are less worrisome from a nonproliferation standpoint and might be missed altogether due to their small scale.

Comparing Latency Measures

One advantage of an ENR-based measure of nuclear latency is that it more closely resembles policymakers' views about who is weapons capable. To further illustrate this point, let's compare the latency indicators for a single year: 1975. Table 3.2 lists the countries identified as being weapons-capable in a formerly secret December 1975 CIA assessment alongside the measures produced by political scientists.[27] This allows us to assess how well the measures generated by scholars match real-world views of weapons capabilities.[28]

There is substantial overlap between the CIA's list of latent nuclear powers and countries with at least laboratory ENR capabilities. Eighty-six percent of those on the CIA's list (twelve of fourteen) were ENR-capable. Two countries without ENR programs were latent according to the CIA: South Korea and Taiwan. Within a few years, however, both of these countries had conducted ENR activities at least on a laboratory scale. Five countries with ENR programs did not have latent nuclear forces in 1975 according to the CIA: Australia, Belgium, the Netherlands, North Korea, and Norway. However, all of them entered discussions about nuclear latency within the US intelligence community around this time.[29] With the possible exception of North Korea, all of these countries could reasonably be classified as latent nuclear powers based on CIA assessments from this era.

---

[27] These are countries that could arm within seven years.

[28] Twenty-six countries scored 7 on Jo and Gartzke's index in 1975. To achieve symmetry, the table lists the top twenty-six countries in Smith and Spaniel's database (2020).

[29] The CIA describes Australia, Belgium, the Netherlands, and Norway as weapons-capable in a January 1966 assessment (US Central Intelligence Agency, 1966). In 1975, the CIA concluded that North Korea could not have a nuclear device within ten years.

Table 3.2 *Comparing measures of nuclear latency in 1975.*

Country	Latency indicator			
	JG	SS	CIA	ENR
Argentina	✓	✓(11)	✓	✓
Australia	✓	✓(5)		✓
Austria	✓	✓(26)		
Belgium	✓	✓(8)		✓
Brazil	✓		✓	✓
Bulgaria	✓	✓(10)		
Canada	✓	✓(12)	✓	✓
Colombia	✓			
Czechoslovakia	✓	✓(13)		
Denmark	✓	✓(23)		
East Germany	✓	✓(6)		
Finland	✓	✓(25)		
Greece	✓			
Hungary	✓	✓(17)		
Iran		✓(15)	✓	✓
Italy	✓	✓(3)	✓	✓
Japan	✓	✓(4)	✓	✓
Mexico	✓	✓(16)		
Netherlands		✓(24)		✓
North Korea				✓
Norway				✓
Pakistan		✓(14)	✓	✓
Poland	✓	✓(18)		
Portugal	✓	✓(19)		
Romania	✓	✓(20)		
South Africa			✓	✓
South Korea	✓	✓(22)	✓	
Spain	✓	✓(7)	✓	✓
Sweden	✓	✓(9)	✓	✓
Taiwan			✓	
Turkey	✓	✓(21)		
West Germany	✓	✓(1)	✓	✓
Yugoslavia	✓	✓(2)	✓	✓

Notes: JG = Jo and Gartzke; SS = Smith and Spaniel;
CIA = Central Intelligence Agency;
ENR = current or past enrichment or reprocessing.
For SS, ranking is in parenthesis.

There is more variation between the CIA's list and the other two latency indicators. Jo and Gartzke's index classifies ten of the countries on the CIA's list as latent nuclear powers but misses four: Iran, Pakistan, South Africa, and Taiwan.[30] More strikingly, sixteen countries with the maximum score on Jo and Gartzke's seven-point indicator – nearly 60 percent of all states that meet this threshold – were not latent according to the CIA. This includes Austria, Colombia, Finland, Greece, Mexico, and Turkey. Based on the available CIA assessments from this era, the US government did not consider these states as capable of arming quickly. They are notably absent from the agency's nuclear proliferation assessments conducted in the mid-1970s, especially when it comes to discussions of threshold capabilities. Others, most notably the six Eastern European nations on Jo and Gartzke's list, did receive attention in relevant documents but had relatively long proliferation timetables. The CIA's timeline for when these countries would have the technological capacity for a nuclear device was: "not in the foreseeable future."[31] "Although several of the Eastern European nations have nuclear power programs," the CIA concluded, they do not "operate fuel reprocessing facilities of significant size."[32] Overall, in 1975, only 35 percent of the most nuclear-capable states according to Jo and Gartzke's index were latent nuclear powers in the eyes of the US intelligence community.

v-CLEAR fares better, which is not surprising given that it directly measures enrichment and reprocessing capabilities. The four highest-scoring countries in 1975 – West Germany, Yugoslavia, Italy, and Japan – were clearly latent nuclear powers at this time according to US government documents. However, because this database also includes the seven indicators from Jo and Gartzke's index, it rates some countries as weapons-capable that the CIA did not consider to be among the most prominent latent nuclear powers. This includes East Germany (#6), Bulgaria (#10), and Mexico (#16). It is notable that South Africa, a country that would actually build nuclear weapons a few years later, is only the fifty-fifth most capable state in 1975, according to v-CLEAR. Bangladesh, Jamaica, the Philippines, Uganda,

---

[30] Missing South Africa is particularly notable because it would go on to assemble a nuclear weapon some time between 1978 and 1982.

[31] However, Czechoslovakia and East Germany appeared in a 1966 CIA assessments of states that could have nuclear weapons within ten years (US Central Intelligence Agency, 1966, 6).

[32] These nations were unlikely to obtain sizable ENR facilities because the Soviet Union probably would not allow them to do so, according to the CIA (US Central Intelligence Agency, 1975b).

and Venezuela – countries that, to my knowledge, have never been classified as capable of arming quickly by the US government – all score higher than South Africa.

In sum, available indicators of nuclear latency measure slightly different things. I focus on ENR capabilities because they are most appropriate for my research objective, but this measure may not be the best indicator of latency in all situations. An active ENR program is crucial for communicating threats in weaponless deterrence, and for making them credible. States that have ongoing ENR programs, then, possess latent nuclear forces that are optimized for deterrence.

The Nuclear Latency Dataset

I use the Nuclear Latency (NL) dataset to identify latent nuclear powers based on their ENR capabilities.[33] The NL dataset emerged from a multiyear collaborative project between the author and the nuclear engineers Garill Coles and Paul Nelson.[34] We set out to identify all uranium enrichment and plutonium reprocessing facilities built globally from 1939 to 2012.

A site becomes a "facility," according to the NL dataset, when a state introduces nuclear materials with the intent to enrich uranium or produce plutonium. The possession of relevant technology without an attempt to make at least small quantities of bomb-relevant materials would not constitute an ENR facility, based on our definition. Swedish scientists, for example, built centrifuges during the early 1970s at the Royal Institute of Technology in Stockholm. We did not find evidence that they used centrifuges to enrich *uranium*, however, even though the technology could have theoretically been used for this purpose. The Swedish experiments achieved separation in a hydrogen-argon mixture (and a hydrogen–deuterium mixture). This site therefore does not meet the threshold necessary for inclusion in the NL dataset.[35]

We ultimately identified more than 250 ENR sites in thirty-three countries. We collected detailed information on each of these facilities. The variables in the dataset include: the country where the facility is located, the years of construction and operation, the type of ENR

---

[33] This dataset is described in Fuhrmann and Tkach (2015). After the initial release of the dataset, I made a number of updates. The version used for the book includes several changes to the years of latency, especially in the case of laboratory-scale activities. For the dates used in the book, see Table 3.4.

[34] The following research assistants helped with data collection: Molly Berkemeier, Yewon Kwon, and Benjamin Tkach.

[35] See Bonnevier (1970, 771).

activity,[36] the scale of the facility,[37] whether a plant was built in secret, and the safeguards status of the site.[38]

Challenges and Solutions

Obtaining comprehensive details about all ENR facilities globally over a period of seventy-three years was difficult. Information about a country's ENR activities is often incomplete or entirely absent in publicly available sources. This is partially because countries sometimes attempt to conceal their sensitive nuclear activities given the national security implications of ENR technology. They may fear that exposure of ENR facilities would invite preventive military attacks or other forms of international blowback, as discussed in Chapter 1. Although countries such as the United States track ENR developments closely, the full extent of what they know does not always seep into the public record.[39] Coverage of ENR activities in primary and secondary sources is uneven across countries. The IAEA includes information on ENR plants in its annual reports, but only for sites inspected by the Agency. Military plants or other undeclared facilities, which constitute a significant percentage of all ENR activities, are excluded from these reports. Nuclear proliferation scholarship provides a wealth of useful information but some countries go largely, if not entirely, unstudied by US-based academics.[40] We know far more about nuclear activities in the United States, Pakistan, and South Korea, for instance, than we do in East Germany, Italy, and Spain based on English-language scholarship.

Laboratory-scale ENR work poses a unique challenge. It is relatively easy to hide laboratory-based activities due to their small scale.

---

[36] The dataset lumps all reprocessing activities into a single category and distinguishes between seven different methods of uranium enrichment: gaseous diffusion, gas centrifuge, electromagnetic isotope separation, chemical and ion exchange, aerodynamic isotope separation, laser isotope separation, and thermal diffusion.

[37] We identified the scale of the facility based on three categories – laboratory, pilot, or commercial. Laboratory activities involve enrichment or reprocessing on a small scale. Pilot plants give countries the ability to separate plutonium or enrich uranium on a larger scale. These facilities could, at least in theory, produce sufficient fissile material for one or more weapons but they are not intended for large-scale fissile material production. Commercial plants enrich uranium or separate plutonium on an industrial scale, giving states the capacity to make copious amounts fuel for nuclear power plants or produce large amounts of fissile material for bombs.

[38] See Fuhrmann and Tkach (2015, 448–449) for a detailed description of the variables in the dataset.

[39] Governments sometimes miss ENR activity as well. Israel missed Libya's gas centrifuge program prior to 2003, for example, because it was not directing its intelligence capabilities in that direction.

[40] See Braut-Hegghammer (2019).

Moreover, experiments may be less likely to attract international attention since they are unlikely to produce enough fissile material for a bomb. The media and nongovernmental organizations committed to nonproliferation may therefore invest less effort in uncovering experimental work. As a result, we have less reliable information about states' laboratory-based activities relative to pilot- or commercial-scale facilities. Most nonproliferation experts recognize that Germany is a latent nuclear power due in part to its industrial-scale uranium enrichment plant in Gronau, located in the northwest along the border with the Netherlands, which has operated since 1985. However, fewer scholars are aware that Wilhelm Groth, a physical chemist who worked on Nazi Germany's nuclear program, enriched uranium on a laboratory scale using a centrifuge in 1942.[41] This is partially because of the secrecy surrounding the latter activities, but also due to the small scale on which they were carried out.

Working in an information-poor environment carries three implications for data collection. First, governments may succeed in keeping their ENR activities secret. This raises the possibility that the dataset is missing some ENR plants. The absence of proof that an ENR plant existed does not necessarily mean that a country was ENR-free. Second, we sometimes have little information about facilities that were known to exist. A source may indicate, for instance, that a country separated plutonium or enriched uranium without revealing when or where the relevant activities took place. Third, there is a surprising amount of conflicting information about states' ENR programs in the literature. Sources commonly disagree about things like a plant's scale or the years that it operated.

To manage these challenges, we consulted a large number of diverse sources. Whenever possible, we reviewed primary documents. This includes memoirs, reports, and journal articles published by scientists who worked on a country's nuclear program.[42] We also reviewed declassified CIA assessments of nuclear capabilities globally. These documents sometimes give us a sense of a state's progress in developing enrichment or reprocessing technology. For example, a formerly top secret special national intelligence estimate from August 1974 titled *Prospects for Further Proliferation of Nuclear Weapons* includes a chart that lists all countries with ENR programs. Documents produced by the IAEA were also helpful for identifying civilian sites. We examined peer-reviewed articles in technical journals to uncover laboratory-scale ENR activities.

---

[41] Walker (1989, 82–83).
[42] A good example is Bain et al. (1997).

And we consulted books and articles produced by scholars that detail countries' nuclear histories. When discrepancies arose, and they often did, we made subjective judgments about which sources seemed more credible. In general, we privileged primary documents and databases over secondary accounts. As another means to enhance the quality of our dataset, we made it (and all of the supporting documentation) publicly available and invited other experts to identify errors and omissions.

Despite our efforts, I cannot rule out the possibility that the NL dataset is missing some ENR plants or has misidentified the exact years that one or more plants operated. However, the NL dataset is the most comprehensive source for information on the global development of sensitive nuclear facilities that is publicly available. It is useful to compare the NL dataset with two other efforts to identify ENR development around the world.

First, the IAEA's Nuclear Fuel Cycle Information System (NFCIS) database provides "an international directory of civilian nuclear fuel cycle facilities worldwide."[43] It contains ninety-seven ENR plants (forty-three enrichment facilities and fifty-four reprocessing sites), compared to more than 250 in the NL dataset. This disparity emerges partially because the NFCIS database focuses on commercial nuclear activities. The IAEA notes that "*some* pilot and laboratory scale facilities are included in the database," implying that its coverage in these areas is incomplete.[44] In addition, the IAEA focuses on civilian plants and relies on information provided by member states through questionnaires.[45] Military sites or other activities that countries deem to be sensitive may therefore be excluded from the NFCIS database.

Second, the political scientist Matthew Kroenig has identified capable nuclear suppliers based on the first year that they operated a plutonium reprocessing or uranium enrichment plant domestically.[46] The scope of this effort differs from the NL dataset: It is not intended to identify all ENR facilities and their periods of operation, just the year that each country operated its first plant. According to this study, nineteen countries are ENR-capable. By contrast, the NL dataset identifies thirty-three states that operated at least laboratory-scale ENR facilities. Kroenig's list of nuclear suppliers omits a number of countries that engaged in important ENR activities. It does not include Canada, for example, which produced plutonium at Chalk River. Nor does it include

---

[43] IAEA (2009, foreword).
[44] Emphasis added. IAEA (2009, foreword).
[45] IAEA (2009, 3).
[46] Kroenig (2009a, 117–118).

Iraq, which operated several ENR facilities from 1982 to 1991. Spain is also absent even though it operated a reprocessing plant at the Juan Vigon National Nuclear Energy Center in the late 1960s and early 1970s.

Although the NL dataset includes more information than other databases, readers may worry that the possibility of missing facilities could bias the results reported later in this book. It is important to remember that secret capabilities cannot deter military conflict, according to latent nuclear deterrence theory. If a country was so effective in concealing its ENR program that it remains unknown to this day, its latent nuclear capacity would not have had much deterrent value. When it comes to deterrence, unknown capabilities are functionally equivalent to having no ENR capacity. The possibility of missing facilities in the dataset, then, is less problematic than it initially appears when it comes to testing my theory.

Identifying the Latent Nuclear Powers

Table 3.3 lists the thirty-three states that obtained at least laboratory-scale ENR capabilities from 1939 to 2012. The table identifies the ENR method(s) that each country pursued. A "✓" indicates that a country separated plutonium or enriched uranium using the method indicated. In some cases, states may have done some research and development (R&D), and made progress toward the requisite ENR threshold, but appear to have fallen short. These cases are denoted with a "□" in Table 3.3. Libya, for example, obtained centrifuges from Pakistan beginning in the late 1990s and set up a covert enrichment plant in al Hashan, located about four miles southeast of Tripoli. However, there is no evidence that it introduced uranium hexaflouride into the centrifuges – a step that must be taken in order to enrich uranium. Libya rises to the level of a latent nuclear power because it separated small amounts of plutonium at the Tajura Nuclear Research Center – not because of its (much more well-known) centrifuge program.

The NL dataset includes information on all ENR facilities, including those built in nuclear weapons states after the point of weaponization. However, countries transition out of nuclear latency once they assemble a bomb. This brings us to the second criterion listed above. How do we know if a country possesses one or more nuclear weapons?

I classify states as nuclear powers in the first year of bomb assembly, even if their weapons were not battle-ready. Determining this date can be difficult for two main reasons. First, states sometimes publicly declare their weapons status by openly testing a nuclear device, like China did in 1964, but testing and weaponization can occur at different times. India

Table 3.3 *Enrichment and reprocessing (ENR) activities by country, 1939–2012.*

| Fissile material | Plutonium | Enriched uranium | | | | | |
Method	Reprocessing	GD	GC	EMIS	CIE	AIS	LIS
Algeria	✓						
Argentina	✓	✓				✓	
Australia			✓				✓
Belgium	✓						□
Brazil	✓		✓			✓	✓
Canada	✓						✓
China	✓	✓	✓				
Czech Republic	✓						
East Germany	✓		□				
Egypt	✓						
France	✓	✓	✓		✓		✓
Germany	✓		✓		✓		
India	✓		✓				✓
Iran	✓		✓				✓
Iraq	✓	✓	✓	✓	✓		✓
Israel	✓		✓				✓
Italy	✓	✓	✓				□
Japan	✓	□	✓		✓		✓
Libya	✓		✓				
Netherlands			✓				□
North Korea	✓		✓				
Norway	✓						
Pakistan	✓	□	✓				
Romania	✓				✓		□
Russia	✓	✓	✓	✓			
South Africa	✓					✓	✓
South Korea	✓				✓		✓
Spain	✓	□					□
Sweden	✓	□					□
Taiwan	✓						□
UK	✓		✓				✓
USA	✓	✓	✓	✓			✓
Yugoslavia	✓		□	✓	□		□

Notes: ✓ = uranium enrichment or plutonium separation achieved; □ = R&D.
GD = gaseous diffusion; GC = gas centrifuge; EMIS = electromagnetic isotope separation; CIE = chemical and ion exchange; AIS = aerodynamic isotope separation; LIS = laser isotope separation.

conducted a so-called peaceful nuclear explosion in 1974 but did not weaponize this capability until many years later. Pakistan tested for the first time in 1998 but assembled a bomb at least a few years prior. Two nuclear powers – Israel and South Africa – never openly tested nuclear weapons, although Israel may have secretly detonated a device in 1979. Second, countries can create ambiguity about their nuclear capabilities. Nonnuclear states sometimes cultivate the perception that they might possess a bomb, a strategy taken by South Africa. The second kind of ambiguity arises when a state has assembled one or more bombs but creates the impression that it might still be nonnuclear. Israel, for example, has maintained a policy of *opacity* for decades, whereby it does not acknowledge possessing nuclear weapons but does not claim to be nonnuclear either.[47]

When the exact point of bomb assembly is unclear, I consider a state to be nuclear-armed when it is more likely than not that it put together a bomb, even if some ambiguity persists. In the face of uncertainty, I err on the side of coding weaponization too early rather than too late. This has an important analytical advantage: It reduces the chance that I attribute deterrence benefits to latent forces that actually result from weapons-in-being. A country pursuing the second type of ambiguity should be classified as a nuclear weapons state – not a latent nuclear power.

Consider the case of Israel. The country probably assembled a bomb by 1967, and Israel's main rivals recognized this, even though the government never confirmed that it was nuclear-armed. Standard deterrence logic, therefore, best accounts for any political benefits that Israel obtained from its nuclear capabilities after the Six Day War in 1967, not the mechanisms of latent deterrence. Classifying Israel as latent post-1967 would therefore stack the deck in favor of latent nuclear deterrence theory. My approach, by contrast, makes it harder to find evidence in favor of the theory.

Table 3.4 shows the years that I classify countries as full and partial latent nuclear powers, based on the criteria I have discussed. It indicates when states possessed operational laboratory or pilot/commercial ENR capabilities, as well as the years of weaponization. As the table shows, twenty-three countries achieved full nuclear latency. Another ten states had partial nuclear latency, operating experimental ENR programs without building larger-scale facilities. Every country that made it to full nuclear latency first spent some time as a partial latent nuclear power. Notice that nuclear latency can turn "on" and "off" over time. Canada,

---

[47] Cohen (1998).

Table 3.4 *Latent nuclear powers and nuclear weapons states by year, 1939–2012.*

Country	Partial latency	Full latency	Assembled bombs
Algeria	1996–2010		
Argentina	1968–73, 1981–83, 1997–	1983–97	
Australia	1968–83, 1992–2007		
Belgium	1960–66	1966–74	
Brazil	1968–85	1985–	
Canada	1942–48, 1967–77 1980–85, 1990–93	1948–56	
China	1958–63	1963–64	1964–
Czech Republic	1977–86, 2004–		
East Germany	1985–90		
Egypt	1987		
France	1949–54	1954–60	1960–
(West) Germany	1942–45, 1949–67	1967–	
India	1959–64	1964–74	1974–
Iran	1974–78, 1985–2003	2003, 2006–	
Iraq	1982–90	1990–91	
Israel	1961–65	1965–67	1967–
Italy	1966–70	1970–90	
Japan	1968–75	1975–	
Libya	1984–90		
Netherlands	1950–73	1973–	
North Korea	1975–89	1989–93	1993–
Norway	1954–61	1961–68	
Pakistan	1973–79	1979–88	1988–
Romania	1985–89, 1999–		
Russia	1941–48	1948–49	1949–
South Africa	1967–1974	1974–78, 1991–98	1978–91
South Korea	1979–82, 1991–2000 2006–		
Spain	1964–67	1967–71	
Sweden	1954–72		
Taiwan	1976–77		
UK	1940–51	1951–52	1952–
USA	1941–43	1943–45	1945–
Yugoslavia	1954–66	1966–78	

for instance, had four different spells of laboratory-scale ENR activity spanning the period from World War II to the 1990s.

A handful of additional states had ENR programs and may have come close to crossing the nuclear latency threshold. Table 3.5 lists these

Table 3.5 *Countries with unverified enrichment and reprocessing (ENR) activity.*

Country	Likely scale	Method
Denmark	Laboratory	Reprocessing, enrichment (centrifuge)
Indonesia	Laboratory	Reprocessing
Mexico	Laboratory	Reprocessing, enrichment (unspecified)
Poland	Laboratory	Enrichment (centrifuge)
Switzerland	Laboratory	Enrichment (laser and chemical)
Syria	Pilot	Reprocessing

cases. Some of these countries carried out basic R&D but I found no evidence that they got to the point of separating plutonium or enriching uranium on a laboratory scale or above. For example, the IAEA indicated that Indonesia possessed an R&D facility associated with reprocessing technology: the Radio-Metallurgy Installation (RMI) in Serpong.[48] Yet I was unable to determine if Indonesia separated any plutonium at this site. Other states listed in Table 3.5 made progress on isotopic separation but did not work specifically on uranium. In the case of Switzerland, Hubert van den Bergh used a laser-based enrichment process to separate sulfur isotopes at the Ecole Polytechnique in 1985.[49] Van den Bergh's process could have been used to enrich uranium in theory but I found no evidence that he or anyone else in Switzerland did so. This case therefore does not meet the NL dataset's definition of an ENR plant described earlier.

The case of Syria is unique. I did not find any evidence of a concerted Syrian ENR program, but I would not be surprised if there was one. We know that Syria was building a nuclear reactor with North Korean assistance from the late 1990s until Israel bombed it in a 2007 surprise attack (I discuss this case in Chapter 6). Syrian leader Bashar al Assad apparently desired this capability in order to build nuclear weapons. To make bombs, however, he would have needed a reprocessing plant to separate plutonium from spent nuclear fuel; the reactor alone would be insufficient to produce fissile material for a bomb. It is odd to go through the trouble of obtaining the reactor in secret without also having a reprocessing capability, or at least plans to obtain it. Based on the information I currently have at my disposal, however, there was not a reprocessing plant of any kind in Syria.

[48] IAEA (2000, 9).
[49] Eerkens and Kim (2010).

Conclusion

This chapter developed the concept of nuclear latency and described a database on global ENR capabilities from 1939 to 2012. It introduced two measures of nuclear latency that I will employ throughout the book. Partial nuclear latency exists when a country has an active laboratory-scale ENR program. When a state gets to the point of operating a pilot or commercial ENR plant, I classify it as having full nuclear latency. Thirty-three countries were partially latent at some point during the nuclear age. Twenty-three of these states made it to the point of full nuclear latency, producing larger quantities of HEU or plutonium. It is more common for states that reach this technological threshold to remain nonnuclear than to go on to build nuclear weapons (thirteen of twenty-three cases).

The chapters that follow will explore the causes and consequences of nuclear latency in world politics, using both of my operational measures. We will start by examining the drivers and constraints that influence the global spread of latent nuclear capabilities in Chapter 4. Then, in Chapters 5–7, we will learn how nuclear latency affects key aspects of strategic stability: crises, military conflict, foreign policy preferences, and intra-alliance bargaining (Chapter 5); preventive war (Chapter 6); and arms races (Chapter 7).

4   Causes of Nuclear Latency:
Why Technology Spreads*

Argentina. Canada. Egypt. Japan. Norway. We learned in Chapter 3 that this seemingly diverse set of countries – and twenty-eight others – developed the technological capacity to make nuclear weapons. Meanwhile, a host of states that had interest in becoming latent nuclear powers, ranging from Mexico to Saudi Arabia to Turkey, ultimately did not. What accounts for this variation? Why do some countries obtain sensitive dual-use nuclear technology while others remain nonlatent?

This book is primarily about the political effects of nuclear latency. To have any hope of correctly identifying those effects, however, we need to understand when and why countries become latent nuclear powers.[1] Nuclear latency emerges because of strategic decisions made by governments, not random chance. This means that latent powers may be different than their nonlatent counterparts in ways besides the obvious disparity in nuclear capabilities. Countries that obtain sensitive nuclear technology, for example, are probably wealthier and militarily stronger than those that do not. Differences such as these could explain patterns we observe between nuclear latency and international outcomes such as military conflict. To avoid reaching misleading conclusions, we must account for the ways in which latent nuclear powers differ from nonlatent states. Doing this requires us to understand when and why countries obtain bomb-making potential.

This chapter takes up this task, identifying the main drivers and constraints of nuclear latency. Doing so enriches our understanding of the role that nuclear latency plays in world politics, in addition to helping us better identify latency's political effects beginning in Chapter 5. We saw in Chapter 2 that many world leaders believe in weaponless deterrence.

* This chapter uses some material that was previously published in Fuhrmann, Matthew. 2019. "Explaining the Proliferation of Latent Nuclear Capabilities," pages 289–315 of: Joseph Pilat (ed.), *Nuclear Latency and Hedging: Concepts, History, and Issues*. Washington, DC: Woodrow Wilson Center for Scholars.
[1] We must do a lot of other things, too. I address those in Chapter 5.

Some of them desired dual-use nuclear technology precisely because having it enhanced their political influence. Latent nuclear deterrence theory therefore sheds light on the causes of latent nuclear forces, in addition to its consequences. But a desire for greater influence is hardly the only factor that explains the international spread of latent nuclear forces. This chapter identifies factors related to national security, domestic politics, and economics that cause countries to covet enrichment and reprocessing (ENR) technology. It also reviews the technological and political constraints that may stymie ENR development. Together, these demand-side and supply-side factors give us a more complete understanding of who gets sensitive nuclear technology.

Based on the drivers and constraints, I identify factors that should be associated with countries becoming latent nuclear powers. Using the Nuclear Latency (NL) database described in Chapter 3, I assess the degree to which these variables are correlated with nuclear latency onset – both the partial and full varieties. The variables most reliably correlated with both stages of latency emergence are a country's military capabilities and having a nuclear-armed rival. I also conduct a qualitative investigation to identify the motives of the twenty-three states that reached full nuclear latency. This analysis indicates that many factors contribute to the international spread of ENR technology, not just one or two. This includes an unabated desire to build nuclear weapons, nuclear hedging, a quest for greater international status, energy security, and profit-seeking.

Causes of Nuclear Latency

To understand any political outcome, we must account for drivers and constraints.[2] Adopting military technologies requires countries to have political interest in the capabilities they afford as well as the technological and organizational capacity to obtain them. International relations scholars often refer to the former as the *demand-side* and the latter as the *supply-side* of military technology diffusion.[3] In the absence of a strong motive, a country is unlikely to become a latent nuclear power. However, being highly resolved to get ENR technology does not guarantee this outcome, as there are significant political and technological barriers that stand in the way. I will start by reviewing

---

[2] See Most and Starr (1989).
[3] For relevant examples, see Sagan (2011), Fuhrmann (2012a), Debs and Monteiro (2017), and Fuhrmann and Horowitz (2017).

the main demand-side drivers of nuclear latency and then turn to a discussion of the supply-side constraints.

Driver #1: Incidental Latency

Building nuclear weapons requires countries to obtain fissile material. It is unlikely that states would be able to acquire sufficient quantities of weapons-grade HEU or plutonium on international markets or as a result of theft.[4] Having ENR technology is therefore essentially a prerequisite for arming. Some countries obtain nuclear latency simply because it is a necessary stop on the way to obtaining bombs. These countries become latent for a brief period but their ultimate goal is to become a full-fledged nuclear power. In these situations, the same factors that motivate countries to build nuclear weapons – especially fears of external aggression – drive the (temporary) emergence of latent nuclear forces.

The United States may provide the clearest example of this motive. Following the Japanese bombing of Pearl Harbor in December 1941, the United States initiated the Manhattan Project. The goal of this program was clear: To deliver a nuclear bomb as quickly as possible as a way of helping the United States prevail in World War II. By 1943, the United States had a significant enrichment capacity in Oak Ridge, Tennessee. Shortly thereafter, a large-scale reprocessing facility came online in Hanford, Washington. Washington chased these ENR capabilities because it was determined to build nuclear weapons. Once the United States entered the war, officials saw latency as a means to an end rather than the ultimate objective. But the United States was nonetheless a latent nuclear power from 1941 to 1945 – after producing fissile material on a laboratory scale but before assembling its first bomb.

Driver #2: Nuclear Hedging

Countries may seek sensitive nuclear technology as part of a hedging strategy. Political scientist Ariel Levite defines hedging as "a national strategy of maintaining, or appearing to maintain, a viable option for the relatively rapid acquisition of nuclear weapons, based on an indigenous technical capacity to produce them within a relatively short time frame ranging from several weeks to a few years."[5] Hedgers are not actively seeking nuclear weapons, just the capability to get them in short order.

---

[4] These things could happen, of course, but have been rare historically.
[5] Levite (2002).

Sensitive nuclear technology plays an essential role in shortening a country's time to a bomb, making it valuable for hedgers. Being able to make fissile material may provide political benefits regardless of a country's motives for producing it. Hedgers are unique in that they seek this capability explicitly for the national security benefits that might come from being ENR-capable.

Hedgers covet fissile material production capabilities, in part, to be prepared in the event of a crisis. They want to have the capacity to arm quickly if a serious national security threat arises.[6] Without ENR capabilities, countries would likely be caught flatfooted during a potential national emergency – an unenviable position to say the least. Hedgers may also seek ENR technology deliberately to shape the behavior of other countries, not just have an insurance policy. Latent nuclear deterrence theory holds that bomb-making capabilities can enhance international influence. We saw in Chapter 2 that government officials around the world embrace this view. Hedgers may become ENR-capable because they believe that doing so will confer leverage over their adversaries and allies. As political scientist Vipin Narang argues, hedging "may be both a latent deterrent to an underlying threat and a coercive tool that a potential proliferator can use vis-à-vis a senior formal ally that generates security benefits."[7]

In addition to providing security benefits, hedging is an attractive strategy because it is less costly than going all the way to a bomb. Aside from the financial and technological burdens of building and maintaining an arsenal, states that proliferate may face international sanctions, especially following the establishment of the nuclear Nonproliferation Treaty (NPT) in 1968. Hedgers may be able to dodge these costs while still having the option to assemble bombs quickly, if necessary.

Nuclear hedging is widespread. Countries ranging from Australia to West Germany pursued ENR technology as a deliberate strategy to shorten the time to a bomb without actually arming. Former Australian Prime Minister John Gorton revealed in 1999 that his country had an unambiguous hedging motive during the 1960s. "We were interested in this thing [the nuclear power plant at Jervis Bay]," Gorton said, "because it could provide electricity to everybody and it could, if you decided later on, it could make an atomic bomb."[8] According to nuclear physicist Otto Haxel, West German Minister of Defense Franz Josef Strauss, "was not stupid enough to believe that the Federal Republic could afford

---

[6] This resembles what Narang (2017) calls insurance hedging.

[7] Narang (2017, 120). On the use of latency for compellence, see Volpe (2017).

[8] AAP Newsfeed (1999).

the construction of nuclear bombs. However, he wanted to retain the opportunity to do so as a trump card in international negotiations."[9] The list of hedgers also includes countries that ultimately built nuclear weapons. At least five of the ten eventual nuclear powers engaged in hedging before weaponizing their previously latent capabilities: France, India, Israel, Pakistan, and South Africa.[10]

The line between hedging and incidental latency can be blurry. The South Korean case illustrates this ambiguity. Many political scientists assume that South Korea had a dedicated nuclear-weapon program under Park Chung-hee in the 1970s.[11] However, a declassified US State Department assessment from November 18, 1975, reveals that Seoul's approach may have been more nuanced: "It may be likely that the ROK is intent on acquiring a weapon as soon as possible, but it also appears possible that the decision to acquire a weapon may not have been firmly taken and that the ROK is essentially developing a contingent military capability for possible activation at a later time."[12]

Driver #3: Prestige and Status

Scholars have argued that military-relevant technologies ranging from satellites to armed drones can enhance a country's status in international politics.[13] Nuclear weapons, in particular, are widely seen as a status symbol in international relations, similar to a national airline.[14] Having a "peaceful" nuclear program can signal technological modernity and relevance, too. Sensitive fuel-cycle technology is especially likely to bring countries esteem. The proliferation significance of fissile material production capacity and the exclusivity of the ENR club could make latent nuclear capabilities attractive for states seeking to enhance their standing internationally or domestically.

Several latent nuclear powers cite prestige-related motives for equipping themselves with latent nuclear forces. Canada maintained its nuclear program after World War II, which included reprocessing activities at the Chalk River Laboratories, in part for prestige-related reasons. As historian Margaret Gowing wrote, "atomic energy had helped to carve a new status for Canada in the post-war world. It had brought

---

[9] Quoted in Radkau (1983, 517). Translated from German by Hankyeul Yang.
[10] Narang (2017, 134).
[11] Singh and Way (2004) and Jo and Gartzke (2007) code South Korea as "pursuing" nuclear weapons.
[12] US Department of State (1975a, 6).
[13] Early (2014), Fuhrmann and Horowitz (2017), and Horowitz et al. (2022).
[14] Sagan (1996, 73–76).

her to the top diplomatic tables and it had demonstrated and enhanced her underlying scientific, technological, and industrial strength."[15] Iran developed its enrichment capacity partially for prestige-related reasons as well. Mohamed ElBaredei, the former Director General of the International Atomic Energy Agency, characterized Iran's motives in 2009: "In my view Iran's nuclear program is a means to an end: it wants to be recognized as a regional power, they believe that the nuclear know-how brings prestige, brings power, and they would like to see the U.S. engaging them."[16] Status-related considerations have also contributed to Brazil's nuclear program. As a US intelligence assessment put it in 1983, "Brazilian leaders clearly see the eventual mastery of nuclear fuel cycle technology as necessary for the great-power status to which they aspire."[17]

Status concerns are especially likely to influence a country's behavior when its neighbors obtain bomb-making capabilities. The regional spread of ENR technology can make neighboring states feel that they need to keep up with the Joneses. As an unnamed official from the United Arab Emirates who the nuclear expert George Perkovich described as "highly-informed" and "militarily experienced" put it in the mid-2000s, "If my neighbor drives in to his driveway with a new, big car and my son points to it and then looks at my old car, he will ask, 'Why don't we have a car like that?' To keep my family's respect I might feel I have to get a car as fine as my neighbors."[18]

Driver #4: Financial Gain and Energy Security

Sensitive nuclear technology attracts attention from the international community in large part because of its bomb-making potential. Yet ENR plants, like all nuclear technology, have legitimate commercial applications as well. In particular, these facilities provide states with the capacity to produce low enriched uranium (LEU) fuel for nuclear power plants.[19]

Countries and private firms may wish to export nuclear fuel to foreign clients. In that case, ENR development may occur because countries see potentially lucrative business opportunities. As a CIA assessment concluded in December 1975, "sales of uranium and uranium-enrichment

[15] Gowing (1974, 328).
[16] Quoted in Krastev (2009).
[17] US Central Intelligence Agency (1983, 8).
[18] Perkovich (2008, 234).
[19] Plutonium could fuel nuclear reactors but this is generally not done today.

services may earn several billion dollars more" over the next five years.[20] Three firms currently dominate the market in enrichment services: Rosatom (Russia), Urenco (Germany, the Netherlands, and the United Kingdom), and Areva (France).[21] The United States was a leader in global enrichment services for much of the nuclear age, but it is no longer a major player in this area. The last US-owned enrichment plant, located in Paducah, Kentucky, closed in 2013.[22] The only US firm providing enrichment services, USEC, filed for bankruptcy shortly thereafter.[23] It emerged from Chapter 11 protection under a new name (Centrus Energy), but its financial difficulties continued.[24]

Many states with nuclear power plants rely on international suppliers to meet their fuel needs. However, two economic considerations could motivate states to produce their fuel domestically.

First, countries that expect to rely heavily on nuclear power to meet their electricity needs might find a domestic fuel-making capacity to be economically desirable. For a state with few nuclear power plants, a large investment in fuel production may be economically unwise. Low nuclear energy producers would need to rely mostly on international clients to achieve economies of scale – the cost savings that results from increased production.[25] As a country's nuclear fuel needs rise domestically, however, it becomes easier to justify a capital-intensive investment in enrichment or reprocessing technology.

Second, countries may worry that geopolitical considerations could lead to disruptions in the market for nuclear fuel. A state that is deeply worried about its energy security may prefer to meet its nuclear fuel needs domestically rather than rely on foreign suppliers, who might raise prices or reduce supplies on short notice. In the United States, some have used the energy security logic to justify continued investment in ENR activities.[26] Concerns about market capriciousness exist, but they should not be overblown. Compared to the oil market, which experienced severe disruptions following the oil embargo of the 1970s, enrichment services have been relatively stable.

Economic and commercial factors have motivated ENR technology development in the past, and this trend could continue moving forward. A clear example of this comes from the European consortium Eurodif,

---

[20] US Central Intelligence Agency (1975a, 10).
[21] Rothwell (2009).
[22] Wald (2013a).
[23] Wald (2013b).
[24] Overly (2014).
[25] Fuhrmann (2012a, 46).
[26] Wald (2011).

which built a uranium enrichment facility in France during the 1970s.[27] According to economic historian Esther Sánchez-Sánchez, three aims drove this endeavor: to meet growing need for enriched uranium in Europe, to ensure a stable supply of fuel and reasonable prices, and to diversify supply sources by reducing reliance on the United States.[28] Some Australian officials have also pointed to economic motives, suggesting that Canberra should export enriched uranium in order to make financial gains. As John Carlson, the former Director General of the Australian Safeguards and Nonproliferation Office, said in 2006, "The Prime Minister [John Howard] has said we have a third of the world's uranium reserves and clearly we need to look at whether we can value-add rather than have the economic advantage of upgrading falling only to other countries."[29]

Constraint #1: Technological Capacity

There are technological hurdles that must be overcome to achieve nuclear latency. The indigenous development of ENR plants can be difficult and time consuming. Although the underlying technology is no longer cutting-edge – much of it has existed for decades – building ENR facilities requires some preexisting capacity in nuclear engineering and related fields. States with considerable wealth and nuclear-specific experience can take a decade or more to successfully build an ENR plant. For example, Urenco, a consortium that includes British, Dutch, and German entities, began a uranium-enrichment program in 1960 and did not have an operational demonstration plant until 1971. Countries with fewer domestic resources may struggle to build ENR plants. Saudi Arabia's underdeveloped nuclear program, for instance, substantially limits its ability to enrich uranium domestically. The country's wealth would probably allow it to build up the requisite knowledge and infrastructure eventually, but this would take years and perhaps decades.

The case of North Korea suggests that just about any country can achieve success with enough motivation and time. Despite being one of the poorest countries in the world, North Korea eventually overcame the requisite scientific and technological challenges. States with greater technological and scientific capacity should have an easier time developing and/or operating sensitive dual-use nuclear plants, but

---

[27] The initial members of Eurodif were France, Belgium, Italy, Spain, and Sweden.
[28] Sánchez-Sánchez (2017a).
[29] ABC News (2006).

history shows that ENR programs are not necessarily beyond the reach of less-developed countries.

Countries can bypass relevant technological hurdles by obtaining foreign assistance. Prior research shows that obtaining international nuclear aid increases the likelihood that nuclear programs will bear fruit.[30] Yet even substantial outside help does not guarantee success. Libya received enrichment-related assistance from Pakistan, for instance, but it was still unable successfully to produce a demonstration plant despite trying for many years.

Constraint #2: Political Coercion

Potential latent nuclear powers are subject to political pressure from other countries who are concerned about weapons proliferation. Given its dual-use nature, obtaining ENR technology is not equivalent to building nuclear weapons. The NPT guarantees the right to produce nuclear energy for peaceful purposes, including the development of ENR plants. But powerful countries such as the United States understand the strategic significance of being able to produce fissile material and generally prefer that countries – both allies and adversaries – do not obtain this capability. For decades, US nuclear cooperation agreements (NCAs) have routinely barred ENR assistance while allowing for other forms of energy aid.[31] United States President George W. Bush proposed international guidelines that limited ENR transfers to countries in compliance with the NPT that already had a large-scale facility in operation.[32]

Superpowers have routinely put pressure on countries that pursued latent nuclear capacity, along with suppliers that wanted to sell sensitive technology. Historian Eliza Gheorghe calls countries seeking to curb the international spread of dual-use nuclear technology *thwarters* and shows that their efforts played a key role in explaining when a program succeeded.[33] During the 1970s, for example, Brazil sought to expand its ENR program with assistance from West Germany. This resulted in considerable blowback from the United States. United States officials told their counterparts in Brasilia that they wanted "the indefinite postponement of the building of the uranium enrichment and irradiated material reprocessing plants."[34] If they moved forward with the planned

[30] Fuhrmann (2012a) and Kroenig (2010).
[31] See Fuhrmann (2012a).
[32] Ford (2005).
[33] Gheorghe (2019). See also Miller (2018).
[34] Brazilian Foreign Ministry (1977b).

ENR expansion, Brazilian officials understood that Washington might respond by canceling plans to supply fuel for the Angra-1 nuclear power plant, placing restrictions on Brazilian exports or the financing of external debt, or threatening "'incalculable' consequences for the country."[35] The United States also told West Germany not transfer ENR plants to Brazil, while voicing no objections over the transfer of other, less sensitive nuclear facilities. In a sign of unity among the superpowers, the Soviet Union send a diplomatic démarche to Bonn making the same demand.[36] Brazil still achieved success with its ENR program – its laboratory-scale centrifuge activities dated back to 1968 and it would go on to enrich uranium on a pilot scale in the mid-1980s – but it ultimately received little ENR aid from West Germany.

The South Korean case also offers a fitting illustration. In the 1970s, France agreed to sell South Korea a plutonium reprocessing plant. After learning of the deal, Washington applied substantial political pressure on Seoul and South Korea eventually agreed to abandon its purchase of the facility. The application of US leverage appears to be decisive in explaining why South Korea did not move beyond laboratory ENR activities. As this case suggests, countries may desire nuclear latency for political or strategic reasons but refrain from moving forward because of actual or anticipated diplomatic blowback.

Constraint #3: Preventive War Risk

Countries can do more than apply political pressure to stop the global spread of ENR technology. They can also use military force to destroy relevant technology and materials, potentially eroding a country's capacity to make fissile material (this is the subject of Chapter 6). An attacker might take such extreme action if it believed that latent nuclear forces would ultimately be weaponized, leading to a dire national security threat. Israel destroyed reactors in Iraq in 1981 and Syria in 2007, and there has been much speculation about a military strike on Iran's nuclear facilities over the past 20 years.[37] Potential latent nuclear powers might fear that they would suffer a preventive military strike if they sought ENR technology. This possibility could deter them from pursuing bomb-relevant technology.[38]

---

[35] Brazilian Foreign Ministry (1977b).
[36] Brazilian Foreign Ministry (1977a).
[37] For an overview of this history, see Fuhrmann and Kreps (2010).
[38] Debs and Monteiro (2017), Fuhrmann (2018), and Spaniel (2019, 158).

There are at least three reasons a country might nonetheless try to become ENR-capable despite the risk of inviting a preventive strike. First, because nuclear facilities can be hidden from plain view, a target might believe that it could conceal its activities from potential attackers. A country might suspect that its nuclear facilities would be bombed if international actors discovered them but proceed anyway – if it believed that its nuclear activities could escape detection. Second, a state's nuclear intentions are not directly observable to others.[39] Even if its ENR facilities are detected, then, a target might believe that it can convince others that its program is entirely peaceful. A third possibility, identified by political scientist William Spaniel, is that the target underestimates the attacker's resolve to strike the target's nuclear facilities.[40] The target might believe that the attacker is not sufficiently threatened by nuclear armament to take on the costs of a preventive strike, emboldening the target to seek ENR technology.

Research Strategy

How important are these drivers and constraints in explaining the development of latent nuclear forces? To find out, I take a two-pronged approach to analyzing historical evidence.

I begin by using statistical analysis to look at broad trends over time. My goal is to identify the factors that are associated with the onset of nuclear latency, based on the preceding discussion of drivers and constraints. Doing this requires me to identify variables that should be closely associated with nuclear latency onset based on each of the arguments. One limitation of this approach is that some arguments expect the same association between an explanatory variable and the emergence of nuclear latency. Knowing which variables are associated with ENR program development, then, does not necessarily tell us which drivers or constraints account for the patterns we observe.

The statistical analysis nonetheless serves important functions. In addition to identifying broad trends, it helps us better understand the fundamental differences between latent nuclear powers and their non-latent counterparts. Knowing this is critical for understanding how the nonrandom assignment of sensitive nuclear technology could influence its political effects. The analysis that follows, therefore, helps to lay the groundwork for my analyses of crises, military conflict, foreign policy

---

[39] Debs and Monteiro (2014) and Spaniel (2019, chapter 7).
[40] Spaniel (2019, chapter 8).

influence, intra-alliance bargaining, preventive war, and arms racing later in the book (Chapters 5–7).

To supplement the statistical analysis, I carried out historical research to determine countries' motives, focusing on the twenty-three states that achieved full nuclear latency.[41] I identified motives based on government officials' public and (when available) private statements and assessments by other scholars, supplemented with circumstantial evidence.[42] This analysis will more directly assess the relative importance of bomb-making, hedging, status considerations, energy security, and financial profits in explaining the adoption of a significant ENR capability. We will find out, for example, how common incidental latency is compared to hedging, and how frequently commercial motives play a role relative to national security considerations.

I focused on the primary motives for ENR development – those factors emphasized by policymakers that seemed to drive a country's nuclear policy. Motives can change over time. I zero in on the period of full nuclear latency onset, seeking to identify the most important drivers of a country's policy in the first year that it obtained an operational pilot or commercial ENR plant. To illustrate, hedging and status considerations motivated the French pursuit of dual-use nuclear technology in the 1940s and early 1950s. But by the time France was making fissile material on a larger scale, in 1954, incidental latency offers the best explanation for its possession of ENR technology.[43]

Dataset, Variables, and Measurement

I assembled a dataset that includes all countries in the world from 1939 to 2010. After accounting for missing data, there are 166 countries in my analysis. The unit of observation in this dataset is the country-year, meaning that each line represents one country in a single year. Because my focus is on the emergence of nuclear latency, I drop countries from the analysis in the first year after they obtain sensitive nuclear technology.[44]

---

[41] This analysis benefited from research assistance provided by Duncan Espenshade.

[42] Useful data sources on countries' nuclear policies include Singh and Way (2004), Jo and Gartzke (2007), Narang (2017), and Bleek (2010).

[43] As discussed in Chapter 7, there is debate about when exactly the French decision to build a bomb became irreversible, with some scholars suggesting it may have come as late as 1958.

[44] For example, in my analysis of partial latency onset, China exits the dataset in 1959 since it first completed laboratory-scale work on enrichment or reprocessing in 1958.

Table 4.1 *Variables influencing nuclear latency onset.*

Variable	Driver/constraint	Expected relationship with latency onset
Prior fatal disputes and crises	Incidental latency	+
	Hedging	+
	Preventive war risk	−
Nuclear-armed rival	Incidental latency	+
	Hedging	+
	Preventive war risk	−
Nuclear-armed ally	Incidental latency	−
	Hedging	−
	Political coercion	+ / −
	Preventive war risk	+
Latent rival	Hedging	+
Status deficit	Status and prestige	+
Regional nuclear latency	Status and prestige	+
Nuclear energy investment	Financial gain	+
	Energy security	+
	Technological capacity	+
Latent ally	Energy security	−
	Technological capacity	+
GDP per capita	Financial gain	+
	Technological capacity	+
Economic growth	Technological capacity	+
Military capabilities	Preventive war risk	+
	Political coercion	+
Military growth	Incidental latency	+
	Hedging	+
Prior civil war	Technological capacity	−
	Political coercion	−
	Preventive war	−
Democracy	Technological capacity	+
	Preventive war risk	+

For each country-year observation, I create a number of independent variables. Table 4.1 lists fourteen explanatory variables that should be especially salient alongside the driver or constraint with which they are associated and the expected direction of the relationship.[45] Most of these variables are associated with more than one argument. Notice that the drivers and constraints sometimes generate conflicting predictions for the same variable.

---

[45] Some of these variables could be associated with arguments other than the ones listed here. I focus on the most plausible links in Table 4.1.

International conflict is one of the principal drivers of nuclear weapons proliferation.[46] Incidental latency expects, therefore, that prior military disputes lead to a greater likelihood of ENR development. Countries that have experienced disputes in the recent past should also be more inclined to hedge without immediately pushing toward a full-blown bomb program.[47] Higher levels of conflict can induce hedging for two main reasons: (1) these states are most in need of the insurance policy that ENR technology provides and (2) given that past conflict generates expectations about future disputes, these countries should value the deterrence benefits that latency may offer. Prior conflict can cut in the other direction too, since it indicates susceptibility to preventive strikes. High conflict involvement in the past means that a country has adversaries who may be willing to act militarily in order to stop or delay weapons proliferation, creating a possible barrier to ENR development.

I generate two measures of a country's conflict history over the preceding five years. The first captures the number of times a country was targeted in a military dispute that resulted in it experiencing at least one fatality, according to the Correlates of War's (COW) Militarized Interstate Dispute (MID) dataset.[48] The second identifies the total number of crises a state experienced based on the International Crisis Behavior (ICB) project.[49]

I create binary indicators for whether a country has a nuclear-armed or latent rival.[50] Having a nuclear-armed rival might be seen as particularly threatening. Not only are states likely to worry about future conflict when they have a strategic adversary with nuclear weapons, they are also outgunned – making the costs of conflict particularly high. These states may race to get the bomb in order to match their rival's arsenal, leading to temporary latent status.[51] Countries with a nuclear-armed rival may also seek sensitive nuclear technology in order to bolster deterrence or obtain a more reliable insurance policy without actually arming. At the same time, these states are also particularly susceptible to preventive strikes because nuclear-armed countries have both the capabilities and determination to stop their rivals from arming.

[46] Singh and Way (2004), Jo and Gartzke (2007), Fuhrmann (2012a), and Debs and Monteiro (2017).
[47] Levite (2002).
[48] I use an updated version of the MID dataset produced by Gibler et al. (2017). I count only cases in which the target was an original member of the dispute, excluding joiners.
[49] Brecher et al. (2017).
[50] Rivalries are based on Dreyer and Thompson (2011). For all relevant variables in this chapter, I use the dates on weaponization and latency described in Chapter 3. The latent rival measure captures whether the rival has partial or full nuclear latency.
[51] Sagan (1996, 57–58). See also Miller (2014a).

The arms-racing logic applies to the international spread of latent nuclear capabilities, in addition to nuclear arsenals. Hedging is likely to be a particularly desirable strategy for countries that have latent rivals. When a country pursues nuclear latency, its adversaries may be unsure of its intentions. The uncertainty generated by a country's pursuit of ENR facilities may compel its rivals to take action. If the rival goes on to proliferate, others will be at a strategic disadvantage if they have to start nuclear programs from scratch. To avoid falling behind, countries might begin ENR programs as soon as their adversaries do so, or shortly thereafter. Reactive ENR development does not necessarily imply that a state is determined to build nuclear weapons – just that it wants to be in a position to do so in the future, if necessary. Having a latent rival can encourage the pursuit of ENR technology explicitly to discourage the adversary from arming.

Alliance relationships can influence ENR development as well. Protection from a nuclear-armed state makes countries less vulnerable to preventive military attacks from third parties.[52] Nuclear powers may also be less inclined to stop a state from crossing the latency threshold when it is an ally. In addition, allies of nuclear-armed countries may be incentivized to seek ENR capabilities in order to extract stronger security guarantees.[53] Yet, states that benefit from nuclear umbrellas may feel more secure than those without this protection, resulting in less of a need for dual-use nuclear capabilities as a hedging strategy or an unambiguous weapons program. Consistent with this expectation, although nuclear powers would be less threatened by an ally's armament than an adversary's, political pressure is likely more effective because the coercer has greater leverage.[54]

Countries are much more likely to provide nuclear energy assistance to their military allies than their nonallies.[55] Allies of existing latent nuclear powers, then, should have an easier time getting technological assistance for an ENR program. On the other hand, these countries may also feel more secure outsourcing their fuel supply needs to another country, given that market disruptions for political reasons are less likely. I account for whether a country has a defense pact with one or more nuclear-armed or latent states.[56]

[52] Debs and Monteiro (2017).

[53] Volpe (2017, 2023).

[54] See Miller (2018).

[55] Fuhrmann (2009b) and Fuhrmann (2012a).

[56] I use version 5.0 of the Alliance Treaty Obligations and Provisions (ATOP) dataset for all of the alliance variables. See Leeds et al. (2002).

Getting sensitive nuclear technology may enhance the international status of any country. Countries should be especially interested in the status-enhancing effects of an ENR program, however, when they believe that they do not get the respect they deserve internationally. A status deficit, then, should be associated with a greater likelihood of becoming a latent nuclear power, according to the prestige logic. I use a measure of this concept developed by political scientist Jonathan Renshon.[57]

The number of latent nuclear powers in a region may influence the status value of ENR technology. As the number of latent states increases, non-ENR adopters are more likely to be perceived as technologically unadvanced, which could fuel perceptions of inferiority among status-conscious leaders. In order to keep up with their neighbors in a perceived competition for social status, countries may seek ENR technology when there are high levels of adoption in the region. Other drivers and constraints might also expect to find an association between regional adoption and ENR development. It might be harder for thwarters to exert pressure, for example, as the number of countries in a region with ENR programs increases. I measure the percentage of other countries in the region that have an active ENR program during a given year, excluding a state's own capabilities from this calculation.[58]

States with plans for nuclear energy investments should be particularly likely to seek ENR technology. Countries with operational nuclear power plants have shown that they can clear a key technological barrier, suggesting that sensitive nuclear technology is within reach. In addition, as a country's domestic nuclear energy production increases, it has a stronger economic rationale for making its own fuel. Large domestic demand makes it easier to generate economies of scale, and also raises the cost of a disruption in the international marketplace for nuclear fuel. I measure a state's investment in nuclear energy based on the number of reactors for electricity production on which a country has begun construction over the preceding five years.[59]

---

[57] Renshon (2017, 158). I use Renshon's standardized community measure. Greater values indicate larger status deficits.

[58] I use COW country codes to identify the following regions: North America (country codes 2–99), South America (country codes 100–199), Europe (country codes 200–399), Africa (country codes 400–599), the Middle East (country codes 600–699), Central Asia (country codes 700–705), East Asia (country codes 706–749), South Asia (country codes 750–799), Southeast Asia (country codes 800–899), and Oceania (country codes 900–999).

[59] I take the natural log of this measure to address its skewed distribution. I add 0.00000001 to this measure prior to conducting the logarithmic transformation, since a log of zero is undefined. I updated this variable from Fuhrmann (2012b) using the International Atomic Energy Agency's Power Reactor Information System database.

A country's national wealth influences whether it has the technological and scientific capacity needed to operate ENR plants. States with higher levels of gross domestic product (GDP) per capita should have more resources and expertise available to master nuclear technology. Moreover, wealthy countries may be more inclined to chase the economic benefits that come with selling nuclear fuel and related services abroad, since they should generally have an easier time breaking into the market.[60] When a country's economy grows over time, it has more resources to devote to things like nuclear technology. I also measure the percentage change in GDP per capita from year $t - 1$ to year t.[61]

Militarily powerful states may be able to withstand political pressure and deter preventive strikes, giving them a greater opportunity to emerge as latent nuclear powers.[62] I measure military power based on a country's share of the global total of six power indicators in a given year: military expenditures, military personnel, energy consumption, total population, urban population, and iron/steel production.[63] Moreover, growing military capabilities can be indicative of a worsening security environment, as well as a sign that a country is seeking to expand its international influence. I account for the percentage change in military capacity between year $t - 1$ and year t, in addition to the current levels.[64]

If states experience civil wars they may place less of a priority on developing nuclear technology since they have other pressing political priorities. Countries may also worry about unstable counterparts possessing sensitive nuclear capabilities, leading them to apply greater political pressure or even consider preventive strikes in those situations. Domestically unstable states therefore have less of an opportunity to become latent nuclear powers. I generate a variable measuring a country's civil war history over the previous five years, excluding the present year.[65]

---

[60] I measure GDP per capita based on the updated World Bank estimates of GDP and population provided in Anders et al. (2020). I exponentiate the two variables (which are logged in the Anders et al. [2020] dataset) before dividing GDP by population, and then log the resulting variable to address its skewed distribution.

[61] I use a nonlogged measure of GDP per capita to construct this variable.

[62] Debs and Monteiro (2017).

[63] This is the widely used COW Composite Index of National Capabilities (CINC). Singer et al. (1972). I take the natural log of this measure to address its skewed distribution.

[64] This measure is based on nonlogged values for CINC scores.

[65] I use version 22.1 of the UCDP/PRIO Armed Conflict Dataset (Gleditsch et al., 2002). The civil war variable includes intrastate and internationalized intrastate conflicts, excluding extrasystemic and interstate conflicts. This variable measures the total number of civil war-years a country has experienced over the prior five years, meaning that this measure accounts for ongoing conflicts, not just onsets.

A country's regime type may be important too. Nondemocratic states are much more likely than democracies to have their nuclear programs targeted militarily.[66] Nonproliferation enforcers may see nondemocracies in possession of nuclear latency as a particularly strong threat to the status quo because leaders in those countries are relatively unconstrained domestically, increasing the likelihood that they could act capriciously. Former US national security adviser Brent Scowcroft, for instance, cited Saddam Hussein's "notoriously mercurial" behavior as a reason for trying to end Iraq's nuclear ambitions.[67] On top of this, nondemocracies may have suboptimal approaches to the management of nuclear programs that stymie technological and organizational capacity.[68] I generate a variable indicating whether a country is a democracy during a given year.[69]

The Correlates of Nuclear Latency Onset

To what extent are the explanatory variables correlated with partial and full nuclear latency onset? To answer this question, I estimate logit models of nuclear latency onset. The models control for time dependence by including covariates that measure the number of years that pass without a country obtaining latency, along with its square and cube.[70] I cluster the standard errors by country.[71]

Figure 4.1 illustrates the results. It reports the average marginal effect (AME) for each independent variable based on the logit models of partial and full latency. The AME emerges from a two-step process. First, for each country-year observation in the dataset, I compute the change in the predicted probability of nuclear latency onset when an independent variable increases by one unit and other factors remain constant.[72] Second, I calculate the mean difference in probability across all country-year observations. The squares and circles in the figure represent the AME for each variable and the horizontal lines are the 95 percent

---

[66] Fuhrmann and Kreps (2010).

[67] Bush and Scowcroft (1998, 306–307).

[68] Hymans (2012) and Braut-Heggehammer (2016).

[69] I consider a country to be democratic if it scores 7 or greater on the widely employed twenty-one-point indicator of a state's regime type from the Polity IV project, which ranges from −10 to +10. Marshall et al. (2009). I coded cases as 0 when countries score −66 on the Polity scale, which indicates a foreign interruption.

[70] Carter and Signorino (2010).

[71] Owing to missing data on the civil war and status measures, the analysis spans from 1951 to 2001.

[72] I do this in Stata version 15 using the "margins" command.

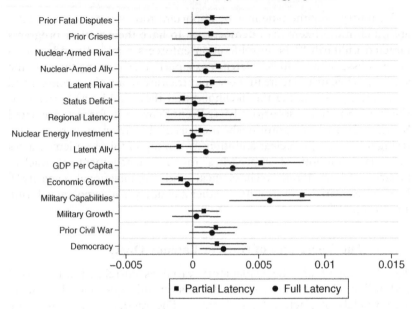

Figure 4.1 Marginal effects of standardized independent variables on partial and full nuclear latency onset.

confidence intervals. If the confidence interval does not include zero, scholars often say that the effect is "statistically significant."

I standardized the coefficients before calculating the AMEs so that they are directly comparable. This enables me to easily identify the relative importance of the independent variables in shaping the probability of latency onset. After standardization, each explanatory variable has a mean of 0 and a standard deviation of 1. The results in Figure 4.1 therefore show the average change in the predicted probability of nuclear latency onset when each explanatory increases by one standard deviation.

As shown in Figure 4.1, only two variables are statistically associated with both partial and full latency: nuclear-armed rival and military capabilities. Military capabilities is the most important variable in influencing the likelihood of nuclear latency onset. An increase in this variable of one standard deviation raises the predicted probability of partial latency onset by 0.83 percentage points and full latency onset by 0.58 percentage points. These increases may seem small. However, because nuclear latency onset occurs infrequently, the baseline probability is exceedingly small. When all independent variables are set to their mean values, the predicted probabilities of partial and full latency onset are 0.060 percent and 0.027 percent, respectively. With these values as a starting place, the AMEs of military capabilities correspond to a nearly fifteen-fold increase for partial latency and a twenty-two-fold increase for full latency. Even after these large increases from a relative standpoint, however, the overall probabilities remain small. With this caveat in mind, these findings suggest that militarily powerful countries are less vulnerable to political coercion and preventive attacks, and they have more resources at their disposal to achieve latency. These considerations together put powerful states in a better position to become latent nuclear powers.

Nuclear-armed rival produces statistically significant but relatively small AMEs.[73] Compared to the AMEs for military capabilities, they are about one-sixth the size in the case of partial latency and one-fifth the size for full latency. Despite the comparatively modest effects, these results indicate that facing potential external nuclear threats reliably motivates states to seek latent nuclear forces. A related variable, latent rival, is statistically associated with partial nuclear latency but the 95 percent confidence barely crosses zero in the case of full latency ($p = 0.071$).

Other explanatory variables are statistically associated with one stage of nuclear latency but not the other. Prior fatal disputes are correlated with partial latency onset, but not the full variety. The AME in the case of partial latency is similar in size to the effect of nuclear-armed rival. Crisis history, another indicator of the security environment, is statistically insignificant in both stages; it could have a positive or negative association with both stages of latency onset, according to this analysis. Overall, then, prior military conflict does not unambiguously result in a greater likelihood of nuclear latency onset. This ambiguous pattern could emerge because military conflict pushes a country in opposing directions. As I highlighted earlier, security threats simultaneously increase a country's desire to be weapons-capable and the resolve of those on the other side of prior conflicts to stop them from achieving that goal. When facing an actual or potential nuclear-armed rival, the demand for latency seems to overtake concerns about counterproliferation interventions, but this does not translate to security threats in general (many of which emanate from nonnuclear states). Moreover, there are important nonsecurity reasons to seek nuclear latency that could be reducing the salience of prior conflict in these statistical models.

There is a clear positive association between GDP per capita and partial nuclear latency onset but not full latency onset. This variable has

---

[73] My approach to calculating AMEs has a drawback for dichotomous variables. Standardizing the coefficients makes the effects directly comparable, but dichotomous variables cannot experience a one standard deviation change in the real world; they change only from 0 to 1, or vice versa.

the second largest effect on partial latency. The AME is about 3.5 times the size of the AMEs for prior fatal disputes and nuclear-armed rival. In the case of full latency, the AME for GDP per capita is also large but the 95 percent confidence interval includes 0, indicating uncertainty about whether the relationship is positive or negative. Combined with the military capabilities findings, these results indicate that supply-side factors are key for understanding which states become latent nuclear powers, a conclusion that is consistent with other research on the international spread of nuclear capabilities.[74]

Two variables pertaining to the domestic political environment – prior civil war and democracy – are similarly significant in one of the two cases. Democracies are unambiguously more likely than nondemocracies to obtain full nuclear latency but this finding does not carry over to partial latency. Based on the ATEs, democracy is the third most important variable in shaping the likelihood of full latency onset, behind military capabilities and GDP per capita. This provides some support for the notion that democracies are less vulnerable to counter-proliferation measures, including preventive military attacks. A history of civil war is positively associated with partial latency onset but not full latency onset. The ATE for civil war is about 20 percent larger than the ATE for fatal dispute history – the next strongest variable in the analysis of partial latency. The positive association here was not anticipated by the drivers and constraints emphasized above. An ex-post explanation could be that domestically vulnerable leaders see nuclear latency as a way to shore up support and increase their hold on power.

The other variables are not statistically associated with either stage of nuclear latency. This does not mean that they are unimportant. As we will see when we get to the qualitative evidence, some of these factors – for example, status and prestige – are key considerations for some countries. But, overall, we have a relatively high degree of uncertainty about the relationship between these variables and the emergence of latent nuclear forces.

Identifying Motives: Looking at the Cases

The preceding analyses usefully identified the correlates of nuclear latency onset. As explained earlier, however, we do not yet know which explanations are the most salient for explaining the global spread of sensitive nuclear technology. To find out, let's turn to the results of the qualitative analysis. For this analysis, I focus on the drivers of nuclear

---

[74] See especially Fuhrmann (2009a, 2012a) and Kroenig (2010).

latency adoption discussed earlier: incidental latency, nuclear hedging, prestige, financial gain, and energy security.

Table 4.2 and Figure 4.2 convey the results. Table 4.2 lists the first year that each country achieved full nuclear latency along with their primary motivations for seeking that capability, based on my survey of the historical record. Figure 4.2 displays how frequently each motive appears as a driving force.

Three caveats are in order before discussing these findings. First, the absence of a motive does not mean that it played no role in a country's ENR program. Everybody understands, for example, that having ENR technology might confer international prestige. I sought to distinguish cases where this recognition played a major role in motivating ENR development from those where it was a minor or trivial consideration. Second, understanding a country's motives can be challenging and I did not always find definitive rationales from leaders for their ENR programs. Sources other than the ones I consulted may produce different answers in the future. Third, the appearance of multiple motives for the same country does not imply that they were equally important. In the case of West Germany, for example, hedging was probably more important during the 1960s than the quest for financial gain.[75] In addition, as mentioned previously, I focus on the motives that existed at the time a country achieved full nuclear latency. Motives can change over time.

Two general conclusions emerge from Table 4.2 and Figure 4.2. First, no single explanation dominates. Instead, all five motives analyzed here find broad support in the historical record. Second, in more than half of the countries, there was not just a single motive for becoming a latent nuclear power. These conclusions together underscore that fully understanding the causes of nuclear latency requires multiple explanations, not just one or two.

Ten of the twenty-three countries that achieved full nuclear latency (44 percent) were already determined to build nuclear weapons.[76] This includes eight countries that ultimately obtained nuclear arsenals, plus Iran and Iraq. The latter two were steadfastly seeking nuclear weapons when their pilot ENR facilities first began operating but reversed course following external shocks: the 1991 Persian Gulf War (for Iraq) and the 2003 Iraq War and changes in domestic leadership (for Iran). For these ten states, the quest for ENR technology was simply a means to obtain nuclear bombs.

---

[75] See Gerzhoy (2015).

[76] I identified these states based on the criteria for unrestrained nuclear programs, which I lay out in Chapter 5.

Table 4.2 *Qualitative evidence for nuclear latency onset in twenty-three countries.*

Country	Year of full latency onset	Primary motivation(s)
Argentina	1983	Hedging Status/prestige Energy security Financial gain
Belgium	1966	Energy security Financial gain Status/prestige
Brazil	1985	Hedging Status/prestige Energy security
Canada	1948	Status/prestige
China	1963	Incidental latency
France	1954	Incidental latency
Germany	1967	Energy security Financial gain Hedging
India	1964	Hedging Status/prestige
Iran	2003	Incidental latency
Iraq	1990	Incidental latency
Israel	1965	Incidental latency
Italy	1970	Energy security Status/prestige Hedging
Japan	1975	Hedging Energy security
Netherlands	1973	Energy security Financial gain Status/prestige
North Korea	1989	Incidental latency
Norway	1961	Hedging Status/prestige Financial gain
Pakistan	1979	Incidental latency
Russia	1948	Incidental latency
South Africa	1975	Energy security Financial gain Hedging Status/prestige
Spain	1967	Energy security Hedging Status/prestige
United Kingdom	1951	Incidental latency
United States	1943	Incidental latency
Yugoslavia	1966	Financial gain Hedging Status/prestige

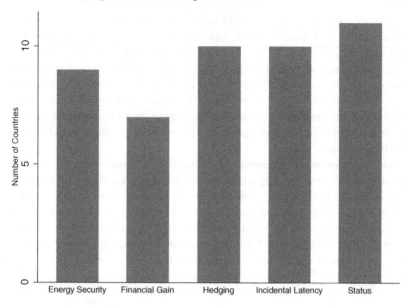

Figure 4.2 Frequency of nuclear latency motives in twenty-three countries.

Incidental latency does not appear alongside other motives in Table 4.2, as it is incompatible with them. It is logically impossible, based on my operationalization of the concept, simultaneously to hedge and have incidental latency. Incidental latency could theoretically exist alongside status and economic considerations. In practice, however, once a state is determined to build a bomb, its quest for an arsenal trumps all other motives for obtaining an ENR capability. States with incidental latency may be motivated by status concerns, such as in the case of France after 1954. But in that case leaders saw prestige value in weapons, not just the technological capability to build them. In some countries, such as the United States prior to India's 1974 nuclear test, commercial motives eventually emerged but these were positive side effects rather than a main driver of getting the capability.

The other thirteen countries had more flexible nuclear policies at the time they began operating pilot scale ENR plants. Hedging appeared as a primary motive in ten cases. Brazil provides one illustration. In 1987, Brazilian General Haroldo Erichsen da Fonseca underscored the logic of hedging. As Brazil's ability to make fissile material advanced, he said, "We do not have the objective of making an atomic bomb, but if it is necessary, we are going to build it."[77] Two eventual nuclear weapons states, India and South Africa, were hedging at the time they achieved full nuclear latency. These countries embraced weaponless deterrence and postponed a final decision on weaponization before ultimately moving on to assembled bombs (see Chapter 2). Yugoslavia eventually launched a serious nuclear weapons program and its activities had a military dimension almost from the beginning, but I consider its motives to be more in line with hedging in the mid-1960s when its pilot-scale ENR plant came online.[78]

Many hedgers understood the potential political value of nuclear latency. As we saw in Chapter 2, leaders from several states – Argentina, Japan, Spain, and others – believed in the viability of weaponless deterrence, suggesting that a desire for greater political influence motivated their development of an ENR capability. Italian leaders understood this as well. Italy flirted with building nuclear weapons but never pursued this option with vigor, instead aiming to reap diplomatic benefits from nuclear latency.[79] Others seemingly wanted to shorten the time needed to make a bomb without an observable (at least to me as an analyst) desire to influence the behavior of other countries.[80] These states expressed a desire to be weapons-capable for national security reasons without conveying a clear sense of why this might be beneficial.

Hedging loomed in the background in other cases without driving a state's nuclear policy. For example, Canada had hints of hedging in the early days of the nuclear age. Ottawa's nuclear program had a military dimension in the beginning: It was part of the Manhattan Project and played a role in the British nuclear weapons program in the aftermath of World War II.[81] At least until the 1950s, some officials in Canada toyed with building indigenous bombs. Gowing notes that there was "greater Canadian interest in the military aspects of atomic energy" in 1950, shortly after Canada became a full latent nuclear power.[82] A few years later, the CIA concluded that Canada might build nuclear weapons: "Canada has the capability to develop [an atomic weapons] program," according to a formerly classified assessment, "and we believe

---

[77] Quoted in *Los Angeles Times* (1987).

[78] This is consistent with Narang (2017). This classification could change as new information emerges in the future. Much about the Yugoslav nuclear weapons program remains unknown.

[79] Nuti (1993).

[80] In some cases, this was to have an insurance policy in case the security environment deteriorated. On insurance hedging, see Narang (2017).

[81] I do not code this as incidental latency because Canada's efforts were not intended to build indigenous nuclear weapons.

[82] Gowing (1974, 326).

it will do so, probably with British assistance, unless it receives defensive atomic weapons from the US."[83] A potential interest in bomb-making may have played a small role in Canada's plutonium program prior to the shuttering of its Chalk River reprocessing plant in 1956, but the status considerations discussed earlier were the primary driver.

A desire for greater international status was a primary motivator of ENR development in eleven of the twenty-three countries that achieved full nuclear latency (48 percent). As shown in Figure 4.2, status is the most common driver of latency adoption by a slight margin. Dutch nuclear physicist Jaap Kistemaker, a leader of the country's enrichment program beginning in the 1950s, underscored the role of status considerations in his country's nuclear program. Only by possessing sensitive nuclear technology, he wrote, "do you matter and do you have a say in the world."[84]

Energy security loomed as a key factor in nine cases (39 percent). This played a role in the Italian ENR program, for example, alongside hedging and status considerations. According to an Italian Foreign Ministry document, officials in Rome feared that the NPT would restrict an indigenous ENR program, and they wanted to ensure independence from the major nuclear suppliers such as the United States in this area.[85]

Profit motives were salient in seven countries, making it the least-frequent driver of nuclear latency onset. When profit motives dominate a country's nuclear program, national security considerations are usually secondary or minimal, as in the cases of Belgium and the Netherlands. In Norway, hedging and financial gain through nuclear exports both played a role, with the latter perhaps being more significant. According to historian Astrid Forland, "during the period of plutonium production, the Norwegians were more keen on making money than bombs."[86] Commercial motives became more important in some nonnuclear states over time, such as Argentina and Brazil, but they did not appear to be the initial driving forces.

Now that we better understand the motives in each case, let's return to a key finding from the statistical analysis: Having a nuclear-armed or latent rival is associated with nuclear latency onset.[87] There are two possible interpretations of this evidence. One is that ENR development follows the logic of incidental latency. In this view, potential nuclear

---

[83] US Central Intelligence Agency (1957b, 7).

[84] Quoted in Voute (2020, 189).

[85] This document is referenced in Nuti (2019, 129).

[86] Forland (1997).

[87] Having a latent rival was statistically associated at the 95 percent level with the first stage of nuclear latency only.

threats motivate countries to race all the way to a bomb. If true, the results would confirm something we already know: Countries build nuclear weapons in response to nuclear threats.[88] A second interpretation is that countries with rivals that have latent or actual nuclear forces might seek ENR technology primarily as a hedging strategy designed, in part, to deter unwanted foreign policy outcomes without actually arming.

A look at the cases reveals that both of these interpretations have merit, but the former provides relatively more explanatory power. Eleven countries had a nuclear-armed or latent rival at the time they first achieved full nuclear latency. Eight of these countries (73 percent) already had dedicated nuclear programs, indicating that their latency was incidental.[89] The other three – Argentina, Brazil, and India – were hedging at the time of full latency onset. In the presence of nuclear threats, therefore, it is much more common for a country to become bent on building a bomb. Importantly, though, some countries rely on latent forces to deter current or potential nuclear threats.

Conclusion

This chapter addressed the causes of nuclear latency onset. As the book aims to provide a comprehensive examination of nuclear latency's role in world politics, pinpointing the reasons for ENR technology diffusion internationally is an important part of the equation. I laid out the main drivers and constraints that countries face when considering whether to seek ENR technology. Based on these factors, the chapter identified variables that should be associated with the emergence of latent nuclear forces and conducted statistical analyses. The chapter also examined qualitative evidence, identifying the main motives for the twenty-three countries that achieved full nuclear latency.

The statistical analysis highlighted the importance of both supply-side and demand-side factors in shaping nuclear latency adoption. A country's military capabilities were strongly correlated with partial and full latency onset from a statistical and substantive standpoint. On the demand front, having a nuclear-armed rival was reliably associated with

---

[88] See, for example, Paul (2000), Singh and Way (2004), Jo and Gartzke (2007), and Debs and Monteiro (2017).

[89] Remarkably, of the ten countries with incidental latency at the time they first became fully ENR capable, eight (80 percent) had a latent or nuclear-armed rival. The two exceptions are Israel and North Korea. Although North Korea is not considered to be a rival of the United States according to the database used in this chapter it arguably should be, as I will discuss in subsequent chapters.

both stages of latency adoption. Some variables – having a latent rival, civil war history, prior fatal disputes, GDP per capita, and democracy – were statistically correlated with one stage of latency onset but not the other.

The qualitative investigation revealed that many factors account for global interest in ENR technology. For ten of the countries, an unabated desire for nuclear weapons motivated their adoption of pilot/commercial ENR plants, making their latency incidental. In the other thirteen cases, a combination of hedging (ten countries), energy security (nine countries), financial gain (seven countries), and status (eleven countries) played a key role.

The combined qualitative and quantitative evidence carries two key implications for analyzing the efficacy of weaponless deterrence. First, the analysis identifies important ways in which latent and nonlatent countries are different. Knowing these differences is critical for evaluating the deterrent effects of nuclear latency. Because countries do not become latent at random, we need to know whether the factors that give rise to ENR development – rather than having the technology per se – account for patterns we observe in the historical data. In the statistical analysis of military conflict carried out in Chapter 5, I will account for differences between latent nuclear powers and their nonlatent counterparts using the explanatory variables analyzed above.

Second, the distinction between incidental latency and hedging serves as a starting point for identifying the countries that should be able to influence their adversaries and allies more effectively. As we saw in Chapter 1, the viability of weaponless deterrence varies based on a country's level of nuclear restraint. States with unrestrained nuclear programs cannot credibly engage in deterrence by proliferation, but they can potentially use deterrence by delayed attack or doubt more effectively than their counterparts with restrained programs. The danger, however, is that unrestrained programs are more likely to invite preventive attacks and other forms of political blowback. Overall, for latent nuclear powers, unrestrained nuclear programs offer higher risks but potentially greater rewards. States that pursue this path will probably experience higher rates of conflict overall, and they will be unable to deter their adversaries from arming, but they may have better luck deterring the most severe uses of military force, such as full scale invasions. Any country whose latency was incidental in the above analysis (see Table 4.2), by definition, had an unrestrained nuclear program. Several others adopted unrestrained programs after the point of latency onset. In Chapter 5, I will identify all of those cases and analyze the efficacy of weaponless deterrence based on a country's level of nuclear restraint.

5   Reaping Rewards: Deterring Conflict and Gaining Influence

World leaders believe that nuclear latency confers political leverage. North Korean leaders, for example, claimed that the means to make fissile material for a bomb gave them a "deterrent," regardless of whether they possessed deliverable nuclear weapons.[1] But does nuclear latency actually generate foreign-policy benefits?

This chapter investigates this issue, presenting new quantitative evidence on the political effects of nuclear latency. It begins by identifying latent nuclear deterrence theory's predictions in three contexts: military conflict, foreign-policy preferences, and alliance leverage. I then describe the research strategy for testing these predictions. I take a design-based approach to causal inference, seeking to identify how developing nuclear latency changes a country's foreign policy fortunes in the decade that follows latency adoption. I use matching and weighting methods to make nonlatent countries as similar as possible to latent ones, and then use difference-in-differences (DiD) estimation to adjust for a time trend.[2] This allows me to compare the foreign-policy outcomes newly latent nuclear powers experience to what we would have expected in a counterfactual situation where these states stayed nonlatent.

The political effects of latent forces depend on a nuclear program's political aims (restrained or unrestrained), the level of latency (partial or full), and the specific foreign policy outcome. When a nuclear program is restrained, obtaining full latency results in greater international influence. This includes fewer crises and fatal military disputes, greater foreign-policy similarity with other countries, and (for US allies) more US troops on their soil. However, these benefits emerge in just some of the years that follow latency adoption and the degree to which they materialize depends on various research design choices. The most tenuous benefit is a reduction in fatal disputes, while the others are more consistently obtained. In the presence of unrestrained nuclear programs,

---

[1] Hecker and Serbin (2023, chapter 4). See other examples in Chapters 1 and 2.
[2] Imai et al. (2023).

by contrast, full nuclear latency generates benefits less reliably and invites some blowback. In addition, compared to full nuclear latency, partial capabilities have smaller effects that are more inconsistently observed and less in line with the theory. Being closer to a bomb, therefore, generally carries more significant consequences for foreign policy and international conflict.

Predictions

Chapter 1 described latent nuclear deterrence theory and identified its general predictions. Recall that countries hoping to gain political leverage from latent nuclear forces face three major challenges. First, punishment costs are delayed, weakening their effect on challengers – if they even anticipate them at all. Second, carrying out threats in weaponless deterrence is costly for the defender, not just the challenger, so challengers may see them as noncredible. Third, merely attempting weaponless deterrence can be dangerous, as it can incite international instability.

To have any hope of succeeding, defenders must mitigate these problems. Three things help them do so: possessing sensitive nuclear technology – specifically uranium enrichment or plutonium reprocessing (ENR) facilities – having restrained political aims, and high stakes.

It is analytically useful to place opportunities for political influence into one of four categories based on whether the defender possesses ENR technology and has on unrestrained nuclear program, as shown in Table 5.1. When the stakes are low, countries in all four categories will struggle to gain leverage from latent nuclear forces. As the stakes rise, however, these groups begin to vary in their ability to effectively practice weaponless deterrence.

When a country has a restrained nuclear program, shifting from being ENR-free (Category 1) to possessing ENR technology (Category 2) increases the viability of latent nuclear deterrence in high-stakes situations. By contrast, when a state has an unrestrained nuclear

Table 5.1 *Categorization of defenders in latent nuclear deterrence.*

	No ENR	ENR
Restrained	Category 1	Category 2
Unrestrained	Category 3	Category 4

program, going from no ENR technology (Category 3) to ENR-capable (Category 4), may not reliably enhance weaponless deterrence. Because this shift can bolster deterrence *and* invite instability, the overall effect is more uncertain.[3] This chapter tests these general predictions in three specific contexts: military conflict, foreign-policy preferences, and leverage within military alliances.

Military Conflict

Military disputes take many forms, ranging from low-level displays of force to full-scale invasions. The three means of influence in weaponless deterrence – proliferation, delayed attack, and doubt – will probably not dissuade potential attackers from instigating low-level conflicts. Challengers anticipate that defenders are unlikely to execute threats when the stakes are small. Threats become more credible as the potential consequences for a country's national security increase. It is believable that a country might expeditiously arm with nuclear weapons (and perhaps carry out a delayed strike) if an adversary attempted to seize some of its territory, whereas this is not a plausible response to the adversary's navy seizing a fishing vessel or other actions that do not put the defender's vital interests at risk.

Countries in possession of sensitive nuclear technology (Categories 2 and 4) are better positioned to deter serious military disputes. Countries possessing ENR technology are on the technological cusp of building nuclear bombs. They have therefore shortened the delay between a potential challenge to the status quo and the imposition of punishment. This increases the expected punishment costs for potential aggressors. Moreover, operating ENR plants sends a warning shot, forcing potential aggressors to consider the possibility of inducing proliferation or inviting a delayed retaliatory strike.

Yet the value of sensitive nuclear technology for deterring serious military disputes depends on a country's political aims. As we saw in Chapter 4, some seek ENR plants because they are bent on building bombs while others demonstrate restraint, taking a wait-and-see

---

[3] These predictions hinge on a key assumption – that governments generally know when their adversaries develop latent nuclear capabilities. According to latent nuclear deterrence theory, nuclear facilities that are unknown to a potential attacker cannot deter its use of military force. Most of the time, countries know when one of their enemies becomes a latent nuclear power. Indeed, history shows that it is difficult for a country to conceal *all* of its nuclear infrastructure, even if some facilities remain covert. On average, then, we would expect to see a relationship between possessing sensitive nuclear facilities and being targeted in military disputes.

approach. A drawback of weaponless deterrence is that obtaining sensitive dual-use technology – which is critical for success – could incite military conflict rather than deter it. Countries that take a restrained approach (Categories 1 and 2) can mitigate this risk to some degree by reassuring their adversaries that nuclear armament is neither inevitable nor imminent. This keeps deterrence by proliferation on the table, but may weaken deterrence by doubt by reducing the perception that the latent nuclear power could already be nuclear-armed.

By contrast, unrestrained nuclear programs carry higher risks and potentially higher rewards. Countries seen as racing to a bomb are more likely to provoke military action against them, possibly eroding any deterrence benefits. At the same time, these countries may have better luck with deterrence by doubt, the mechanism that can impose the highest expected costs on potential attackers. This is because the punishment time delay is shorter, and nuclear use is more costly than mere armament.

This leads to two predictions about military conflict.

- **Military Conflict Prediction 1** When a country has a restrained nuclear program, going from no ENR technology (Category 1) to being ENR-capable (Category 2) lowers the risk of serious military conflict.
- **Military Conflict Prediction 2** When a country has an unrestrained nuclear program, going from no ENR technology (Category 3) to being ENR-capable (Category 4) less reliably lowers the risk of serious military disputes. Because this shift can bolster deterrence *and* invite instability, the overall effect on military conflict is more uncertain.

Foreign-Policy Preferences

The political effects of nuclear latency may extend beyond the realm of open military conflict. If latent nuclear deterrence theory is correct, we may see changes in the general foreign-policy orientation of a country when a counterpart obtains sensitive nuclear technology. Former US Secretary of State Henry Kissinger's claim that Iran's nuclear latency causes others to "reorient" their foreign policies toward Tehran, which I highlighted in Chapter 2, exemplifies this line of thinking.[4]

The divergence of foreign-policy preferences between two countries can create a threatening atmosphere. Prior studies have shown that

[4] Kissinger (2012).

foreign policy dissimilarity is associated with military disputes.[5] Adopting foreign policies and rhetoric that heighten ideological divisions can therefore encourage the target state to seek nuclear weapons. To be sure, many of the countries that sought nuclear forces in the post–Cold War era opposed the US-led international order. This includes India, Iran, Libya, North Korea, and Syria. To stave off nuclear weapons proliferation, then, others may refrain from exacerbating foreign-policy differences with an ENR-capable state.

The most likely means of influence outside of a military conflict environment is deterrence by proliferation. When a challenger is contemplating the use of military force, it may consider a latent nuclear power's potential to arm and eventually carry out a nuclear strike in the event of serious escalation. If war is not an immediate consideration for the challenger, however, this possibility may not enter its mind, weakening deterrence by delayed attack and doubt. In its general foreign-policy interactions with an ENR-capable state, a challenger is more likely to worry about inducing nuclear weapons proliferation.

The exclusive reliance on deterrence by proliferation has two implications for foreign-policy preferences. First, it is essential that nuclear armament by the defender would impose costs on the challenger. This is likely to be true when future military conflict is possible but may not be the case otherwise. For example, Iraq does not want neighboring Iran to build nuclear weapons but, sitting more than 3,000 miles away, Vietnam is less worried about this possibility. Second, it is especially important for an ENR-capable country seeking political leverage to show restraint. Being seen as steadfastly coveting nuclear weapons would undermine deterrence by proliferation, rendering the most likely means of influence feeble. Moreover, racing to build nuclear weapons could trigger foreign-policy actions that exacerbate tensions with other countries.

As with military conflict, there are limits to the kinds of foreign-policy actions a country can hope to influence. Yet a country's broad foreign-policy preferences typically stem from big issues, such as its position in relation the current international order. In general, then, latent nuclear deterrence can influence foreign-policy congruence – particularly when two states have a history of military conflict. In that case, a challenger's change in foreign policy may be seen as particularly threatening for the defender, making proliferation threats more credible.

This leads to four predictions about foreign-policy preferences. The first two suggest that one state's obtainment of ENR technology causes changes in another's preferences, regardless of restraint. The latter two

---

[5] Gartzke (2000) and Bailey et al. (2017).

expect that these changes in foreign-policy orientation should increase the similarity of preferences between the two countries if the latent state's program is restrained and reduce preference similarity if the program is unrestrained. Among states with a history of conflict, the challenger will generally respond to the defender's obtainment of nuclear latency, but the change will be desirable only if the defender has a restrained program.

- **Foreign-Policy Preferences Prediction 1** When a country has a restrained nuclear program, going from no ENR technology (Category 1) to being ENR-capable (Category 2) changes the foreign-policy preferences of other states with which future military conflict is possible.
- **Foreign-Policy Preferences Prediction 2** When a country has an unrestrained nuclear program, going from no ENR technology (Category 3) to being ENR-capable (Category 4) changes the foreign-policy preferences of other states with which future military conflict is possible.
- **Foreign-Policy Preferences Prediction 3** When a country has a restrained nuclear program, going from no ENR technology (Category 1) to being ENR-capable (Category 2) increases foreign-policy similarity between the ENR-capable state and those with which future military conflict is possible.
- **Foreign-Policy Preferences Prediction 4** When a country has an unrestrained nuclear program, going from no ENR technology (Category 3) to being ENR-capable (Category 4) does not increase – and may decrease – foreign-policy similarity between the ENR-capable state and those with which future military conflict is possible.

Alliance Leverage

Countries believe they can use weaponless deterrence to extract greater concessions from their powerful allies, not just influence their enemies (see Chapter 2). Allies of the United States, in particular, have frequently threatened to arm with nuclear weapons in order to gain leverage over Washington.[6] For example, Japanese leader Eisaku Sato used a proliferation threat to compel Richard Nixon to return the island of Okinawa in the late 1960s.[7]

---

[6] The most comprehensive study addressing this issue to date is Volpe (2023). See also Volpe (2017).
[7] See Volpe (2023).

Like in the case of foreign-policy influence, the main mechanism in play here is deterrence by proliferation; deterrence by delayed attack and doubt are unlikely to be viable. Countries can use proliferation threats to gain influence over allies under three conditions: the defender has a successful ENR program, the ally is sufficiently threatened by the defender's obtainment of nuclear weapons, and the defender has not already decided to launch an unrestrained weapons program. Meeting the second condition may appear difficult in an alliance relationship. However, the United States generally opposes the spread of nuclear weapons to both allies and adversaries, even if it finds the possibility of armament by the latter more threatening.[8]

There are many ways in which the United States could bolster its defense commitments to allies. Conventional troop deployments can be particularly effective as a means of reassurance within alliances.[9] Allies often seek a greater number of US troops on their soil as a signal of a stronger defense commitment. If countries meet the above conditions, they should be successful in gaining additional US troops. Yet launching an unrestrained nuclear program can make the United States think about withdrawing its forces, as the case of South Korea in the 1970s shows.[10]

- **Alliance Leverage Prediction 1** When a US ally has a restrained nuclear program, going from no ENR technology (Category 1) to being ENR-capable (Category 2) increases the number of US troops on the ally's soil.
- **Alliance Leverage Prediction 2** When a US ally has an unrestrained nuclear program, going from no ENR technology (Category 3) to being ENR-capable (Category 4) does not increase – and may reduce – the number of US troops on the ally's soil.

Stages of Nuclear Latency

This chapter, like Chapter 4, will analyze two stages of nuclear latency: partial and full. Latent nuclear deterrence theory expects that both partial and full nuclear latency can potentially generate foreign-policy benefits. However, full latency should have stronger political effects than partial capabilities, for three reasons.

First, countries that have an operational pilot plant are closer to a bomb and therefore would have a shorter lag time for inflicting punishment. This reduced time lag increases the expected punishment costs.

---

[8] On the consistent US opposition to nuclear weapons proliferation, see Kroenig (2014a).
[9] Reiter (2014).
[10] Lanoszka (2018, chapter 5).

Second, operating a pilot plant sends a stronger signal to other countries than just laboratory-scale ENR work. Small-scale activities carried out in a laboratory are more prone to being missed by foreign governments. And, if they are detected, officials might not see them as a shot across the bow, since they are less worrisome from a nonproliferation standpoint.

Third, full latency potentially enables all three means of influence: proliferation, delayed attack, and doubt. States with partial latency only, by contrast, may be forced to rely mostly on deterrence by proliferation. Being at least a couple of years from a bomb, these countries would struggle credibly to threaten a delayed nuclear attack or cultivate the perception that they are already nuclear-armed. Delayed attack would be viable in situations where military conflict is expected to last a long time – longer than it would take the country to arm – and if the adversary is particularly farsighted. Doubt could be on the table for a state with partial nuclear latency if the adversary overestimates its progress toward a bomb, but is otherwise unlikely to confer much leverage.

This expectation stands in contrast to political scientist Tristan Volpe's "sweet spot" theory of bargaining with nuclear latency.[11] He argues that developing the capacity to produce fissile material can give a country political leverage, a claim that is consistent with latent nuclear deterrence theory. Volpe posits, however, that getting too close to a bomb weakens the leverage a state derives from nuclear latency by making it harder to signal restraint. As countries start making plutonium or highly enriched uranium on a larger scale, he argues, their adversaries come to view nuclear armament as inevitable, rendering proliferation threats ineffective.[12] Based on this line of thinking, full nuclear latency may be less effective than partial capabilities.

How to Test the Predictions

Testing the aforementioned predictions presents major challenges. As we saw in Chapter 4, nuclear latency arises due to strategic decisions made by governments – not random chance. Patterns we observe between nuclear latency and foreign-policy outcomes, therefore, could be driven by the underlying factors that motivate countries to seek latency. How, then, can we assess whether nuclear latency and these outcomes are causally connected? The strategy that a researcher adopts to address this question can carry major implications for a study's ultimate conclusions.

[11] Volpe (2017).
[12] Volpe's analysis focuses on what I call deterrence by proliferation and does not examine the other two mechanisms.

Consider research on the deterrent effects of nuclear weapons. A flurry of studies over the past four decades have analyzed historical data to assess the relationship between nuclear weapons and international conflict.[13] Several analyses find that nuclear weapons are not associated with a lower likelihood of experiencing military conflict.[14] Some even report that having an arsenal *increases* a country's vulnerability to disputes.[15] Others find that building nuclear weapons lowers a country's risk of being targeted.[16] This variation emerges, in part, because scholars make different choices when it comes to research design – particularly strategies for assessing causality.[17] This is true of research on the political effects of nuclear latency as well, although fewer studies have examined this relationship.

Prior Approaches: Observable Confounders and Two-Way Fixed Effects

I am aware of seven published studies that use statistical analysis to estimate the political effects of nuclear latency. A 2015 study that I carried out with political scientist Benjamin Tkach found that nuclear latency was associated with a lower probability of being targeted in military disputes.[18] Consistent with this conclusion, political scientist William Spaniel reported that higher levels of latent nuclear capacity are correlated with a lower probability of having military disputes reciprocated.[19] Along similar lines, Eleonora Mattiacci, Rupal Mehta, and Rachel Whitlark found that having nuclear latency increases the number of cooperative overtures a country receives from the United States.[20] The other four studies, by contrast, found that latency did not provide benefits for deterrence or political influence more generally.[21] Based on these analyses, we do not yet have consensus in scholarship about the political effects of nuclear latency. It is not clear, however, that any of these studies can credibly draw conclusions about causality.

---

[13] For a review of this literature, see Gartzke and Kroenig (2016).
[14] For example, Gartzke and Jo (2009), Sobek et al. (2012), Fuhrmann and Sechser (2014), and Bell and Miller (2015).
[15] Geller (1990) and Rauchhaus (2009).
[16] Kroenig (2018), Narang and Mehta (2019), and Lee et al. (2022).
[17] The fact that nuclear weapons have heterogeneous effects on military conflict based on a state's posture is also important for explaining this variation. See Narang (2014).
[18] Fuhrmann and Tkach (2015).
[19] Spaniel (2019, chapter 4).
[20] Mattiacci et al. (2022).
[21] Horowitz (2013), Mehta and Whitlark (2017a), Smith and Spaniel (2020), and Jones et al. (2023).

Prior research addresses the nonrandom assignment of nuclear latency by controlling for observable confounders, like a state's conflict history, military/economic capabilities, and alliances. But some confounding factors cannot easily be incorporated into a statistical model because they are unobservable to analysts or difficult to measure. The possible existence of unmeasured confounders makes it difficult to draw conclusions about causality based on prior research. This problem is well known. As Tkach and I put it in our 2015 study, "We have shown that there is a correlation between these two variables, but more work is needed to understand whether this is a causal relationship."[22] We emphasized throughout the article that our findings are "far from definitive" and should be seen as "preliminary."[23]

We can potentially get closer to identifying a causal relationship by using fixed effects to account for unmeasured differences between cases. A common approach in social science research is to include country fixed effects to account for time-invariant confounders, like culture and geography, and year fixed effects to adjust for common shocks, like the end of the Cold War. When there are just two units and two time periods, using unit and year fixed effects is equivalent to a classic DiD design.[24] Scholars have routinely extended this framework when they have multiple units and time periods, as is usually the case in international relations research. The literature refers to this approach as the two-way fixed effects (TWFE) DiD estimator.[25] This estimator has been widely used for causal inference in many fields. In top finance and accounting journals, for example, there are 366 papers that use this design – and most of them have been published since 2010.[26] It is easy to see why political scientists Kosuke Imai and In Song Kim call the TWFE DiD estimator the "default methodology for estimating causal effects from panel data" in the social sciences.[27]

In prior research, I used the TWFE DiD estimator to examine the deterrent effects of nuclear latency.[28] Consistent with latent nuclear deterrence theory, I found that developing sensitive nuclear technology lowers a country's vulnerability to uses of military force under certain conditions. But we need to be skeptical when interpreting this evidence.

---

[22] Fuhrmann and Tkach (2015, 457).
[23] Fuhrmann and Tkach (2015, 445, 453, 455).
[24] Angriest and Pischke (2009, 228).
[25] See, for example, Goodman-Bacon (2021).
[26] Baker et al. (2022). These are papers where the treatment adoption is staggered, meaning that it is adopted at different points in time.
[27] Imai and Kim (2021, 1).
[28] Fuhrmann (2017).

Recently, social scientists have identified problems with the TWFE DiD estimator, especially in situations where countries adopt the treatment at different points in time, as is the case with nuclear latency.[29] Scholars using this approach typically want to identify the average treatment effect (ATE) or average treatment effect on the treated (ATT). However, thanks to a series of papers published in the past few years, it is now clear that this is not what you get when using the standard TWFE DiD estimator.[30] The coefficient generated by the TWFE DiD estimator is difficult to interpret and it is not clear how the counterfactual outcomes are estimated.[31] As economist Andrew Goodman-Bacon shows, it represents a weighted average of all possible two-by-two DiD that compare a group that changes treatment status (i.e., the treatment group) to a group whose treatment status remains constant (i.e., the control group).[32] The control group could be one of three types: (1) a group that is never treated, (2) an eventually treated group before treatment, or (3) a treated group that remains treated in subsequent periods.

Using already-treated units as controls has major implications for interpreting evidence. Unless the treatment effects are constant over time – which seems unlikely in the case of nuclear latency – the TWFE DiD will be biased in the presence of staggered treatment adoption. Alarmingly, in this situation, it is possible to produce the wrong sign on the treatment effect, meaning that the findings could reflect the opposite of reality.[33]

A Solution: Matching/Weighting Methods and Difference-in-Differences

There are a growing number of possible solutions to the problems with the TWFE DiD estimator, ranging from the synthetic control method to two-stage DiD (2sDiD).[34] I use a design-based approach to causal inference developed by Imai, Kim, and Erik Wang: DiD with matching

---

[29] See, for example, Imai and Kim (2021), Imai et al. (2023), and Goodman-Bacon (2021).

[30] Goodman-Bacon (2021), Imai and Kim (2021), and Imai et al. (2023).

[31] Imai et al. (2023).

[32] Goodman-Bacon (2021). Group size and treatment variance determine the weights.

[33] Baker et al. (2022, 2).

[34] See Gardner (2022) on 2sDiD. For applications of the synthetic control method in international relations research see, for example, Lipscy and Lee (2019) and Imamverdiyeva and Shea (2022).

or weighting (DiDMW).[35] This procedure does not rely on strong parametric assumptions, meaning that the effects of the treatment can be nonlinear within the same unit over time. It also transparently identifies the relevant counterfactuals used to produce the treatment effects and provides helpful diagnostic tools.

In DiDMW we take a three-step approach to identifying treatment effects.[36] First, for each treatment onset, researchers identify potential control observations – known as the *matched set* – that have identical treatment histories over a set number of years, which is determined by the user. If we set the number of lags to 2, for example, we will identify units that shared treatment histories over the preceding two years. Spain first operated a pilot reprocessing plant in 1967. With a two-year lag, potential control cases would be countries that were also nonlatent in 1965 and 1966 but, unlike Spain, did not experience the onset of treatment the following year. Second, the analyst refines the matched set using matching or weighting procedures. This process makes the control cases as similar as possible to those that become latent. Third, the researcher uses the DiD estimator to account for a potential time trend.

This procedure, like any DiD approach, hinges on the assumption of parallel trends. This assumption holds that the difference in outcome values between treated and control units would have remained constant over time in a hypothetical world where the treated units remained untreated. This assumption is impossible to test directly, since it is based on a counterfactual we never observe. However, researchers typically examine the viability of this assumption by looking at the trend among treated and control cases *prior to treatment adoption*. If the trends are parallel pretreatment, we have greater confidence that this would have continued in the absence of treatment. By contrast, nonparallel trends pretreatment would undermine our confidence that this assumption is credible. As we will see below, refinement through matching or weighting increases the homogeneity between treated and control units and produces trends that are relatively parallel pretreatment.

Note that DiDMW has a key advantage when it comes to testing latent nuclear deterrence theory: It allows for countries to switch their treatment status over time, and become treated more than once. States often eliminate enrichment and reprocessing capabilities after obtaining them, as we saw in Chapter 3. Italy, for example, shuttered its pilot-scale

---

[35] Imai et al. (2023). The authors do not use this acronym but I adopt it for ease of presentation.
[36] Imai et al. (2023, 9–10).

reprocessing program in 1990 after possessing this capability for two decades. This kind of shift is important for the theory since ENR plants must be operational in order to generate deterrence benefits. I therefore need a method that can allow for previously latent states to become nonlatent as time passes, and potentially shift back to latency again. Other approaches for dealing with treatment adoption at different points in time assume that a policy intervention continues for all periods once it is "turned on."

This method allows me to conduct an event study, examining how nuclear latency influences military conflict over a set number of years following treatment adoption or termination. I will determine how nuclear latency influences foreign-policy outcomes in year t, the year of treatment adoption, year $t + 1$, year $t + 2$, and so on. This usefully allows me to examine the immediate and longer-run effects of nuclear latency, which could be different. Prior research on nuclear latency, by contrast, does not distinguish latent nuclear powers based on how long they have been capable of making bombs.

Datasets

Testing the predictions requires four distinct datasets. The first two use the country-year as the unit of observation. For the analysis of military conflict, the dataset contains information on all countries in the world from 1929 to 2010, like in the previous chapter. I analyze a subset of this dataset for the alliance leverage analysis, focusing only on the seventy countries that had a formal alliance with the United States from 1950 to 2010.[37]

To test the predictions about foreign-policy preferences, we need information on both challengers and targets. The other two datasets therefore analyze country-pairs – known as "dyads" in international relations scholarship – from 1946 to 2010. One version of the dyadic dataset is "directed," meaning that the same dyad is include twice with the ordering of countries reversed. For example, the US–Russia dyad is included along with the Russia–US dyad. This is appropriate when the ordering of countries matters, like for testing Foreign-Policy Preferences Predictions 1 and 2. In the directed-dyad dataset, I distinguish between the state that is trying to gain influence (the target) and the state whose preferences I will measure (the challenger).

---

[37] I include both defensive and offensive alliances based on the Alliance Treaty Provisions and Obligations (ATOP) database (Leeds et al., 2002).

The second dyadic dataset has one observation for each country-pair in a given year, making it "nondirected." This is more appropriate for testing Foreign-Policy Preferences Predictions 3 and 4 because the outcome does not change based on the ordering of the countries. Both versions of the dyadic dataset include only country-pairs that experienced at least one military dispute during the period of study, since the predictions require the possibility of future conflict.

Outcomes of Interest

This chapter examines three foreign-policy outcomes at the conceptual level: military conflict, foreign policy congruence, and alliance leverage. Operationally, I analyze five variables – two each for military conflict and foreign-policy congruence, and one for alliance leverage.

The first indicator of military conflict measures the number of crises a country perceived in a given year based on the International Crisis Behavior (ICB) dataset.[38] This is a good measure for the theory because it captures whether leaders perceive a time-sensitive threat to their basic values that they think could escalate to serious military hostilities.[39] The number of crises per year ranges from 0 to 7 with a mean of 0.089. Second, I measure the number of times each year a country experienced one or more fatalities during a dispute in which it was targeted, based on the Correlates of War's (COW) Militarized Interstate Dispute (MID) dataset.[40] This variable ranges from 0 to 6 with a mean of 0.038. Fatal disputes and crises are both rare events in this sample, with the former having less variation.

I use two measures of foreign policy preferences based on data produced by political scientists Michael Bailey, Anton Strezhnev, and Erik Voeten.[41] Using votes in the UN General Assembly, they measure a state's preferences toward the US-led international order. I construct a variable indicating how much a challenger country's preferences have changed relative to the target's. In particular, this variable captures the absolute value of the difference between the challenger's change in preferences between year $t - 1$ and year t minus the absolute value of

[38] Brecher et al. (2017). I use Version 14 of the ICB dataset.
[39] Beardsley et al. (2020).
[40] Targets are those that did not take the first militarized action in a dispute. I include cases in which both the initiator and target were original members of a dispute, excluding joiners, such as China during the Korean War. I account for the year in which a dispute was initiated, not every year that a dispute was ongoing. As before, I use an updated version of the MID dataset produced by Gibler et al. (2017).
[41] Bailey et al. (2017).

the difference between the target's change in preferences between year $t - 1$ and year t. Positive values indicate that the challenger's foreign policy preferences changed more than the target's. Negative values, by contrast, mean that the challenger's preferences changed less than the target's. The theory expects to see positive values after the target obtains nuclear latency.

A second measure from Bailey, Strezhnev, and Voeten captures the foreign policy congruence of two countries by taking the absolute value of the difference between each state's ideal point. The resulting variable ranges from 0 to 5.1, with larger values indicating more dissimilar foreign policies. The theory expects that this variable should take on smaller values, meaning that two states' foreign policies become more similar, if at least one of them obtains nuclear latency.

This measure provides a more fine-grained picture of a bilateral relationship compared to violent conflict and crises. Military disputes occur infrequently, as noted earlier, and the absence of hostilities does not necessarily imply that a relationship between two countries is harmonious. We may therefore miss changes in a bilateral relationship from year-to-year by looking only at military conflict.

To illustrate, consider the relationship between Russia and the United States from 1946 to 2010.[42] Figure 5.1 shows the number of crises these two countries experienced during this period along with the difference in their foreign policies. Both measures indicate that the US–Russian relationship improved after the Cold War ended, but the indicator of foreign-policy similarity provides a more complete picture than crises. The measure of foreign-policy congruence shows that the bilateral relationship began to improve dramatically following the rise to power of Mikhail Gorbachev in 1985, and that relations worsened after a "honeymoon" period following the Soviet Union's collapse in 1991. By contrast, we miss this nuance when looking at crises; this variable has the same value (0) from 1984 to 2010.

The outcome of interest in the analysis of alliance leverage is the total number of US troops stationed on a country's territory in a given year.[43] In the sample of US allies, this variable ranges from 0 to 326,863 with a mean of 7,687. I take the natural log of troops to address the variable's skewed distribution.[44]

---

[42] Bailey et al. (2017) also use this example to illustrate the advantages of their measure.
[43] Allen et al. (2022).
[44] Because a log of zero is undefined, I add 0.000000001 to this measure prior to conducting the logarithmic transformation.

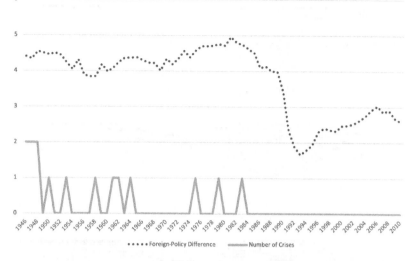

Figure 5.1 Relationship between Russia and the United States, 1946 to 2010.

Treatment

The "treatment" in this chapter is nuclear latency. As in all of the book's analyses, I measure this concept according to the Nuclear Latency (NL) database (see Chapter 3 for details). When analyzing military conflict and alliance leverage, this variable captures whether a country is latent in a given year. The analysis of foreign policy preferences accounts for the capabilities of two countries, not just one. When using directed dyads, I measure whether the target (not the challenger) has nuclear latency in a given year. For nondirected dyads, I consider a unit to be "treated" if at least one country in the dyad has nuclear latency in a given year.

Recall that I identify two stages: partial and full nuclear latency. The former includes laboratory-scale ENR work only, while the latter captures having an operational pilot or commercial plant. As I have argued previously, whether a country is a partial or full nuclear power carries implications for latent nuclear deterrence. In particular, the deterrent effects partial latency should be weak compared to having full-fledged latent nuclear forces.

I create treatment variation plots to illustrate how the adoption of nuclear latency varies across countries and over time.[45] Figure 5.2

---

[45] On treatement variation plots, see Imai et al. (2023).

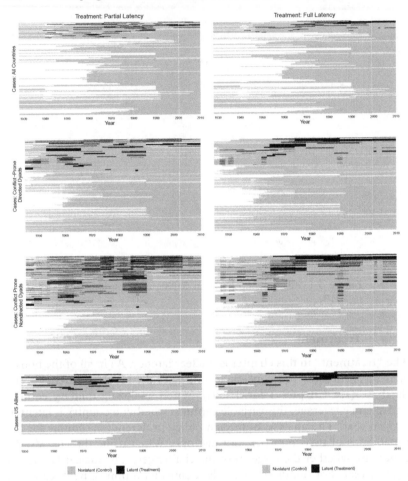

Figure 5.2 Treatment variation plot showing spatial–temporal variation in nuclear latency.

shows the treatment variation plots for full and partial nuclear latency in the four unique samples. These plots intuitively illustrate how the DiDMW procedure calculates causal effects by comparing treated and untreated units. The rows in each figure represent countries and the year is displayed along the horizontal axis. The black shading indicates that a country was latent during a particular year, while the gray shading means that it was nonlatent. White spaces reveal that the country (or dyad) did not exist at that particular point in time.

The figure shows that the majority of countries are never treated in the monadic dataset (the top row), but a sizable percentage are latent at some point during the period of study – 11 percent for full latency. Among those that are treated, the treatment frequently turns "off" and "on." Treatments can turn off if a country shutters previously operational ENR plants, or if it builds nuclear weapons. We can also see that some countries remain treated for decades while others are latent for just a few years. The bottom row of Figure 5.2 shows the treatment variation in the sample of seventy US treaty allies. Fourteen of the seventy US allies (20 percent) are fully latent at some point during the time period analyzed here.

The second and third rows of Figure 5.2 show the treatment variation in the two dyadic datasets. The horizontal bars are thinner in these plots, indicating a greater number of observations in the sample. The percentage of treated units here increases substantially. In the nondirected dyad dataset, more than half of the cases feature a state with latency at some point. These samples include conflict-prone dyads only. Countries are more likely to seek nuclear latency when they face external security threats, causing latency to be overrepresented compared to what we see in the monadic versions.

Moderating Variable

Testing the aforementioned predictions requires a measure of nuclear restraint. Latent nuclear deterrence theory expects that the effect of ENR capabilities on foreign-policy outcomes will vary based on whether a country has an unrestrained program. To account for this, I specify restraint as a moderating variable using the DiDWM procedure.

I identify unrestrained nuclear programs – those that were unambiguously intended to produce weapons – based on three criteria.[46] First, the

---

[46] Unrestrained programs bear resemblance to what other scholarship calls nuclear weapons "pursuit," but I set a slightly higher bar for inclusion. Singh and Way (2004, 866) define pursuit as follows: "states have to do more than simply explore the possibility of a weapons program. They have to take additional further steps aimed at acquiring nuclear weapons, such as a political decision by cabinet-level officials, movement toward weaponization, or development of single-use, dedicated technology." Bleek (2017, 3) similarly defines pursuit as "active programs authorized by leaders with the aim of acquiring nuclear weapons or the capacity to construct them on short notice. In order to qualify as pursuit, leaders do not need to have decided whether they will take the final step in the proliferation process." These definitions include cases where leaders have ambiguous intentions and are not necessarily pushing all the way toward a bomb, such as Brazil. What I call an unrestrained nuclear program is closer to what Narang (2017) calls an active "weaponization strategy." Like me, Narang distinguishes hedging from the active pursuit of nuclear weapons.

leadership made a political decision to build nuclear weapons. Second, there is a concerted national effort to prioritize bomb development backed by broad domestic support for weaponization. Third, there is no indication that the state might stop its race to build nuclear weapons if some event – for example, an improvement in the international security environment – were to happen in the future.[47] Programs that do not meet these criteria are restrained, based on my classification scheme, even if leaders were partially motivated by a desire for nuclear weapons now or at some point in the future.[48]

These criteria are designed to distinguish Manhattan Project-style programs from other nuclear ventures in terms of a country's political intentions. Unconditional nuclear programs need not be designed to produce a bomb as quickly as possible, like in the Manhattan Project, but the goal of the political leadership must clearly be to get one.[49] These programs have entered the point of no return, absent some unanticipated domestic or international shock.

Table 5.2 lists the states with unrestrained nuclear programs based on my criteria and the years during which they had this status. Sixteen of the thirty-three countries with ENR programs – just under 50 percent – had unrestrained nuclear programs at some point. This includes the ten full latent nuclear powers identified in Chapter 4 whose latency was merely incidental from the beginning. Of the six others, three achieved partial latency only (Libya, South Korea, and Taiwan) and three initiated unrestrained programs after operating pilot-scale ENR plants (India, South Africa, and Yugoslavia). One country on this list, Syria, did not achieve partial or full nuclear latency, according to publicly available information.

A number of countries had nuclear weapons-related activities that did not rise to the level of having an unrestrained program, based on the information at my disposal. Table 5.2 also lists these cases.[50]

Variables for Matching and Weighting

For all five-foreign policy measures, I use matching and weighting procedures to increase the homogeneity of treated and untreated units.

---

[47] I continue to classify programs as unrestrained once eventual nuclear powers assemble their first bomb.

[48] Countries with unrestrained programs had incidental latency, while many of the states with restrained programs were hedgers (see Chapter 4).

[49] For a typology that accounts for the speed at which a country seeks to build a bomb, among other things, see Narang (2017).

[50] I identify nuclear weapons activities based on Singh and Way (2004), Jo and Gartzke (2007), Bleek (2010), Muller and Schmidt (2010), Narang (2017), Mehta (2020), and my own knowledge of these cases.

Table 5.2 *Countries with unrestrained nuclear weapons programs and other weapon-related activities, 1942–2010.*

Unrestrained nuclear weapons program		Some weapon-related activities	
Country	Year(s)	Country	Decade(s)
China	1955–2010	Algeria	1980s–1990s
France	1954–2010	Argentina	1960s–1990s
India	1972–2010	Australia	1950s–1970s
Iran	1987–2003	Brazil	1950s–1990s
Iraq	1981–1991	Canada	1940s
Israel	1955–2010	Chile	1970s–1990s
Libya	1970–2003	Egypt	1950s–1980s
North Korea	1970–2010	Germany	1940s–1950s
Pakistan	1972–2010	Indonesia	1960s
Russia	1945–2010	Italy	1950s
South Africa	1978–1991	Japan	1940s–1970s
South Korea	1972–1974	Nigeria	1980s
Syria	2000–2007	Norway	1940s–1960s
United Kingdom	1946–2010	Romania	1980s
United States	1942–2010	Spain	1960s–1970s
Yugoslavia	1982–1987	Sweden	1950s–1960s
		Switzerland	1940s–1960s
		Taiwan	1970s–1980s

In particular, I use Mahalanobis distance matching with up-to-ten matches, propensity score matching with up-to-ten matches, propensity score weighting, and covariate balancing propensity score (CBPS) weighting.

I weight or match latent and nonlatent cases based on the variables that should influence latency adoption, as described in Chapter 4. To review, this includes: conflict history (prior fatal disputes and prior crises), having a nuclear-armed or latent rival, being an ally with a superpower or latent state, having a status deficit, the degree of latency in a country's region, nuclear energy investment, GDP per capita, economic growth, military capabilities, military growth, domestic instability, and democracy. In the analysis of alliance leverage, I also use a variable that measures the average number of US troops deployed in a country over the previous five years. The goal is to make latent and nonlatent states as similar as possible across these observable metrics.

I measure these variables at the dyadic level in the analyses of foreign-policy preferences and similarity. When using nondirected dyads, these variables generally take on whatever value is higher between the two states in the dyad. There are two exceptions: I calculate the power ratio in the dyad based on the share of capabilities controlled by the weaker state and I measure democracy based on the difference in the two states' polity scores. In addition, I adjust for whether the two states in the dyad are military allies, the total number of fatal disputes and crises they experienced over the previous five years, and the average foreign-policy congruence over the preceding five years. In the directed dyad dataset, I include the monadic variables mentioned previously for both the challenger and target. I also adjust for the challenger's share of capabilities in the dyad, the difference in polity scores, the presence of a bilateral military alliance, the number of prior crises and fatal disputes in the dyad over the previous five years, and the average change in the challenger's foreign-policy preferences over the prior five years.

Causal Quantity of Interest

I will use DiDMW to generate the ATT of nuclear latency onset for both restrained and unrestrained programs. This will tell us how a state's adoption of latency changed foreign-policy outcomes relative to a counterfactual in which it did not obtain ENR technology. The standard errors around the ATTs will be calculated based on 1,000 weighted bootstrap samples.[51]

This procedure requires me to specify two integers: leads (F) and lags (L). Here, F indicates the number of years after treatment for which the ATT is calculated. I choose a value of $F = 10$, allowing me to assess the causal effect of nuclear latency up to ten years after ENR facilities come online. This is analytically desirable because the deterrence effects of latency could increase over time, as a country's capabilities mature and its timeline to a bomb shortens.

Here, L is the number of lags for which the researcher adjusts. I select a value of $L = 2$, adjusting for two lags of treatment history. In addition, I include two lags for all of the confounding variables except those that are already measured over the previous five-year period.[52]

---

[51] On the standard error calculation, see Imai et al. (2023, 597–598). Given the way the standard errors are calculated, there will be minor fluctuations each time the simulations are run. In cases where the confidence interval is very close to zero, an ATT may be statistically insignificant in one run but significant in the next.

[52] Some adjustments are necessary due to the data not being linearly independent. In the analysis of directed dyads, I cannot include lags for the variable measuring the difference in polity scores when using propensity score matching, propensity score weighting, and CBPS weighting. For nondirected dyads, I am able to include only one lag of GDP per capita in some refinement methods when partial latency is the treatment. Further adjustments are necessary in some of the robustness tests, particularly when the number of lags increases. The variables that include information

I would ideally like to calculate the average effect of treatment reversal for latent nuclear powers that become nonlatent (ART), in addition to the ATT. The ART focuses on latency termination, comparing how shuttering ENR facilities influences a state's propensity to experience conflict relative to a counterfactual where it remained latent. However, as we can see from Figure 5.2, there are too few cases to generate reliable calculations of the ART, especially in the monadic dataset. Compounding the issue further, countries that build nuclear weapons after being latent would need to be dropped from this analysis. Otherwise, two different behaviors – closing ENR plants while remaining nonnuclear and building nuclear bombs – would be classified as the same treatment, leading to misleading inferences.

Assessing Covariate Balance and the Parallel Trend Assumption

Figures 5.3 and 5.4 show the covariate balance for all of the potential confounders after using the refinement methods, along with the balance without any refinement. Figure 5.3 uses partial latency as the treatment and Figure 5.4 uses full latency. The lines in these charts represent the standardized mean difference between treated and untreated units for each variable in the two years preceding the onset of nuclear latency. A difference of zero would indicate that the treatment and control groups have identical values after the relevant adjustments.

When there is no refinement, covariate balance is poor. This makes sense given what we learned in Chapter 4: Latent nuclear powers are different than their nonlatent counterparts. Mahalanobis distance matching modestly improves covariate balance, but considerable imbalance remains most of the time. Propensity score matching does better, but the biggest improvement comes from the two weighting methods. Propensity score weighting and CBPS weighting eliminate most (but not all) of the imbalance in all four datasets. However, across all refinement methods, the covariates are still heavily imbalanced in the dataset of US allies when partial latency is the treatment. We therefore need to be particularly circumspect when interpreting the effects of partial latency on US troop deployments.

The main analyses presented below are based on CBPS weighting – the refinement method that generally produces the best covariate balance. Later, I will examine how the findings change when using alternate

over the previous five years are prior crises, prior fatal disputes, nuclear energy investment, and prior civil wars. See Chapter 4 for details on how these are measured.

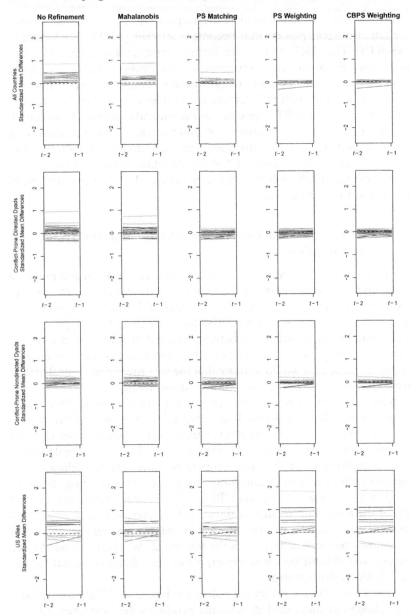

Figure 5.3 Covariate balance with partial latency as treatment.

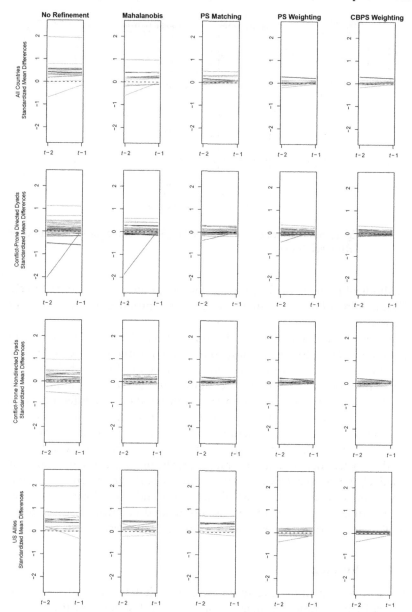

Figure 5.4 Covariate balance with full latency as treatment.

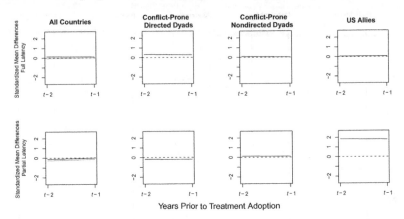

Figure 5.5 Covariate balance for lagged outcome variables based on CBPS weighting.

methods of refinement. In general, however, I am most confident in the findings when I use refinement methods that produce the best covariate balance.

To assess the parallel trends assumption, Figure 5.5 shows the covariate balance for just the lagged dependent variables based on CBPS weighting.[53] Although these variables appeared in Figures 5.3 and 5.4, it was not possible to differentiate them from the other confounders.

There are some fluctuations in the mean standardized differences over time. However, these differences are close to zero and relatively constant leading up to the year of treatment adoption. The biggest exception to this is in the dataset of US allies: The standardized mean difference in the lagged dependent variable is stable in pretreatment years but relatively far from zero when partial latency is the treatment.[54] Overall, this evidence increases my confidence that trends would have continued in this direction even if the eventually treated countries had remained nonlatent – a critical assumption on which a DiD design rests.

Findings

We can now examine the findings. For each foreign-policy outcome, I start by presenting the main results. Next, I describe how the findings change when I alter various aspects of the research design.

---

[53] All of these variables measure outcomes over the previous five-year period.
[54] This is true for all covariates, as shown in Figure 5.3.

I conduct five main robustness tests.[55] First, I use alternate lag structures, adjusting for one, three, and four lags of treatment history and the confounding variables instead of two.[56] Second, I use alternate methods of refinement: propensity score weighting, propensity score matching with up-to-five and up-to-ten matches, and Mahalanobis distance matching with up-to-five and up-to-ten matches.[57] Third, I take a simplified approach to calculating weights, focusing on the most basic factors affecting a country's demand and capacity for latency.[58] Fourth, I used an alternate measure of nuclear restraint based on whether a country had an active weaponization strategy according to political scientist Vipin Narang's data.[59] Fifth, I used listwise deletion instead of the default procedure for handling missing data, removing any observation from the dataset that has missing data for one or more variables.

Military Conflict

Figures 5.6 and 5.7 show the ATTs for international crises and fatal disputes. Each figure shows the effects based on a nuclear program's political aims (restrained or unrestrained) and two stages of nuclear latency (partial and full). In all four scenarios, the figures show the ATTs in the year of treatment adoption ($t + 0$) and then over the next ten years ($t + 1$ to $t + 10$).

The results provide qualified support for Military Conflict Prediction 1. For countries with restrained programs and partial nuclear latency, the estimated causal effects are statistically insignificant (see Figures 5.6c and 5.7c). Merely conducting laboratory-scale ENR work, therefore, does not reduce a country's vulnerability to crises or fatal disputes in the presence of a restrained program. However, achieving full latency in this scenario causes a reduction in the number of crises and fatal disputes – at least in some years after treatment adoption.

---

[55] I include several other tests for the dyadic analysis only, which are described later in the chapter.

[56] As before, I include lags for the variables measured in year t but not variables that already include information over the preceding five years.

[57] When assessing covariate balance in Figures 5.3 and 5.4, I used up-to-ten matches for the two matching methods. I added up-to-five matches for each refinement method to see if this change influences the findings.

[58] I included only GDP per captia, whether a country has a latent or nuclear-armed rival, prior crises, prior fatal disputes, and a lagged dependent variable measured over the prior five years. In the analysis of crises and fatal disputes, the conflict history variables are the lagged dependent variables.

[59] Narang (2017).

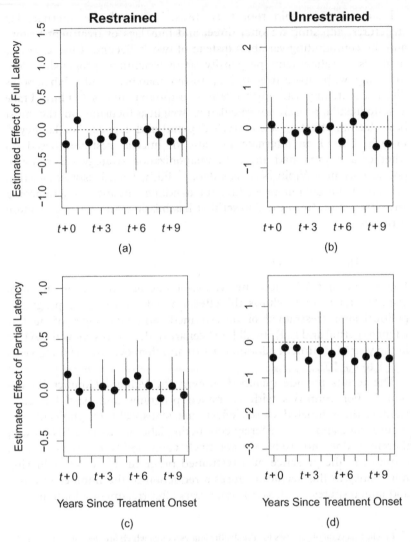

Figure 5.6 Average treatment effect of nuclear latency on crises.

When a nuclear program is restrained, countries experience a statistically significant reduction in crises during five of the years that follow full latency onset (see Figure 5.6a). When the ATTs are statistically significant, the causal effects range from −0.19 to −0.15. Noninteger effects of this size are nonintuitive and may seem small. Recall, however, that crises occur infrequently (the mean is 0.089). In more than

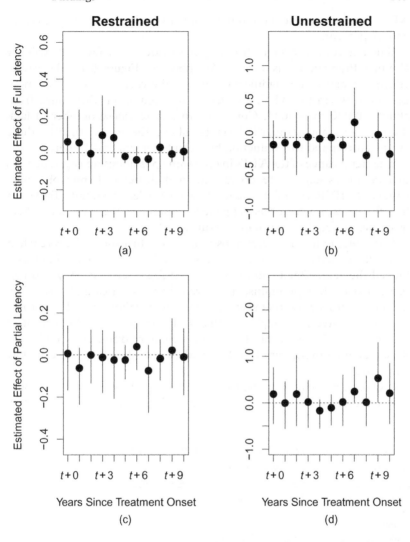

Figure 5.7 Average treatment effect of nuclear latency on fatal disputes.

90 percent of the years in the sample, countries do not experience any crises. Given the distribution of this outcome variable, it is unlikely that a one-unit shift in any dichotomous explanatory variable would produce an effect greater than one in either direction. To illustrate the size of the causal effects, imagine there is a state whose expected number of crises is one standard deviation above the mean (0.43). For this country, the

ATTs represent a reduction in the number of crises between 35 percent and 42 percent.

When it comes to fatal disputes, the evidence in favor of Military Conflict Prediction 1 is weaker. As shown in Figure 5.7a, the causal effects are statistically significant in two of the years following treatment adoption. When the ATTs are statistically significant, they range from about -0.020 to -0.034. Compared to a state whose number of fatal disputes was one standard deviation above the mean (0.258), these effects correspond to a reduction between 8 percent and 13 percent.

The significance of the ATTs in only some postadoption years suggests that countries experience crises and fatal disputes despite obtaining large-scale ENR capabilities and showing nuclear restraint. Table 5.3 lists the cases in which this happened. Looking at these cases can help us contextualize the quantitative results.

According to the theory, serious military conflict should be rare when a fully latent state exercises nuclear restraint. Table 5.3 shows that this is indeed the case. When countries achieved full nuclear latency and had restrained nuclear programs, there were just six crises and three fatal disputes over a period that spanned more than eighty years. These cases are concentrated in a single country: India accounts for 33 percent of the crises and 100 percent of the violent military disputes in Table 5.3. When it comes to Military Conflict Prediction 1, therefore, there are just a few outliers.

A quick examination of the cases in Table 5.3 helps us to understand why military conflict occurred even though countries were seemingly

Table 5.3 *Crises and fatal disputes experienced by fully latent countries with restrained nuclear programs.*

Target country	Year	Conflict name
Crises		
India	1965	Kashmir II
India	1971	Bangladesh War
Iran	2006	Nuclear crisis II
Japan	2009	North Korean nuclear crisis IV
Netherlands	1999	Kosovo War
South Africa	1975	War in Angola
Fatal disputes		
India	1964	Second Kashmir War
India	1965	Operation Desert Hawk
India	1967	Fighting along Kashmir ceasefire line

well positioned to succeed in deterrence. According to latent nuclear deterrence theory, obtaining large-scale ENR capabilities and showing nuclear restraint partially mitigates the challenges in latent nuclear deterrence, but does not eliminate them. It is therefore possible to experience serious military conflict despite implementing the theory's solutions, as discussed in Chapter 1.

Misperception of the latent nuclear power's intentions played a role in several of these cases, especially those involving India. Based on my criteria, India had a restrained nuclear program during the 1960s and early 1970s. However, some officials in Islamabad believed that an Indian nuclear bomb was inevitable as early as the 1960s, a point that I will revisit in Chapter 7. This perception weakened weaponless deterrence in two ways: taking deterrence by proliferation off the table and encouraging Pakistan to take military action sooner rather than later.

Consider the 1965 Second Kashmir War. Pakistan launched a military campaign to foment rebellion in Indian-controlled Kashmir, hoping to ultimately wrest the disputed territory away from its South Asian rival. Things did not go according to plan for Pakistan, as it encountered stiff resistance from Indian forces. After about two weeks of fighting, Islamabad called for a ceasefire. As noted in Chapter 2, the CIA concluded in February 1965 – six months before 30,000 Pakistani forces crossed the Line of Control in Kashmir – that India could build a bomb within one year of a political decision. Morrice James, the British High Commissioner to Pakistan during the war, believed that that the Pakistanis gambled partially because the window for military action was closing: "India's military strength was increasing and India had even talked of a nuclear weapon."[60] Based on this line of thinking, India was going to get nuclear weapons – possibly very soon – and this may have been Pakistan's last chance to alter the status quo in Kashmir. Rather than deterring conflict, India's latent nuclear capacity may have induced it. As George Perkovich put it, this may be "the first case of nuclear proliferation in one country (India) prompting an adversary to undertake military action to 'beat' the anticipated effects of nuclear deterrence."[61]

Disagreement about political aims played a role in the second Iranian nuclear crisis as well. The possibility of war over its nuclear program triggered a crisis for Iran in 2006. I classify Iran's program as restrained beginning in 2003, but some officials in Israel and the United States believed that Iran was bent on arming well after that point (I discuss

---

[60] Quoted in Baja (2013, 375).
[61] See Perkovich (1999, 108). He makes it clear that this claim is a bit speculative and that more research is needed to confirm or refute it.

this case further in Chapter 6). When that view exists, based on latent nuclear deterrence theory, serious crises can ensue – and that is what happened here. Notably, the crisis for Iran ended after the US intelligence community released an assessment in December 2007 indicating that Iran had stopped trying to build nuclear weapons, making its program restrained.[62]

For latent nuclear deterrence to be successful, the possibility of future nuclear armament must be brought to the forefront. The theory emphasized one way to do this: by developing large-scale ENR facilities. However, some of the cases in Table 5.3 show that the possibility of nuclear armament was a distant consideration, despite the defender's possession of this technology. This is because other crisis actors and events drowned out the latent nuclear power's bomb-making potential. In the fourth North Korean nuclear crisis, which began in 2009, officials in Pyongyang seemed to focus on perceived US threats – not the potential consequences of their actions for Japan's nuclear future. Similarly, the Netherlands participated in the 1999 NATO-led bombing of Yugoslavia and was technically part of the Kosovo crisis but it was not one of the principal actors. There is little reason to expect that Yugoslav leaders would have focused on Dutch retaliation of any kind, let alone its potential to engage in weaponless deterrence. A clear lesson emerges from these two cases: In multilateral interactions where a potential challenger's focus is on a superpower, the nuclear capabilities of weaker defenders are likely to be downplayed or ignored altogether.[63]

South Africa's nuclear latency did not prevent it from experiencing a crisis in 1975 when a civil war broke out in Angola following the country's independence from Portugal. The Soviet Union provided support to the People's Movement for the Liberation of Angola (MPLA), a Marxist group, generating fears of a Communist takeover of the region among officials in South Africa.[64] Some scholars have argued that the presence of Soviet-backed troops in the region contributed to South Africa's decision ultimately to build a small nuclear arsenal.[65] It is unclear if Soviet officials anticipated a connection between their support of the MPLA and the possibility of South African nuclear armament. Moscow may have calculated that supporting a rebel group

---

[62] See the description of this crisis from the ICB project at www.icb.umd.edu/dataviewer/?crisno=448.

[63] This previews a problem we will see more of in Chapter 7: In arms races, third parties frequently complicate latent deterrence.

[64] See the description of this crisis from the ICB project at www.icb.umd.edu/dataviewer/?crisno=260.

[65] Liberman (2001) and van Wyk (2019).

in a neighboring country would be insufficient to induce a South African bomb since it did not involve actions within the country's national borders. In any case, some scholars have argued that South Africa's latent nuclear forces helped limit Communist expansion in the region even if South Africa was unable fully to eliminate it.[66]

Let's now evaluate Military Conflict Prediction 2, which is about the effects of nuclear latency in the presence of unrestrained nuclear programs. According to latent nuclear deterrence theory, having an unrestrained program simultaneously makes things better and worse for gaining international influence. As a result, the deterrence benefits may be less reliably obtained and there should be more uncertainty surrounding latency's political effects.

Figures 5.6 and 5.7 broadly support this expectation. When it comes to full nuclear latency, none of the ATTs for crises are statistically significant (see Figure 5.6b). For fatal disputes, the ATTs are statistically significant in two of the years following full latency onset (see Figure 5.7b), the same number we saw for restrained programs. These causal effects range between -0.25 and -0.23, which are more than ten times larger than the weakest effect generated by restrained programs.

The findings for partial latency underscore unrestrained programs' competing effects particularly well (see Figures 5.6d and 5.7d). There is a reduction in crises during three of the years following partial latency adoption but an increase in fatal disputes in two of the years. Partial latency is more consequential for international conflict than full latency when a state has an unrestrained program, but the effects are not uniformly positive for the partially latent state.

It is also notable that the confidence intervals around the ATTs are much larger when a nuclear program is unrestrained. For example, the confidence interval around the ATT of full nuclear latency on the number of fatal disputes in year $t + 9$ is nearly eight times larger when a program is unrestrained ([-0.27, 0.35] compared to [-0.046, 0.034]). Based on the 95 percent confidence intervals, unrestrained nuclear programs could conceivably generate much larger reductions in military conflict than restrained ones. But unrestrained programs might also increase the number of disputes rather substantially, based on the upper-bound confidence interval. This is what we would expect if unrestrained programs have potentially larger deterrence effects while also providing incentives for others to use preventive military force and inflaming bilateral relations more generally.

---

[66] van Wyk (2019, 165) and Liberman (2001, 61).

Robustness Tests

Table 5.4 reports the results of the robustness tests for crises and fatal disputes. The results for full latency appear above the results for partial latency, while restrained programs appear on the left and unrestrained programs appear on the right. The table reports the number of years in which the causal effects are statistically significant for each change to the research design, as well as the direction of the causal effects. For comparison, I include the original results from Figures 5.6 and 5.7 in the top row. Since I examine the causal effects from year

Table 5.4 *Robustness test results for military conflict.*

	Restrained		Unrestrained	
	Crises	Fatal disputes	Crises	Fatal disputes
Full latency				
Original (Figures 5.6 and 5.7)	5 (−)	2 (−)	0	2 (−)
$L = 1$, 1 lag for confounders	7 (−)	0	0	2 (−)
$L = 3$, 3 lags for confounders	3 (−)	1 (−)	0	0
$L = 4$, 4 lags for confounders	7 (−)	2 (−)	0	0
Propensity score weighting	5 (−)	0	0	2 (−)
Propensity score matching, 10 matches	3 (−)	2 (−)	1 (−)	0
Propensity score matching, 5 matches	0	0	0	1 (−)
Mahalanobis distance matching, 10 matches	0	0	1 (−)	0
Mahalanobis distance matching, 5 matches	0	2 (+)	0	0
Listwise deletion	4 (−)	0	1 (−)	0
Fewer variables for matching/weighting	5 (−)	0	0	0
Restraint: Alternate measure	4 (−)	0	1 (−)	2 (−)
Partial latency				
Original (Figures 5.6 and 5.7)	0	0	3 (−)	2 (+)
$L = 1$, 1 lag for confounders	0	0	5 (−)	1 (+)
$L = 3$, 3 lags for confounders	0	0	5 (−)	2 (+)
$L = 4$, 4 lags for confounders	0	0	5 (−)	2 (+)
Propensity score weighting	0	0	4 (−)	2 (+)
Propensity score matching, 10 matches	0	0	4 (−)	1 (−)
Propensity score matching, 5 matches	0	0	4 (−)	1 (+)
Mahalanobis distance matching, 10 matches	0	1 (−)	1 (−)	1 (−)
Mahalanobis distance matching, 5 matches	0	0	2 (−)	1 (+)
Listwise deletion	0	0	5 (−)	1 (+)
Fewer variables for matching/weighting	0	0	3 (−)	1 (+)
Restraint: Alternate measure	0	0	0	2 (+)

Note: The table shows the number of statistically significant ATTs in each scenario. The maximum possible number is eleven. The positive and negative signs indicate the direction of the ATTs.

$t + 0$ to year $t + 10$ the maximum possible number of significant effects is 11.

Modifications to the research design produce some fluctuations in the number of years where the causal effects are statistically significant. The most notable changes emerge for full nuclear latency; the initial findings for partial latency are relatively stable.

Overall, the robustness tests strengthen the evidence for Military Conflict Prediction 2. Unrestrained programs generate more uncertain effects for deterrence than the initial results implied. The apparent benefits of having full nuclear latency and an unrestrained nuclear program are weaker than the initial findings suggested. The causal effects are statistically significant in only four of the eleven robustness tests for fatal disputes. In four robustness tests, however, the ATT for crises is statistically significant in one year, compared to zero years in the main analysis.

On the other hand, the robustness tests weaken the case for Military Conflict Prediction 1. The ATTs for restrained programs and fatal disputes are not statistically significant in the majority of robustness tests. The initial evidence that full nuclear latency reduces the number of fatal disputes in two postadoption years is sensitive to changes in the method of refinement, the lag structure, or other research design changes.

The results for crises, by contrast, are relatively stable in the presence of a restrained program. In the majority of follow-on tests, the causal effects are statistically significant and negative between three and seven postadoption years. The exceptions to this are when I used propensity score matching with up-to-five matches and Mahalanobis distance matching (up-to-five and up-to-ten matches), when none of the causal effects were statistically significant. This may initially seem damaging for the theory. Yet, as shown in Figures 5.3 and 5.4, the two matching methods produce relatively poor covariate balance compared to the two weighting methods, giving me more confidence in the latter. When using both CBPS weighting and propensity score weighting, there is evidence that full nuclear latency reduces the number of crises a state experiences in at least some postadoption years, regardless of the number of lags adjusted for and other research design choices.

The robustness tests underscore that the evidence for Military Conflict Prediction 1 is stronger for crises than fatal disputes. Although I did not expect this before carrying out the analysis, there are two possible post-hoc explanations. One is that crises more closely capture the key concept: serious conflict. Military disputes that result in fatalities would appear unambiguously serious. Yet the MID dataset contains some episodes that did not generate major national security threats and/or occurred without a specific decision to use force on the part of national leaders.[67] To illustrate, one fatal MID in the dataset involves a 2004 incident in which Israeli forces accidentally killed three Egyptian troops along the border, mistaking them for Palestinian militants.[68] Many fatal MIDs are undoubtedly serious, but there is heterogeneity in the level of threat they posed. The crises I study, by contrast, tap directly into leaders' perceptions of national security threats. A case would be included only if a leader perceived a threat to their country's basic values that could escalate to a serious military confrontation.

Another explanation for the less consistent results is that fatal disputes have less variation to analyze. Most of the time, countries do not experience any crises or fatal disputes, including in the years immediately preceding the adoption of nuclear latency. Fatal disputes are relatively more infrequent than crises. A lack of variation can make it harder to find statistically significant effects, particularly when comparing outcomes a small number of years before-and-after treatment adoption using DidWM.[69] This could at least partially account for the mixed evidence shown in Table 5.4, particularly for fatal disputes. I will now turn to foreign-policy outcomes where we have bigger variation.

Foreign-Policy Preferences

Figure 5.8 shows the ATTs of foreign-policy preferences using directed dyads. This analysis accounts for directionality: It distinguishes between challengers and targets, examining whether nuclear latency obtainment by the latter affects the former's foreign-policy preferences. Positive effects here mean that the challenger changes its foreign policy preferences more than the target does from one year to the next. Negative effects indicate the opposite: that the target changes its preferences more than the challenger.

Figure 5.8 provides supporting evidence for Foreign-Policy Preferences Prediction 1, which expects positive effects when the target becomes latent and has a restrained program, but only in the case of full latency. The ATTs are statistically significant and positive in the first three years after full latency onset and then for three of the next seven years (see Figure 5.8a). The statistically significant causal effects range from 0.082 to 0.18. These numbers do not have an

---

[67] Scholars have pointed out other contexts in which the MID dataset is suboptimal. See, for example, Downes and Sechser (2012).

[68] This description is based on the MID narratives available from the Correlates of War project at https://correlatesofwar.org/data-sets/mids/.

[69] Imai et al. (2023, 603).

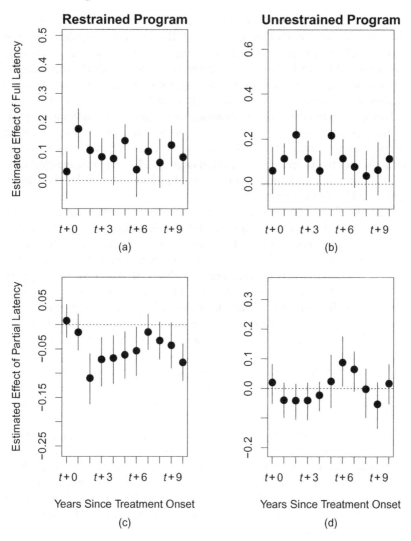

Figure 5.8 Average treatment effect of the target's nuclear latency on the challenger's foreign-policy preferences.

intuitive interpretation, so it is important to put them in perspective. From a starting place of one standard deviation above the mean (0.18), these effects correspond to increases in the outcome variable of 46 percent and 100 percent. The target getting full latency, then, doubles the challenger's change in foreign-policy preferences when the ATT is largest.

It also helps to compare these changes to cases in the dataset. In 1992, the year after the Soviet Union collapsed, Russia's foreign policy changed by 0.45 relative to the United States. This is more than twice as large as the biggest ATT in Figure 5.8. In 2009, the year Barack Obama became US president, US foreign policy changed relative to Cuba by 0.080, a change that is similar to the weakest statistically significant ATT.

However, partial latency is insufficient to change a challenger's preferences (see Figure 5.8c). The ATTs are negative in six posttreatment years, meaning that the challenger's preferences change less than the target's after the target obtains partial latency. The statistically significant effects range in size from -0.11 to -0.05, which are smaller than those generated by full latency.

The ATTs are also positive for full latency when a target has an unrestrained program, as expected by Foreign-Policy Preferences Prediction 2 (see Figure 5.8b). Like for restrained programs, the causal effects are statistically significant and positive the first three years after the target obtains full latency and for three of the next seven years. The size of the effects range from 0.11 to 0.22 in years when they are statistically significant, making them slightly larger than the case of restrained programs. From a starting point of one standard deviation above the mean, these effects translate to increases of 61 percent and 122 percent.

Partial latency, by contrast, moves the challenger's foreign policy preferences in just one posttreatment year (see Figure 5.8d). In that year, the ATT is 0.09 – weaker than the smallest effect produced by full latency.

These findings show that the target's obtainment of full nuclear latency changes the challenger's foreign-policy preferences for both restrained and unrestrained programs. However, we do not yet know if these changes move the challenger's preferences closer to – or farther away from – the target's. Are the changes shown in Figure 5.8 desirable for the target or not? To find out, let's turn to the analysis of nondirected dyads and the similarity of preferences.

Figure 5.9 displays the ATTs of nuclear latency on the similarity of foreign policy preferences in a dyad. Recall that the outcome variable in this analysis is the absolute value of the difference in foreign-policy preferences between the two states. Thus, negative effects mean that latency makes foreign policy preferences in a dyad more similar, while positive effects indicate more divergent preferences.

The results are generally in line with Foreign-Policy Preferences Prediction 3. When a nuclear program is restrained, the adoption of full nuclear latency by at least one state in a dyad causes foreign-policy

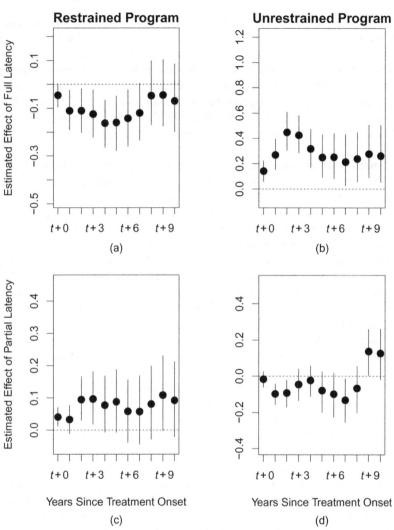

Figure 5.9 Average treatment effect of nuclear latency on the similarity of foreign-policy differences in a dyad.

preferences to become more similar (see Figure 5.9a). The causal effects are statistically significant for the first six years after full latency onset. However, the causal effects become insignificant beginning in year $t + 7$. The benefit of greater foreign policy alignment that fully latent states obtain, therefore, decays over time.

When the causal effects are statistically significant, the point estimates range from -0.11 to -0.16. For two countries that had a level of foreign policy similarity one standard deviation above the mean, these causal effects correspond to an improvement between 4 percent and 6 percent.[70] These effects are substantively meaningful but much smaller than what we see following the transformation of a bilateral relationship. As you can see in Figure 5.1, for example, the distance between US and Russian foreign policy preferences shrank by 1.54 points from 1990 to 1992.

Partial nuclear latency does not help countries increase the similarity of their foreign-policy preferences in the presence of nuclear restraint. On the contrary, the ATTs for partial latency are statistically significant and positive for three posttreatment years. This means that the onset of partial latency in a dyad makes foreign-policy preferences more dissimilar. When significant, the causal effects range from 0.041 to 0.097. Although the theory did not expect the positive and statistically significant result here, the pattern is consistent with the view that countries need full nuclear latency in order to gain greater international influence; partially latent forces are insufficient for this purpose.

The evidence is similarly in line with Foreign-Policy Preferences Prediction 4. When countries have unrestrained programs, one state's obtainment of full nuclear latency immediately causes foreign-policy preferences in the dyad to become more dissimilar. The worsening of foreign-policy alignment continues for the next ten years. The size of these effects is larger than what we saw for restrained programs. The ATTs range from 0.14 to 0.45. For a dyad that is one standard deviation above the mean in terms of its foreign-policy congruence, these effects translate to an increase in dissimilarity between 5 percent and 18 percent. For perspective, following the 1959 Cuban Revolution, which brought Fidel Castro to power, the difference between US and Cuban foreign-policy preferences increased by 2.79.[71] And the gap between US and Iranian foreign policy increased by 0.58 the year after the 1979 Islamic Revolution, compared to the value the year prior.

The effects of partial latency in the presence of an unrestrained program are more ambiguous. The causal effects are statistically significant in four posttreatment years. In three of these years the effect is negative, meaning that bilateral relations improve, and in one it is positive. There is a time dimension here: The effects start off in the negative direction in the two years after latency adoption and then turn positive as time

---

[70] These percentages are larger if we start with a smaller value, like the mean.
[71] This is based on a comparison between 1958 and 1960.

passes and some of these states approach full latency. From a substantive standpoint, the statistically significant causal effects range from -0.097 to 0.14. These effects are weaker than those generated by both full nuclear latency scenarios but stronger that what emerged from partial latency combined with a restrained program.

In sum, full nuclear latency can provide foreign-policy leverage or worsen bilateral relations, depending on the nuclear program's aims. Full nuclear latency improves foreign-policy alignment when a program is restrained and decreases alignment when a program is unrestrained. The results from the directed-dyad analysis (Figure 5.8) suggest that the challenger's changes in foreign-policy preferences – not just movement by the newly latent target – account for the changes in preference similarity in the dyad. The effects are largest shortly after latency emerges – when the ATTs for both the target's preferences and preference alignment in the dyad are statistically significant – and then fade away over time. Partial latency produces effects that are more ambiguous and less in line with the predictions.

Robustness Tests

Table 5.5 summarizes the results of the robustness tests for the two dyadic analyses. In addition to the analyses described earlier, I did several dyad-specific robustness tests. I used an alternate sample that included all dyads within 400 miles and those with a superpower (the United States or the Soviet Union until 1991). Future conflict might be possible in these dyads, even if they did not experience a dispute during the period of study. I also adjusted for additional dyadic nuclear variables. For the directed dyad analysis, I added variables measuring whether the challenger state possessed nuclear weapons or latency; in the case of nondirected dyads, I accounted for whether at least one state had nuclear weapons. Finally, for the analysis of nondirected dyads, I modified the coding of restraint to consider a dyad unrestrained if either country has an unrestrained program, not just the latent state.

There are fluctuations in the number of years where the causal effects are statistically significant across these follow-on tests, like in the case of military conflict. The evidence for the first two-foreign policy predictions is broadly similar. In the case of full latency, the causal effects were significant in six posttreatment years for both restrained and unrestrained programs. Across the robustness tests, changes in the the target's foreign-policy preferences are statistically significant between four and eleven posttreatment years if the program is restrained and between one and seven years if it is unrestrained.

Table 5.5 *Robustness test results for foreign-policy preferences.*

	Restrained		Unrestrained	
	Target's preferences	Preference similarity	Target's preferences	Preference similarity
Full latency				
Original (Figures 5.8 and 5.9)	6 (+)	6 (−)	6 (+)	11 (+)
Propensity score weighting	5 (+)	6 (−)	7 (+)	11 (+)
Propensity score matching, 10 matches	6 (+)	6 (−)	7 (+)	6 (+)
Propensity score matching, 5 matches	7 (+)	3 (−)	6 (+)	5 (+)
Mahalanobis distance matching, 10 matches	9 (+)	0	7 (+)	7 (+)
Mahalanobis distance matching, 5 matches	9 (+)	0	6 (+)	7 (+)
$L = 1$, 1 lag for confounders	8 (+)	6 (−)	3 (+)	10 (+)
$L = 3$, 3 lags for confounders	11 (+)	5 (−)	3 (+)	11 (+)
$L = 4$, 4 lags for confounders	4 (+)	3 (−)	5 (+)	11 (+)
Listwise deletion	4 (+)	0	4 (+)	5 (+)
Fewer variables for matching/weighting	10 (+)	2 (−)	2 (+)	11 (+)
Restraint: Alternate measure	6 (+)	6 (−)	6 (+)	11 (+)
Restraint: Adjust nondirected dyads	N/A	5 (−)	N/A	8 (+)
Adjusting for dyadic nuclear weapons	6 (+)	6 (−)	6 (+)	7 (+)
Alternate sample: Neighbors and superpowers	5 (+)	8 (−)	1 (+)	3 (+)

	Restrained		Unrestrained	
	Target's preferences	Preference similarity	Target's preferences	Preference similarity
Partial latency				
Original (Figures 5.8 and 5.9)	6 (−)	3 (+)	1 (+)	3 (−), 1 (+)
Propensity score weighting	6 (−)	3 (+)	1 (+)	3 (−), 1 (+)
Propensity score matching, 10 matches	6 (−)	3 (+)	2 (−)	1 (−)
Propensity score matching, 5 matches	5 (−)	0	5 (−)	1 (−)
Mahalanobis distance matching, 10 matches	3 (−)	11 (+)	3 (+)	1 (−), 2 (+)
Mahalanobis distance matching, 5 matches	2 (−)	11 (+)	5 (+)	1 (−), 2 (+)
$L = 1$, 1 lag for confounders	5 (−)	7 (+)	1 (+)	2 (−), 2 (+)
$L = 3$, 3 lags for confounders	6 (−)	8 (+)	0	3 (−), 1 (+)
$L = 4$, 4 lags for confounders	6 (−)	2 (+)	1 (+)	2 (−), 2 (+)
Listwise deletion	10 (−)	2 (+)	0	5 (−)
Fewer variables for matching/weighting	5 (−)	6 (+)	2 (+)	2 (−), 2 (+)
Restraint: Alternate measure	6 (−)	4 (+)	1 (+)	3 (−), 1 (+)
Restraint: Adjust nondirected dyads	N/A	4 (+)	N/A	1 (−)
Adjusting for dyadic nuclear weapons	6 (−)	9 (+)	1 (+)	5 (−)
Alternate sample: Neighbors and superpowers	3 (−)	0	3 (+)	2 (+)

Notes: The table shows the number of statistically significant ATTs in each scenario. The maximum possible number is eleven. The positive and negative signs indicate the direction of the ATTs. N/A means not applicable.

There is relatively stable support for Foreign-Policy Prediction 4 too, as the ATTs are broadly similar to what I found in the initial analysis. Foreign-policy alignment gets worse when a fully latent state has an unrestrained program in at least three posttreatment years. In six of the robustness tests, the ATTs are significant in all eleven years, as in the main analysis.

The evidence in favor of Foreign-Policy Prediction 3 appears to weaken in Table 5.5, as all the ATTs for full latency are insignificant in three of the robustness tests. However, it is important to contextualize these results.

Two of these cases involve Mahalanobis distance matching. This refinement method produced worse covariate balance than the other methods, as shown in Figure 5.4, giving me more confidence in the other approaches. The findings are virtually identical when using propensity score weighting, which produced similar covariate balance to the main refinement method, CBPS weighting. The causal effects are also insignificant when I use listwise deletion, eliminating any case from the analysis that has missing data for at least one variable. Listwise deletion eliminates thirteen dyadic observations with full latency onset – 14 percent of the total number in the main analysis. The eliminated dyads include six fully latent states: Canada (seven cases), Belgium (one case), Japan (one case), the Netherlands (two cases), Spain (one case), and Yugoslavia (one case). The results for listwise deletion suggest that these cases are important in producing the main results. Given the relatively small number of full latency onsets to begin with, I prioritized DiDMW's default procedures for handling missing data, which allow me to include all of the cases.

Alliance Leverage

Are US allies able to extract stronger defense commitments by virtue of having latent nuclear forces? The answer is: sometimes. Figure 5.10 displays the ATTs for partial and full nuclear latency in the presence of restrained and unrestrained nuclear programs.

Alliance Leverage Prediction 1 expects that nuclear latency causes US allies to receive a greater number of American troops on their soil when they have restrained nuclear programs. Figure 5.10 shows that this happens in the case of full nuclear latency but there is a time lag. In the first seven years post full latency, the causal effects are significant just once (year $t + 4$). The ATTs become statistically significant and the confidence intervals move farther away from zero in years $t + 8$, $t + 9$, and $t + 10$. These findings support the emerging view that having

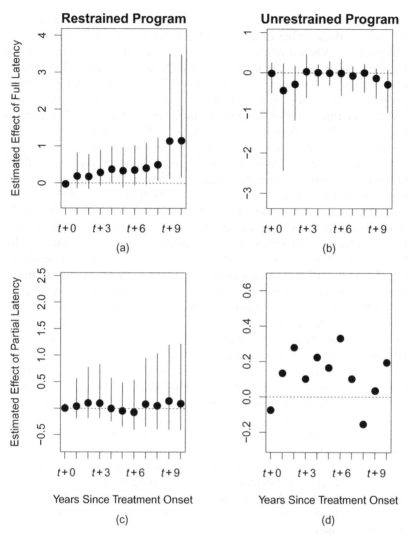

Figure 5.10 Average treatment effect of nuclear latency on US troop deployments.

nuclear latency can help countries influence their allies, not just their adversaries.[72]

The effects are substantively large, with point estimates ranging from 0.37 to 1.15 in years where the ATTs are statistically significant. Given

[72] Volpe (2017, 2023).

the logged dependent variable, adopting full nuclear latency causes an increase in the number of deployed US troops between 37 percent and 115 percent. When it comes to alliance leverage, then, the causal effects increase over time as the latent state's capabilities mature. This stands in contrast to the results on foreign-policy similarity and restrained programs, where the effects of full latency emerged quickly and then faded over time. It also diverges from Volpe's "sweet spot" theory of bargaining with nuclear latency described earlier, which expects greater success before a state starts producing fissile material on a large scale.[73]

Does the benefit of more US troops continue after ten years of full latency for countries with restrained programs? To find out, I reran the main analysis while setting F to 20, enabling me to examine what happens in the twenty years following full latency adoption. The ATTs are statistically significant for another five years (from $t + 11$ to year $t + 15$) after my initial analysis ended. Between years $t + 16$ and $t + 20$, the effects are statistically significant just once. Based on this analysis, fully latent US allies see more troops on their soil for an extended stretch of time – for eight consecutive years – once their capabilities mature, but this benefit emerges more inconsistently after fifteen years pass.

The ATTs for partial nuclear latency are statistically insignificant across all years when states have restrained nuclear programs. This is consistent with the preceding analyses, where partially latent forces were often insufficient to gain greater political leverage. The relatively poor improvement in covariate balance after CBPS weighting (and all other refinement methods) when partial latency is the treatment should induce caution when interpreting this evidence (see Figure 5.3).

The story is different when we turn to unrestrained nuclear programs. Consistent with Alliance Leverage Prediction 2, fully latent US allies are unable to obtain more US troops when their political aims are unrestrained. It is important to mention, though, that only two US allies had unrestrained programs during the period I study: France and Pakistan. The insignificant ATTs could emerge due to the small number of relevant cases.

In the case of partial latency, the ATTs for unrestrained programs are negative and statistically significant in nine years after partial latency adoption. Substantively, the increases in troops during these years range from 4 percent to 33 percent – smaller than the increases generated by full nuclear latency and restrained programs. These ATTs are driven by a single case. Pakistan is the only US ally that had an unrestrained program

---

[73] Volpe (2017).

at the time it first obtained partial latency (France first obtained partial latency in the 1940s, before my analysis of troop deployment begins).

The alliance leverage findings bring to light on alternative mechanism that could explain the findings pertaining to military conflict and foreign-policy preferences. Latent nuclear powers could be less vulnerable because they receive more conventional military aid from their allies, which in turn bolsters extended deterrence and results in greater international influence more generally.[74] Based on this line of thinking, concerns about fomenting nuclear proliferation, inviting a (delayed) nuclear attack, or doubt about what exactly a country possesses have little to do with foreign-policy influence. Instead, the already-nuclear-armed ally's signals of support for the latent nuclear power deters third-party countries and confers leverage.

Does this alternative logic account for the reduction in crises and increase in the similarity of foreign policy preferences that we observed earlier? It may be one part of the story, but there are at least two reasons to question whether it drives the earlier findings.

First, if compelling stronger support from the United States were the full story, we would have expected to see the strongest causal effects for conflict and foreign-policy preferences at the same time as (or shortly after) the number of troops increased. But this is not what we observe. Allies do not reliably obtain more US troops until they have been fully latent for several years. However, the other foreign-policy benefits generally kick in earlier. For example, countries with restrained programs experience a reduction in the number of crises they experience in the same year they obtain full nuclear latency and then during three of the next five years.

Second, there is considerable qualitative evidence in favor of the mechanisms at the heart of latent nuclear deterrence theory. As we saw in Chapter 2, many leaders buy in to the notion of weaponless deterrence as a means of international influence. New case evidence presented in Chapters 6 and 7 will further amplify this view, showing how deterrence by proliferation, delayed attack, and doubt translated to international influence in particular episodes.

Robustness Tests

Table 5.6 shows the robustness tests for US troop deployments. The results are fairly stable for partial latency: Restrained programs never produce significant ATTs and unrestrained programs reliably increase the number of troops between six and nine posttreatment years.

[74] I thank Andrew Coe for pointing out this alternative mechanism.

Table 5.6 *Robustness test results for alliance leverage.*

	Restrained US troops	Unrestrained US troops
Full latency		
Original (Figure 5.10)	4 (+)	0
Propensity score weighting	6 (+)	0
Propensity score matching, 10 matches	3 (+)	2 (−)
Propensity score matching, 5 matches	0	0
Mahalanobis distance matching, 10 matches	0	5 (−)
Mahalanobis distance matching, 5 matches	0	0
$L = 1$, 1 lag for confounders	7 (+)	0
$L = 3$, 3 lags for confounders	0	0
$L = 4$, 4 lags for confounders	7 (+)	7 (−)
Listwise deletion	7 (+)	6 (+), 1 (−)
Fewer variables for matching/weighting	8 (+)	4 (−)
Restraint: Alternate measure	3 (+)	0
Partial latency		
Original (Figure 5.10)	0	9 (+)
Propensity score weighting	0	9 (+)
Propensity score matching, 10 matches	0	6 (+), 2 (−)
Propensity score matching, 5 matches	0	6 (+)
Mahalanobis distance matching, 10 matches	0	7 (+)
Mahalanobis distance matching, 5 matches	0	6 (+)
$L = 1$, 1 lag for confounders	0	7 (+)
$L = 3$, 3 lags for confounders	0	6 (+)
$L = 4$, 4 lags for confounders	0	6 (+)
Listwise deletion	0	6 (+)
Fewer variables for matching/weighting	0	8 (+)
Restraint: Alternate measure	0	9 (+)

Note: The table shows the number of statistically significant ATTs in each scenario. The maximum possible number is eleven. The positive and negative signs indicate the direction of the ATTs.

There are more-significant differences when we look at full latency. There is always a time delay before the statistically significant effects for restrained programs kick in, but they sometimes emerge sooner than in the main analysis – as early as year $t + 3$. However, like in some of the preceding analyses, the ATTs for restrained programs are statistically insignificant when I use Mahalanobis distance matching (up-to-five and up-to-ten matches) and propensity score matching (up-to-five matches only). For US troop deployments, like the other outcomes, the matching methods that produce insignificant ATTs produce much worse covariate balance than the two weighting methods. As before, the results are most in line with the theory when I use the refinement methods that produce the best covariate balance: CBPS weighting and propensity score weighting.

There is also no support for Alliance Leverage Prediction 1 when I adjust for three lags of treatment history and the confounders. Yet using three lags produces worse covariate balance than adjusting two lags, as I did in the main analysis. Notice the strongest results for the theory emerge when I adjust for four lags.[75] In that case, full latency increases the number of troops in seven of the posttreatment years when the program is restrained and reduces the number of troops in seven years when the program is unrestrained. Increasing the number of lags beyond two, therefore, does not always produces insignificant ATTs and can sometimes strengthen the evidence for the theory.

The robustness tests generally strengthen support for Alliance Leverage Prediction 2. In the presence of an unrestrained program, full nuclear latency onset sometimes produces insignificant ATTs, as in the main analysis. In five of the robustness tests, the causal effects are negative and statistically significant. When using listwise deletion, however, the ATTs are positive in six years and negative in one.

Revisiting the Mechanisms: Proliferation, Delayed Attack, and Doubt

Three mechanisms underlie latent nuclear deterrence theory: proliferation, delayed attack, and doubt. One limitation of the preceding analysis is that it does not offer a direct test of latent nuclear deterrence theory's logic. It suggests that nuclear latency is causally connected to foreign policy outcomes, but it does not definitively prove that this is because of proliferation, delayed attack, and/or doubt.

The theory does not expect that one mechanism is "better" or "worse" than the others. As the qualitative evidence presented in Chapter 2 showed, leaders believe in all three forms of influence, and they sometimes perceive them to operate simultaneously. At the same time, the salience of a mechanism can vary based on the foreign-policy context. Which one is most important based on the quantitative evidence presented earlier?

In the cases of foreign policy preferences and US troop deployments, deterrence by proliferation is the most viable mechanism on logical grounds, as I discussed when laying out the predictions at the beginning

---

[75] The covariate balance here is also worse than when using two lags.

of the chapter. By contrast, all three mechanisms are theoretically viable for deterring international crises and fatal disputes. Here, accounting for a country's political aims – particularly whether its nuclear program was unrestrained – helps us understand which mechanism is doing the work. If ENR capabilities lower the rate of crises or military conflict in the presence of a restrained program, deterrence by proliferation and delayed attack are the most likely mechanisms. Deterrence by delayed attack or doubt would most likely be responsible for the same effect in the presence of an unrestrained program.

Latent nuclear powers see some reduction in crises and fatal disputes when they have unrestrained programs, although this result varies based on various research design choices. Deterrence by proliferation cannot account for these effects. They likely emerge at least partially because of doubt, but deterrence by delayed attack could also explain the reduction in military conflict for this group. Countries more-reliably deter conflict when they have restrained programs, particularly in the case of crises. Doubt is not a viable mechanism for these states, so the result is best explained by proliferation and/or delayed attack. The analysis does not tell us whether proliferation or delayed attack is most responsible for this effect; both are likely part of the story.

Overall, the analysis in this chapter provides suggestive evidence in favor of all three mechanisms. It is notable that deterrence by doubt does not drive all of the foreign-policy benefits that latent nuclear powers accrue, given that this mechanism is the most familiar to scholars of nuclear proliferation.[76] The three mechanisms ultimately work together to enhance a country's international influence. Depending on the context, however, one mechanism may be more salient than the others.

Conclusion

Identifying the foreign-policy effects of nuclear programs is difficult. Nuclear capabilities emerge because of strategic decisions made by governments, not random chance. Patterns we observe between nuclear programs and foreign-policy outcomes like military conflict could therefore be driven by third variables, known in statistics as confounders. A positive association could emerge, for example, because the countries that get nuclear weapons or latency live in neighborhoods rife with military conflict – not necessarily because deterrence does not work.[77]

---

[76] Deterrence by doubt is analogous to what some scholars call opaque nuclear proliferation. See, for example, Cohen and Frankel (1990) and Hagerty (1993).

[77] This is also a point made in Bell and Miller (2015).

This chapter addressed this challenge by taking a design-based approach to causal inference.[78] I first identified a set of control observations that had the same treatment history as countries that became latent. Next, I used weighting and matching procedures to make the untreated and treated units as similar as possible. Then, I used a DiD estimator to account for a time trend. This research design brings us closer to identifying the causal effects of nuclear latency relative to other published studies.

In this chapter, I examined five foreign-policy outcomes: crises, fatal disputes, the challenger's foreign-policy preferences, foreign-policy similarity, and US troop deployments. I studied how these outcomes changed in the ten years after countries obtained nuclear latency (in addition to the year of latency onset) compared to an alternative scenario where they had remained nonlatent. For each outcome, I analyzed how restraint moderated the effect of nuclear latency. In addition, I distinguished between two stages of nuclear latency: partial and full.

The findings were often supportive of latent nuclear deterrence theory. However, the strength of the evidence varied based on the foreign-policy outcome and various modifications to the initial research design. The findings point toward three general conclusions.

First, full nuclear latency can confer influence when countries have restrained programs – at least in some postadoption years. The initial results showed that becoming fully latent with a restrained program lowered the number of crises and violent disputes a state experienced, changed the target's foreign-policy preferences, increased the similarity of foreign-policy preferences in a dyad, and led to more troop deployments for US allies. These findings require unpacking, as the overall picture is nuanced.

A reduction in fatal disputes was the least consistent benefit in the main analysis, occurring in only two postlatency years. In many of the robustness tests, none of the causal effects were statistically significant. There was a greater and more-reliable reduction in the number of crises: The causal effects were statistically significant in five of the years I analyzed. Across the robustness tests, the causal effects were significant between three and seven years, except for when I used refinement methods that produced poor covariate balance, in which case none of the effects were significant. A qualitative look at the data showed that both fatal disputes and crises were rare for fully latent states with restrained programs. Such states experienced just six crises and three fatal disputes from 1929 to 2010. This highlights a key limitation of the method

---

[78] Imai et al. (2023).

I used in the context of military conflict: There is relatively low variation, making it harder to find statistically significant effects.

Full nuclear latency had more-consistent effects on foreign-policy preferences, which may be because this outcome provides a more fine-grained measure of bilateral relations. When a state obtained full nuclear latency and had a restrained program, foreign-policy similarity with potential adversaries increased for the next six years. This finding is reasonably robust. As in the case of crises, however, support for the theory weakens considerably when I used refinement methods that produced poor covariate balance. Listwise deletion, which eliminates thirteen cases of full latency onset, also produced no statistically significant effects in the analysis of preference similarity.

There was also evidence that one state's obtainment of nuclear latency changes the other's foreign-policy preferences. This is important because it shows that the improvement in foreign-policy similarity arises because the latent nuclear power causes a change in the other state's policies, not because the latent power moderates its own behavior. These effects were also strongest in the first half of the period I analyzed. They were statistically significant in 80 percent of the first five years following latency onset ($t + 1$ to $t + 5$), and 40 percent of the next five ($t + 6$ to $t + 10$). In the robustness tests, between four and eleven of the causal effects were statistically significant, showing that the target's obtainment of nuclear latency moves the challenger's foreign-policy preferences at least some of the time.

Increases in troop deployments start to kick in as time passes for fully latent US allies with restrained programs. In the main analysis, the causal effects are statistically significant and positive in year $t + 4$ and years $t + 8$ through $t + 10$. In many of the robustness tests, this benefit emerges sooner, as early as year $t + 3$, and for a greater number of years. Yet, there is always a delay of at least a handful of years before these countries see an increase in troops on their soil. Interestingly, this is the opposite of what happens for foreign-policy preferences among adversaries, where the benefits emerge right away and fade over time. The evidence supporting the theory weakens when I use refinement methods that worsen covariate balance, and when I adjust for three lags of treatment history and the confounding variables, which also worsens covariate balance compared to two lags.

The second conclusion is that combining full nuclear latency with an unrestrained program generated fewer benefits and invited greater risks, which is also in line with the theory. Developing fully latent nuclear forces in the presence of an unrestrained program less-reliably lowered the risk of fatal disputes or crises – in at-most two postadoption years, and in many cases zero years. The confidence intervals for unrestrained programs are much larger, indicating greater uncertainty about the estimates. This is consistent with the theory's claim that unrestrained nuclear programs generate competing effects for deterrence: They strengthen some means of influence (deterrence by delayed attack and doubt) while weakening others (deterrence by proliferation), and provide adversaries with incentives to attack.

Having an unrestrained program while possessing latent nuclear forces made foreign-policy preferences less congruent. This effect is relatively persistent. Foreign-policy preferences become more dissimilar in the year of full latency onset and continue for the next ten years. Across the robustness tests, at least some (and often all eleven) of the causal effects are positive and statistically significant. Like in the case of restrained programs, we also see statistically significant changes in the other state's foreign-policy preferences, providing evidence that greater dissimilarity does not emerge just because the latent nuclear power adjusts its policies. In the robustness tests, the changes in preferences were statistically significant between one and seven postadoption years. These effects tend to be more consistent in the first five years after full latency adoption, as in the case of restrained programs.

There is no evidence that states with full latency and unrestrained programs get more US troops on their soil. None of the causal effects were statistically significant in the main analysis, or in any of the robustness tests.

Third, partial nuclear latency generates smaller effects that are more-inconsistently observed and less in line with the theory. In virtually every test, partial latency did not generate benefits when a program was restrained, and in some cases it made the country worse off. When the program was unrestrained, a partially latent country reaped some benefits. The biggest one was an increase in troop deployments on the soil of US allies, but this is driven by one country: Pakistan. When they exist, the benefits and costs were usually smaller and less-consistently obtained than in the case of full latency. Being closer to a bomb, therefore, is more beneficial for countries hoping to gain political leverage from a nonweaponized nuclear program.

This evidence is overall supportive the view that latent nuclear forces can buy international influence. As we learned in Chapter 2, many world leaders believe this to be true. Yet garnering influence does not come easy, as it depends on satisfying some key conditions. And, even when those conditions are met, the benefits of achieving nuclear latency emerge in just some posttreatment years. When combined with an unrestrained program, nuclear latency generates greater risks. Chapter 6 focuses on one of those risks: preventive military attacks.

6   Backlash: Explaining Preventive Attacks*

Iraq began a quest to ramp up its nuclear capabilities in the 1970s. To help the Iraqis get their nuclear program off the ground, France supplied a research reactor, which became known as *Osiraq*, along with 13 kg of highly enriched uranium to fuel it.[1] Although this facility was provided exclusively for peaceful purposes, some foreign officials – particularly in Israel – suspected that Iraqi leader Saddam Hussein, who rose to the presidency in 1979, had more sinister intentions. Israeli Prime Minister Menachem Begin concluded that Iraq could not be trusted with dual-use nuclear technology. On June 16, 1981, eight Israeli F-16 fighter jets bombed the Osiraq reactor just before it became operational, fully destroying it.

This episode serves as a warning to states pursuing latent nuclear forces: Nuclear programs can invite military conflict, in addition to deterring it. This chapter explains when nuclear programs provoke preventive uses of military force. It places the spotlight on two variables at the heart of latent nuclear deterrence theory: ENR technology and the challenger's perceptions of the potential proliferator's intentions. An ENR-capable state with an unrestrained nuclear program is a recipe for a crisis. Countries are more likely to consider using military force to stop or delay armament in that situation.

However, there are significant barriers to launching preventive strikes against an ENR-capable country. Such a state can engage in weaponless deterrence more effectively than an ENR-free counterpart, and the odds of operational success go down once a country has expansive nuclear capabilities. Once a crisis arises, then, states that lack sensitive nuclear technology are more vulnerable to preventive strikes. Yet ENR-capable countries can still suffer attacks if an adversary believes that the potential proliferator is making a mad dash to a bomb. Ultimately, the best way

---

* This chapter builds on some ideas I initially conveyed in Fuhrmann (2018).
[1] Fuhrmann (2012a, 117).

for a country to avoid preventive strikes is to convince others that it is not bent on getting nuclear weapons.

The following pages unpack these claims. This chapter will delve into the history of preventive strikes. The first step is to lay the groundwork by defining what constitutes a preventive strike, providing the universe of cases, and describing what we already know about why countries target nuclear programs. I will then describe latent nuclear deterrence theory's expectations and examine four cases to illustrate the theory's logic: Israel's preventive strike against Syria's nuclear reactor (2007) and US responses to nuclear programs in Iran (2002–2015), North Korea (1994), and Syria (2007). The case studies will show that leaders were thinking along the lines that latent nuclear deterrence theory expects as they contemplated the use of military force.

What Constitutes a Preventive Strike?

I define preventive attacks based on one of my earlier studies: "the state-sanctioned use of force against materials, commodities, or infrastructure related to a nuclear weapons program that has the intention of delaying a country's acquisition of nuclear bombs."[2] Actions must involve physical destruction to be classified as preventive strikes. Destruction can occur as a result of airstrikes or acts of sabotage. Cyber attacks that destroy physical assets, like the joint American–Israeli Stuxnet attack against Iran's Natanz enrichment plant beginning in 2008, are included – but I do not count nonkinetic cyber incidents that are intended to infiltrate networks and steal data.[3] Preventive attacks can be covert, meaning that the attacking government carries them out in secret and denies involvement, or conspicuous uses of military force.[4]

Strikes against nuclear programs can occur during ongoing wars or in peacetime. I focus exclusively on peacetime cases – those in which concerns about nuclear proliferation motivated the initial use of force.[5] Peacetime cases take two main forms: "bolt from the blue" limited preventive strikes (such as Israel's bombing of the Iraqi Osiraq reactor

---

[2] Fuhrmann and Kreps (2010, 834).

[3] I exclude targeted assassinations of nuclear scientists from my conception of a preventive attack.

[4] As I will discuss later, however, latent nuclear deterrence theory expects that covert attacks are more permissible than overt ones.

[5] I do this because my objective is to explain the onset of nonproliferation-induced conflict. On top of this, once countries are already at war they face a fundamentally different calculus, as the costs of striking nuclear infrastructure are substantially reduced. Fuhrmann and Kreps (2010, 834) acknowledge and discuss this issue but study both peacetime and wartime cases. On the distinction between intrawar strikes and peacetime attacks see also Reiter (2006).

in 1981) or larger-scale conflicts where the attacker's aims go beyond just targeting nuclear programs (such as the 1991 Persian Gulf War). I exclude strikes against nuclear facilities that occur doing ongoing wars if the target's nuclear program did not contribute to the conflict's onset. Iraq's bombing of Iran's Bushehr nuclear power plant during the Iran–Iraq War, for example, falls outside the scope of my analysis.

I focus on attacks against nonnuclear targets, excluding cases where there is consensus that the target is already nuclear-armed. My focus here is on how nonweaponized nuclear programs influence international conflict – not nuclear arsenals. I therefore do not include Iraq's firing of Scud missiles at the Israeli Dimona plant during the 1991 Persian Gulf War or US preventive war threats against North Korea in 2017. In both of these cases, the attacker knew without a doubt that the target was already nuclear-armed.

I examine the serious consideration of preventive strikes, in addition to attacks that are carried out. Analysts cannot always observe policies that a government considers but ultimately does not carry out, making it difficult to identify the full set of cases in which a country came close to launching preventive attacks. Three main actions constitute serious consideration of attacking a nuclear program: making a decision to strike that is later reversed, seeking cooperation from a third-party to bomb nuclear facilities, or advocating for preventive military action during internal deliberations.[6]

Table 6.1 lists the cases the meet the above criteria.[7] Peacetime consideration of preventive strikes has occurred in eighteen country-pairs since 1945. Many of these cases spanned multiple years, and some involved joint operations between two potential attackers. Attackers considered targeting ten different potential proliferators – fifty-eight percent of the countries that pursued nuclear weapons.[8] Strikes against nuclear facilities happened in six of the cases in which attackers seriously considered using force. The majority of cases in which countries consider using force, therefore, do not lead to preventive strikes.

What We Know about Targeting Nuclear Programs

Prior research helps us understand why countries use military force in the name of nonproliferation. Before reviewing the predictions of

---

[6] Fuhrmann and Kreps (2010, 834–835).

[7] I identify the universe of cases using an updated version of a database that I previously compiled with political scientist Sarah Kreps. Fuhrmann and Kreps (2010). This database ends in 2000. I extend it through 2020 based on Whitlark (2021) and my own updates.

[8] This is based on information on pursuit compiled by Bleek (2010).

Table 6.1 *Peacetime preventive strike cases, 1945–2021.*

Target	Attacker	Consideration years	Attack years
China	USA	1961–64	None
	Taiwan	1963	None
India	Pakistan	1984	None
Iran	Israel	2003–21	2007–12, 2020–21
	USA	2003–21	2007–10
Iraq	Israel	1977–81	1979, 1981
	USA	1990–91, 1998, 2002–03	1991, 1998, 2003
	UK	1998, 2002–03	1998, 2003
Israel	Egypt	1967	None
	USSR	1967	None
North Korea	USA	1994, 2003	None
	South Korea	1991, 1993–94	None
Pakistan	India	1982, 1984, 1986–87	None
	Israel	1979–87	None
South Africa	USSR	1976	None
Syria	Israel	2006–07	2007
	USA	2007	None
USSR	USA	1945–49	None

latent nuclear deterrence theory, it is worthwhile to summarize other arguments about preventive war. These explanations do not compete with latent nuclear deterrence theory. It is counterproductive, in my view, to claim that other arguments are "wrong" and my theory is "right." Instead, they together give us a richer understanding of why countries target nuclear programs. I will explain the ways in which latent nuclear deterrence theory is compatible with other arguments in the following section. The first step, though, is to lay out what we know from prior research.

Adversarial Relations and Threat Perceptions

The degree to which a target's nuclear armament threatens an attacker's national security influences the likelihood of a preventive strike. When the perceived threat is high a country may target its counterpart's nuclear facilities militarily. By contrast, if a country does not perceive that nuclear armament would pose a major national security threat, there is little reason for it to take on the risks of a preventive strike.[9]

---

[9] Feaver and Niou (1996, 215).

A 2010 study that I conducted with political scientist Sarah Kreps confirmed that adversarial relations play a key role in this context. We found that a history of violent conflict and dissimilar foreign-policy interests substantially increased the likelihood that a potential attacker will consider targeting a proliferator's nuclear facilities.[10] We also found that authoritarian regimes were more susceptible to preventive military action, as countries view autocratic leaders armed with nuclear weapons as more capricious and dangerous than their democratic counterparts.

Threat perceptions can vary among leaders in the same state, not just across countries. In the United States, for example, Jimmy Carter generally worried more about nuclear proliferation than Richard Nixon. Political scientist Rachel Whitlark shows that leader-level variation in beliefs about nuclear proliferation can help explain when countries target nuclear programs militarily. Leaders are especially likely to consider preventive strikes, she argues, when they believe that nuclear proliferation will lead to dire consequences for international stability, and that the target will be undeterrable if it obtains a bomb.[11] John F. Kennedy was more enthusiastic about bombing Chinese nuclear facilities than Lyndon Johnson, based on this argument, because Kennedy had more pessimistic views about how a nuclear-armed China would behave in the future.

Conventional Retaliation and the Distribution of Military Power

Countries contemplating preventive strikes consider the target's possible military responses. A preventive attack becomes less likely, all else equal, when the target can inflict greater amounts of punishment on the attacker via conventional retaliation.[12] Credible military responses raise the expected costs of attacking relative to the benefits, making preventive action less likely. International relations scholar Jan Ludvik argues that the threat of conventional retaliation is sufficient to deter the targeting of nuclear facilities.[13] He finds that preventive strikes have *never* occurred when the target threatened a retaliatory conventional response. The small number of preventive strikes to date – including Israel's attacks against Iraq and Syria – have targeted relatively weak countries that were incapable of inflicting substantial conventional punishment on the attacker. On the other hand, the high costs of attacking played a role in deterring the United States from targeting the Chinese nuclear program in the 1960s and North Korean facilities in the 1990s.

[10] Fuhrmann and Kreps (2010, 848).
[11] Whitlark (2021).
[12] Feaver and Niou (1996, 215).
[13] Ludvik (2019). See also Ramberg (2006).

The theory of nuclear proliferation developed by economist Alexandre Debs and political scientist Nuno Monteiro similarly spotlights the role of conventional retaliation.[14] Their argument emphasizes the balance of conventional military capabilities between the target and attacker. Preventive war threats are most likely to work, they argue, when the target is weak relative to the attacker. In that case, the expected costs of war for the attacker are small in relation to the benefits. As the target becomes more powerful relative to the target, however, preventive attacks become more costly and therefore less likely, allowing nuclear proliferation to occur unimpeded. Lyle Goldstein similarly focuses on the balance of power, arguing that asymmetric nuclear rivalries are particularly prone to instability.[15] But relatively strong states, he argues, can deter preventive attacks with credible threats of large-scale conventional retaliation.

Normative and Political Blowback

There are nonmilitary costs of taking preventive military action as well.[16] The United Nations charter prohibits using military force to address nonimminent threats. At least some international law experts see preventive strikes against nuclear programs, in particular, as illegal.[17] And some domestic and international actors view this type of action as morally reprehensible. NSC 68, which laid out US security policy in the beginning of the Cold War, exemplifies this view: "It goes without saying that the idea of 'preventive war' – in the sense of a military attack not provoked by a military attack upon us or our allies – is generally unacceptable to Americans."[18] Countries that target an adversary's nuclear facilities in peacetime, therefore, might invite political and diplomatic blowback. Attacks could result in economic sanctions, strained alliance relationships, inflamed relations with third-party rivals, diplomatic isolation, or weakened domestic popularity for leaders. These costs can make countries think twice about targeting nuclear programs by raising the costs of striking.

Shimon Peres, who was then Israel's opposition leader, did not support the 1981 Osiraq strike because he worried that it would leave his country alone, "like a tree in the desert."[19] The attack did indeed

---

[14] Debs and Monteiro (2017).
[15] Goldstein (2006).
[16] The ideas in this paragraph are drawn from Fuhrmann (2018, 120–121). See also Goldstein (2006) and Ramberg (2006).
[17] Sloss (2003).
[18] Quoted in Fuhrmann (2018, 120–121).
[19] Quoted in Perlmutter et al. (2003, 69).

result in political censure, including a UN Security Council Resolution that condemned Israel for violating "norms of international conduct."[20] A few decades later, Israel refrained from attacking nuclear facilities in Iran, in part, because the United States – Israel's most important partner – favored a diplomatic settlement. The potential for political blowback also loomed over US discussions about attacking Chinese nuclear facilities in the 1960s. The United States became more reluctant to strike after the Soviet Union refused to green-light the operation, as Washington did not want to inflame relations with its superpower rival.[21]

Nuclear Progress

How close the target is to a bomb shapes the likelihood of a preventive strike. I have argued in previous work that preventive attacks become more likely once the potential proliferator obtains the means to produce fissile material.[22] The need for military action increases once the target is ENR-capable, as the potential attacker faces a ticking clock and may have exhausted other options to stop weaponization. Nuclear progress – specifically whether the target already possesses ENR technology – is particularly central to the theory of preventive war developed by political scientists Muhammet Bas and Andrew Coe. They argue that preventive strikes should happen "if and only if" the attacker's intelligence estimates indicate that target's program is nearing the point of successful weapon assembly.[23] Attacks should not occur early in the target's nuclear program, according to their theory, because the risk of armament is small and the potential attacker prefers to monitor the situation and delay the consequences of striking.[24]

Latent Nuclear Deterrence Theory and Preventive Strikes

The preceding discussion underscores that numerous factors can contribute to military attacks against nuclear programs. What does latent nuclear deterrence theory tell us about when preventive strikes will occur?

---

[20] United Nations Security Council (1981).

[21] Goldstein (2006, 10).

[22] Fuhrmann and Kreps (2010, 843).

[23] This assumes that nuclear armament would have a large effect on the balance of power relative to the costs of attacking. See Bas and Coe (2016, 669).

[24] Bas and Coe (2016, 667).

Provoking Crises: Rivalries, ENR Technology, and Unrestrained Programs

Countries will consider preventive military action only if the potential proliferator is an adversary. An attack is implausible outside of an adversarial relationship because the threat posed by nuclear armament would not justify the costs of a preventive strike, as the research I have discussed shows. In the presence of a rivalry, two factors central to latent nuclear deterrence theory influence the use of preventive military force. The first is whether the target is in possession of sensitive nuclear technology. Like Bas and Coe, I argue that ENR facilities play a critical role in this context, in part, because they influence how close a country is to a bomb.[25] The second key variable is the potential attacker's perceptions of its counterpart's nuclear intentions.

We can say that ENR technology is a double-edged sword. Becoming ENR-capable can bolster weaponless deterrence, leading to a lower risk of conflict. But producing fissile material can also induce security threats for other countries, potentially triggering proliferation-related crises. Other countries' perceptions of the latent state's nuclear intentions influence the degree to which ENR programs induce instability.

There is little need for a preventive strike when an ENR-capable country has a restrained nuclear program because the target would not arm as long as peace persists. Targets in this situation can use deterrence by proliferation to dissuade military attacks without prompting serious concerns about their nuclear intentions. Striking the target's nuclear facilities would merely make matters worse by hardening its resolve to build nuclear weapons. The downside for targets in this situation, however, is that the two other mechanisms of weaponless deterrence – delayed attack and doubt – would be harder to employ successfully. These means of influence work better when a challenger believes that the target is very close to a bomb or might already be in possession of one, a perception that is difficult to cultivate with a restrained nuclear program.

Hence, ENR capabilities are more likely to trigger proliferation-related crises, according to latent nuclear deterrence theory, when other countries believe that the latent nuclear power has an unrestrained nuclear program. The perceived inevitability of nuclear armament combined with the target's shortened proliferation timeline creates a sense of urgency for potential attackers. Those states might calculate that their last chance to stop nuclear proliferation is rapidly approaching,

---

[25] Bas and Coe (2016).

necessitating a final policy decision. Kicking the proverbial can down the road is no longer a viable response.

Instability can also arise when the potential target of a preventive attack has an unrestrained nuclear program and does not possess sensitive nuclear technology. This situation is less likely to prompt a crisis because there is less urgency for the attacker. The target, lacking ENR capabilities, would be years or decades away from a bomb.

Bomb-Making Capacity as a Deterrent

The news is not entirely bad for ENR-capable countries with unrestrained nuclear programs. Serious consideration of a military response does not always prompt actual strikes, as Table 6.1 underscores. The Soviet Union, for example, thought about attacking South Africa's nuclear installations in the 1970s but ultimately refrained from using military force. The likelihood of carrying out plans for an attack depends partially on the target's ENR capacity. Although the target's mastery of ENR technology increases the probability of a crisis, it also makes preventive strikes less attractive for potential attackers. It does so in three main ways.

First, ENR-capable states have the potential to engage in weaponless deterrence even if they have unrestrained programs. Beliefs in the inevitability of nuclear proliferation take deterrence by proliferation off the table, but deterrence by delayed attack or doubt could still operate. These targets can therefore more effectively use the prospect of an eventual nuclear strike to deter preventive attacks.

Second, preventive strikes are less likely to be successful when the target is already ENR-capable. Once states advance to the point of mastering ENR technology, their nuclear infrastructure is relatively expansive. A successful preventive attack, therefore, would have to destroy multiple facilities – not just a single chokepoint, as in the 1981 raid on Osiraq. Potential proliferators with advanced nuclear programs are also more likely to have unknown nuclear capabilities, as they have had more time to develop and disperse relevant technologies and materials. This is a major problem for potential attackers given that secret capabilities cannot be destroyed in a preventive strike. Also, ENR-capable states have spent years (or decades) building up an indigenous knowledge base. Any facilities that are destroyed, therefore, could be rebuilt relatively quickly.[26] For all of these reasons, states with ENR programs can deter preventive strikes by *denial* with greater ease, not just punishment.

[26] Fuhrmann (2018, 119).

Third, by the time a state has mastered ENR technology, many of its key nuclear facilities are likely to be operational. Bombing a live nuclear reactor or reprocessing plant could result in the dispersal of radioactive materials, triggering something analogous to the 2011 Fukushima disaster in Japan. Concerns about radioactive contamination can dissuade countries from targeting these plants.[27] Attackers may prefer to strike early, before a potential proliferator's key nuclear sites are operational. The possibility of environmental contamination can have a particularly strong deterrent effect if the potential attacker has operational nuclear reactors or other sites with radioactive materials on its own soil. In that case, bombing nuclear sites could prompt retaliatory strikes that lead to an environmental disaster for the country that attacked first. Operational nuclear plants can therefore deter conflict, a phenomenon that former US State Department analyst Bennett Ramberg calls "mutually assured radioactive contamination."[28]

The Success–Necessity Tradeoff

Preventive strikes are therefore more likely to be successful at an acceptable cost early in a target's nuclear program, before it gets to the point of possessing ENR plants.[29] But attackers will probably be more uncertain about a target's nuclear intentions when its program is in the pre-ENR phase. This exposes a conundrum for potential attackers that I refer to as the success–necessity tradeoff. As the need to take military action becomes greater, the probability that strikes will succeed by delaying or ending a weapons program declines.

Attackers could respond to the success–necessity tradeoff in two ways. First, they could attack early – before the target obtains the ability to make fissile material for a bomb. Second, the attacker could wait until the target obtains ENR capabilities and attack as a last ditch effort to stop nuclear armament.[30] The first option prioritizes the success side of the ledger, while the second privileges necessity.

In the presence of beliefs about the inevitability of nuclear armament, striking early is more likely if the target's development of nuclear weapons poses an existential threat to the attacker. Waiting may be too

---

[27] Fuhrmann (2018, 121).

[28] Ramberg (2019).

[29] The ideas in this section draw on the two windows for preventive strikes discussed in Fuhrmann (2018, 121–123).

[30] Bas and Coe (2018) make a similar argument about the timing nonproliferation deals. They contend that deals can occur early in a proliferator's nuclear program or as it approaches the point of bomb assembly. However, according to their argument, preventive war threats lack credibility at the early stage.

risky in that scenario, as the attacker would not want to be in a situation where it was too late effectively to stop the target from arming. The nonlatent deterrence costs, such as conventional retaliation and political blowback, also influence whether striking early is an attractive option. If the attacker believes that the nonlatent deterrence costs are small, it will be more likely to gamble by taking early action. By contrast, if attacking a country before it is ENR-capable would cause stiff blowback – including, potentially, a big war – an attacker is likely to postpone a decision, hoping that military action can be avoided in the end.

Prioritizing necessity over success, however, ultimately makes preventive strikes less likely. Once the target is ENR capable, preventive military action is more costly for the attacker and less likely to succeed. In addition, the costs of attacking relative to the stakes may be higher since "easier" cases might result in preventive strikes earlier in the target's program. Attacks can still occur against ENR-capable states that make a mad dash to a bomb. In that case, a country might attack as a "Hail Mary" effort to delay nuclear proliferation despite the potential punishment costs and risks of failure, or if it believed that the ENR-related obstacles could be mitigated.

The Six Day War illustrates how a mad dash to a bomb by an ENR-capable target can fuel preventive strikes. Egyptian leader Gamal Abdel Nasser warned throughout the early to mid-1960s that Israeli nuclear armament would prompt a preventive war. In May 1967, Egyptian planes flew over Dimona – Israel's most sensitive nuclear facility – in an apparent show of force. Historians Isabella Ginor and Gideon Remez argue that the war, which occurred one month later, was an attempt to stop Israel from arming.[31] Oleg Grinevsky, who worked in the Soviet Foreign Ministry, lends credence to this view, claiming that "In Egypt's military plans Dimona was marked as one of the main targets" and only Israel's swift military victory "saved Dimona from annihilation."[32] In the end, Egypt may have fueled the very thing it was trying to stop.[33]

Why Preventive Strikes Can Happen Despite Deterrence

When attacks would be likely, preventive war threats can deter countries from moving closer to a bomb.[34] For example, because targets know that sprinting to a bomb might invite a swift military response, they are less

---

[31] Ginor and Remez (2007, 30–31). Others dispute this view, arguing that Israel's nuclear program played little role in the 1967 war.
[32] Quoted in Ginor and Remez (2007, 31).
[33] On Israel's nuclear intentions prior to the Six Day War, see Cohen (2007).
[34] Debs and Monteiro (2017), Fuhrmann (2018), and Spaniel (2019, 158).

likely to go down that path. Along similar lines, a country might refrain from pursuing ENR capabilities if it believed that doing so would invite a preventive strike. The variables at the heart of latent nuclear deterrence theory, therefore, are endogenous to the risk of preventive war.

As Debs and Monteiro have shown, however, it is nonetheless possible for countries to find themselves in situations where their nuclear programs could be targeted militarily.[35] As I discussed in Chapter 4, there are at least three reasons we might observe preventive attacks even though credible preventive war threats can sometimes keep countries from taking actions that would put them at risk. First, a target might have confidence that it could keep its activities secret, shielding them from military attacks. If this belief ends up being wrong, however, the target could find itself on the receiving end of a preventive strike. Second, a target might believe that it could convince others that its intentions are peaceful.[36] This perception could prompt a country at risk of a preventive strike to develop ENR capabilities, believing that others would perceive a restrained program. But if the attacker instead perceives more sinister intentions, the ENR developer could find itself in the danger zone. Third, the target might misperceive the attacker's resolve, believing that it is not sufficiently threatened to take military action.[37]

Covert Action versus Overt Military Force

High stakes are generally required for latent nuclear deterrence to succeed. This is because threats to arm or use nuclear weapons become more believable as dispute severity increases. Conflict severity affects the targeting of nuclear programs as well. Covert action, cyber attacks, or low-level acts of sabotage may still occur against ENR-capable targets, even if traditional airstrikes are off the table.

Consider the logic of weaponless deterrence. As I explained in Chapter 1, threats to arm become credible following a military dispute because: (1) the target wants to protect itself to avoid suffering a similar fate in the future; (2) foreign aggression provokes nationalist sentiment; and (3) the target may withdraw from international nonproliferation commitments. These outcomes are most likely to emerge if the attacker humiliates the target. Conventional airstrikes against a country's nuclear

---

[35] Debs and Monteiro (2014). See also Spaniel (2019, chapter 7).
[36] This is possible because intentions are not directly observable to others. See Debs and Monteiro (2014) and Spaniel (2019, chapter 7).
[37] Spaniel (2019, chapter 8).

facilities – which are often among a state's most prized possessions – is likely to humiliate a country, creating strong pressures to arm. Potential attackers anticipate this possibility, which is why deterrence by proliferation can be effective. However, covert actions and lower-level acts of sabotage may not trigger intense pressures for proliferation because they enable the target to save face. Acting covertly also allows countries to control escalation, preventing the emergence of a large-scale war.[38] With a higher degree of escalation control, threats to use nuclear weapons become less credible too, weakening deterrence by delayed attack and doubt.

Latent nuclear deterrence, therefore, is most viable against major overt uses of military force. Lower-level forms of conflict and covert action are more permissible, as the Iran case discussed later will illustrate.

Research Strategy

Preventive strikes are rare. There are only a few peacetime uses of military force to delay nuclear proliferation (see Table 6.1). The kinds of statistical tests I conducted in Chapter 5 are not reliable with such a small universe of cases. This chapter therefore takes a qualitative empirical approach. I conduct case studies to more directly evaluate the theory's causal logic. The case discussions will illustrate the theory's mechanisms, while also bringing to light important nuances in the historical record.

Returning to the two-by-two framework introduced in Chapter 5, Table 6.2 places the cases of preventive attack consideration into one of the four categories based on two variables: the target's ENR status and whether its nuclear program was restrained or unrestrained. I code the target's ENR capabilities using the Nuclear Latency (NL) dataset, focusing on full nuclear latency.[39] I identify nuclear restraint based on the potential attacker's perceptions rather than the target's behavior. In an ideal world, I would have done this for dyadic statistical analysis in Chapter 5 too. But this task is labor intensive and sometimes unfeasible due to the lack of relevant documents and secondary sources. However, because there are just twenty relevant country-pairs here, it is manageable to incorporate a qualitative assessment of the attacker's perceptions into my coding of nuclear restraint. The table also differentiates whether preventive attacks were carried out covertly or overtly.

[38] Carson (2018).
[39] I focus on full nuclear latency because the evidence in Chapter 5 indicated that it was more consequential than partial latency. However, the overall pattern is not dramatically different if I instead code ENR status based on partial latency.

Table 6.2 *Case evidence for preventive strikes.*

	No ENR	ENR
Restrained	Category 1 USA–Syria: 2007 USA–Iran: 2004–05	Category 2 USA–Iran: 2003, 2006–07[a]
Unrestrained	Category 3 Israel–Iraq: 1977–81[a,b] Israel–Iran: 2004–05 Israel–Syria: 2006–07[b] UK–Iraq: 1998, 2002–03[b] USA–Iraq: 1998, 2002–03[b]	Category 4 Egypt–Israel: 1967 India–Pakistan: 1982, 1984, 1986–87 Israel–Iran: 2003, 2006–10[a] Pakistan–India: 1984 ROK–DPRK: 1991, 1993–94 Taiwan–China: 1963 USA–China: 1961–64 USA–Iraq: 1990–91[b] USA–DPRK: 1994, 2003 USA–USSR: 1947–49 USSR–South Africa: 1976 USSR–Israel: 1967

Notes: [a] Covert attack occurred. [b] Overt attack occurred.

Table 6.2 reveals a concentration of cases in Category 4. Latent nuclear deterrence theory anticipated this possibility. According to the theory, the combination of sensitive nuclear technology and unrestrained nuclear programs is particularly likely to generate a crisis. By contrast, Categories 1, 2, and 3 have far few opportunities for preventive strikes. The small number of cases in these categories underscores why statistical comparisons of the strike rates is problematic; a small number of changes in the future could produce radically different findings.

The table confirms that Categories 3 and 4 offer the most viable pathways to preventive strikes, as the success–necessity tradeoff expects. The barriers to success are higher in Category 4 but so is the need to for military action, as a decision on how to respond to the target's nuclear ambitions can no longer be put off. Although the preventive strike rate is larger in Category 3 than in Category 4, noncovert attacks have occurred in both groups. By contrast, noncovert attacks did not occur in Categories 1 or 2.

I will analyze one case from each of the four categories in Table 6.2: United States–Syria (Category 1), United States–Iran (Category 2),

Israel–Syria (Category 3), and United States–North Korea (Category 4). When presenting the evidence, I weave the two cases involving Syria into a single narrative. These cases provide useful variation on the outcome of interest. In two of the cases, countries refrained from attacking despite giving the option serious consideration (United States–Syria and United States–North Korea). One of the episodes involved airstrikes to destroy a nuclear facility (Israel–Syria). And the fourth case featured a covert cyber attack but did not involve traditional uses of military force (United States–Iran).

Predictions

Table 6.3 summarizes the evidence we should expect to find in each case if latent nuclear deterrence theory is correct. The expectations vary along three main dimensions: (1) the attacker's perceptions of the target's nuclear intentions, (2) beliefs about the likelihood of operational success, and (3) and the perceived costs of carrying out a preventive strike.

Beliefs in the inevitability of nuclear armament should harden resolve to attack In the Israel–Syria and United States–North Korea cases, while perceptions of restraint should weaken the case for striking in the other two cases. Concerns that an attack would not be successful should contribute to the nonattack decisions in the cases of the United States–Iran and United States–North Korea, along with higher expected costs of striking stemming from the targets' ENR capabilities. In the two cases where the theory expects weaponless deterrence to be viable (United States–Iran and United States–North Korea), different mechanisms should be at play.

Deterrence by proliferation should be salient in the United States–Iran case because Washington was not convinced that armament was inevitable – at least after 2003. By contrast, since North Korea had an unrestrained program, deterrence by delayed attack or doubt should be more salient in this case. The relatively low expected costs of striking, combined with awareness that waiting for the target to become ENR-capable would make a strike more costly, should motivate the decision to attack early in the Israel–Syria case.

Table 6.3 previews the findings from my investigation. As shown in the table, the predictions are largely confirmed. Although senior officials sometimes disagreed on these points, as the following discussion will make clear, leaders' beliefs were usually consistent with the theory's expectations. There is evidence in support of each prediction in three cases (United States–Syria, United States–Iran, and Israel–Syria). In the United States–North Korea case, three of the predictions are only

Table 6.3 *Expectations for preventive strikes in four case studies.*

Category number	Case	LND theory's expectations	Prediction confirmed?
1	USA–Syria	• Perceptions of nuclear restraint reduced the need for an attack. • Officials believed operational success was likely. • LND does not raise the costs of attacking.	Yes Yes Yes
2	USA–Iran	• Perceptions of nuclear restraint reduced the need for an attack. • Officials have concerns about operational success. • LND raises costs of attacking. • DbP is more relevant than DbDA or DbD. • Covert action preferred to traditional military attack.	Yes Yes Yes Yes Yes
3	Israel–Syria	• Perceptions of nonrestraint heighten need for attack. • Officials believed operational success was likely. • LND does not raise the costs of attacking. • Awareness that waiting to attack would increase costs. • Attacker sees target's nuclear armament as existential threat.	Yes Yes Yes Yes Yes
4	USA–North Korea	• Perceptions of nonrestraint heighten need for attack. • Officials have concerns about operational success. • LND raises costs of attacking. • DbD and DbDA are more relevant than DbP. • Concerns about radioactive fallout raise costs of striking.	Yes Partially Partially No Partially

Notes: LND = latent nuclear deterrence; DbP = deterrence by proliferation; DbDA = deterrence by delayed attack; DbD = deterrence by doubt.

partially confirmed and one is refuted. This case adds important nuances to latent nuclear deterrence theory, particularly when it comes to the conditions under which deterrence by doubt is viable.

The Iranian Nuclear Crisis, 2002–2015

The United States helped kick-start Iran's ambitions in the 1960s, providing Tehran with a research reactor, enriched uranium to fuel it, and hot cells for experimental work on plutonium separation.[40] This nuclear assistance, which was provided through the US "Atoms for Peace" program, occurred when Iran and the United States were military allies. But the two countries suddenly turned from friends to foes following the 1979 Islamic Revolution in Iran. Twenty-three years later, in August 2002, Iran's nuclear program triggered serious anxiety in the United States. An Iranian dissident group revealed the existence of a secret uranium enrichment plant in Natanz as well as a heavy water production facility in Arak. In the years that followed, Iran's enrichment capabilities continued to expand, augmenting the country's bomb-making capacity.

The possibility of an Iranian bomb troubled officials in Washington. There was bipartisan consensus in the United States that Iran's acquisition of nuclear weapons could produce a number of undesirable effects. As President Obama said in a 2015 speech, "Among U.S. policymakers, there's never been disagreement on the danger posed by an Iranian nuclear bomb."[41] United States officials worried, in particular, that an Iranian bomb would limit US freedom of action in the Middle East, encourage Tehran to adopt a more assertive foreign policy, trigger a regional arms race, and generally raise the risk that nuclear weapons would be used in war. President George W. Bush put things in especially stark terms when he said at an October 2007 press conference, "if you're interested in avoiding World War Three, it seems like you ought to be interested in preventing them from having the knowledge necessary to make a nuclear weapon."[42]

These fears prompted the United States seriously to consider preventive strikes against Iran as Tehran's enrichment capacity brought it closer to a bomb. Despite a period of sustained tension, however, there was not a serious military confrontation. The United States instead relied

---

[40] On the history of this nuclear assistance and the reasons for it, see Fuhrmann (2012a, 82–89).
[41] Obama (2015).
[42] Bush (2010, 418).

on other foreign-policy tools. Washington led an international effort to impose stiff economic sanctions on Iran over its nuclear activities. The United Nations Security Council passed multiple resolutions sanctioning Iran between 2006 and 2010 and demanded that Tehran halt its uranium enrichment activities. The United States and its partners ultimately achieved a diplomatic settlement with Iran in 2015, formally known as the Joint Comprehensive Plan of Action (JCPOA). This agreement, which lifted sanctions on Iran in exchange for limits on the country's sensitive nuclear activities, brought an end to the Iranian nuclear crisis – at least temporarily. On May 8, 2018, President Donald Trump withdrew the United States from the JCPOA, prompting Iran to accelerate its sensitive nuclear activities. Iran's nuclear future now remains uncertain.

I focus on the period between the public revelation of Iran's Natanz enrichment plant in 2002 and the conclusion of the JCPOA in 2015. Why did the United States refrain from an overt preventive attack even though this option remained on the table throughout the Bush and Obama administrations? Latent nuclear deterrence theory helps us better understand the answer.

A Train without Brakes? Perceptions of Iranian Intentions

United States officials were suspicious of Iran's intentions following the exposure of the secret nuclear plants in 2002. The covert nature of these activities raised serious doubts in Washington that Iran's program was strictly for electricity and medical isotope production, as its leaders claimed. As Condoleezza Rice, the US national security adviser, asked rhetorically, "If they were ostensibly pursuing nuclear technologies for peaceful purposes, why would they have anything to hide?"[43] Bush adopted this line of thinking as well. He called the Natanz and Arak facilities, "two telltale signs of a nuclear weapons program."[44]

In October 2003, however, Iran agreed to suspend all enrichment and reprocessing activities in exchange for political and economic incentives. This deal seemingly revealed flexibility in Iran's nuclear posture and eased US concerns to some degree. But the agreement collapsed following the election of Mahmoud Ahmadinejad as president in June 2005. By April 2006, Iran had enriched uranium to a level sufficient to fuel a nuclear power plant. Ahmadinejad proclaimed that Iran had

---

[43] Rice (2011, 165).
[44] Bush (2010, 415–416).

"joined the club of nuclear countries."[45] Ten months later, he implied that nothing could derail Iran's march toward a bomb. "The train of Iranian nation is without brakes and rear gear," Ahmadinejad said.[46] Iran rejected diplomatic overtures during this period, fueling the perception among some US officials that Iran was racing to build nuclear weapons. Bush concluded, "There was only one logical explanation: Iran was enriching uranium to use in a bomb."[47]

United States intelligence at this time supported these skeptical views. According to CIA director Michael Hayden, prior to 2007, the intelligence community concluded that Iran was "determined" to get nuclear weapons.[48] There was little doubt about Iran's nuclear intentions in Washington.

The situation changed dramatically following the conclusion of a US National Intelligence Estimate (NIE) in September 2007. Departing from the previous judgment, the NIE stated, "We judge with high confidence that in fall 2003, Tehran halted its nuclear weapons program."[49] The NIE also made it clear, however, that the path to a bomb remained open: "We also assess with moderate-to-high confidence that Tehran at a minimum is keeping open the option to develop nuclear weapons." Iran's nuclear future was uncertain, according to this assessment. Tehran clearly wanted to maintain the *capacity* to build nuclear bombs, but there was no firm evidence that it was racing to proliferate as quickly as possible.

United States officials continued to worry about what Iran might do in the future. "Given its past pursuit of a secret nuclear weapons program," Rice argued, "it would not be unreasonable to assume that Tehran might intend to pursue one again."[50] United States Vice President Dick Cheney, who initially argued that the administration should simply ignore the NIE, argued that work on weapons design and the weaponization of fissile material "are easily resumed," meaning that Iran's program still generated cause for concern.[51] At this point, though, Iran did not have an unrestrained nuclear program.

Almost everyone agreed that the 2007 intelligence assessment weakened the case for a preventive attack against Iran. As Bush later wrote,

[45] Tait and MacAskill (2006).
[46] CBS News (2007).
[47] Bush (2010, 416).
[48] Hayden (2011).
[49] Rice (2011, 617) briefly mentions the 2007 assessment.
[50] Rice (2011, 618).
[51] Cheney and Cheney (2011, 478). Rice (2011, 617) mentions Cheney's initial argument regarding the NIE.

"It tied my hands on the military side." "After the NIE," the President added, "how could I possibly explain using the military to destroy the nuclear facilities of a country the intelligence community said had no active nuclear weapons program?"[52] Secretary of Defense Robert Gates echoed this view, arguing in the spring of 2008 that "the president's own conditions for preemptive war had not been met, our own intelligence estimate would be used against us, and we would be the ones isolated, not Iran."[53]

Officials in the Obama administration similarly suspected that Iran might be coveting a bomb, but they also saw signs of restraint. United States officials publicly revealed another secret uranium enrichment plant in September 2009. This one, located in the city of Qom, was buried in a mountain, 260 feet below the surface.[54] The revelation of this facility revived the post-2002 perceptions of Iran's possible military aims. As Obama put it, "Everything about the facility – its size, configuration, and location on a military installation – indicated Iran's interest in shielding its activities from both detection and attack, features inconsistent with a civilian program."[55] Secretary of State Hillary Clinton also questioned Iran's claims that its intentions were fully peaceful: "their scientists were working in secret in hardened bunkers built deep inside mountains, enriching uranium at levels and quantities that led reasonable people to harbor well-founded suspicions of their intentions."[56] She told Yoweri Museveni, the President of Uganda, in April 2010, "it is hard not to have suspicions."[57]

Despite these suspicions, Obama administration officials did not see an Iranian bomb as inevitable, nor did they believe that Tehran was presently sprinting to a bomb. As Deputy Secretary of State William Burns indicated, "we had no firm evidence of a revival of Iran's earlier weaponization efforts."[58] There was nonetheless considerable uncertainty about Iran's intentions. "We could never be entirely sure" that they didn't have a weapons program, Burns said.[59] The belief that Tehran was on the fence regarding its nuclear program raised the costs of military action and created an opening for a diplomatic breakthrough. By 2012, due partially to international sanctions on Iran that Clinton

[52] Bush (2010, 419).
[53] Gates (2014, 191).
[54] Reuters (2012).
[55] Obama (2020, 471).
[56] Clinton (2014, 419).
[57] Clinton (2014, 428).
[58] Burns (2019, 347).
[59] Burns (2019, 347).

described as "crippling," US officials perceived an opportunity to reach a deal that kept Tehran nonnuclear.[60]

Inducing an Iranian Bomb

The perceived flexibility in Iran's nuclear posture made deterrence by proliferation potentially viable. Concerns about fomenting nuclear proliferation ultimately contributed to US military restraint. A secret study carried out during the Bush presidency reportedly concluded that bombing Iran would be counter productive. As Hayden, the CIA director, put it, Bush's advisers believed that striking the Iranians "would drive them to do what we were trying to prevent."[61] Washington recognized that a military strike would have exacerbated Tehran's insecurity, thereby heightening its need for a nuclear deterrent. An attack may also have induced Iran to withdraw from the nuclear Nonproliferation Treaty (NPT) or refuse to have its facilities inspected by the International Atomic Energy Agency (IAEA), which would lower the barriers to proliferation.[62]

Gates, the only cabinet-level national security official to serve under both Bush and Obama, clearly articulated the logic of deterrence by proliferation. In a May 2008 meeting, as Bush was contemplating military action, Gates explained why a preventive strike was a bad idea. He said, "a strike by the United States or Israel would end divisions in the Iranian government, strengthen the most radical elements, unify the country behind the government in their hatred of us, and demonstrate to all Iranians the need to develop nuclear weapons."[63] Cheney countered by suggesting that people would blame the Bush administration for not stopping Iran if it went on to build nuclear weapons. In response, Gates interjected, "people might also say that we not only didn't stop them from getting nuclear weapons *but made it inevitable*" by attacking.[64] After the meeting concluded, Gates followed up to amplify this view, telling Bush, "A military attack by either Israel or the United States will, I believe – having watched these guys since 1979 – guarantee that the Iranians will develop nuclear weapons, and seek revenge."[65]

Rice seemed to adopt this line of thinking as well. She wrote, "Most experts believed that limited military action might actually strengthen

---

[60] Clinton (2014, 441–442).
[61] Quoted in Broad (2012).
[62] Broad (2012).
[63] Gates (2014, 190).
[64] Gates (2014, 191). Emphasis added.
[65] Gates (2014, 192).

the regime – provoking a unifying nationalist response and undermining the reformers." Rice further revealed that US officials "repeatedly" explained this to Israeli leaders, who were anxious to launch a preventive strike, to underscore that military action would backfire.[66]

This perspective persisted during the Obama administration. According to Colin Kahl, who served as deputy assistant to the US president and national security to the vice president from 2014 to 2017, "Obama regularly talked about a military strike buying a few years but motivating Iran to go all the way to deter a future attack." Kahl added that "while Obama was willing to use force as a last resort if Iran made a mad dash for the bomb, he strongly believed that only a diplomatic solution – not a military one – offered an enduring solution to the proliferation challenge posed by Iran."[67] Burns provided a similar characterization of the president's thinking. "Obama was unconvinced by the logic or necessity of force at this stage," Burns indicated.[68] He explained the reason for this assessment: the Iranians "would undoubtedly regroup, take their program fully underground, and very likely make a decision to weaponize, with wide popular support in the aftermath of a unilateral U.S. or Israeli strike."[69]

These statements provide unambiguous evidence that deterrence by proliferation influenced officials' thinking as they contemplated preventive strikes during the Bush and Obama years. Concerns about inducing an Iranian bomb by attacking were widespread among US policymakers. This was not just a couple of voices expressing a minority opinion. As journalist Christiane Amanpour said in April 2012, "*Many* American officials who I have spoken to fear that if there is an attack on the nuclear program there, that is what could turn them into making that decision to actually go military" and arm with nuclear weapons.[70]

Deterrence by proliferation influenced officials outside of the United States as well. Russian Foreign Minister Sergei Lavrov told Rice in late 2005 that military pressure on Iran would backfire. "Then they will expel the inspectors and we will have no way to monitor the program," Lavrov said.[71] Carl Bildt and Erkki Tuomioja, the foreign ministers of Sweden and Finland, expressed similar thinking in 2012. They wrote, "It is difficult to see a single action more likely to drive Iran into taking the final decision to acquire nuclear weapons than an attack on the country.

---

[66] Rice (2011, 624).
[67] Email correspondence with the author, September 18, 2017, and January 30, 2018.
[68] Burns (2019, 355).
[69] Burns (2019, 355).
[70] Amanpour (2012). Emphasis added.
[71] Rice (2011, 422).

And once such a decision was made, it would only be a matter of time before a nuclear-armed Iran became a reality [because Iran was already a latent nuclear power]."[72]

Things might have played out differently if Washington believed that Iran was sprinting toward the bomb. Actions such as withdrawing from the NPT, expelling international inspectors, or diverting large quantities of nuclear material from civilian plants may have produced a latent nuclear deterrence failure, if those moves caused the United States to believe that nuclear proliferation would be immediate and inevitable in the absence of military intervention. Foreign officials such as Israeli Defense Minister Ehud Barak understood this as well. "It is clear to them," Barak said, "that if they break the IAEA and start moving toward a nuclear explodable device or weapon, America will contemplate action."[73] That US officials saw an Iranian bomb as possible but not inevitable in the absence of conflict made deterrence by proliferation viable.

Uncertain Prospects for Success

Advocates of military action against Iran often suggest that the United States (or Israel) could erode Tehran's nuclear capacity with relative ease. John Bolton wrote in 2015, before he became national security adviser, "The United States could do a thorough job of destruction, but Israel alone can do what's necessary."[74] However, it was far from obvious that preventive strikes could have degraded Iran's nuclear capacity to a degree that was acceptable to US policymakers.

President Bush acknowledged that he was not confident in the odds of success. "There were many reasons I was concerned about undertaking a military strike on Iran," he wrote, "including its uncertain effectiveness."[75] Key military advisers shared this view. Admiral Michael Mullen, the Chairman of the Joint Chiefs of Staff, explained the difficulty of conducting a successful preventive strike during a 2008 meeting with Bush and his national security team.[76] In January 2012, journalist Bob Schieffer asked General Martin Dempsey, Mullen's successor, whether the military could destroy Iran's nuclear capacity using conventional weapons only. Dempsey replied, "Well, I certainly want them to believe

---

[72] Bildt and Tuomioja (2012).
[73] Amanpour (2012).
[74] Bolton (2015).
[75] Bush (2010, 419).
[76] Gates (2014, 191).

that that's the case," suggesting that he did not, in fact, have complete confidence the military could do it.[77]

That Iran had advanced dual-use capabilities greatly complicated a preventive strike, as latent nuclear deterrence theory expects. By the time the United States was seriously considering a preventive strike, Iran had extensive knowledge about uranium enrichment. Any enrichment facilities that were destroyed, therefore, could be rebuilt relatively quickly. Burns made this argument explicitly: "They had the knowledge to enrich, and there was no way you could bomb, sanction, or wish that away."[78] He further indicated that Iran's ENR-related progress by 2013 – when it was spinning around 19,000 centrifuges – made it virtually impossible to eliminate the country's enrichment capacity. "Maybe we could have gotten to a zero enrichment outcome a decade earlier, when they were spinning a few dozen centrifuges," Burns said.[79]

Unlike the 1981 Israeli raid against Iraq's nuclear reactor – when destroying a single facility could substantially curtail the program – multiple sites would need to be located and destroyed in order for a raid against Iran to be operationally successful. As Rice put it, "One could not destroy the nuclear program by just attacking a few targets."[80] There were now redundancies built into Iran's program, with key technologies and materials dispersed across the country. In November 2011, Barak claimed that Iran was nine months away from entering a "zone of immunity," a point at which it would be impossible to stop weaponization militarily due to all of the program's redundancies.[81]

Given the advanced state of its nuclear program, Iran had time to harden critical infrastructure, making it less vulnerable to attack. The enrichment facility at Qom would be the most difficult to destroy, given that it is buried deep in a mountain. The United States possesses a bunker buster called the Massive Ordnance Penetrator (MOP), designed to be delivered with B-2 stealth bombers, that might be able to destroy the centrifuges located there. But there is some debate about whether the MOP could get the job done. One anonymous US official characterized destroying Qom as "hard but not impossible."[82]

For all these reasons, US officials believed that, in the best-case scenario, a preventive strike could have set Iran's nuclear program back

---

[77] Schieffer followed up to ask, "Well, is it?" Dempsey's response was telling: "I absolutely want them to believe that that's the case." See Tau (2012).
[78] Burns (2019, 362).
[79] Burns (2019, 362).
[80] Rice (2011, 624).
[81] Zakaria (2011). See also Pollack (2013, 199).
[82] Reuters (2012).

by a few years. Officials in both the Bush and Obama administrations did not see military force as an enduring solution to the problems posed by Iran's nuclear program. As Gates said, "we needed a long-term solution, not just a one-to-three year delay."[83] Given that an attack would increase Iran's appetite for a nuclear arsenal – and that operational success was far from certain – there was a real possibility that the net effect of using military force would be to increase the likelihood of an Iranian bomb, especially in the medium to long term.

Covert Action and Preventing Escalation

The United States resisted a traditional military attack on Iran's nuclear facilities, but the crisis was not completely conflict-free. Iran and the United States experienced lower-level militarized disputes during the crisis. In January 2005, for instance, US planes violated Iranian airspace, apparently to collect intelligence on the country's nuclear activities; US forces also conducted military operations in the Persian Gulf in March 2007 and, the next month, sent planes over Iranian territory at low altitudes as signals of resolve. Most significantly, the United States secretly carried out the Stuxnet cyberattack against the Natanz enrichment plant in joint operation with Israel called "Olympic Games." The United States and Israel began developing Stuxnet in 2005 and first deployed the cyberweapon at Natanz in 2007, although this operation did not become public until three years later.[84] The worm infiltrated computer systems at Natanz and caused centrifuges to suddenly speed up or slow down, causing them to self-destruct.[85]

These kinds of disputes are possible, according to latent nuclear deterrence theory, because postconflict threats to build nuclear weapons may lack credibility. The United States likely calculated that Iran would not race to obtain a nuclear arsenal just because of American displays of force or even the Stuxnet attack. These actions did not pose a large enough threat to Tehran to justify a race to a bomb. "Olympic Games" certainly irked the Iranians – they reportedly fired people after centrifuges ceased working – but it did not provoke a strong sense of nationalism or insecurity.[86] The covert nature of the attack allowed Iranian leaders to avoid or deflect the reality that its nuclear program had been attacked, reducing pressures for escalation. In the end, Iran's

---

[83] Gates (2014, 190).
[84] Reuters (2013).
[85] Sanger (2012).
[86] Sanger (2012).

development of sensitive nuclear technology may have invited low-level disputes but it did not trigger a traditional preventive strike.

United States leaders saw the Stuxnet operation as a way to prevent airstrikes against Iran's nuclear facilities. Obama told his advisers that Israel would bomb Iran if "Olympic Games" did not work.[87] This was an outcome the United States wanted to avoid. As Secretary of State John Kerry indicated, "The priority at that moment was convincing Israel to refrain from bombing Iran – at least temporarily."[88] To keep the Israelis at bay, Washington needed to demonstrate that it took the threat posed by Iran's nuclear program seriously. Involving Israel in "Olympic Games" was the only way to do this, according to US officials.[89] The Stuxnet cyberattack had its intended effect in the eyes of US policymakers. "This campaign helped deflect Netanyahu's push to bomb," Burns said.[90]

Conventional Punishment: Another Disincentive to Strike

Washington was concerned about Iranian conventional retaliation, not just punishment via weaponless deterrence. United States officials were well aware that Iran could take damaging retaliatory actions immediately following an attack against its nuclear facilities. Drawing a distinction between Israel's September 2007 strike in the Middle East, Gates told Bush, "Iran was not Syria – it would retaliate."[91] He believed that Iranian countermeasures could threaten US interests in Iraq and Lebanon, put oil supplies at risk, tank any hope of a peace process in the region, and possibly provoke a war between Hezbollah and Israel. Concerns about what might happen in Iraq seemed especially salient. If Israeli planes used Iraqi airspace to bomb Iranian nuclear plants, Gates and other US officials feared, "the Iraqi government might well tell us to leave the country immediately."[92]

Obama talked about the possibility of conventional retaliation as well. He worried that military action against Iran's nuclear program "could plunge the Middle East – and the United States – into yet another conflict at a time when we still had 180,000 highly exposed troops along Iran's borders, and when any big spike in oil prices could send the

---

[87] Sanger (2012).
[88] Kerry (2018, 495).
[89] Sanger (2012).
[90] Burns (2019, 355)
[91] Gates (2014, 190).
[92] Gates (2014, 190).

world economy deeper into a tailspin."[93] After analyzing what a military confrontation with Iran might look like, Obama acknowledged he felt "weighed down by the knowledge that if war became necessary, nearly everything else I was trying to achieve would likely be upended."[94]

This raises the question: How important were these factors in deterring a US attack relative to weaponless deterrence? It is difficult to reach a definitive answer. Senior US officials usually laid out more than one reason they opposed a preventive strike. As Bush acknowledged, there were "many reasons" he decided not to authorize an attack.[95] It is clear that concerns about fomenting nuclear armament and doubts about operational effectiveness contributed to restraint, as the theory predicted. So did the possibility of Iran inflicting military and economic pain on the United States through conventional retaliation. Obama underscored the salience of both considerations in 2015, saying that he preferred a diplomatic settlement to a preventive strike "not just because of the costs of war, but also because a negotiated agreement offered a more effective, verifiable and durable resolution."[96] Leaders typically did not rank-order the factors based on their relative importance, making it difficult to know what weighed most heavily on their minds.

On top of this, officials disagreed about the costs of attacking Iran. Cheney, for example, viewed the danger of undermining progress in Iraq as the greatest deterrent but he did not seem persuaded by the logic of deterrence by proliferation.[97] For others across two administrations, latent nuclear deterrence theory played a central role in their thinking. Some even suggested, in contrast to Cheney, that the theory may offer the most compelling explanation for US restraint. After articulating seven possible consequences of attacking Iran, journalist Jeffrey Goldberg – who interviewed Obama on Middle East foreign-policy issues multiple times – concluded, "Again, what I worry about, at bottom, is that an Israeli attack would inadvertently create conditions for an acceleration of the Iranian nuclear program."[98]

At this point, then, we can conclude that latent nuclear deterrence theory helps us better understand this case – but it only tells part of the story. No single theory or explanation can fully account for US behavior during the crisis over Iran's nuclear program. We may be able to offer

[93] Obama (2020, 454).
[94] Obama (2020, 454).
[95] Bush (2010, 419).
[96] Obama (2015).
[97] Gates (2014, 192).
[98] Goldberg (2012). This is also the first of four paradoxes associated with a preventive strike articulated by Pollack (2013, 185).

a clearer answer about the relative importance of different factors in the coming years, as formerly classified materials become public.

The First North Korean Nuclear Crisis, 1994

In July 1989, US newspapers made a troubling revelation: North Korea had built a plutonium reprocessing plant at its Yongbyon nuclear complex. This facility, combined with a small nuclear reactor at the same site, gave North Korea the means to make plutonium for nuclear bombs.[99] North Korea's possession of sensitive nuclear technology heightened concerns about Pyongyang's intentions in the United States and elsewhere.

The IAEA sought to verify the country's compliance with its NPT commitments, but Pyongyang was not fully cooperative. In March 1993, as international pressure mounted, North Korea announced that it was withdrawing from the NPT.[100] North Korea reversed this decision three months later, but ultimately refused to grant IAEA inspectors the access they needed to determine the full scope of the country's nuclear actions and capabilities. In May 1994, North Korea started removing spent fuel rods from their Yongbyon reactor. United States Secretary of Defense William Perry later recalled, "This action brought the crisis to a head." As he explained, "If North Korea reprocessed this spent fuel, they could produce in a few months enough plutonium to make six to ten bombs."[101] On June 14, 1994, North Korea booted international inspectors from its territory and withdrew from the IAEA.[102]

United States officials took this as a sign that North Korea was bent on building nuclear weapons. Perry summed up his thinking at the time: "We're only guessing what their intentions were. They never told us why they were doing it. But it was inescapable that they were heading for nuclear weapons when they sent the inspectors out, we believed."[103] A North Korean nuclear arsenal seemed inevitable in the absence of external intervention.

The possibility of North Korea becoming a nuclear power threatened US national security. As Perry said, "I thought at the time, and the president thought at the time, that it would be a catastrophe if North Korea got nuclear weapons."[104] United States officials were worried, in

---

[99] Albright (1994).
[100] Sanger (1993).
[101] Perry (2015, 106).
[102] Sanger (1994).
[103] PBS (2003c).
[104] Interview with the author, April 27, 2021.

particular, that a North Korean nuclear arsenal would raise the risk of a catastrophic war, trigger an arms race in East Asia, weaken the NPT, and lead to sales of sensitive technology to terrorists or states of proliferation concern.[105]

These circumstances – the development of ENR technology by a country seen as racing toward a bomb in the presence of strong opposition to nuclear armament – are ripe for a crisis, according to latent nuclear deterrence theory. Consistent with this expectation, the United States considered preventive military action to stop North Korean nuclear armament. President Clinton wrote in his memoirs that he was "determined to stop North Korea from developing a nuclear arsenal, even at the risk of war."[106]

The Pentagon had a detailed plan. It called for cruise missile strikes against the Yongbyon reactor at night, to minimize the loss of life. This would have been a limited attack against a single facility with the goal of eliminating plutonium that could be used to build six to ten nuclear weapons. "We didn't want to extend our action beyond getting that reactor," Perry said.[107] It was widely understood, however, that a limited strike could ultimately lead to war. As Robert Gallucci, who was the chief US negotiator during the North Korea crisis, characterized the situation, "I think, in everybody's mind, we were moving on a course that not inevitably, but most likely would move us to the use of military force. That seemed the direction we were heading . . . It could easily have led to a war, by miscalculation, or by the North Koreans preferring the uncertainty of a conflict to the certainty of enormous concessions."[108]

In the end, however, the United States did not attack North Korea. The two countries concluded an agreement in October 1994, known as the Agreed Framework, that brought an end to the first North Korean nuclear crisis. Under the terms of the deal, Pyongyang agreed to freeze its plutonium production capabilities in exchange for oil and two electricity-producing nuclear reactors.[109] The following sections examine the degree to which latent nuclear deterrence theory helps us understand US restraint during the 1994 standoff.

---

[105] Whitlark (2021, 195).
[106] Clinton (2004, 591).
[107] Interview with the author, April 27, 2021.
[108] PBS (2003b).
[109] This agreement held throughout the 1990s but it ultimately collapsed. Pyongyang withdrew from the NPT in 2003 and tested its first nuclear weapon three years later.

Uncertain Nuclear Capabilities and Deterrence by Doubt

The preceding discussion implies that the US objective during the 1994 crisis was to prevent North Korea from obtaining a nuclear bomb. However, there are some indications that North Korea may have been nuclear-armed during this standoff – more than a decade before its first nuclear test in 2006. According to a 2002 CIA estimate, the intelligence community "has assessed since the early 1990s that the North has one or possibly two weapons using plutonium it produced prior to 1992."[110] Gates, who headed the CIA from 1991 to 1993 and later became secretary of defense, said in June 1994, "it is *highly probable* that the North Koreans already have one or two nuclear devices."[111] A top secret Soviet assessment similarly concluded in February 1990 that North Korea was already in possession of an assembled nuclear bomb.[112] South Korean intelligence indicated that North Korea contemplated carrying out a nuclear test in March 1992 but ultimately scrapped the idea.[113]

Others recognized that North Korea *might* have been nuclear-armed in the 1990s but believed that it probably was not. Perry told me that he "thought it was more likely than not that the North Koreans did not have a nuclear weapon."[114] There was uncertainty on two fronts: whether North Korea had sufficient plutonium and, if it did, whether it had successfully weaponized that material. "Putting those two things together," Perry said, "my judgment at the time is they probably did not have nuclear weapons." He also acknowledged, however, "They might very well have."[115] James Clapper, who directed the Defense Intelligence Agency during the crisis held a similar view. He was personally (as opposed to institutionally) "skeptical they ever had a bomb," adding that "we didn't have smoking gun evidence either way."[116] In his view, the intelligence community's conclusions reflected the "worst-case alternative."[117]

Regardless of their ultimate conclusions, US officials were uncertain about North Korea's nuclear capabilities during the 1994 crisis. Those who believed that North Korea was nuclear-armed could not rule out the possibility that it was still nonnuclear, and vice versa. The ambiguity over North Korea's nuclear capabilities came through during a discussion

[110] US Central Intelligence Agency (2002).
[111] Quoted in Sigal (1998, 93).
[112] Mazarr (1995b, 56).
[113] Wit et al. (2004, 38).
[114] Interview with the author, April 27, 2021.
[115] Interview with the author, April 27, 2021.
[116] Quoted in Sigal (1998, 93).
[117] Quoted in Sigal (1998, 93).

between Perry and South Korean Defense Minister Rhee Byong Tae on April 20, 1994. According to a declassified summary of the meeting, Rhee told Perry that he was "confused because he read that some believe that North Korea already has one or two bombs." Rhee then asked, "So what is our objective? To freeze the program? Or to prohibit North Korea from owning any bomb?"[118]

This kind of uncertainty has the potential to dissuade military attacks. As deterrence by doubt suggests, the mere possibility of atomic punishment can make a country think twice about using military force. Potential attackers discount punishment costs based on their likelihood of being imposed. Because a nuclear attack can inflict such severe damage to property and human life, however, the expected punishment costs can still be substantial even if a country believes that the odds of nuclear possession are long, say five-to-one. Did deterrence by doubt play a role in the crisis with North Korea?

The possibility of a North Korean nuclear attack loomed in the background as the United States considered attacking Yongbyon. An editorial in *The New York Times* in December 1993 raised the prospect of nuclear retaliation: "If the new intelligence assessment is correct, and North Korea actually has a bomb or two, Pyongyang's response [to a US attack] could be disastrous."[119] Leon Sigal also highlighted the risk of nuclear punishment in his comprehensive book on the crisis, writing that "neither the United States nor South Korea wanted to take that risk [of war], especially with a potentially nuclear-armed North."[120]

Some US officials similarly acknowledged the potential for North Korean nuclear retaliation. Immediately after saying that the 1994 crisis was "such a serious point" due to the risk of war, Gallucci mentioned North Korea's nuclear capabilities: "We didn't know whether North Korea then had nuclear weapons."[121] Mitchell Reiss, who served as assistant executive director to the Korean Peninsula Energy Development Organization (KEDO) – the agency tasked with implementing the Agreed Framework, wrote in 1995 that "a preemptive strike might invite the real, if low, possibility of a nuclear response from Pyongyang."[122] Referring to the one to two nuclear bombs that North Korea might possess, Perry said, "we knew about them and thought about them" during the crisis.[123]

---

[118] US Department of Defense (1994).
[119] *The New York Times* (1993).
[120] Sigal (1998, 9).
[121] PBS (2003b).
[122] Reiss (1995, 259).
[123] Interview with the author, April 27, 2021.

However, North Korea's conventional capabilities – not the one to two nuclear weapons it might have possessed – weighed most heavily on the minds of US officials. As Perry put it, "it's not that we were unconcerned about the one or two bombs, but they were overshadowed."[124] Conventional forces had a greater deterrent effect on the United States for two main reasons.

First, given the size of North Korea's army and the weapons it amassed along the North–South border, it could inflict greater damage with its conventional capabilities than one to two nuclear weapons. "The thing that we feared," Perry said, "was that North Korea, if provoked, would make a conventional attack on South Korea."[125] He went on to explain why this scenario was worrisome: "given the size of their army and the relative size of the South Korean and American forces at the border, we thought there was every likelihood they could get to Seoul before you could stop them ... [There were] 10-20 million people in that immediate vicinity of Seoul at that time. So we thought that ... would have been a disaster."[126]

United States estimates indicated that a second Korean War might kill or wound one million civilians and 300,000 to 750,000 US and South Korean troops.[127] To put these figures in perspective, if a nuclear bomb the size of the one North Korea tested in 2006 (0.5 kt) detonated in the air above Seoul, it would kill an estimated 14,160 people and injure another 10,750. This test was a fizzle, meaning that the weapon failed to generate its expected yield. North Korea's second nuclear test in 2009 was more successful, generating a yield of 6 kt. A bomb that size detonated above Seoul would result in nearly 50,000 fatalities and around 64,000 injuries.[128] Although these casualty estimates are substantial, the damage North Korea could inflict with conventional capabilities alone back in 1994 was greater.

Second, US officials believed that conventional retaliation was much more likely than a nuclear response from North Korea. General Gary Luck, who commanded US forces in South Korea saw a conventional invasion as inevitable if the United States bombed Yongbyon: "If we pull an Osirak," he said, "they will be coming south."[129] Perry likewise indicated, "The looming factor was the near certainty that they might

---

[124] Interview with the author, April 27, 2021.
[125] Interview with the author, April 27, 2021.
[126] Interview with the author, April 27, 2021.
[127] Wit et al. (2004, 102, 181).
[128] I generated these estimates using the NUKEMAP simulator developed by Alex Wellerstein.
[129] Wit et al. (2004, 104).

invade South Korea with the conventional forces."[130] By contrast, nuclear retaliation was possible but far from certain. This led US officials to discount North Korea's nuclear capabilities relative to its conventional firepower. The biggest concern, according to Perry, was not "the one or two nuclear weapons they *might* have, but the million or so troops they *did* have, we knew they had."[131]

It is important to underscore that North Korea's conventional capabilities make this a unique case. Pyongyang had a huge conventional army and the South Korean capital, where about half the country's population lived at the time, was within 25 miles of the border. "I can't think of another place quite like that," Perry said.[132] Given these circumstances, conventional retaliation swamped concerns about a possible nuclear attack. United States officials thought about the possibility that North Korea was nuclear-armed, but its nuclear capabilities did not play a decisive role in the outcome.

I asked Perry if the one to two nuclear weapons North Korea possibly had would have played a bigger role if Pyongyang had dramatically weaker conventional forces. He responded: "My present view on that looking back is the answer is probably."[133] The North Korean case therefore shows that a country's conventional capabilities shape the extent to which nuclear deterrence by doubt influences crisis outcomes. Latent nuclear forces are likely to play a greater role – at least when it comes to deterrence by doubt – when the damage they could inflict exceeds what the country could do with its conventional weapons alone.

This applies to traditional nuclear forces as well. An unambiguous nuclear weapons capability, like the one the United States has maintained since 1945, will also be less relevant in situations where the nuclear power can credibly threaten to inflict large amounts of pain and/or impose its will using its conventional forces only.[134] For example, US nuclear weapons did not play a role in the 1994 Haiti crisis – during which the United States used military force to restore the country's democratically elected leader, Jean-Bertrand Aristide, to power – because Washington's conventional forces were more than enough to get the job done. That conventional forces trumped the risk of nuclear retaliation during the North Korean crisis, then, reflects a fundamental reality of nuclear threat-making rather than a limitation unique to latent nuclear deterrence.

[130] Interview with the author, April 27, 2021.
[131] Interview with the author, April 27, 2021.
[132] Interview with the author, April 27, 2021.
[133] Interview with the author, April 27, 2021.
[134] Sechser and Fuhrmann (2017).

The Perils of Pushing Too Hard: Deterrence by Proliferation in Action

Deterrence by proliferation is unlikely to work, according to latent nuclear deterrence theory, when the potential attacker believes that the target is already determined to get nuclear weapons. United States officials perceived that North Korea had an unrestrained nuclear program in 1994 – particularly after Pyongyang expelled international inspectors from its territory and pulled out of the IAEA. As expected, the prospect of fomenting nuclear proliferation did not play a major role in inducing US restraint during its interactions with North Korea in the 1994 crisis.

After the conclusion of the Agreed Framework, however, US perceptions of North Korean intentions changed. Some officials in Washington no longer believed that Pyongyang was racing to a bomb – at least not with the same vigor that it was in 1994. This created an opportunity for deterrence by proliferation to influence US behavior. During the late 1990s, the risk of hardening North Korea's resolve to get nuclear weapons by issuing military threats shaped how Washington approached Pyongyang.

In November 1998, President Clinton tasked Perry, who stepped down as Secretary of Defense in January 1997, to lead a review of US policy toward North Korea. Perry traveled to North Korea in May 1999 as part of this policy review process and issued a report that laid out the review team's findings and recommendations five months later.[135] The final report articulated a plan for countering the challenges North Korea posed to US national security. It called for a negotiated settlement whereby North Korea verified that is not pursuing nuclear weapons and ended its long-range missile program in exchange for the United States normalizing bilateral relations and rolling back economic sanctions.

Perry's thinking as he led the policy review reflects the logic of deterrence by proliferation. He understood why North Korea might want nuclear weapons. "They feared the United States was going to make a unilateral military attack to overthrow the regime," Perry said.[136] He further recognized that threatening North Korea would reinforce this fear, thereby encouraging the very thing that the United States was trying to stop – the development of North Korean bombs. As Perry put it, taking tough action to stop nuclear armament "can be very counterproductive."[137] He therefore pursued an alternative approach to address the North Korean threat: "I was looking for a way of putting

---

[135] Perry (1999).
[136] Interview with the author, April 27, 2021.
[137] Interview with the author, April 27, 2021.

them in a position where they did not feel threatened," Perry said, as this would make them much more willing to be nonnuclear. This had a major influence on his overall approach to North Korea. As Perry put it, "It was a primary factor in my thinking."[138]

United States policy on North Korea shifted when President George W. Bush assumed office in January 2001. Some of Bush's advisers – most notably Secretary of State Colin Powell – were inclined to continue the approach outlined in the Clinton-era policy review.[139] But the president seemed to favor a different approach. Early in his first term, Bush compared North Korean leader Kim Jong Il's actions to his daughters throwing food on the floor when they were little to get attention. He told his advisers, "The United States is through picking up his food."[140]

North Korea began taking actions that suggested it had unrestrained nuclear ambitions. At the end of 2002, the government announced that it was restarting the Yongbyon reactor and declared to the IAEA that the Agency did not have jurisdiction over its nuclear facilities.[141] Around this time, new intelligence indicated that North Korea had a covert uranium enrichment capability. Bush called this "a startling revelation" which underscored that North Korea "had cheated on the Agreed Framework."[142] North Korean officials confirmed the existence of the previously secret enrichment plant to visiting US officials in October 2002.[143] Three months later, North Korea formally withdrew from the NPT. In April 2003, North Korean official Li Gun told US Assistant Secretary of State James Kelly that Pyongyang had at least one nuclear weapon and then reportedly asked, "Now what are you going to do about it?"[144]

These actions once again took deterrence by proliferation off the table and hardened Bush's resolve to take a more hawkish approach. In February 2003, Bush told Chinese leader Jiang Zemin that he would be forced to consider a preventive military strike against North Korea if the issue could not be addressed diplomatically.[145] Diplomatic efforts continued through the Six Party Talks – which included China, Japan, Russia, and South Korea, in addition to the United States and North Korea – but did not yield a decisive breakthrough. North

---

[138] Interview with the author, April 27, 2021.
[139] Rice (2011, 160).
[140] Bush (2010, 423).
[141] Rice (2011, 163).
[142] Bush (2010, 423).
[143] Rice (2011, 161623).
[144] CNN (2003a).
[145] Bush (2010, 424).

Korea ultimately conducted six nuclear tests between October 2006 and September 2017.

Would a Strike Have Worked? Questioning Operational Success

United States officials were confident that the military could successfully destroy the Yongbyon reactor with cruise missiles. North Korean air defenses and hilly terrain in the area posed complications, but policy-makers believed that these challenges could be overcome.[146] As then-Assistant Secretary of Defense Ashton Carter put it, "The technical military facts were not very much in dispute."[147]

The bigger problem from an operational standpoint was the plutonium that North Korea had already separated – and the one to two nuclear weapons that it might already possess. General John Shalikashvili, Chair-man of the Joint Chiefs of Staff, and CIA Director James Woolsey told White House officials in November 1993 that they did not know where the existing plutonium was located and therefore could not guarantee its destruction.[148] There was also plutonium – enough for six to ten nuclear weapons – presently in the spent fuel at the Yongbyon reactor. This material could be moved to another location and separated to make bombs. United States officials aimed to destroy the reactor before North Korea had an opportunity to move this plutonium, but there was no guarantee this plan would be successful.[149]

A bomb's worth of plutonium takes up little space. President Clinton made this clear in a 1995 speech: "a lump of plutonium the size of a soda can is enough to build a bomb."[150] It is therefore relatively easy to conceal plutonium once it has been separated from spent nuclear fuel, or to move it on short notice. Finding this material or the bombs that may have already been assembled in North Korea seemed close to impossible.[151] Air Force Chief of Staff Merrill McPeak aptly summed up the challenge: "We can't find nuclear weapons now, except by going on a house-to-house search."[152]

For some US officials, this problem weakened the case for using military force. After describing the challenge of the unaccounted for plutonium, Joel Wit, Daniel Poneman, and Robert Gallucci – all of

[146] Wit et al. (2004, 107).
[147] Quoted in Sigal (1998, 75).
[148] Wit et al. (2004, 106–107).
[149] Wit et al. (2004, 103).
[150] See also Wit et al. (2004, 211).
[151] Reiss (1995, 259).
[152] Quoted in Sigal (1998, 76).

whom served in government during the crisis – concluded, "At best, the attack might delay the problem without eliminating it."[153] Reiss expressed a similar view: "Nothing less than the military defeat, occupation, and inspection of the entire country would eliminate the North's nuclear weapons program."[154] Even some advocates of a preventive attack acknowledged this problem. Former National Security Adviser Brent Scowcroft and Arnold Kanter, who previously served in the State Department, penned an op-ed in June 1994 calling for military strikes against North Korea. But they admitted that the policy for which they were advocating came with a major drawback: "The approach we have outlined is designed to prevent a bad problem from becoming worse. By itself, it cannot deal with the one or two nuclear weapons North Korea may already have."[155]

Recognition that a military attack could probably not fully eliminate North Korea's stock of fissile material weakened the case for attacking. Had North Korea not already produced fissile material, however, the odds of success would have been greater, as latent nuclear deterrence theory expects. Given that it was now in possession of separated plutonium, though, Washington was less optimistic that an Osiraq-like attack would fully solve the problem.

Radioactivity Raises the Stakes

Public commentary on the first North Korean nuclear crisis frequently invokes the possibility that bombing the Yongbyon reactor could result in radioactive contamination. For example, Robert Manning, who previously worked as an adviser in the State Department and the Pentagon, wrote in 1994 that there was a "high probability that an Osirak-like preemptive strike would spew radioactive fallout all over Northeast Asia."[156] United States officials recognized this risk as well. Perry requested a study to assess whether the US military could bomb the reactor without generating radioactive fallout. Ashton Carter, who led this study, recalled that the possibility of creating "a Chernobyl-like radiological plume downwind" by striking the reactor was "an obviously important concern."[157]

The Pentagon's study concluded, however, that a cruise missile attack could "entomb the plutonium," as Carter put it, without causing a

[153] Wit et al. (2004, 211).
[154] Reiss (1995, 259).
[155] Scowcroft and Kanter (1994).
[156] Manning (1994, 68). For another example, see Sigal (1998, 9).
[157] PBS (2003a).

radiological disaster. According to Carter, "We were very confident we could avoid that."[158] Perry wrote in his 2015 memoirs that it was "safe" to strike the Yongbyon reactor because the analysis showed "no appreciable radiological plume."[159] He later added, "the advice that I got from the experts who were studying this was that we could do that in such a way that that would not be a significant danger."[160]

This judgment may be due, in part, to the relatively low "burnup" – a term for the amount of uranium that is burned in a reactor – at Yongbyon.[161] Lower burnup translates to less radioactive spent nuclear fuel. A 2017 analysis by energy experts David von Hippel and Peter Hayes concluded that the total inventory of radioactive cesium-137 in the Yongbyon reactor is 3.7 PBq – compared to almost 3,000 PBq in the Japanese Fukushima plant where a disaster occurred following an tsunami in March 2011.[162] Given the small amounts of radioactive material present, an attack on the reactor would not disperse cesium-137 beyond the areas immediately surrounding Yongbyon.

The possibility of causing a radiological disaster nonetheless influenced the thinking of some current and former policymakers. Scowcroft and Kanter advocated for an attack against the reprocessing plant – instead of the reactor – in part because of the lower risk of disseminating radioactive material.[163] Although North Korea had previously separated plutonium from spent nuclear fuel at this facility, there was no nuclear material present at the height of the crisis (aside from possible nuclear waste tanks).[164] Wit, Poneman, and Gallucci argued that radiological risks affected the timing of a preventive strike.[165] They suggested that an attack would have to occur after North Korea started to move spent fuel to the reprocessing facility, presumably to avoid hitting the reactor or the spent fuel pool.

A second (and more worrisome) radiation-related concern had to do with North Korean retaliation. United States and South Korean officials feared that Pyongyang would respond to a strike against its nuclear facilities by targeting nuclear power plants in South Korea. Most of South Korea's nuclear power plants were located along the coast, potentially enabling North Korean sea-based attacks or acts of

---

[158] PBS (2003a).
[159] Perry (2015, 106).
[160] Interview with the author, April 27, 2021.
[161] NRC (2018).
[162] von Hippel and Hayes (2017).
[163] Scowcroft and Kanter (1994).
[164] Ibid.
[165] Wit et al. (2004, 103).

sabotage.[166] The South's nuclear power plants burned much more uranium than the Yongbyon reactor, meaning that attacking them could cause greater radioactive fallout. Officials in both Seoul and Washington were aware that North Korean counterattacks on these facilities could release "severe local radiation."[167] When it comes to the potential for radioactive contamination, then, the possibility of a retaliatory strike on South Korea's nuclear facilities had a greater deterrent effect than whatever environmental damage might occur on North Korean soil.[168]

Syria's Reactor in the Desert, 2007

In the spring of 2007, Israel approached the United States with surprising news. Israeli intelligence had discovered a nuclear reactor in Syria being built with North Korean assistance, and the facility was almost operational. Israel had already come to the conclusion that the reactor must be taken out militarily. It was willing to act unilaterally, if necessary, but preferred that the United States carry out the operation. Prime Minister Ehud Olmert made a direct appeal to Bush. "George," he said, "I'm asking you to bomb the compound." Bush replied, "Give me some time to look at the intelligence and I'll give you an answer."[169]

Bush's foreign-policy team quickly got to work. United States officials ultimately debated two main options for dealing with the Syrian reactor. The first was immediately to destroy it militarily, either in a unilateral attack or together with Israel. The second involved diplomacy. Washington would inform the UN and the IAEA of the secret nuclear facility and, after building international support, compel the Syrians to dismantle the facility.[170] During internal deliberations, there was near consensus among national security officials that diplomacy was the best path, with Cheney being the sole voice in favor of a preventive strike.

Bush ultimately selected the diplomatic option. The president phoned Olmert in mid-July to convey his decision. The Israeli leader was clearly disappointed. "Your strategy is very disturbing to me," Omert told Bush.[171] At the end of the conversation, the president essentially green-lit a unilateral Israeli strike. "We will not get in your way," Bush said.[172]

---

166 Wit et al. (2004, 104).
167 Wit et al. (2004, 104). See also Reiss (1995, 259).
168 von Hippel and Hayes (2017).
169 Bush (2010, 421).
170 Cheney and Cheney (2011, 471).
171 Bush (2010, 422).
172 Katz (2019b).

Less than two months later, Israel took matters into its own hands, carrying out airstrikes that razed the Syrian nuclear reactor.

Assessing the Danger

Israeli officials viewed Syria's nuclear program as a threat to their country's existence. Once Olmert found out about the reactor he knew, according to remarks he made later, that "nothing would be the same." He believed that the Syrian reactor posed a threat "at the existential level" that was "of an unprecedented order of magnitude."[173] The Israeli prime minister conveyed this sentiment to Bush when he solicited US help in taking out the facility.[174]

Israel is particularly vulnerable to a nuclear strike owing to its small geographic size and population. An airburst detonation of a 1 Mt warhead above Jerusalem would kill an estimated 618,000 Israelis – about 7 percent of the country's population – and render a large proportion of its land uninhabitable.[175] Given this catastrophic potential, Israeli leaders worry about an adversary obtaining even rudimentary nuclear capabilities. Since 1981, Israel has pursued the Begin Doctrine – named after the country's sixth prime minister – which holds that Israel's enemies cannot be allowed to obtain a nuclear bomb. Olmert's views of Syria's nuclear program were consistent with this longstanding doctrine.

The shared border heightened the perceived danger of a Syrian bomb, as the close proximity of the two countries shortens warning time and makes weapons delivery easier. Olmert believed that Syria could successfully drop a nuclear bomb from a plane, like the United States did during World War II, despite the vulnerability of Syrian aircraft to Israeli air defense systems. "When their planes take off, they are above Israel within one minute," he said. "They don't need to have a missile."[176]

United States officials also viewed Syria's nuclear ambitions as a national security threat. Cheney was particularly vocal about the danger. The vice president told Bush on June 14 that nuclear proliferation "was still our biggest long-term security challenge. It was clearly the ultimate threat to the homeland."[177] He went on to say that Syria (along with Iran) "constituted a major threat to America's interests in the Middle East" due to its sponsorship of terrorism and its facilitation of enemy

---

[173] Harel and Benn (2018).
[174] Bush (2010, 421).
[175] These figures are based on the NUKEMAP simulator: https://nuclearsecrecy.com/nukemap/.
[176] Katz (2019b, location 1462).
[177] Cheney and Cheney (2011, 469–470).

combatants into Iraq.[178] However, unlike their Israeli counterparts, most US officials did not see Syria's nuclear program as an existential threat. After all, Israel – not the United States – would be the most likely target of Syrian nuclear forces, were it to obtain them. Israeli officials recognized this disparity in threat perception. "The risk [posed by Syria's nuclear program] will always be greater for Israel while the US interest will always be different," according to David Ivry, the chief of the Israeli air force during the 1981 Osiraq strike.[179]

An Easy Job: Perceptions of Operational Success

United States and Israeli officials were united in the view that taking out the Syrian nuclear reactor would be relatively easy.[180] Bush said, "As a military matter, the bombing mission would be straightforward. The Air Force could destroy the target, no sweat."[181] Cheney agreed: "We certainly had the capacity to take it out with ease," he wrote in 2011.[182] Amos Yadlin, who headed the Military Intelligence Directorate (known as Aman for short) in the Israel Defense Forces, similarly indicated that he "wasn't worried about operational success of the attack."[183] "A few planes are all we need to get it done," Yadlin said.[184] For the Aman head, who helped carry out the bombing of the Osiraq reactor in 1981 as a pilot, eliminating the Syrian facility would be easier than the mission in Iraq 26 years prior.[185]

This confidence stemmed at least partially from Syria's nascent nuclear capabilities, as latent nuclear deterrence theory expects. The country did not have a known reprocessing plant, which would be needed to make weapons-usable plutonium from fuel burned in the reactor. Nor did it possess other technologies that are part of the fuel cycle, like uranium conversion or enrichment plants. Two nuclear reactors – the second of which was a small research reactor with little direct proliferation significance – represented the entirety of Syria's

---

[178] Cheney and Cheney (2011, 470).
[179] Katz (2019b, location 1297).
[180] This assumes that conventional munitions would be used to destroy the facility in a traditional military strike. Officials were not confident that acts of sabotage could eliminate the reactor. As Elliott Abrams, the US deputy national security adviser during this episode, recalled, "there was no covert option that would get enough explosives to the site." See Katz (2019b, location 818).
[181] Bush (2010, 421).
[182] Cheney and Cheney (2011, 468).
[183] Trevithick (2018).
[184] Katz (2019a).
[185] Katz (2019b, location 2093)

nuclear program in 2007. Taking out a single plant, therefore, could essentially eliminate its capacity to make a bomb. The reactor was an easy target since it was mostly above ground and not well defended with air defense systems.

Policymakers contrasted the nuclear programs in Iran and Syria based on the existence of sensitive nuclear technology. The Syrian program was much easier to target militarily, officials acknowledged, due to its relatively underdeveloped state.[186] As General Michael Herzog, who was chief of staff to the Israel minister of defense at the time of the al Kibar raid, put it, "The Iranian project is not built around a single reactor [like Syria's], but rather combines the uranium and plutonium tracks within a broad framework of human capital, know-how, facilities, and infrastructures."[187]

The emphasis on human capital underscores that Syria's nuclear program was less "survivable" than Iran's partially due to the relative lack of indigenous knowledge. Officials, even those who supported preventive strikes, knew that Iran had the domestic capacity to rebuild ENR sites that may have been destroyed in a short amount of time, possibly one to three years. Syria, on the other hand, did not. Rather than building up its indigenous human capital, Damascus worked with North Korea to build the reactor. If Israel or the United States destroyed Syria's reactor, it would not have been able to rebuild it without substantial outside help. And, as some of my prior research shows, foreign suppliers are reluctant to help countries rebuild their facilities following preventive strikes.[188] By eliminating that reactor, therefore, Israel and the United States knew they had a chance to level a decisive blow against Syria's nuclear program.

Despite their optimistic assessments, officials – particularly those in Israel – recognized that the mission would become much harder as Syria's nuclear program advanced. There was widespread recognition among Israeli national security officials that the nuclear reactor could not be bombed once it became operational, as this would lead to an environmental disaster. After Israel uncovered the reactor in Syria, Mossad director Meir Dagan said to Olmert that there was time pressure because striking the the facility once it started "burning" nuclear fuel would lead to radioactive contamination along the Euphrates River.[189] This became a major concern for the prime minister. He told a group

---

[186] Katz (2019b, location 217).
[187] Herzog (2018).
[188] Kreps and Fuhrmann (2011).
[189] Clements (2012).

of Israeli military officers, "We can't allow the reactor to go hot and we are already in the midst of planning how to take care of it."[190] When Barak downplayed the danger of striking a hot reactor during a national security meeting in the summer of 2007, others in the room were horrified. According to those present, Gideon Frank, the head of the Israeli Atomic Energy Commission, "blanched and nearly fainted."[191] Israeli officials countered Barak's assertion and explained why striking a was a nonstarter: "For every baby who is born in the next 200 years along the Euphrates with a deformity or a genetic defect, they will blame us straightaway."[192] Echoing this view, Yadlin later said, "No one wanted to be responsible for radioactive material leaking into the Euphrates River and then adversely affecting the lives of generations of Syrians and Iraqis."[193] For Israel, then, attacking early was essential.

Sizing Up Intentions: Was Syria Racing to a Bomb?

Israeli officials were convinced that Syria had a nuclear weapons program and that it was racing to build a bomb. They expressed no doubt about Syria's intentions. "We were able to say with certainty: This reactor is intended to produce plutonium – and for military purposes only," says Yadlin.[194] According to Amnon Sufrin, who headed the intelligence division at the Mossad, intelligence officials told Olmert, "There are no more question marks. Now there are only exclamation points."[195] Given this perception, Israel believed that Syrian nuclear armament would be inevitable in the absence of a military attack.[196]

This view hardened Israel's resolve to launch a preventive strike. After learning about Syria's gambit, Olmert asked his intelligence officials, "what do we do with this [reactor]?" They answered clearly and unambiguously: "We destroy."[197]

The United States, by contrast, was much more uncertain about Syria's intentions. United States intelligence concluded with high confidence that the al Kibar site was a nuclear reactor. However, the CIA had only low confidence that it was part of a nuclear weapons program. The agency reached this conclusion, according to Hayden, because it

---

[190] Katz (2019b, location 1265).
[191] Harel and Benn (2018).
[192] Harel and Benn (2018).
[193] Katz (2019b, location 1188).
[194] Sagir (2017)
[195] Harel and Benn (2018).
[196] Katz (2019b, location 2275).
[197] In Omert's telling, the roles were reversed and he said, "We destroy it." Harel and Benn (2018).

"could not identify the other essentials of a weapons program," including a reprocessing facility or a site dedicated to weaponizing the plutonium.[198] The absence of an ENR capability of any kind in Syria was indeed curious. The country would have needed a reprocessing facility to get bomb-usable plutonium from the reactor's spent nuclear fuel. That US intelligence could not find one raised doubts about the seriousness of Syria's efforts, and also suggested that Damascus was years away from a bomb if it had, in fact, decided to build one. This underscores a tenet of latent nuclear deterrence theory: ENR capabilities become a focal point for assessing a country's intentions and time to a bomb.

The intelligence community's conclusion had a critical effect on the US decision not to carry out a preventive strike. Bush put it plainly: "Mike's report clarified my decision." The president later told Olmert, "I cannot justify an attack on a sovereign nation unless my intelligence agencies stand up and say it's a weapons program."[199] If Syria was not racing to a bomb, there was not an urgent need for a preventive strike. Attacking anyway would invite domestic and international blowback, something about which Bush worried. As Abrams later wrote, "The president thought that the 'low confidence' judgment would leak, as it surely would have, and the United States would have been attacked for conducting the bombing raid despite the 'low confidence' report."[200]

The experience in Iraq magnified these concerns. The intelligence community concluded in the lead up to the March 2003 Iraq War that Saddam Hussein had a concerted nuclear weapons program. The Iraqi dictator's nuclear ambitions became part of the justification for going to war to overthrow his regime. Following the war, however, it became clear that US intelligence had been wrong; there was not a nuclear weapons program in Iraq. United States officials were reluctant to launch a preventive attack against another Middle Eastern country over concerns about nuclear proliferation when the CIA was not confident that a bomb program existed.[201]

Weaponless Deterrence: Nowhere in Sight

Having sensitive nuclear technology can give countries a viable weaponless deterrence option. That Syria did not have any known ENR

[198] Hayden (2011).
[199] Bush (2010, 421). Rice corroborates this assessment. See Rice (2011, 708).
[200] Abrams (2013).
[201] Katz (2019b, location 1519).

capabilities essentially took weaponless deterrence off the table, as the theory expects. Unlike the cases of Iran and North Korea, I was unable to find evidence that US or Israeli officials thought about any form of latent nuclear deterrence during this crisis. Concerns about fomenting proliferation did not appear to be a significant barrier to attacking, nor did the possibility of a delayed nuclear strike. And there was little ambiguity in this case: nobody feared that Syria might already be in possession of a bomb.

Officials in the United States and Israel identified several possible costs of carrying out a preventive strike. A big concern was Syrian conventional retaliation and the possibility of an eventual war.[202] The United States had little appetite for another protracted military conflict in the Middle East. According to Eliot Cohen, who was a State Department official under Rice, "Many in the Administration were deeply reluctant to start what they thought would be a third Middle Eastern war."[203] United States officials also raised normative concerns about carrying out an unprovoked attack. As Gates told the president, "We don't do 'Pearl Harbors'."[204] Bush similarly worried that "bombing a sovereign country with no warning or announced justification would create severe blowback."[205] The lack of US credibility on WMD-related issues in the aftermath of the Iraq War posed another barrier to attacking Syria.[206] However, Syria's ability to inflict punishment on the United States or Israel via weaponless deterrence was not among the potential costs that senior officials cited.

The absence of evidence in the available public record, of course, does not mean that officials never considered the possibility of weaponless deterrence. It is notable, though, that many of the same officials – Gates, Rice, Hayden, and others – talked openly about latent nuclear deterrence in the context of Iran. One key difference between these two countries is that Iran possessed advanced ENR capabilities and could make fissile material for a bomb while Syria's nuclear program was still in a pre-ENR state.

---

[202] Israel believed it could blunt Syrian leader Bashar al Assad's response by giving him a "deniability zone." As General Yossi Baidatz, a senior Israeli intelligence official, characterized the strategy, Assad would show restraint and not retaliate as long as Israel did not "stick the reactor in his face." Katz (2019b, location 1702). By conducting the operation quietly and not admitting involvement (at least initially), Israel believed that it could control escalation by allowing Assad to save face. This view proved to correct, as Syria did not retaliate after Israel bombed the reactor.

[203] Makovsky (2012).

[204] Gates (2014, 173).

[205] Bush (2010, 421).

[206] Gates (2014, 173).

Weighing the Success–Necessity Tradeoff

Overall, the perceptions of Israeli officials were conducive to an early preventive strike against Syria's nuclear reactor. Olmert and most of his advisers believed that Syria was racing to build a bomb. They also recognized that Syria's pre-ENR status made a successful attack more likely, and that the operation would become harder and potentially costlier as Damascus' nuclear capabilities expanded. Given that Syria apparently lacked a plutonium reprocessing capability, it would most likely have been several years away from a bomb in 2007. However, because Olmert saw Syria's nuclear program as an existential threat, waiting was too risky. He prioritized success over necessity.

The situation was different in the United States. Officials in Washington also felt that a preventive strike would be relatively easy given that Syria possessed just one relevant nuclear plant. They knew that attacking early would very likely derail Syria's nuclear program, possibly permanently. But most US policymakers did not believe that Syria was racing to a bomb, nor did they see this possibility as an existential threat. This led many of them to place an emphasis on necessity over success. They emphasized that the situation was not urgent. As Gates put it, "I also thought we had both time and options other than an immediate military strike."[207] Gates and others were prepared to take military action later, if necessary, but did not favor a strike at a time when Syria was so far away from a bomb with uncertain intentions and no detectable reprocessing capability.

There was one cabinet-level official in the United States who saw things close to the way Olmert did: Cheney. The vice president was particularly vocal about the national security threat posed by Syria's actions and he seemingly believed that Damascus would obtain a bomb without external military action, despite the CIA's "low confidence" conclusion. These views led Cheney to favor an immediate military strike, like his Israeli counterparts.[208] He argued that the United States should "attack the site, the sooner the better," according to Gates.[209] Even within the same country, then, varying perceptions about national security threats and a potential proliferator's intentions can produce different policy recommendations.

Conclusion

This chapter investigated preventive strikes against nuclear programs. It identified the cases in which countries have considered using military

---

[207] Gates (2014, 173).
[208] Cheney and Cheney (2011, 470).
[209] Gates (2014, 173).

force to stop or delay nuclear weapons proliferation during peacetime. The chapter then probed latent nuclear deterrence theory by examining four of these cases: United States–Iran, United States–North Korea, Israel–Syria, and United States–Syria. The case studies generated four main findings that are largely – but not entirely – consistent with the theory.

First, pursuing sensitive nuclear technology while seemingly racing to a bomb provoked nonproliferation-related crises. Countries frequently considered preventive strikes when an adversary had the capacity to make fissile material, a key ingredient for a bomb, and was apparently bent on arming. Twelve cases of preventive strike consideration – 67 percent of the total number – fit this profile. This evidence is consistent with a key finding from Chapter 5: ENR-capable states reap fewer benefits and may invite insecurity when they launch unrestrained nuclear programs.

Second, a state's perceptions of a potential proliferator's intentions influenced whether nuclear programs provoke or deter military conflict. Israeli officials were highly motivated to strike Syria's nuclear reactor in 2007 because they believed that Damascus was bent on arming. Perceptions of nonrestraint played a role in bringing the United States to the brink of attacking North Korea in the mid-1990 as well. By contrast, US officials were unsure whether Syria and Iran were racing to a bomb, which lessened the perceived need for a preventive attack.

Third, states in possession of sensitive nuclear technology can engage in weaponless deterrence more effectively than their non-ENR-capable counterparts. In the two cases where the target of military force had the means to make fissile material (United States–Iran and United States–North Korea), at least one of the means of latent nuclear deterrence weighed on the minds of officials contemplating an attack. In the United States–Iran case, multiple officials across Republican and Democratic administrations worried that attacking Iranian nuclear facilities would backfire by motivating Tehran to more feverishly push toward a bomb. Deterrence by proliferation was viable in this case because many US officials did not perceive that Iran was racing to arm after 2003. When it came to North Korea, some US officials and other commentators opposed a military attack in 1993–94 on the grounds that Pyongyang might already be in possession of one to two nuclear weapons. However, others – most notably Secretary of Defense Perry – indicated that North Korea's conventional forces were the biggest deterrent. Perry further revealed that deterrence by proliferation was a primary factor in his thinking about North Korea in the late 1990s, after the nuclear crisis had subsided. By contrast, in the case of Syria – a country that lacked

ENR technology – I found no evidence that US or Israeli policymakers thought seriously about deterrence by proliferation, delayed attack, or doubt. If such evidence exists, it is far less pervasive than it is in other cases, based on information that is currently publicly available.

Fourth, the perceived likelihood of operational success in a preventive strike declines as a state's nuclear program advances. ENR-capable countries are more likely to have expansive nuclear programs and substantial indigenous knowledge. Succeeding therefore requires destroying several key facilities, and razed infrastructure can be rebuilt relatively quickly. This reality raised the barriers to attacking in the United States–Iran case. Some officials similarly worried about operational success during the North Korea crisis, as well as causing environmental contamination by attacking a reactor. These concerns were not universally shared, however, and some appeared confident that the reactor should be safely destroyed with relative ease. When it came to Syria, many in Israel and the United States acknowledged that the early stage of Syria's nuclear program – the reactor it was constructing in secret was not yet operational – made operational success easier. Destroying a single nuclear plant may be enough to deal a serious blow to its bomb-making capacity, officials believed, with a smaller risk of environmental contamination. Attacking early depends on the perception of an existential threat if the target obtains nuclear weapons. In the absence of such a threat perception, officials are likely to prioritize necessity over success, waiting to strike until the target makes a mad dash for a bomb. Perceptions of an existential threat contributed to Israel's decision to attack, while a less extreme threat perception led the United States to prioritize necessity over success.

These conclusions are subject to three important caveats. First, latent nuclear deterrence theory helps us better understand the history of preventive strikes against nuclear programs, but it is by no means the only relevant explanation. Factors emphasized by other research, including threats of conventional retaliation, also play a key role in this context. Fully explaining when countries consider using military force to delay nuclear proliferation requires drawing on multiple factors, not just those emphasized by latent deterrence. Second, there is a small number of relevant cases. As a result, our understanding of preventive strikes could change in the future on the basis of a small number of incidents, possibly just a single attack. Third, because the cases I examined occurred relatively recently, we do not yet have access to many relevant government documents. The story could evolve as formerly classified documents emerge in the coming years and decades.

7   Arms Races: Deterring Weapons Proliferation

Saudi Crown Prince Mohammed bin Salman drew international attention in March 2018 when he proclaimed that if Iran "developed a nuclear bomb, we will follow suit as soon as possible."[1] Around the same time, media reports indicated that Saudi Arabia coveted dual-use uranium enrichment technology that could be used to make nuclear fuel – or, potentially, material for bombs. Many observers around the world took this as evidence that Saudi Arabia was bent on obtaining nuclear weapons. A CNBC headline, for example, seemingly left little doubt about bin Salman's intentions: "Saudi Crown Prince Threatens to Develop a Nuke as Kingdom Seeks Foreign Nuclear Technology."

However, neither Saudi Arabia's pursuit of sensitive nuclear technology nor the Crown Prince's comments imply that Saudi Arabia has a dedicated bomb program. His statement was conditional: Saudi Arabia will build nuclear weapons, he said, *only if Iran does*. Otherwise, as the Crown Prince stated, "Saudi Arabia does not want to acquire any nuclear bomb."[2] Thus, bin Salman's words represented a deterrent threat to Iran. He was signaling to Iranian officials something like, "you will pay a big price if you build a bomb, but if you keep your nuclear powder dry we will too." Framed in this way, Saudi Arabia was posturing to stop Iran from building nuclear weapons – not necessarily revealing a desire to obtain a bomb imminently.

Bin Salman's apparent strategy is hardly unique. Countries frequently seek sensitive nuclear technology in order to gain leverage. Their goal is not necessarily to build nuclear weapons. It is instead to use the *possibility* of obtaining the bomb in order to stop an adversary from weaponizing its nuclear program. Does this strategy work?

This chapter provides the answer. According to latent nuclear deterrence theory, it is possible for countries to deter an arms race by (implicitly) threatening to "go nuclear" if their rival arms. But doing so

---

[1] Quoted in Sanger and Broad (2018).
[2] Quoted in Reuters (2018).

depends on meeting several conditions: possessing enrichment or repro-cessing (ENR) technology, stakes high enough to make the defender's proliferation threat credible and sufficiently costly for the potential challenger, and having a restrained nuclear program. On top of this, weaponless deterrence in this context becomes more difficult if the potential challenger has third-party rivals that already possess nuclear weapons or are racing to build them.

I conducted six cases of potential nuclear armament to evaluate the theory's causal logic. In each of these cases, one country (the defender) attempted to stop another (the challenger) from arming by threatening to build its own nuclear weapons. Only one case, Brazil, met all of the theory's conditions for success. The possibility of inducing an Argentine bomb contributed to Brazilian nuclear restraint, as the theory expects. Despite facing a third-party threat from the United Kingdom, Brazil's bomb-making potential similarly encouraged Argentina to keep its nuclear powder dry. In the other cases, deterrence by proliferation failed because one or more of the theory's conditions was not met. These cases illustrate that, when it comes to nuclear armament, meeting the conditions for successful weaponless deterrence can be challenging in practice.

Understanding Nuclear Proliferation and Arms Races

Arms races figure prominently in international relations scholarship.[3] Most research focuses on the consequences of arms races for war and instability, leaving their causes relatively underexplored.[4] Yet a number of studies seek to understand why countries develop and field military technologies – drones, aircraft carriers, missiles, nuclear weapons, and others.[5] Decisions about whether to obtain military capabilities are complex. Many factors – not just one or two – shape whether military technologies spread internationally. Technological constraints, foreign assistance, bureaucratic politics, international norms and law, status considerations, and national security threats all play a role in this context.

One factor is particularly relevant for this chapter's analysis: the capabilities of adversaries. Many scholars and policymakers have argued that countries obtain military capabilities when their rivals do so. This argument, sometimes called "domino theory" or "reactive proliferation,"

---

[3] For a review of this literature, see Sample (2021).
[4] See Glaser (2000) and Rider (2009).
[5] See, for example, Sagan (1996), Hymans (2006), Solingen (2007), Horowitz (2010), Fuhrmann and Horowitz (2017), and Early et al. (2022).

is particularly prominent in the nuclear weapons context.[6] In this view, one country's development of nuclear weapons causes others to follow suit. The US Manhattan Project, for example, immediately prompted the Soviet weapons program and eventually contributed to the Chinese and North Korean nuclear arsenals. This line of thinking pervades public discourse about nuclear weapons. In the words of nuclear experts William Potter and Gaukhar Mukhatzhanova, many people assume "that one state's nuclearization is likely to trigger decisions by other states to 'go nuclear' in quick succession," often invoking "imagery and metaphors of nuclear dominoes and proliferation chains."[7]

Studies evaluating domino theory typically focus on how one state's possession of nuclear weapons influences the likelihood that its rivals explore, pursue, or acquire a similar capability. Yet the logic can be extended to a situation where a country faces a nuclear-capable rival who has not already armed. We saw evidence in Chapter 4 that countries were statistically more likely to obtain latency when they had a latent (or already-nuclear-armed) rival. The next step is to find out whether these states go further and actually assemble nuclear bombs.

At least one other scholar has considered that the presence of a nuclear-capable rival could be positive from a nonproliferation standpoint. Political scientist George Quester introduced the concept of "no-first proliferation."[8] This idea holds that, when a pair of countries each has bomb-making capabilities, neither will arm first because they know that this will cause the other to follow suit. However, we do not fully understand what it takes to make this strategy successful. Drawing on latent nuclear deterrence theory, I identify the conditions that influence whether nuclear latency deters nuclear armament.

Latent Nuclear Deterrence Theory and Nuclear Armament

Latent nuclear deterrence theory expects that countries can potentially leverage their nuclear programs to deter their adversaries from arming. But doing so is challenging. For starters, just one mechanism – deterrence by proliferation – has the potential to stop a country from building nuclear weapons. Deterrence by delayed attack and doubt lack viability because threats to carry out nuclear attacks in retaliation for possessing (or attempting to possess) nuclear weapons are not

---

[6] See Sagan (1996) and Miller (2014a).
[7] Potter and Mukhatzhanova (2008, 139).
[8] Quester (1991, 225).

credible. These two mechanisms, therefore, cannot compensate for the weaknesses of proliferation threats as an instrument of deterrence, as they can for military conflict.

To succeed in halting another state's armament, countries must meet three conditions. At this point in the book, these conditions should be familiar. Let's briefly review the conditions for success in the context of nuclear weapons proliferation.

First, having sensitive nuclear technology is critical for deterring armament by another country. States with operational ENR facilities could build a bomb quicker than their non-ENR-capable counterparts. Having this technology therefore makes it difficult for the challenger to elude punishment: A potential proliferator knows that if they go nuclear their opponent could follow suit relatively quickly. The punishment costs would be discounted less than if the defender lacked an ENR capability since the challenger knows that any advantage it gained would be short lived. On top of this, operating an ENR plant allows countries to communicate a simple message: "if you build a bomb, I can do it too."[9]

The scale of a state's ENR program may influence how useful it is for halting armament by another country. Laboratory-scale ENR capabilities may bolster deterrence, but larger-scale fissile material production programs should have greater value. The ENR programs that could reasonably produce enough material for at least one bomb generate shorter time lags for the imposition of punishment and send a stronger signal to foreign observers. Government officials might not notice or care if another country is producing small quantities of plutonium or enriched uranium in a laboratory.

The stakes represent a second key condition. When it comes to deterring nuclear armament, a rivalry between the challenger and the defender raises the stakes in ways that increase the likelihood of success. A defender's threat to arm is more credible among rivals because the challenger's possession of nuclear weapons would constitute a substantial nuclear security threat. Moreover, the defender's implementation of the threat would impose greater costs on the challenger compared to a situation where the two countries were not rivals.[10]

A third condition for success is having a restrained nuclear program. Reassuring other states that nuclear proliferation is not inevitable is

---

[9] This assumes that others will know about a state's operational ENR capability. As in the case of military conflict, secret capabilities cannot deter.

[10] Chapter 5 showed that deterrence by proliferation can work among allies when the United States is the target of a threat. But the United States is a unique case. Because of its superpower status, Washington generally opposes the spread of nuclear weapons to everyone, both allies and adversaries. See Kroenig (2014a).

essential for deterring nuclear armament, since deterrence by doubt or delayed attack are not viable in this context. Failing to do so puts countries in a perilous situation: They will not be unable to deter rivals from arming while at the same time amplifying their adversaries' incentives to build bombs. Having an ENR-capable rival with an unrestrained program is therefore a scenario primed for nuclear proliferation.

Third parties can play the role of spoiler when it comes to deterring armament with proliferation threats. Showing nuclear restraint may not dampen another country's resolve to seek an arsenal if it faces nuclear threats from a third party. The prospect of inducing an Indian bomb, for instance, did not restrain China's program because Chinese leaders were mostly worried about nuclear threats emanating from the United States and the Soviet Union. Anything India may have done to reassure China about its intentions, then, would probably not have stopped Chinese weaponization. Successful weaponless deterrence in this context therefore depends on all of a country's rivals having nuclear restraint (this includes not already possessing assembled weapons), not just one.

Research Strategy

Testing the theory in the context of nuclear armament presents a challenge that is similar to the one described in Chapter 6: There are very few relevant cases. Only ten countries have built nuclear weapons. I therefore do not have enough variation to carry out a rigorous statistical test of the predictions along the lines of what I did in Chapter 5. Instead, I take the same approach as in Chapter 6. I probe the theory's causal mechanisms by examining key cases of deterrence by proliferation. My research objective is to assess whether leaders were thinking along the lines that latent nuclear deterrence theory suggests as they contemplated their nuclear futures.

This chapter's analysis focuses on the behavior and thinking of countries that could challenge the status quo by arming with nuclear weapons. I classify potential proliferators as countries with full nuclear latency according to the Nuclear Latency (NL) database. These states had the technological foundation for a bomb program and could have conceivably armed. I pair each of these countries with their strategic rivals.[11] The rivals seek to stop the potential proliferators from arming,

---

[11] I identify rivalries based on Colaresi et al. (2007). For the purpose of my analysis in this chapter, I consider two cases to be rivalries even though they are not included in the Colaresi et al. (2007) database: United States–North Korea and France–Soviet Union. If I excluded these cases, France and North Korea would shift from Category 3 to Category 1 in Table 7.1.

preserving the status quo if they are successful. The presence of a rivalry induces high stakes, as I have described.

Table 7.1 places each potential proliferator into one of four categories based on its rival's ENR status and the political aims of the rival's nuclear program (restrained or unrestrained). I identify a program as unrestrained based on the challenger's perceptions of the target's intentions, as in Chapter 6. However, there is a key difference: I place a potential proliferator in one of the unrestrained categories (3 or 4) if *any* of its rivals have an unrestrained program. To appear in Category 1 or 2, therefore, *all* of the potential proliferator's rivals must have restrained nuclear programs. This is to account for the role that third-party rivals can play in stymieing effective deterrence by proliferation. As before, I classify countries in possession of nuclear weapons as having unrestrained programs, in addition to nonnuclear states that meet the criteria first spelled out in Chapter 5. I similarly consider whether a potential proliferator has at least one ENR-capable rival. If it does, the potential proliferator appears in Category 2 or 4, even if other rivals are ENR-free. Thus, the relevant categories for this chapter's analysis are as follows.

- **Category 1** No rivals possess sensitive nuclear technology and all rivals have restrained nuclear programs.
- **Category 2** At least one rival possesses sensitive nuclear technology and all rivals have restrained nuclear programs.
- **Category 3** No rivals possess sensitive nuclear technology and at least one rival has an unrestrained program.
- **Category 4** At least one rival possesses sensitive nuclear technology and at least one rival has an unrestrained program.

The table classifies a rival as ENR-capable if it had full nuclear latency in a given year. However, it also identifies the cases where a rival had partial latency. If I classified rivals with at least partial latency as ENR-capable, one case would shift from Category 1 to Category 2 and eight cases would shift from Category 3 to Category 4 for at least one year.

Potential proliferators can shift between groups over time. For example, China moved from Category 3 to Category 4 after India achieved full nuclear latency in 1964. Table 7.1 also shows that countries can end up in Category 1 for two reasons: Their rivals lack full ENR capabilities or they do not have any rivals in a given year. The end of the Argentine-Brazilian rivalry, for instance, explains why Brazil shifts from Category 2 to Category 1 after 1985.

Table 7.1 shows that some of the categories have just a handful of proliferation opportunities, underscoring the difficulty in making

Table 7.1 *Case evidence for nuclear armament.*

	Rival no ENR	Rival ENR
Rival restrained	**Category 1** Belgium: 1966–74 (Rival: none) Brazil: 1986–2010 (Rival: none) Canada: 1948–56 (Rival: none) Germany: 1967–2010 (Rival: East Germany) Israel: 1965–67[a] (Rivals: Egypt, Iraq, Jordan, Syria) Italy: 1970–90 (Rival: none) Japan: 1975–95 (Rival: none) Netherlands: 1973–2010 (Rival: none) Norway: 1961–68 (Rival: none) South Africa: 1974–78[a], 1991–98 (Rivals: Angola, Mozambique, Zambia, Zimbabwe) Spain: 1967–71 (Rival: Morocco) USA: 1943–44 (Rivals: Germany[b], Japan)	**Category 2** Brazil: 1985 (Rival: Argentina)
Rival unrestrained	**Category 3** Argentina: 1983–84, 1986–97 (Rivals: Brazil[b], Chile, UK) China: 1963 (Rivals: India[b], Russia, Taiwan, USA) France: 1954–60[a] (Rivals: West Germany[b], USSR) India: 1965–74[a] (Rivals: China, Pakistan[b]) Iran: 2003, 2006–10 (Rivals: Egypt, Iraq, Israel, Saudi Arabia) Iraq: 1990–91 (Rivals: Egypt, Iran[b], Israel, Kuwait, Saudi Arabia, Syria) Japan: 1996–2010 (Rival: China) North Korea: 1989–93[a] (Rivals: South Korea[b], USA) Pakistan: 1979–88[a] (Rivals: Afghanistan, India) Russia: 1948–49[a] (Rivals: China, Poland, UK[b], USA, Yugoslavia) UK: 1951–52[a] (Rival: Russia) USA, 1945[a] (Rivals: Germany[b], Japan, Russia[b])	**Category 4** Argentina: 1985 (Rivals: Brazil, Chile, UK) China: 1964[a] (Rivals: India, Taiwan, Russia, USA) India: 1964 (Rivals: China, Pakistan)

Notes: [a]Potential proliferator assembled a nuclear weapon. [b]Rival had partial nuclear latency.

meaningful statistical comparisons across these groups. It is especially significant that just one country – Brazil – appears in Category 2. This is where deterrence by proliferation is most likely to be successful. The presence of a single case here reveals that meeting the conditions for success has been difficult over the past seventy years. Moreover, the existence of two rivals with full nuclear latency is fleeting. When this situation emerged (Categories 2 and 4), it persisted for just a single year. Historically, one of two things happened to render this state of the world short-lived: One or both of the ENR-capable rivals went on to build nuclear weapons, or the rivalry ended swiftly.

Nuclear armament occurred in Categories 1, 3, and 4. The latter two were particularly dangerous from a nuclear proliferation standpoint, as latent nuclear deterrence theory expects. Seven of the twelve countries in Category 3 armed and three of the other five had unrestrained nuclear programs at least some of the time they were in this group. Two of the three countries in Category 4 armed or launched an unrestrained program. In Category 1, by contrast, four of the thirteen countries built nuclear weapons or were racing to a bomb. Some states in Category 1 did not have any rivals, reducing their need for nuclear weapons on national security grounds. Others had rivals but those states were incapable of credibly stopping nuclear weapons proliferation by threatening to arm, removing a key barrier to armament.

I examine six of the cases shown in Table 7.1: Argentina, Brazil, France, India, Pakistan, and South Africa. These cases represent all four categories. They provide variation on key variables: the rival's nuclear capabilities, perceptions of the rival's intentions, the existence of third-party nuclear threats, and whether the country ultimately build nuclear weapons. Brazil is a critical case for evaluating latent nuclear deterrence theory since it is the only one that satisfies all of the conditions for success. I therefore spend the most time on this case. Because the cases of Argentina and Brazil are inexorably linked, I examine both of them together. I take the same approach for India and Pakistan.

Predictions

Table 7.2 lists the evidence that latent nuclear deterrence theory expects in all six cases, along with a summary of the findings. Sitting in Category 2, the Brazilian case should turn up "smoking gun" evidence in favor of the theory. Brazilian leaders should perceive proliferation threats based on Argentina's ENR capabilities, especially after Buenos Aires achieved full nuclear latency in 1983, allowing them to understand the consequences of arming. Moreover, if the theory is correct, the

Table 7.2 *Expectations for nuclear armament in six case studies.*

Category number	Case	LND theory's expectations	Prediction confirmed?
1	South Africa Rival: Nigeria	• Officials see rival's nuclear response as noncredible.	Yes
1 and 2	Brazil Rival: Argentina	• Officials take notice of rival's nuclear capabilities. • Officials perceive flexibility in rival's nuclear policy. • Officials worry that weaponization could cause rival to arm (pre-1985).	Yes Yes Yes
3	France Rival: West Germany Third party: USSR	• Officials take notice of rival's nuclear capabilities. • Officials worry that weaponization could cause rival to arm (pre-1955). • Warning relations reduce concerns about rival arming (post-1955). • Third party's building of nuclear weapons encourages armament.	Yes Yes Yes Yes
3	Pakistan Rival: India	• Officials take notice of rival's nuclear capabilities. • Officials perceive rival's nuclear program as unrestrained. • Rival's nuclear program causes officials to race to a bomb.	Yes Yes Yes
3 and 4	Argentina Rival: Brazil Third party: UK	• Officials take notice of rival's nuclear capabilities. • Officials perceive flexibility in rival's nuclear policy. • Officials worry that weaponization could cause rival to arm (pre-1985). • Third party's building of nuclear weapons encourages armament.	Yes Yes Yes Partially
3 and 4	India Rival: Pakistan Third party: China	• Officials do not worry about rival's nuclear response (pre-1973). • Officials take notice of rival's nuclear capabilities (especially post-1979). • Officials perceive rival's nuclear program as unrestrained (post-1972). • Third party's building of nuclear weapons encourages armament.	Yes Yes Yes Yes

possibility of inducing an Argentine bomb should have helped rein in Brazil's nuclear program. In order for this to be true, Brazilian officials must also perceive flexibility in Argentina's nuclear policy.

Argentina came close to meeting the theory's criteria for success. It had an ENR-capable rival with a restrained nuclear program (Brazil). However, Argentina ends up in Categories 3 and 4 because it also faced a third-party nuclear threat from the United Kingdom. The theory expects Argentine leaders to take notice of Brazil's bomb-making potential, particularly once it achieved full nuclear latency in 1985. Officials should reveal an understanding that pushing toward weaponization would be costly, as it might compel Brazil to follow suit. Yet the perceived nuclear threat from the United Kingdom should push Argentina toward a bomb anyway, especially after the country's defeat in the 1982 Falklands War.

South Africa had several rivals, but none of them were ENR-capable, putting it in Category 1. Nigeria attempted to halt South Africa's nuclear weapons program by threatening to build nuclear weapons. The theory expects this attempt at deterrence by proliferation to fail because Nigeria did not have the technological capabilities needed to make its threat credible.

The French case appears in Category 3. France had a longstanding rivalry with (West) Germany that persisted until 1955, ten years after the end of World War II. West Germany obtained partial nuclear latency in the late-1940s but did not become fully latent until 1967. Bonn's bomb-making capabilities were therefore not yet optimized for success at the time France first assembled a nuclear bomb in 1960. France also faced a third-party nuclear threat from the Soviet Union, which first became nuclear-armed in 1949. The theory expects French officials to worry about inducing a West German bomb as Bonn expanded its ability to produce fissile materials. But three factors should cut against the viability of weaponless deterrence: West Germany only made it to partial latency, the Franco-German rivalry ended in 1955, and the threat from the Soviet Union created incentives to arm irrespective of possible West German responses.

India and Pakistan used proliferation threats in hopes of keeping the other country nonnuclear. The theory expects failure in both cases, which appear in Categories 3 or 4. Pakistan obtained partial nuclear latency in 1973 and became fully latent six years later. This should make it difficult for Pakistan to make its proliferation threats credible prior to India's 1974 nuclear test. As Pakistan's ENR capabilities advance, particularly after 1979, Indian officials should view these threats as more believable. At that point, however, leaders in New Delhi should be undeterred due to perceptions that Pakistan was bent on arming.

On top of this, a third-party nuclear threat from China should push India toward a nuclear weapon. India had the capabilities needed to make proliferation threats credible at least since 1964, when it obtained full nuclear latency. However, the perception of an unrestrained nuclear program in Islamabad should erode India's ability to deter Pakistani nuclear armament, if the theory is correct.

The evidence is largely supportive of these expectations. The biggest surprise is that Argentina's rivalry with the United Kingdom did not render Brazil's attempts at deterrence by proliferation feeble. Although the Falklands War accelerated Argentina's nuclear program, it did not result in an Argentine bomb. In the end, there is stronger support for weaponless deterrence in this case than the theory expected. Although the evidence is supportive of the theory overall, this does not imply that latent nuclear deterrence comes easily. On the contrary, the case evidence will illustrate the many ways that deterrence by proliferation can fail.

Success Story: Arms Racing and Weaponless Deterrence in Latin America

Policymakers and scholars frequently point to Argentina and Brazil as success stories for nuclear nonproliferation. The two Latin American states were once embroiled in a rivalry that lasted more than a century. As their strategic competition persisted after World War II, leaders in both countries invested in sensitive dual-use nuclear technology. Many international observers feared that Argentina and Brazil would weaponize their latent nuclear capacity, setting off a regional arms race. In the end, however, they agreed to keep their nuclear powder dry. In 1991, both countries signed a treaty formally forswearing nuclear weapons and establishing a regional organization to verify compliance.

Latent nuclear deterrence theory helps us better understand this outcome. Argentina and Brazil refrained from arming partially because they recognized that doing so would trigger an arms race. Finding evidence from Argentina in support of the theory is somewhat unexpected. The environment was less favorable in this case because of the third-party nuclear threat Argentina faced from the United Kingdom. In the pages that follow, I will discuss the conditions for success in the context of these two cases. I will then present evidence that government officials were thinking along the lines the theory expects.

The Rivalry

Argentina and Brazil had a strategic rivalry from 1817 to 1985.[12] There was a size disparity – Brazil had a larger population but Argentina had a higher GDP per capita – that led both countries to fear that they would be exploited by the other.[13] Armed conflict did not erupt between the two countries during the nuclear age, but there were some serious points of tension. From 1967 to 1979, for example, they were embroiled in a dispute over the Itaipu Dam.[14] The Itaipu dispute was "so emotional," according to Oscar Camilión, who served as Argentina's Foreign Minister and Defense Minister, "because it was a question of boundaries, a territorial question."[15] Tensions remained high even after Argentina and Brazil settled the Itaipu conflict. As one indication of this, on two occasions in 1985, Brazilian military planes flew over Argentina's most sensitive nuclear facility – the Pilcaniyeu enrichment plant – in apparent shows of force.[16]

The relationship between the two countries was not among the most severe post-1945 rivalries in international politics owing to the absence of war. It is clear, though, that apprehension and competition characterized the bilateral relationship as the two countries ramped up their nuclear programs. Luiz Felipe Lampreia, an advisor to the Brazilian foreign minister, recalled that "there was a climate of almost paranoid tension."[17] He added, "The establishments in both countries – the bureaucracies and the military – were very much inclined toward an antagonistic relationship. The military [in Brazil] had been formed under the idea that the most likely war scenario came from Argentina . . . There was, therefore, fertile ground for contentious disagreements to get out of control."[18] Reubens Ricupero, who headed the Americas Department in the Brazilian Foreign Ministry in the 1980s, conveyed a similar view when he said, "during most of their history Brazil and Argentina had a difficult relationship . . . In some moments even the hypothesis of war had been mentioned."[19] Sebastiao do Rego Barros, a seasoned Brazilian

---

[12] Colaresi et al. (2007, 38).

[13] Mallea et al. (2012, 39).

[14] Argentina contested the development of this dam, which Brazil was building jointly with Paraguay, because it could alter the flow of the Parana River, an important waterway that ends in Argentina. See DeYoung (1977).

[15] Mallea et al. (2012, 39).

[16] Mallea et al. (2012, 127).

[17] Mallea et al. (2012, 40).

[18] Mallea et al. (2012, 15–16).

[19] Mallea et al. (2012, 121).

nuclear negotiator, likewise acknowledged that the "atmosphere was very tense" while also asserting that he was "shocked when I learned that the situation between Brazil and Argentina was being compared with the one between India and Pakistan," presumably because those countries had fought multiple wars since their independence in 1947.[20]

The strategic competition meant that threats to build nuclear weapons were meaningful; carrying them out would be costly for the other side. To be sure, during the period of their rivalry, neither country wanted the other to arm with nuclear weapons. Brazilian diplomat Roberto Abdenur captured the prevailing feeling on both sides when he wrote in a formerly secret government document, "it appeared important to me that the two countries at some time examine the question of how to prevent the search for autonomy in the fuel cycle from degenerating into a nuclear race in the worst sense of the expression."[21]

As the 1980s progressed, relations between the two countries began to warm. By 1987, Ricupero indicated that there was "great harmony" in the relationship, adding that "when we started it seemed unimaginable that we could arrive at that point."[22] The improvement of bilateral relations made deterrence by proliferation less viable after the late 1980s. As we will see later, however, credible threats to build nuclear weapons contributed to emergence of a more-cooperative environment.

The Race for Sensitive Nuclear Technology

Argentina was the first country in Latin America to harness sensitive nuclear technology. It produced a laboratory-scale reprocessing facility that operated from 1968 to 1973. In 1978, Argentine officials announced a plan to build a larger-scale reprocessing plant at the Ezeiza Atomic Center, just outside of Buenos Aires. Shortly thereafter, however, the country turned its attention toward uranium enrichment technology, carrying out experimental work in this area by the early 1980s. In 1983, Carlos Castro Madero, the Chairman of Argentina's National Atomic Energy Commission, announced to the world that his country had achieved success with a pilot-scale enrichment plant. This plant continued to operate until 1997, at which time Argentina shifted its attention to a new indigenously developed enrichment process known as *Sigma*. Buenos Aires now operates a commercial-scale enrichment facility using this technology.

[20] Mallea et al. (2012, 50).
[21] Abdenur (1985).
[22] Mallea et al. (2012, 121).

Brazil initially lagged behind in the nuclear sector, but it was determined eventually to match Argentina's capabilities. A 1968 Brazilian document reveals that Brasilia perceived a potential vulnerability from the moment Argentina's ENR program got off the ground. The document concluded that "Argentina is five years ahead of the Brazilian nuclear program," and that the "race to the full development between Argentina and Brazil is an incentive that exists in the minds of many Brazilian institutions and which serves as a stimulus and point of comparison."[23] In 1974, the Brazilian government concluded that it "should not postpone a decision on the question of the second [nuclear] reactor and of the uranium enrichment plant" given that Argentina "already possesses a chemical reprocessing plant."[24] This sentiment continued through the late 1970s, a period that Lampreia characterized as "a delicate moment" since "there was the awareness that Argentina had an advantage because it had started first in this technological race."[25]

Brazil first succeeded with a laboratory-scale enrichment program in 1979, more than a decade after Argentina. Despite this success, it remained determined to equalize Argentina's advancements. Luiz Augusto de Castro Neves, who served in the Brazilian National Security Council during the 1980s, made an explicit connection between Argentina's nuclear program and Brazil's efforts. He recalled a meeting in which a technician "wrote $y = fx$ on the blackboard and said: 'Brazil is y and Argentina is x, because what we do will depend very much from the behavior of the Argentine variable.'"[26] In 1982, Brazilian Congressman Herbert Levy told US officials that Brazil could not allow Argentina to have "its hands with exclusivity an instrument so threatening as the capability to produce atomic bombs." He went on to warn, "the moment would come when they [Argentina] would possess the necessary technology with certain exclusivity" in the absence of action by Brazil.[27] The CIA reached a similar conclusion during this period. A December 1985 document concluded that "Argentina's surprise announcement in late 1983 of an enrichment capability has greatly spurred the Brazilians."[28]

---

[23] Argentine Ministry of Foreign Relations (1968).
[24] Silveira (1974b).
[25] Mallea et al. (2012, 41–42).
[26] Mallea et al. (2012, 117).
[27] Levy (1982).
[28] US Central Intelligence Agency (1985a).

Throughout the 1980s Brazil made progress in the development and operation of enrichment plants using the gas centrifuge process.[29] In 1987, the government announced that it had mastered this enrichment technology at its Aramar facility.[30] Brazil now possesses a large-scale enrichment plant in Resende, near Rio de Janeiro.

A Signal and Focal Point

According to latent nuclear deterrence theory, ENR capabilities are significant because they shorten the time it would take to build a bomb and communicate a "shot across the bow" to other countries. Sensitive nuclear technology had these expected effects in the case of Argentina and Brazil.

For ENR programs to have political effects, the intended audience must know about them. Argentina and Brazil carried out key nuclear activities in secret beginning in 1979.[31] As a result, complete assessments of ENR capabilities were not always available in real time – but each country eventually learned about the other's progress. Argentina's reprocessing activities were conducted openly but the government concealed its enrichment work. According to Neves, Argentina's 1983 enrichment announcement caught Brazil by surprise. "There was an expectation on our part that sooner or later Argentina would develop reprocessing technology because it was more compatible with its line of reactors," he said, but "no one knew of the enrichment intentions."[32] Brazil seems to have learned about this for the first time from a letter sent by President Reynaldo Bignone shortly before Castro Madero's public revelation.[33] Officials in Argentina, by contrast, knew about Brazil's centrifuge program from a very early stage.[34] Brazilian President José Sarney deployed Ambassador Ricupero to inform Argentine President Raúl Alfonsín of Brazil's enrichment breakthrough prior to the 1987 public announcement.[35] But this meeting merely confirmed the broad contours of what Argentine officials apparently already knew.

Assessments of both states' nuclear proliferation potential focused heavily on their ENR capabilities. A 1967 Argentine analysis concluded that it would take "at least ten years" for Brazil to build a bomb in

[29] Dunlap (2018).
[30] Mallea et al. (2012, 18).
[31] Mallea et al. (2012, 65).
[32] Mallea et al. (2012, 72).
[33] Mallea et al. (2012, 70).
[34] Mallea et al. (2012, 22).
[35] Mallea et al. (2012, 190).

part because it "lacks uranium and has no plutonium."[36] The CIA reached a similar conclusion in 1968, noting that "The largest gap [in Brazil's bomb-making capacity], of course, is the lack of fissionable material, with the production via gas centrifuges apparently being a long way away."[37] As each side learned about the other's ENR-related advancements, however, the proliferation timelines shortened considerably. In January 1982, Castro Madero said publicly, "I believe that Brazil and Argentina can make an atomic bomb in a short time, say 3 to 5 years."[38] At the time of Argentina's 1983 enrichment announcement, Brazil estimated that Buenos Aires "could have a nuclear device by the mid-1980s."[39]

More than just shortening proliferation timelines, ENR advancements made the prospect of nuclear weapons proliferation front page news – literally. Following Argentina's 1983 announcement, for instance, the Brazilian Newspaper *Folha de São Paulo* ran a story on its front page indicating that Argentina "was now in a position to build a nuclear weapon."[40] Given the attention afforded to ENR breakthroughs, both countries were forced to consider the possibility of nuclear armament in ways that they otherwise would not. They now understood that if they misstepped and threatened their ENR-capable adversary, nuclear armament may result. This left at least some officials feeling unsettled. According to Lampreia, who was part of the foreign minister's cabinet in the late 1970s, Argentina's 1978 announcement about the Ezeiza reprocessing plant "caused great concern." He characterized it as "perhaps the moment of greatest anxiety in the bilateral relationship."[41] Feeling anxious about the future can compel a country to change its behavior. By raising the specter of armament, then, Argentina's deployment of sensitive nuclear technology bolstered latent nuclear deterrence.

A diplomatic overture made by Brazil in the aftermath of Argentina's 1983 enrichment announcement underscores that ENR advancements can produce behavioral changes by heightening the risk of nuclear armament in the near future. Less than one month after Castro Madero informed the world of Argentina's enrichment breakthrough, Brazilian Foreign Minister Saraiva Guerreiro proposed to his Argentine counterpart that both countries forswear peaceful nuclear explosions (PNEs).[42]

---

[36] Argentine Naval Intelligence Service (1967).
[37] US Department of State (1968).
[38] FBIS (1982b).
[39] Coutto (2014, 317).
[40] Mallea et al. (2012, 18).
[41] Mallea et al. (2012, 55–56).
[42] Mallea et al. (2012, 91).

This timing could be coincidental, but at least one official drew a causal connection between the two events. Recounting the situation years later, Neves said, "Undoubtedly the Argentine announcement that it had succeeded in developing the process of uranium enrichment by gaseous diffusion must have influenced the Brazilian posture to make that initial tentative offer."[43] Based on this line of thinking, Argentina's enrichment breakthrough heightened concerns in Brazil about an Argentine bomb, making Brasilia willing to restrain its own capabilities if Buenos Aires agreed to do the same.

Flexible Nuclear Futures

Scholars sometimes characterize the competition between Argentina and Brazil as an arms race in which both countries were actively pursuing nuclear weapons.[44] There were indeed reasons to think that Argentina and Brazil might be on a path toward bomb development. Neither country ratified the nuclear Nonproliferation Treaty (NPT) until the 1990s – more than twenty years after it entered into force.[45] And officials in each government seemed to covet a nuclear bomb. Oscar Camilión, said, "it is likely that some actors in the Argentine nuclear policy may have contemplated nuclear development as a possible opening into areas that would permit a military balance in view of the difference of population regarding Brazil."[46] In Brazil, there were voices advocating for a bomb as early as the 1950s.[47] In a particularly well-known episode, Brazilian General Leônidas Pires Gonçalves, the Minister of the Army, advocated for bomb development in remarks to the media in the mid-1980s.[48] Lampreia, who claims to be "friends with General Leônidas to this day," later said, "He [the general] does not hide that if he could

---

[43] Mallea et al. (2012, 92). Brazil temporarily backtracked on this idea after making the initial offer, but a renouncement of PNEs was formally codified in a 1991 bilateral nonproliferation agreement.

[44] For example, Singh and Way (2004) classify both countries as pursuing nuclear weapons – a step beyond mere exploration in their nuclear proliferation database.

[45] Brazilian documents indicate that staying outside the NPT was not an indication of a concerted nuclear weapons program in either country. Argentine Naval Intelligence Service (1967) and Brazilian Embassy (1978).

[46] Mallea et al. (2012, 39).

[47] Luiz Cintra do Prado, a former head of Brazil's Nuclear Energy Commission, said in 1954, "It is high time that the Ministry of War deems convenient for Brazil to start making its own bomb." See Argentine Naval Intelligence Service (1967). A US document from 1968 indicates that Marcelo Damy De Sousa Santos, president of the National Commission of Nuclear Energy in the early 1960s, "aspired to be a Brazilian [Homi] Bhabha," a reference to the physicist widely seen as the father of India's nuclear bomb. US Department of State (1968).

[48] Vazquez (1985).

decide, Brazil would have gone forward to acquire nuclear weapons."[49] Shortly thereafter, a press report indicated that there were holes at Serra do Cachimbo, which were possibly for nuclear testing.[50]

Importantly, however, neither country made a political decision to build and deploy nuclear weapons. They did not have Manhattan Project-style programs at any point in their nuclear histories. Their objective instead was to get close to a bomb without actually building one.[51] Argentina and Brazil were willing to weaponize their programs if national security threats required that action – but not as long as the status quo persisted.

Brazil pursued a strategy along these lines as early as 1967. In October of that year, Minister of External Relations José de Magalhaes Pinto said in a National Security Council meeting that although the nuclear program is peaceful in nature "in case of any emergency we would be able to use what we already possess." President Marshal Artur da Costa e Silva gave a one-word reply: "obviously."[52] Neves indicated that this approach continued during the ensuing decades. He recalled that ENR technology was important because it "would give Brazil the capability to go forward toward building a nuclear explosive, in case it wanted to do so, or there would be a decision to that effect."[53] The CIA similarly observed that the heads of the military services believed that their country "should master the nuclear fuel cycle and that, then, only 'a political decision' would be necessary to determine whether to develop nuclear weapons."[54] The story is similar in Argentina. As Roberto Ornstein, a longtime official in Argentina's atomic energy commission, put it, "Argentina wanted to master as many nuclear technologies as it could" but the ultimate goal was not weaponization.[55]

Foreign perceptions of intentions matter mightily in latent nuclear deterrence. Neither side had a unified belief that the other was racing to build nuclear weapons. Camilión said that Argentina "understood that there was no race to obtain the 'nuclear toy'... between the two countries," using a euphemism for a bomb.[56] Adolfo Saracho conveyed a similar sentiment: "It was not felt that Argentina should fear any Brazilian intention to proceed to the atom bomb despite the declarations

[49] Mallea et al. (2012, 103).
[50] *Folha de São Paulo* (1986).
[51] Narang (2017, 118) reaches a similar conclusion.
[52] Brazilian National Security Council (1967).
[53] Mallea et al. (2012, 134).
[54] US Central Intelligence Agency (1985a).
[55] Mallea et al. (2012, 57).
[56] Mallea et al. (2012, 49).

of certain Brazilian military."[57] Even after the discovery of a possible nuclear test side in 1986, Ornstein expressed confidence that Brazil was not on the cusp of arming. "There was no indication," he said, "that Brazil was about to conduct a nuclear test."[58]

At various points, each country perceived some uncertainty about the other's nuclear intentions. Following Argentina's 1978 announcement that it was planning to build a large-scale reprocessing plant, for example, Brazilian officials could not definitively rule out the possibility that Buenos Aires coveted nuclear bombs. Neves later reported that "there was some anxiety" about this news while Lampreia characterizes this as "a time of short tempers" when there was "much reciprocal disquiet."[59] In April 1982, Brazilian intelligence reportedly concluded that it was "impossible" to know for sure whether Argentina wanted nuclear weapons.[60] On the Argentine side, Ornstein reported that Brazil's secret activities created "some doubt about whether there was some ulterior motive."[61] The CIA likewise concluded in 1984 that "Brazilian officials have grown more mistrustful of Argentina's nuclear intentions."[62]

However, initial fears about the other country's intentions were ultimately overcome. The same Argentine and Brazilian officials quoted in the preceding paragraph said that their once-fearful perceptions of the other side's intentions became more innocuous. Neves noted that the anxiety his country felt was "quickly dispelled" and Lampreia similarly said, "we were able to dispel those apprehensions."[63] Ornstein's ultimate conclusion was that Brazil's ENR activities were "not really something worrisome."[64]

Why did Argentina and Brazil perceived mostly innocuous nuclear intentions in the end? Gradually, over a period spanning more than a decade, the two countries instituted a series of measures to allay one side's concerns about the other's nuclear intentions. The establishment of bilateral confidence building measures on both sides increased transparency and fostered trust.[65]

---

[57] Mallea et al. (2012, 149).
[58] Mallea et al. (2012, 132).
[59] Mallea et al. (2012, 56, 61).
[60] Mallea et al. (2012, 186).
[61] Mallea et al. (2012, 74).
[62] US Central Intelligence Agency (1984a, 6).
[63] Mallea et al. (2012, 56, 61).
[64] Mallea et al. (2012, 74).
[65] This was not the only reason officials felt reassured. For example, Neves claimed that Brazil did not worry about Argentine's enrichment program because it lacked an industrial plant capable of large-scale production of highly enriched uranium. See Mallea et al. (2012, 72–73).

Historic Confidence-Building Measures

As early as 1975–77, Argentina and Brazil were looking for ways to credibly signal peaceful nuclear intentions through bilateral actions. As Camilión described it, the idea at that time was to establish "a mechanism to permit the two countries to build trust regarding the possible applications of nuclear energy or possible temptations in the nuclear development of the other party."[66] After the resolution of the Itaipu dispute in 1979, Argentina approached Brazil about concluding a nuclear cooperation agreement (NCA).[67] The Brazilian government indicated a willingness to proceed "[e]ventually, and with great caution" in making "direct contacts" with Argentine officials to identify areas of nuclear cooperation.[68] The two countries concluded an NCA in 1980 that tried to carve out areas of cooperation on "feasible and symbolic things," according to Camilión.[69] He clearly laid out the motivations for the modest terms of the deal: "It was understood that once cooperation between Brazil and Argentina in the industrial field started the gates would be open for the two countries to become as transparent as possible in communicating their respective nuclear programs to the neighbor so that the fear of an armaments race would be dispelled."[70]

The 1980 NCA, according to Ornstein, "never produced anything concrete for the two parties."[71] However, it helped lay the groundwork for future cooperation. In November 1985, President Alfonsín of Argentina and President Sarney of Brazil met for the first time in Foz do Iguaçu and formed a working group to coordinate nuclear policy.[72] This meeting created momentum toward providing mutual assurances through a system of bilateral safeguards. Cooperation in this area was important, as Saracho explained, because "some opinions came up in both countries ... showing warlike frenzy." Mutual assurances were intended to "avoid suspicion about our nuclear intentions," Saracho added.[73] A proposal intended to build mutual confidence was the only one for which there was broad support in the mid-1980s. Brazilian officials, according to a formerly secret document from January 1985,

---

[66] Mallea et al. (2012, 49–50).
[67] Neves (1979a).
[68] Subiza (1979).
[69] For more on Brazil's incentives to sign this agreement, see Neves (1979b). Camilion's statement appears in Mallea et al. (2012, 67).
[70] Mallea et al. (2012, 67).
[71] Mallea et al. (2012, 77).
[72] Mallea (N.D.). A joint statement issued after the meeting is available in Sarney and Alfonsín (1985).
[73] Mallea et al. (2012, 103).

wanted to "get rid of certain misinterpretations and mistrust on what are the true objectives of the Brazilian nuclear program."[74]

Brazil, in particular, wished to proceed cautiously.[75] Neves noted that cooperation "had to be very gradual because ... there was not yet a clear idea about the adoption of those reciprocal safeguards, and their effects on the respective nuclear programs or on the position of the two countries in the international context."[76] The two sides therefore focused on incremental steps to build trust, a classic recipe for fostering cooperation.[77]

Each side invited officials from the other country to visit its sensitive nuclear sites. Argentina pursued this strategy in March 1980 when it hosted a Brazilian delegation at the pilot reprocessing plant under construction in Ezeiza.[78] Neves reported that the visit to Ezeiza "quickly dispelled" the anxiety that initially existed over the reprocessing plant and Argentina's intentions.[79] Later, in July 1987, Brazilians visited Argentina's enrichment plant in Pilcaniyeu. Brazil reciprocated by inviting Argentine officials to its own enrichment facility in Aramar. These visits represented a remarkable degree of transparency. This helped to allay fears in Brazil that Argentina secretly coveted nuclear weapons, and vice versa. According to Neves, "if they [the Argentines] were showing us one of the most sensitive aspects of the nuclear fuel cycle, the isotopic enrichment of uranium, this meant that they wanted to have greater transparency with us."[80]

Argentina and Brazil eventually formalized bilateral nonproliferation agreements. In November 1990, the leaders of each country concluded a declaration on common nuclear policy at Foz do Iguaçu.[81] This led to the 1991 Treaty of Guadalajara, which banned nuclear testing, prohibited bomb development or possession, and created a joint system of accounting and control of nuclear materials to ensure compliance. The Guadalajara agreement also established a regional organization – the Brazil–Argentina Agency for Accountability and Control (ABACC) – to implement these mandates.[82] Both countries ratified the Treaty

---

[74] Abdenur (1985). This statement is attributed to the presidential adviser Danilo Venturini.
[75] Brazilian documents highlight a reluctance to agree to a deal on nuclear explosives. See Abdenur (1985).
[76] Mallea et al. (2012, 119).
[77] See Axelrod (1984).
[78] Batista (1980).
[79] Mallea et al. (2012, 56).
[80] Mallea et al. (2012, 144).
[81] IAEA (1990).
[82] IAEA (1991).

of Tlatelolco, which established a Latin American regional nuclear weapons free zone, in 1994. In 1995, Argentina acceded to the NPT and Brazil did so three years later.

Third-Party Nuclear Threats

Brazil did not have a strategic rivalry with a nuclear-armed state. The country's only post-1945 rivalry was with Argentina. To the extent that Brazil's nuclear program was externally focused, therefore, it was Argentina-centric. There was not a third-party capable of spoiling the opportunity for success in weaponless deterrence by pushing Brazil to arm.

The situation was different in Argentina. Since 1965, Argentina has had a strategic rivalry with the United Kingdom – a country that first tested a nuclear weapon in 1952.[83] The two countries fought a war over the disputed Falkland Islands in 1982. Argentina seized and temporarily held the islands as a fait accompli. But British forces ultimately intervened militarily and regained control over the territory, resulting in a humiliating defeat for Buenos Aires. During the war, Britain deployed nuclear depth charges aboard the ships that it sent to the South Atlantic and deployed Vulcan bombers – which were not armed with atomic forces but had a longstanding nuclear role – to nearby Ascension Island.[84] These actions raised the possibility that Argentina might feel vulnerable to nuclear blackmail, motivating it avoid such an outcome in the future by arming.

At the time, foreign officials saw this as a real possibility. As the war unfolded, Washington worried that a decisive military defeat at the hands of the British would leave Argentina feeling humiliated. A memo sent by staffers to Robert McFarlane, President Ronald Reagan's national security adviser, on May 28 indicated that Britain "can probably secure the Island and inflict a humiliating defeat on the Argentines within the week, although at greater cost than they or others apparently realize. That kind of victory ... will come at great cost to us, the British, and the Western world over the long run."[85] One of those costs, according to this memo, is that "A nuclear weapons capability would be virtually guaranteed, as both Brazil and Argentina would seek ultimate security in nuclear arsenals." A story in *The New York Times* on May 23 made a similar claim: "No matter what the outcome of the Falklands conflict,

---

[83] Colaresi et al. (2007, 38).
[84] Sechser and Fuhrmann (2017, 167–168).
[85] Fontaine et al. (1982).

Argentina is now more likely than ever to develop an atomic bomb as a sign of military strength."[86]

The war did harden the resolve of some Argentine officials to seek nuclear weapons. On June 24, 1982, Castro Madero said publicly that the war enabled an Argentine program to weaponize nuclear technology: "from now on [Argentina] reserves for itself the right to undertake the development of the euphemistically so-called nonproscribed military uses. Until today the safeguard agreements signed by Argentina have not permitted it to undertake nuclear energy development for military purposes."[87] His announcement of successful uranium enrichment came about a year and a half later. Eduardo Santos, the former head of the atomic energy commission, drew an explicit connection between the 1983 announcement and the Falklands defeat: "For us, it was revenge for Malvinas [Argentina's name for the Falkland Islands]."[88]

In the end, though, the perceived threat from the United Kingdom did not push Argentina over the proverbial nuclear cliff. As the following evidence will show, Brazil's nuclear program remained relevant to Argentina's calculations despite the third-party threat from the United Kingdom. This could be partially because Brazil was relatively more important in influencing Argentina's nuclear program. This stands in contrast to other cases involving third parties depicted in Table 7.1. In the case of China, for instance, India's potential to arm was less important than countering perceived nuclear threats from the already-nuclear-armed Soviet Union and United States.

Confessions: How Proliferation Threats Influenced Leaders' Thinking

We learned in Chapter 2 that Argentina and Brazil embraced weaponless deterrence. Both countries attempted to send a message: "Stop or I'll proliferate." The preceding evidence shows that Brazil (and to a lesser extent Argentina) satisfied the conditions that are necessary for deterring nuclear armament by another country. But did proliferation threats actually influence the thinking of officials in both countries?

---

[86] Gwertzman (1982).

[87] FBIS (1982c).

[88] This statement appears in a PowerPoint presentation obtained and translated by Christopher Dunlap. The statement is quoted in Dunlap (2018, 12). In follow up email exchanges with Dunlap and Santos, it appears that this statement was mostly about restoring lost prestige rather than punishing the United Kingdom.

The evidence points in the affirmative direction. Policymakers in Argentina and Brazil acknowledged that the possibility of fomenting an arms race deterred them from weaponizing their nuclear capabilities.

Castro Madero admitted on at least two occasions that Brazil's capacity to build nuclear weapons restrained his country's nuclear program. On January 11, 1982 – before the Falklands War with the United Kingdom – Castro Madero explained why Argentina was not going to weaponize its nuclear program. "It would confer some prestige upon he who owns the atomic bomb," he said, "but that prestige would be short-lived because such a development in Latin America would set off a race among all other countries to catch up."[89] Argentina's defeat in the Falklands War heightened the country's sense of insecurity and vulnerability to nuclear blackmail. Reports surfaced in the aftermath of the war indicating that Argentina may now build a bomb. However, Castro Madero's thinking seemingly remained unaltered. On November 1, seven months after the Falklands conflict, he explained that Buenos Aires was going to keep its nuclear powder dry because "we know that any Latin American country that begins an atomic energy buildup for belligerent purposes will be immediately imitated by the rest of the countries."[90]

Around the same time, the CIA also raised the possibility of deterrence by proliferation. It noted that "Argentina could also be deterred by the prospect that an overt test could easily lead to a nuclear arms race with Brazil."[91] A memorandum issued by the agency two years later (1984) similarly concluded that Argentina would consider reining-in its nuclear activities if "The nuclear rivalry with Brazil appeared to be getting out of control."[92] It further noted that Argentina's failure to credibly signal peaceful intentions would increase Brazil's resolve to explore its "own nuclear options – outside safeguards – that have potential military applications."[93]

Brazilian officials were thinking along similar lines. A formerly secret January 1985 memorandum from Ambassador Roberto Abdenur to Saraiva Guerreiro, the Minister of State, speaks to Brazil's thinking at the time.[94] The memo recounts a conversation between Adbenur and an Argentine official, Jorge Sábato. Abdenur told his counterpart that Brazil was going to continue to seek "the domination of the

---

[89] FBIS (1982b).
[90] FBIS (1982a).
[91] US Central Intelligence Agency (1982a).
[92] US Central Intelligence Agency (1984a, 6).
[93] US Central Intelligence Agency (1984a, 6).
[94] Abdenur (1985).

fuel cycle" for peaceful purposes. At the same time, he made it clear that Brazil would not develop nuclear explosives – even for ostensibly peaceful purposes. Abdenur left little doubt about his motivation for exercising restraint. "If either side manufactured a nuclear device meant for peaceful applications," he reportedly told Sábato, "this in itself would only inevitably lead to a nuclear race." The Brazilian diplomat further indicated that both countries saw the situation in this same light: "I affirmed that in this sense the Argentinian nuclear program did not contemplate the hypothesis of nuclear explosives, because this in itself would only raise apprehension in Brazil and in other countries." Abdenur wrote that "Sábato agreed with my observations."

A decade earlier, when Brazil had less-developed nuclear capabilities, it did not convey this level of confidence in the viability of deterrence by proliferation. After India's 1974 nuclear test, Brazilian officials privately wondered if Argentina would follow suit. A Brazilian government document stated that Argentine might "seek admission into the select group of nuclear powers, *believing itself to be the only Latin American in a position to do so.*"[95] Because Brazil could not credibly threaten to match Buenos Aires' armament, Brazilian officials saw an Argentine bomb as plausible. As Brazil's ENR program advanced, however, concerns of fueling a nuclear arms race played a bigger role in inducing both countries to exercise restraint.

Nuclear parity between the two countries played a key role in freezing the situation in the mid-to-late 1980s. Deterrence by proliferation worked because both Argentina and Brazil had ENR programs capable of producing bombs in a similar amount of time. Brazil's 1987 enrichment breakthrough, in particular, eroded resistance to cooperation in Brasilia and made the subsequent nonproliferation arrangements possible. Ricupero unequivocally spelled out this logic. Referring to the mastery of enrichment technology in 1987, he said, "It is as if we had tied the game. With the game tied, no one was ahead of anyone; it would be easier than before to freeze the situation." "The Brazilian announcement [on enrichment] helped us to say," Ricupero added, "'well, now that we are on par with each other, let us forget it!'"[96]

Declassified documents support this view, revealing that Brazil was reluctant to make nonproliferation concessions during the period where Argentina's ENR capabilities were superior. A 1985 memorandum from Foreign Minister Olavo Setúbal to President Sarney indicated that agreeing to reciprocal nuclear inspections "was considered to be

[95] Silveira (1974c). Emphasis added.
[96] Mallea et al. (2012, 142).

possibly be premature at this moment," adding that "its implications in relation to our interest in maintaining relative parity with Argentina on nuclear affairs would have to be carefully studied."[97] Achieving parity mattered, in part, because it eroded any advantage that one country might obtain by arming first, thereby bolstering deterrence by proliferation. It also allowed both countries to declare victory to their domestic constituencies, making them more likely to come to the negotiating table.

There were other factors that contributed to nonarmament in the cases of Argentina and Brazil. During the 1980s, both countries transitioned to democracy, had key leadership changes, and placed more emphasis on economic development.[98] The end of their rivalry also lessened the need for a nuclear arsenal to deter military threats.[99] All of these things mattered and, on the basis of the available evidence, we cannot say with confidence that one was much more important than the others. The evidence does show, however, that concerns about catalyzing nuclear proliferation contributed to nuclear restraint.

Hollow Warning Shot: Halting South Africa's Nuclear Ambitions

South Africa emerged as a potential proliferator in the 1960s when it began sensitive nuclear activities.[100] The country began enriching uranium on a laboratory scale in 1967 using an indigenously developed aeordynamic isotope separation process. By 1975, South Africa had a larger-scale pilot plant using this technology in operation in Valindaba, known as the "Y-Plant." This facility produced highly enriched uranium (HEU) for the first time in 1978. An even larger semi-commercial-scale facility, known as the "Z-plant," came online in Valindaba around 1986. As South Africa's nuclear program began accumulating fissile material, foreign officials feared that it might be on the cusp of building nuclear weapons.

---

[97] Historical Archive of the Minister of Foreign Affairs of Brazil (1985). See also Setúbal (1985).

[98] For studies that focus on the role of these factors in causing nuclear proliferation, see Hymans (2006), Solingen (2007), Way and Weeks (2014), and Fuhrmann and Horowitz (2015).

[99] Paul (2000, 99–112).

[100] The information in this paragraph draws on the coding sheet for South Africa used to construct the Nuclear Latency database. See Fuhrmann and Tkach (2015). The coding sheets for each country are available at www.matthewfuhrmann.com/datasets .html.

At least one country – Nigeria – responded to South Africa's nuclear advances with an apparent attempt at weaponless deterrence. In 1980, President Shehu Shagari said that Nigeria would build nuclear weapons unless South Africa dismantled its nuclear sites.[101] This statement appeared in press reports, suggesting that Shagari hoped to communicate a message to officials in Pretoria, not just move forward with his country's nuclear program in response to a perceived external threat. He seemingly hoped that the prospect of inducing a Nigerian bomb would compel South African leader Pieter Botha to stop short of weaponizing his country's nuclear capabilities, or roll back progress that had already been made toward that end.

Unfortunately for Nigeria, Shagari's threat failed to produce this effect. At the time of his threat, South Africa had already assembled its first nuclear weapon but this may not have been known to officials in Lagos. In any case, Pretoria showed little interest in mothballing any of its sensitive nuclear sites as Nigeria demanded. South Africa went on to build a small nuclear arsenal of around seven bombs, before dismantling them by the early 1990s. Why was Nigeria's threat insufficient to stop South Africa's armament?

A Noncredible Threat

South Africa would have found Nigerian proliferation undesirable given the tense relationship between the two countries. Nigeria was one of the most vocal critics of South Africa's apartheid regime and Lagos supported the African National Congress (ANC), a then-banned opposition party that opposed white minority rule.[102] Neither country had diplomatic representation in the other from the time of Nigerian independence in 1960 until the end of apartheid in the early 1990s.[103] During this period, Nigeria worked to undermine South Africa's political and diplomatic interests in international fora. In the mid-1970s, for example, Lagos led an effort to expel South Africa from the International Atomic Energy Agency.[104] At the same time, South Africa and Nigeria were not technically rivals at the time of Lagos' proliferation threat, as shown in Table 7.2.

Nigeria had the political will to carry out its proliferation threat. Around the time of President Shagari's warning message, other key

---

[101] FBIS (1981).
[102] Nagar and Paterson (N.D., 8).
[103] Bayer (2006).
[104] Nagar and Paterson (N.D., 17).

Nigerian officials expressed a desire to obtain nuclear weapons. Defense Minister Iya Abubakar said in April 1980, "Nigeria will develop nuclear technology for peaceful purposes and eventually become a nuclear power ...Nigeria is a great country and it needs a strong, invincible and unassailable defence capability."[105] In addition to the status motives reflected in Abubakar's statement, officials believed that building nuclear weapons would strengthen Nigeria's foreign policy and contribute to racial equality in the nuclear sphere.[106]

However, Nigeria lacked the technological capacity to build nuclear weapons. The country began building its nuclear infrastructure in the 1970s, passing legislation to form the Nigerian Atomic Energy Commission (NAEC) and establishing two university-based nuclear research centers.[107] However, these initiatives did not result in quick technological breakthroughs. It was not until 2004 – twenty-four years after Shagari's proliferation threat – that the country began operating its first research reactor.[108] To put this in perspective, Pakistan operated its first research reactor in 1963, about twenty-seven years before assembling its first nuclear bomb.[109] Needless to say, Nigeria never got to the point of mastering sensitive nuclear technology – a key requirement for making credible threats in latent nuclear deterrence. Media reports in 2004 indicated that Pakistan sought to help Nigeria "strengthen its military capability," including acquiring "nuclear power."[110] But there is no definitive evidence that Nigeria received uranium enrichment technology from Pakistan, like Iran, Libya, and North Korea did.

Given the lack of an ENR program in Nigeria, its proliferation threat rang hollow. Even if South Africa thought that Nigeria could eventually build nuclear weapons, the long punishment delay – likely twenty years or more – rendered weaponless deterrence ineffective. And Nigeria's lack of progress in developing sensitive nuclear technology made its threat appear less serious, since a resolved proliferator would invest heavily in an ENR program. It is not surprising, then, that the prospect of a Nigerian bomb apparently had little impact on South African nuclear decisionmaking in the late 1970s and early 1980s. Although many key documents pertaining to South Africa's nuclear program remain inaccessible to scholars, I have not see any evidence that the

---

[105] Quoted in Sillah (1985, 24).
[106] Ejiogu (2013, 262).
[107] Ejiogu (2013, 262).
[108] Chakrov and Hanlon (2018).
[109] Fuhrmann (2012a, 193).
[110] Borger (2004).

prospect of fomenting a Nigerian bomb made officials think twice about weaponization.

France and the Prospect of a West German Bomb

The French nuclear program dates back to the immediate aftermath of World War II. President Charles de Gaulle created the French Atomic Energy Commission (CEA) in October 1945.[111] France initially engaged in hedging, developing the dual-use capabilities needed to make a bomb without deciding to do so. It initiated laboratory-scale ENR activities in the late 1940s and separated plutonium at a pilot-scale reprocessing plant at Fontenay-aux-Roses in 1954, achieving full nuclear latency.

Germany had a clear influence on French behavior in the early days of its nuclear program.[112] With the horrors of World War II fresh on their mind, many French officials were deeply concerned about the prospect of German rearmament. These officials did not want to see Germany equipped with conventional weapons – let alone a nuclear arsenal.[113] Paris reluctantly came to accept the conventional rearmament of West Germany after the United States began pushing for this outcome in 1950. However, according to the French army, it was "inconceivable" to allow Germany to obtain nuclear weapons.[114] Paris sought ways to prevent a German nuclear bomb.

It found an apparent solution in May 1952, when France and Germany – along with five other countries in Europe – signed the European Defense Community (EDC) treaty. This agreement prevented the use of fissile material for military purposes, essentially requiring all of the signatories to refrain from building nuclear weapons. Political scientist Jacques Hymans aptly summarizes France's motives for entering into the EDC treaty: "the French had signed away the right to sovereign nuclear weapons in exchange for the certainty that Germany could never have them either."[115] The logic of latent nuclear deterrence is reflected in this line of thinking: French nuclear armament would increase the likelihood of an eventual West German bomb, so France decided to keep its nuclear program peaceful.

---

[111] Jurgensen and Dominique (2020, 146).
[112] The US-occupied portion of Germany became known as "West Germany" beginning in 1949.
[113] Hymans (2006, 90–91).
[114] Rouanet (1965, 436–437).
[115] Hymans (2006, 91).

Shortly after concluding the EDC treaty, however, France began to seek advantages over West Germany. French diplomats laid out a clear strategy: "We first tie up Germany, then we tie ourselves up in the name of equal rights, then we rack our brains to try to untie ourselves."[116] Prime Minister Pierre Mendes France, who entered office in June 1954, embraced this approach. Thinking back on the situation in the fall of 1954, he later told a colleague, "it was disagreeable to me to see France on the same footing as Germany ... it was intolerable that France suffer discriminatory treatment by the Americans and English and find itself reduced to the rank of Germany."[117] France took a stop toward "untying" itself in August 1954, when parliament rejected the EDC treaty.[118] Shortly thereafter, in December of that year, France created the Bureau of General Studies within the CEA to examine the desirability of nuclear armament.[119] According to historian Georges-Henri Soutou, "there is no doubt" that Mendes France decided to get nuclear weapons at the end of 1954.[120]

Mendes France fell from power in February 1955, just two months after his nuclear armament decision. Subsequent French leaders continued on a path toward nuclear armament with varying degrees of enthusiasm. Some of them – particularly Guy Mollet, who served as prime minister from 1956 to 1957 – personally opposed building nuclear weapons but did not stop the program.[121] In June 1957, the CIA concluded that France was beginning to produce quantities of plutonium sufficient for a bomb and could manufacture three nuclear weapons by the end of 1958.[122] Ten months later, Prime Minister Felix Gaillard secretly ordered preparations for a nuclear test to occur in 1960.[123]

Charles de Gaulle, who was now unequivocal in his support of a French nuclear bomb, returned to power in in June 1958. Without de Gaulle, there was a possibility that France might be content with being a latent nuclear power, like India after it carried out a "peaceful" nuclear test in 1974.[124] This kind of thinking existed in West Germany as late as February 1958. At that time, Friedrich Zimmerman, head of the CSU political party and friend of Defense Minister Josef Strauss, said, "the French intended only to carry their efforts to a point short

---

[116] Quoted in Jurgensen and Dominique (2020, 153).
[117] Quoted in Hymans (2006, 102).
[118] Hymans (2006, 93).
[119] Richelson (2007, 199).
[120] Jurgensen and Dominique (2020, 119).
[121] Hymans (2006, 111–112).
[122] US Central Intelligence Agency (1957a).
[123] Tertrais (2007).
[124] Tertrais (2007).

of production" and then they would use their latent nuclear forces for bargaining leverage.[125] Once de Gaulle assumed power, however, there was no doubt that a French nuclear arsenal would soon emerge. On July 5, 1958, de Gaulle told US Secretary of State John Foster Dulles, "one thing is certain: we will have nuclear weapons."[126] De Gaulle carried out his promise in February 1960 when France detonated a nuclear device in the Sahara Desert, becoming the world's fourth nuclear power.

West Germany's Bomb Making Potential and French Nuclear Policy

French nuclear armament occurred in the shadow of advancements in West Germany's nuclear program. Germany carried out laboratory-scale ENR work during World War II. In 1942, German physical chemist Wilhelm Groth enriched a small amount of uranium using a centrifuge.[127] When the war ended, the Allied powers placed restrictions on German nuclear research but allowed laboratory-scale work to resume in 1952.[128] With restrictions lifted, Germany began research that included "a marked interest in plutonium" – and France was well aware of this work.[129] In the 1950s, West Germany also began carrying out research on uranium enrichment using a jet nozzle process.[130] The country's centrifuge program also got off the ground around this time after German scientists who developed technology in the Soviet Union were allowed to return home.[131] West Germany lagged considerably behind France in terms of nuclear capabilities throughout this period, but its nascent ENR capabilities signaled interest in developing the *capacity* to build a bomb.

Some French officials worried that arming with nuclear weapons would cause West Germany to follow suit. The CIA provided unambiguous evidence that deterrence by proliferation influenced the calculus of at least some leaders in Paris. A 1957 assessment by the agency listed three "obstacles" that might prevent French nuclear armament. One of them was that "Some French officials are also concerned that production by France will influence other countries, notably West Germany, to follow its example."[132] This concern influenced the thinking of US

---

[125] US Department of State (1958a).
[126] Jurgensen and Dominique (2020, 143).
[127] Walker (1989, 82–83).
[128] Soutou (1996, Chapter 2).
[129] Soutou (1996, Chapter 2).
[130] Fuhrmann and Tkach (2015). See the coding sheet for Germany in the Nuclear Latency database available at www.matthewfuhrmann.com/datasets.html
[131] Zentner et al. (2005, 13).
[132] US Central Intelligence Agency (1957a, 5).

policymakers as well. In a 1961 letter to British Prime Minister Harold Macmillian, John F. Kennedy wrote, "If we were to help France acquire a nuclear weapons capability, this could not fail to have a major effect on German attitudes ... [if we aid France] the likelihood that the Germans would eventually wish to acquire a nuclear weapons capability would be significantly increased."[133]

In the end, however, the prospect of West German nuclear armament did not dissuade France from embarking on a path toward a bomb and eventually testing a nuclear device in 1960. France pushed full steam ahead despite West Germany's apparent shot across the bow. This happened, in part, because the Franco-German strategic rivalry came to an end in the mid-1950s, removing a key condition for successful latent nuclear deterrence.

Bilateral Relations Warm

As Mendes France authorized a French bomb in 1954, relations between France and West Germany were warming. Although they got off to a rocky start, Mendes France and German Chancellor Konrad Adenauer forged a productive relationship after meeting in La Celle-Saint-Cloud on October 19, 1954. Soutou notes that this meeting "laid the foundations for the beginning of genuine Franco-German cooperation."[134] The next day, the French and West German leaders met in Paris along with representatives from seven other countries.[135] Agreements concluded at the Paris Conference admitted West Germany into NATO and the Brussels Treaty, which created the Western European Union in 1948. The delegates also agreed to end the occupation of West Germany and allow the country to rearm with conventional forces. To assuage international concerns about its nuclear intentions, West Germany pledged not to build nuclear weapons on its territory.[136] After the Paris Conference, France and West Germany agreed that the Soviet Union – not each other – posed the greatest external threat.[137] The strategic rivalry between the two countries that had persisted since 1756 was finally coming to an end.[138]

---

[133] Kennedy (1961).

[134] Soutou (1996, 27–29).

[135] The other countries were Belgium, Canada, Italy, Luxembourg, the Netherlands, the United Kingdom, and the United States.

[136] US Department of State (1958b, 725)

[137] Soutou (1996, 27–29).

[138] Colaresi et al. (2007) code the rivalry as ending in 1955.

Around this time, France began to embrace cooperation with West Germany in the nuclear sector. French officials worried that the United Kingdom and the United States would engage in "reckless" nuclear cooperation with West Germany that could enable nuclear proliferation.[139] France viewed civilian nuclear cooperation as a means to avoid such an undesirable outcome. As one French diplomat put it, "The best way to control [West Germany's nuclear program] is to participate."[140] Cooperating with West Germany, based on this line of thinking, would enhance France's political leverage and give it more information about German nuclear aims and progress. Mendes France himself embraced this strategy, believing that it would facilitate closer bilateral relations and keep his country "usefully informed on the progress of the German atomic effort."[141] In December 1954, shortly before Mendes France's weaponization decision, the CEA proposed building a uranium enrichment plant jointly with West Germany.[142] France now sought to cooperate with its former rival by developing sensitive dual-use technology – a remarkable turn of events given the state of Franco-German relations just a few years earlier.

The 1956 Suez crisis created additional momentum toward reconciliation between France and West Germany. After Egyptian leader Nasser nationalized the Suez Canal, British, Israeli, and French forces launched a joint military operation to reclaim it. Their campaign invited international blowback: The Soviet Union issued a nuclear threat to compel Israel, France, and the United Kingdom to withdraw their forces while the United States applied economic pressure.[143] In the end, the attempt to regain control over the canal failed. This episode amplified fears among some Western European officials that the United States could not be trusted to address a growing Soviet nuclear threat.[144] Leaders in France and West Germany now felt a renewed desire to settle past differences and foster closer political ties. On the same day their defeat in Egypt became official, Mollet met with Adenauer in Paris. Adenauer agreed that France could continue its bomb program, paving the way for the creation of the European Atomic Energy Community (Euratom) the following year.[145] At this same time, Mollet secretly proposed "military nuclear cooperation" with West Germany.[146]

---

139 Soutou (1996, Chapter 2).
140 Soutou (1996, Chapter 2).
141 Soutou (1996, Chapter 2).
142 Soutou (1996, Chapter 2).
143 Sechser and Fuhrmann (2017, 225–226).
144 Jurgensen and Dominique (2020, 153).
145 Jurgensen and Dominique (2020, 120).
146 Jurgensen and Dominique (2020, 139).

Along with Italy, France and West Germany formed the so-called FIG (France–Italy–Germany) project to jointly produce nuclear weapons in November 1957. The FIG project took a step forward on April 8, 1958, when the participants formally agreed to jointly fund an enrichment facility at Pierrelatte and reiterated their desire to cooperate in the military applications of the atom.[147] However, de Gaulle canceled the FIG project when he returned to power. This decision is somewhat puzzling given de Gaulle's rhetoric and behavior toward West Germany.[148] Like other post-1954 French leaders, de Gaulle saw West Germany as an important ally – not a strategic threat.

De Gaulle believed that West Germany was the "*most important* [country with which] to have close relations," according to the CIA.[149] He wanted to work closely with Bonn in a cooperative manner in order to address shared threats and challenges. As De Gaulle wrote in his memoirs, "Germany, as it is, does not threaten us at all. We even consider that with its capabilities, energy and resources, it is an essential element of the life and progress of Europe and the world."[150] He continued to convey support for defense-related cooperation – including in the area of nuclear weapons – even after canceling the FIG project. Historian Marc Trachtenberg recounts a 1960 meeting in which de Gaulle made this clear to Adenauer: "The defense of Europe could not depend on the vagaries of American political life," he wrote, "and this meant that France and West Germany had to be able to defend themselves by coming together and developing a nuclear capability."[151]

Given de Gaulle's embrace of West Germany, he didn't view the possibility of nuclear weapons proliferation as a punishment. On the contrary, he seemed to welcome a German bomb – and believe that one would inevitably be built.[152] De Gaulle told Adenauer that it was "more than probable" that West Germany would eventually build its own nuclear arsenal.[153] In April 1963, he repeated something similar to US Secretary of State Dean Rusk: West German leaders "will do as they please" with respect to nuclear weapons, he said, "and neither you nor

---

[147] Bini and Londero (2017, 109).

[148] His decision may have reflected a general aversion to sharing nuclear weapons with other countries – not necessarily a Germany-specific aversion to cooperation in this domain. See Bini and Londero (2017, 109).

[149] US Central Intelligence Agency (Director of Central Intelligence) (1963, 12). Emphasis added.

[150] de Gaulle (1975a, 82).

[151] Trachtenberg (2012, 85).

[152] De Gaulle's view changed over time. By 1964, he was far less enthuiastic about a German bomb. Trachtenberg (2012, 86).

[153] Quoted in Trachtenberg (2012, 85).

we will be able to prevent them from doing so."[154] De Gaulle's beliefs about West Germany and its nuclear program doomed deterrence by proliferation to fail. Two of latent nuclear deterrence theory's conditions for success were absent here: West Germany could not inflict pain on France by building nuclear weapons once the two states shifted from rivals to partners, and de Gaulle saw a German bomb as inevitable.

What if the Franco-German rivalry had persisted? In that alternative universe, would France have been deterred from carrying out its first nuclear test in 1960 by the prospect of motivating West Germany to follow suit? It is impossible to know for sure but there is one key reason to suspect not. Yet another factor cut against the efficacy of weaponless deterrence: the presence of relevant third-party states that were already armed with nuclear weapons.

Third-Party Nuclear Threats

The Soviet nuclear threat loomed large for many French officials, especially after the Suez crisis. In 1950, one year after the first Soviet nuclear test, de Gaulle referred to "the heavy Soviet threat on the horizon."[155] In the eyes of French leaders, NATO's adoption of a "New Look" policy of massive retaliation in 1954 made nuclear weapons a centerpiece of international relations. According to Soutou, France now felt that it "would be practically disarmed with regard to the USSR if it did not also equip itself with nuclear weapons."[156] An independent nuclear arsenal was necessary, based on this view, because French policymakers doubted that the United States could be fully trusted to defend their country in the event of a Soviet nuclear attack. De Gaulle famously expressed his doubts about the reliability of US defense commitments. He asked President Kennedy in 1961 if the United States would "be ready to trade New York for Paris."[157]

Although they were allies, the United Kingdom – one of the other three countries armed with nuclear weapons prior to 1960 – also shaped French nuclear behavior. Soutou notes that the United Kingdom was "the essential benchmark for comparison at the time for the French."[158] Given that the British possessed nuclear weapons, French elites believed that they needed them too, or else Paris would not have any influence

---

[154] Quoted in Trachtenberg (2012, 82).
[155] de Gaulle (1975b, 348).
[156] Jurgensen and Dominique (2020, 119).
[157] Kennedy and de Gaulle (1961).
[158] Jurgensen and Dominique (2020, 119).

within NATO or in international affairs more generally.[159] A desire for greater status and international influence clearly influenced the French push toward nuclear armament. As Mendes France put it, "My idea was to keep the atomic bomb as a negotiating tool."[160]

In sum, the Franco-German case did not meet several requirements of success in weaponless deterrence. Only one of the four conditions at the heart of latent nuclear deterrence theory held in this case. West Germany developed laboratory-scale ENR capabilities in the 1950s that gave it a foundation for a bomb program. France took notice and understood the significance of these developments, as the theory would lead us to expect. However, as bilateral relations warmed, the perceived punishment costs declined; French leaders began to see a West German bomb as inevitable; and third-party nuclear states pushed Paris toward weaponization. It is notable that the possibility of German nuclear armament caused France to forswear nuclear weapons in the early 1950s. As the decade unfolded, though, the conditions necessary for success eroded, leading to a failure of deterrence by proliferation.

Runaway Train? Deterrence by Proliferation in South Asia

Before assembling nuclear bombs in the late 1980s, India and Pakistan spent time as latent nuclear powers. India opened up a big lead over Pakistan in the early years of the nuclear age, carrying out laboratory work on plutonium reprocessing beginning in the late 1950s. By 1964, after inaugurating a pilot reprocessing plant in Trombay, India had the means to make plutonium on a larger scale. Pakistan sought to match India's capabilities and eventually succeeded. Laboratory-scale reprocessing activities emerged by 1973 at the Pakistan Institute of Nuclear Science and Technology (PINSTECH). Pakistan developed a larger pilot reprocessing plant at PINSTECH during the 1980s, as well as a small-scale enrichment plant in Sihala, which was operational by 1979.

India's Nuclear Thinking and Behavior

Pakistan used proliferation threats with the apparent intention of deterring Indian weaponization. Most famously, then-Defense Minister Bhutto declared in 1965, "If India builds the bomb, we will eat grass

---

[159] Jurgensen and Dominique (2020, 119).
[160] Quoted in Hymans (2006, 102).

or leaves, even go hungry. But we will get one of our own."[161] He went on to repeat this threat on other occasions, including during a speech at the UN in January 1967.[162] These threats did not stop India from exploding a nuclear device.

On May 18, 1974, India conducted a nuclear detonation at an army base in Pokhran using plutonium produced in the Trombay reprocessing plant. This was a watershed moment – both for relations between India and Pakistan and global nonproliferation policies. India dubbed this nuclear test a "peaceful nuclear explosion," and it did not immediately seek to develop and deploy combat-ready nuclear weapons.[163] For New Delhi, this test was primarily about demonstrating scientific prowess and gaining international status rather than fielding a new military capability.

Some officials and foreign policy commentators recognized that India's 1974 nuclear test would probably compel Pakistan to follow suit. According to a June 1974 note produced by the US State Department's intelligence agency, an unnamed Indian analyst believed, "India's explosion would induce Pakistan to develop its own nuclear weapons capability," leaving New Delhi worse off than if it had not tested.[164] Patrick Moynihan, the US ambassador to India, told Indira Gandhi after the test that she had made a mistake. "Madame Prime Minister," Moynihan recalled saying, "the Mughals next door are not going to sit idle. Sooner or later, you will be condemned to [be] sandwiched between two nuclear neighbors, China and Pakistan."[165] Moynihan turned out to be correct. Just days after India's nuclear test, Bhutto made it clear that Pakistan now had no choice: It must race to build a nuclear bomb.[166] However, the possibility of fomenting a Pakistani bomb did not dissuade India from testing in 1974.[167]

Eyes on China

India had its focus on another adversary, who was already nuclear-armed: China. On October 16, 1964, China conducted its first nuclear test, becoming the fifth country to successfully build a bomb. This event catalyzed India's push to carry out its own test. A little more than a month later, on November 27, 1964, Indian Prime Minister Lal Bahadur

---

[161] Quoted in Khan (2012, 7).
[162] Khan (2012, 69).
[163] For details on the posttest delay in weaponization, see Kampani (2014).
[164] US Department of State (1974).
[165] Quoted in Khan (2012, 119).
[166] Quoted in Khan (2012, 121–123).
[167] Indian officials apparently did not systematically consider the costs and benefits of carrying out the PNE. See Perkovich (1999, 177).

Shastri publicly endorsed a nuclear explosives program for the first time.[168] Shortly thereafter, in an apparent effort to stymie the growth of China's nuclear capabilities, Shastri said, "we will have to reconsider what we will do" if China develops a nuclear delivery system."[169] Some Indian bomb advocates perceived that Beijing's nuclear capability posed a national security threat, coming just two years after India's defeat in the Sino-Indian War.[170] Others wanted to match China's accomplishment for reasons of international status and prestige reasons.[171] In any case, from a nuclear standpoint, the eyes of Indian officials were on China more than Pakistan in the pre-1974 period.

It was easy to overlook Pakistan's nuclear program in the years leading up to India's first nuclear test. Islamabad had not achieved even partial nuclear latency by the time Gandhi authorized the test in 1972. As a result, the same problems that plagued Nigerian leaders in their attempt to deter South African armament stymied Pakistan's efforts. Pakistan lacked the the capabilities needed to make its proliferation threats credible. Moreover, without an active ENR program, Islamabad did not force New Delhi to consider its bomb-making potential by conveying a shot across the bow.

Pakistan launched a weapons program in 1972, shortly after its defeat in the 1971 Indo-Pakistani War. But India did not know that Pakistan was seeking nuclear bombs at the time of the 1974 test.[172] New Delhi recognized Islamabad's nuclear ambitions only after its ENR program expanded. This coincided with India stepping up its monitoring of Pakistan's activities beginning in 1974.[173] By 1979, when Pakistan's enrichment plant at Sihala began operating, Indian intelligence concluded that Islamabad could have a nuclear bomb in one to two years.[174] The US State Department thought that Pakistan might be content to use its ENR potential as a "bargaining chip" and remain nonnuclear.[175] Yet India now began to take Pakistan's proliferation threats seriously and initiated countermeasures, including work on delivery systems and plans for a second nuclear test in 1982 and 1983, which ultimately was not carried out.[176]

---

[168] Fuhrmann (2012a, 163).
[169] Simons (1965).
[170] Fuhrmann (2012a, 164).
[171] Perkovich (1999, 176).
[172] Perkovich (1999, 168).
[173] Joshi (2017).
[174] Joshi (2017).
[175] US Department of State (1979).
[176] Joshi (2017).

Perceptions of Nonrestraint

Indian officials began to see Pakistan's nuclear program as unrestrained, undermining the viability of deterrence by proliferation. A 1981 report issued by the Indian embassy in Islamabad concluded, "it is very likely that Pakistan will succeed in exploding a nuclear device, possibly this year." The report further noted that Pakistani president Muhammad Zia-ul-Haq, who ousted Bhutto in a 1977 coup, was "extremely keen to explode the nuclear device" as soon as possible.[177] Prime Minister Rajiv Gandhi conveyed this sentiment publicly in May 1985, plainly saying, "We feel they [Pakistan] are developing a nuclear weapon," referring to their bomb program as "persistent."[178]

Between the late 1980s and early 1990s, Indian officials came to recognize that Pakistan was not just pursuing nuclear weapons – it now possessed one or more assembled bombs. Kavel Ratna Malkani, the spokesman for India's Bharatiya Janata Party (BJP), said unambiguously in January 1993, "They have the bomb."[179] Western intelligence services now had this view as well.[180]

Indian Prime Minister P. V. Narasimha Rao authorized nuclear testing in December 1995. The United States detected preparations for the test and pressured Rao's government to hold off. According to a US State Department analysis, an Indian test would trigger an arms race in the region: "Pakistan's leaders will come under great domestic political pressure to respond in some way, either by detonating a nuclear test explosion or by taking some other major step to demonstrate a significant nuclear weapon and/or missile capability."[181] Indian leaders surely understood this too, but they already saw Pakistan as a nuclear weapons state. Officials in New Delhi did not fear a Pakistani response – if anything, they welcomed it. They felt that Pakistani testing would reduce the international blowback that India experienced, and possibly expose limitations in Pakistan's nuclear forces.[182]

The consequence of prompting Pakistani weaponization or testing therefore had little bite in New Delhi. India temporarily delayed testing in the face of US pressure before ultimately detonating five nuclear bombs at Pokhran in May 1998, prompting the same number of Pakistani explosions about two weeks later.

---

[177] Prahladan (2017).
[178] Associated Press (1985).
[179] Gargan (1993).
[180] Gargan (1993).
[181] US Department of State (2013).
[182] Perkovich (1999, 419).

Pakistan's Quest for Nuclear Weapons

By the early 1970s, India's latent nuclear forces were well primed for weaponless deterrence. Unlike Pakistan, India had by this time demonstrated the ability to make significant quantities of fissile material. During the 1980s, as Pakistan's nuclear program advanced, Indian leaders explicitly tried their hands at deterrence by proliferation. Prime Minister Rajiv Gandhi told a group of American reporters in June 1985 that India "would have to really rethink all of our policies" if Pakistan assembled a nuclear bomb.[183] Raja Ramanna, a physicist who led India's nuclear program, similarly proclaimed that India could make nuclear weapons and "if anyone tries to twist our hand we could flex our muscles too."[184] Khurshid Alam Khan, the Minister of State for External Affairs, sent an analogous warning Pakistan: "They will come to their senses if they have an opportunity of knowing what we possess."[185] These verbal threats coincided with an announcement that India would soon operate a large nuclear reactor capable of producing plutonium for bombs.[186]

Yet the possibility of fomenting an Indian bomb did not cause Pakistan to put the brakes on its nuclear weapons ambitions prior to India's 1974 test, nor did it stop its eventual armament. Officials in Islamabad believed that India had already inserted nuclear weapons into South Asia through its 1974 nuclear test.[187] In their eyes, India's program was essentially unrestrained. India's warnings were therefore incapable of swaying Pakistan's behavior. Pakistan held off nuclear testing until India's second round of tests in 1998, but by that point Islamabad had already possessed nuclear weapons for several years.

Beliefs about Indian Intentions

India's bomb-making potential influenced Pakistani officials who believed that New Delhi had a flexible nuclear policy and was not bent on building a bomb. For these officials, pushing too hard for nuclear weapons would be counterproductive because it would fuel an arms race with India. I. H. Usmani, the head of the Pakistani Atomic Energy Commission (PAEC), was a prominent proponent of this view. He worried about reactive nuclear proliferation: Pakistan's push to build a nuclear weapon would prompt India to follow suit, and vice versa.[188]

---

[183] Quoted in Perkovich (1999, 268).
[184] Quoted in Perkovich (1999, 270).
[185] Weisman (1985).
[186] Weisman (1985).
[187] Weisman (1985).
[188] Khan (2012, 91).

Usmani explicitly endorsed a strategy of deterrence by proliferation. After China's nuclear test in 1964, he argued that India should have "placed before the international community all components of their device and declared that India has the capability of conducting a nuclear explosion any time it wants" but would not do so.[189] This would send a message to the existing nuclear powers: disarm or face the possibility of another country joining your ranks.

A more powerful faction led by Prime Minister Bhutto and some of his closest allies in government held a different view. In the years preceding India's 1974 nuclear test, they perceived New Delhi's program as unrestrained. Bhutto wrote in 1969, "It appears that she [India] is determined to proceed with her plans to detonate a nuclear bomb."[190] Agha Shahi, who served as Pakistan's foreign minister, concurred. He recalled thinking during the 1960s, "We are now moving into a nuclear age. India is going to develop nuclear weapons."[191]

Belief in the inevitability of an Indian bomb had two effects on the decision-making of Bhutto and his allies. First, it eliminated a key cost of weaponization. Pakistan's behavior could not induce an Indian bomb, in this view, because New Delhi was going to build one regardless. Second, it raised the expected costs of staying nonnuclear. By not arming, Pakistan would face an Indian nuclear monopoly and be vulnerable to blackmail. As a result, Bhutto and his allies pushed hard for a bomb. The Pakistani leader ultimately removed Usmani as head of the PAEC. And, as noted previously, Pakistan began a nuclear weapons program in 1972 and pushed even more vigorously for a bomb after India's 1974 nuclear test.

After 1974, Pakistan essentially viewed India as a nuclear power – even though India did not move to weaponize its nuclear capabilities until the late 1980s. As political scientist Vipin Narang put it, "no one in Pakistan believed it [India's 1974 nuclear test] was peaceful."[192] In a letter to Indian leader Indira Gandhi dated June 6, 1974, Pakistani Prime Minister Bhutto wrote, "It is well established that the testing of a nuclear device is no different from the detonation of a nuclear weapon ... the acquisition of a capability, which has direct and immediate military consequences, becomes a permanent factor to be reckoned with."[193] During a meeting with his advisers a few days later, Bhutto underscored his perception of India's capabilities: "The explosion has introduced a

---

[189] Quoted in Khan (2012, 92).
[190] Khan (2012, 61).
[191] Khan (2012, 61).
[192] Narang (2022, 204).
[193] Quoted in Perkovich (1999, 185–186) and Khan (2012, 119).

qualitative change in the situation between the two countries. Pakistan will not succumb to nuclear blackmail."[194]

India's 1974 test similarly influenced China's views about deterrence by proliferation in South Asia. Pakistan had previously sought nuclear assistance from China, but officials in Beijing refused. According to the CIA, Bhutto understood China's logic: "Peking has in the past turned down requests with the argument that such cooperation might provoke Moscow to give New Delhi a nuclear capability." In the aftermath of India's first nuclear test, however, he recognized that "this argument no longer applies."[195] Since the possibility of inducing an Indian bomb could no longer influence China's calculus, Bhutto renewed his request for aid. This time China agreed, ultimately providing a bomb design and uranium enrichment technology to Pakistan in the 1980s.[196]

Conclusion

How does nuclear latency influence weapons proliferation and arms racing? Latent nuclear deterrence theory expects that countries can deter armament under three conditions: they possess ENR technology, the potential proliferator is a rival, and none of the latent state's rivals have unrestrained programs. This chapter evaluated the theory by examining six case studies of potential nuclear armament. It turned up evidence that was largely consistent with the theory.

Deterrence by proliferation dissuaded others from arming when the theory's conditions were satisfied. However, only the case of Brazil met the requisite requirements. Officials in Brasilia understood that racing to a bomb would backfire by triggering reactive weaponization by Argentina. Argentine leaders held a similar view, despite facing pressures to build nuclear bombs due to the country's rivalry with a nuclear-armed United Kingdom. It is difficult to assess the importance of weaponless deterrence relative to other factors, even in these successful cases. Officials were thinking along the lines that latent nuclear deterrence theory expects, but multiple factors were pushing in the same direction. Deterrence by proliferation did not single-handedly cause Argentina and Brazil to remain nonnuclear. Instead, it was one factor among several that contributed to this outcome.

The other cases illustrated four main pathways to deterrence by proliferation failure. The first is if the potential proliferator did not

[194] Quoted in Khan (2012, 121–123).
[195] US Central Intelligence Agency (1974).
[196] Kroenig (2009b).

have any rivals with significant ENR capabilities, rendering proliferation threats noncredible. This applied to Nigeria's efforts to stymie South Africa's nuclear program in the early 1980s and Pakistan's attempts to halt Indian weaponization beginning in the mid-1960s. Second, bilateral relations between the potential proliferator and the ENR-capable rival warmed, reducing the expected punishment costs if the rival armed too. This played the biggest role in the Franco-German case during the 1950s. Some French officials opposed building nuclear weapons on the grounds that doing so would cause West Germany to follow suit. However, this argument carried less weight as the rivalry between the two countries ended and leaders in Paris began to embrace cooperation with Bonn. Third, the ENR-capable rival had an unrestrained nuclear program. As shown by Pakistani assessments of Indian nuclear intentions, proliferation threats have little deterrence value if the challenger believes that the threat-maker is going to arm regardless of what the challenger does. Worse than that, believing that a rival is racing to a bomb can trigger an arms race. Fourth, the potential proliferator faced a third-party nuclear threat that overshadowed the rival's potential response. This played a role in French and Indian nuclear decision making, as both countries were trying to match the capabilities of rivals that were already nuclear armed (the Soviet Union and China).

These conclusions amplify what we learned in the preceding chapters. When countries have restrained nuclear programs, obtaining ENR capabilities can enhance their influence in high-stakes interactions. However, becoming ENR-capable in the presence of an unrestrained nuclear program can incite instability, encouraging others to obtain nuclear weapons. This chapter, like the others, also indicated that full nuclear latency is more helpful than partial latency for gaining influence without arms. West Germany's laboratory-scale ENR activities drew significant attention in France during the 1950s. Yet, in most of the other cases, larger ENR programs attracted greater attention internationally and communicated more effective proliferation threats.

One limitation of this chapter is that it analyzed a small number countries – those that had full nuclear latency – as potential challengers to the status quo. I focused on the twenty-three states that obtained large-scale ENR programs as potential proliferators because they were the strongest candidates to arm. It is impossible for countries without this capability to indigenously build nuclear weapons – unless they are able to steal or buy sufficient fissile material from another state. However, limiting the focus of my analysis to this subset of countries comes with an analytical downside. The cases I studied might be "hard" ones for deterrence, as states that get the means to produce fissile material are already more determined to get nuclear weapons. This is a common challenge in international relations research when scholars study military or economic coercion.[197] Deterrence by proliferation might work before a potential challenger obtains full nuclear latency. For example, Saudi Arabia might be deterred from moving toward nuclear weapons by the possibility that this would trigger an Iranian bomb. This chapter cannot tell us whether latent nuclear powers gain influence in this kind of situation, just whether they can dissuade countries that are already fully latent from arming.[198] My analysis might therefore under-report the potential deterrence benefits of nuclear latency in the armament context.

---

[197] See, for example, Fearon (2002), Miller (2014b), and Morgan et al. (2014).

[198] Whether Iran would be deterred from arming based on Saudi Arabia's nuclear response does fall within the scope of this chapter's analysis.

What is the role of nuclear technology in international relations? Ever since the US bombing of Hiroshima and Nagasaki in August 1945, scholars have examined how nuclear weapons influence international peace and stability. At this point, it is widely recognized that the international spread of nuclear weapons is consequential. Another reality is less widely acknowledged in scholarship: Having the technological capacity to make nuclear weapons influences a country's political fortunes even if it does not ultimately arm.

Nuclear technology can serve peaceful and military ends. It enables countries to generate electricity, produce medical isotopes, and conduct basic research, in addition to making nuclear bombs. Many countries have developed the technological building blocks needed to make nuclear weapons. Just ten of them went on to build and deploy nuclear forces, including China, Russia, and the United States. The others stopped short of a full-blown nuclear arsenal. These so-called latent nuclear powers have "peaceful" nuclear programs that give them the potential foundation for a bomb program. They do not possess nuclear weapons but could make them quickly if they so desired, giving them a capability known as nuclear latency. From Latin America, to the Middle East, to East Asia, latent nuclear powers shape the international landscape.

This book is about this group of countries. It has sought to provide a comprehensive assessment of nuclear latency in world politics. The book has addressed the key questions about this underappreciated subject. How many countries have obtained nuclear latency, and who are the latent nuclear powers? Why do countries obtain latent nuclear capabilities? How does the spread of nuclear latency influence international peace and security? Does having nuclear latency give countries greater international influence? Or is nuclear latency merely a recipe for military conflict, arms races, and other forms of global instability?

I introduced a framework – latent nuclear deterrence theory – to help answer these questions. Nuclear latency can produce both desirable and unwanted effects for the countries that develop it. The theory helps us better understand when latent nuclear forces confer influence, and when they invite instability. To do so, it first explains how it is possible to use latent nuclear forces for international leverage. The theory then identifies major challenges that countries face when they seek to use nuclear latency to enhance their influence and describes potential solutions to these barriers.

It is clear how a country armed with nuclear weapons could gain influence over other countries: The nuclear-armed state could threaten to launch a devastating military attack if others threaten its vital national interests. By contrast, how a state that is close to a bomb but does not yet possess one could have international leverage is not immediately obvious and requires deeper explanation. There are three mechanisms through which latent nuclear powers could gain political influence over other countries. I call them deterrence by proliferation, delayed attack, and doubt.

In deterrence by proliferation, countries threaten to arm with nuclear weapons if another state takes some undesirable foreign-policy action. This is a political threat rather than a military one. Countries raise the possibility of building a destructive military technology but not necessarily using it in combat. The other two means of influence, by contrast, involve more-traditional forms of military punishment. In deterrence by delayed attack, a nonnuclear country raises the possibility of an eventual nuclear strike in the event of war. After suffering a serious military attack, a latent nuclear power could swiftly assemble a nuclear weapon and then use it in a counterstrike. Punishment could be delayed by hours, days, weeks, months, or even years – depending on the country's nuclear capabilities. Deterrence by doubt can operate as a country gets very close to a bomb, as was the case in India and Pakistan during the 1980s. At that point, other countries may think that the country could already be nuclear-armed even though it is, in fact, nonnuclear. This uncertainty can make others think twice before mounting an invasion or other kind of military attack.

Three major challenges make it difficult to gain influence without arms via these three mechanisms. First, there is a time delay between a foreign-policy infraction and the imposition of the threatened punishment. This necessitates that countries have keen foresight. The time gap also provides opportunities to stop a counterpart's nuclear armament after a challenge to the status quo, and results in discounted punishment costs. Second, implementing threats is costly for the threatener, not just the country that would experience punishment. This can make threats in weaponless deterrence appear unbelievable. Third, seeking nuclear latency can invite insecurity by catalyzing preventive military strikes, arms races, and other countermeasures.

To have any hope of succeeding in latent nuclear deterrence, countries must mitigate these challenges. Doing so depends on three main factors: a state's nuclear capabilities, the intentions of leaders, and the salience of the issue at stake. When it comes to capabilities, I focus on the technology that gives countries the ability to produce the most essential ingredient for a bomb: fissile material. As for intentions, I distinguish unrestrained nuclear programs from restrained ones. An unrestrained program is one in which leaders have made a final decision to build nuclear weapons – one that is not reversible in the absence of an unexpected domestic or international shock. Relevant examples include the US Manhattan Project, China's campaign to obtain a nuclear capability after 1954, and Iraq's nuclear program once Saddam Hussein rose to power. When a program is restrained, a country is not bent on arming but it may flirt with this possibility, like in the cases of Argentina, Germany, and Japan.

In high-stakes situations, countries with restrained nuclear programs might be able to enhance their international influence by obtaining uranium enrichment or plutonium reprocessing (ENR) capabilities, which enable them to make fissile material. However, if countries race to build nuclear weapons, this same capacity can provoke an international backlash.

This book has evaluated these claims in several foreign policy contexts, presenting new quantitative and qualitative evidence. It has examined what world leaders think about weaponless deterrence, focusing on the beliefs of government officials in ten latent nuclear powers. After enhancing the plausibility of weaponless deterrence with this case evidence, the book has quantitatively examined how obtaining nuclear latency changed a country's fortunes, focusing on serious military conflict (international crises and fatal disputes), foreign-policy alignment (the challenger's foreign-policy preferences and preference similarity among adversaries), and leverage within military alliances (US troop deployments). I have taken a design-based approach to causal inference, identifying how a state's adoption of nuclear latency changed these outcomes in future years compared to the counterfactual where the country stayed nonlatent. The book has also examined how nuclear latency influenced preventive military attacks and arms races, two key forms of global instability. It has analyzed four cases where countries considered using military force to stop nuclear weapons proliferation and six cases of potential nuclear armament. In addition, the book has devoted a chapter to the causes of nuclear latency, addressing why states covet latent nuclear forces and the constraints they face in building them.

The backbone of the book's empirical analysis is a newly updated database – the Nuclear Latency (NL) dataset – that contains information on all publicly known ENR facilities built globally from 1939 to 2012.[1] To make fissile material – plutonium or weapons-grade highly enriched uranium (HEU) – countries need ENR facilities; ENR plants are widely seen as the most sensitive nuclear technology due to the bomb-making potential that they provide. Yet these plants can also be used in a nuclear energy program to make fuel or recycle waste. According to my database, thirty-three countries had ENR programs at some point during the nuclear age. Twenty-three of them had facilities that, at least in theory, could have produced enough fissile material for at least one bomb, giving them what I call full nuclear latency. The other ten had a laboratory-scale ENR capability, or partial nuclear latency.

Much of the evidence is supportive of latent nuclear deterrence theory. Three broad findings have emerged from the book's quantitative and qualitative analyses. First, many world leaders have faith in weaponless deterrence, believing that nuclear latency gives them greater political leverage. Second, the degree to which this is true in practice depends on the stage of latency a country reaches. Partial nuclear latency generated relatively few political benefits, but moving beyond laboratory-scale ENR programs more reliably enhanced a country's foreign-policy influence. Third, a state's motives are important for understanding the political effects of nuclear latency. When countries had restrained nuclear programs, nuclear latency conferred some international influence. Yet the benefits did not always materialize. Sometimes they were present in fewer than half of the years I studied, depending on the foreign-policy outcome and various methodological choices.[2] Unrestrained programs generated fewer and less consistent foreign-policy benefits when countries obtained nuclear latency. Worse than that, they sometimes fueled crises and arms races.

Overall, these findings underscore that there are not simple answers to questions about nuclear latency in world politics. Latent nuclear forces influence international peace and stability in nuanced but important ways. Obtaining bomb-making capabilities can be a path to greater security but it is one laden with obstacles and the prospects for success are uncertain.

---

[1] This database builds on Fuhrmann and Tkach (2015).
[2] Details about the sensitivity of the findings are in Chapter 5.

Learning about Latency: Lessons for International Politics

The term nuclear latency is relatively new to the international relations lexicon.[3] Yet the underlying concept is nearly as old as the atomic age. Government reports, news stories, and academic studies have long acknowledged the significance of some countries being technologically close to a bomb, using phrases like "threshold state," "near-nuclear status," or "virtual nuclear arsenal" to describe this phenomenon.[4]

Much of the early thinking focused on the undesirable effects of latent nuclear forces. The 1946 Acheson–Lilienthal Report, an early US government attempt to grapple with the international spread of nuclear technology, highlighted the problem of latency.[5] Knowing that countries with nuclear energy programs could build weapons with relative ease, the report called for international control over fissile-material production, leaving individual countries without the technology needed to make the most essential ingredient for a bomb. The international community did not adopt this proposal, however, and many states launched ENR programs in the ensuing years and decades.

As dual-use nuclear technology spread around the world, some began to wonder whether nuclear latency could produce desirable foreign-policy effects. The idea of a latent deterrent is more than fifty years old. In 1966, the journalist Leonard Beaton wrote that having the capacity to make nuclear weapons without actually possessing them could become "a bargaining counter of some importance," adding that "the military and political usefulness of this status remains to be explored."[6]

Interest in nuclear latency is growing today. Journalists and government officials around the globe frequently call attention to near-nuclear status as an important feature of contemporary international politics, particularly when referencing countries such as Iran, Japan, and South Korea. Scholars have taken on this issue with renewed vigor as well. Over a recent ten-year period (2013–2022), more than 500 books and articles addressed nuclear latency, at least in passing.[7] However, this is

---

[3] The earliest mentions I have found come from reports produced by scientists at Los Alamos National Laboratory for the US Department of Energy during the 1990s. One example is Canavan (1998).

[4] See, for example, Schelling (1962), US Central Intelligence Agency (1981a), Quester (1991), Hagerty (1993), Mazarr (1997a), and Cohen and Pilat (1998).

[5] Pilat (2014).

[6] Beaton (1966, 16).

[7] Some examples include Fuhrmann and Tkach (2015), Mehta and Whitlark (2017a), Volpe (2017), Narang (2017), Pilat (2019), Saunders (2019), and Mattiacci et al. (2022).

just a small fraction – about 1 percent – of the books and articles that mentioned nuclear weapons during this same period.[8]

Although knowledge about nuclear latency has thankfully accumulated over the past several decades, how exactly latent nuclear forces influence peace and stability, if at all, remained unclear. Claims about nuclear latency by journalists and policymakers often have a speculative flavor. And scholarship up until this point produced conflicting findings, with some studies reporting that nuclear latency deters military conflict or confers influence and others concluding that it is either irrelevant or destabilizing.

This book has taken a deep dive on the subject of nuclear latency, striving to clarify the role that nuclear technology plays in world politics. Ten lessons emerge from the preceding chapters. These lessons carry implications for nuclear deterrence, proliferation, disarmament, and international relations more generally. Taken together, they challenge some widely held views while also confirming insights from earlier thinking.

Lesson #1: Countries Practice Nuclear Deterrence without Assembled Bombs

In January 2004, the nuclear scientist Sigfried Hecker joined a group of fellow Americans on a trip to North Korea.[9] At the time, there were widespread concerns about North Korea's nuclear ambitions. Ten years earlier, the North Koreans struck a deal with the United States and its allies, known as the Agreed Framework, to freeze weapon-related activities in exchange for economic and political inducements. But North Korea restarted previously shuttered nuclear facilities in 2002 and formally withdrew from the nuclear Nonproliferation Treaty (NPT), an international agreement binding countries to refrain from obtaining nuclear weapons, the next year.

Pyongyang wanted the visiting Americans to bring a message back to Washington: It had nuclear weapons. North Korean officials showed the Americans their nuclear complex at Yongbyon, which housed facilities for making plutonium – a critical ingredient for a bomb. As a former director of the Los Alamos National Laboratory, where the United States assembled its first atomic bombs, Hecker had the technical bona fides to assess North Korea's capabilities. While at Yongbyon, he asked

---

[8] These figures are based on a search I carried out in Google Scholar on February 2, 2023.
[9] This story draws on my conversations with Sigfried Hecker on April 4, 2022, and Hecker and Serbin (2023).

the North Koreans to see some of the plutonium they claimed to have produced. They agreed, presenting Hecker with a sealed glass jar containing 200 grams of plutonium in metal form. Picking up the jar, Hecker could tell by its weight and warmth that the material inside was, in fact, plutonium.

After the visit to Yongbyon, Hecker and his colleagues met with North Korean Ambassador Ri Gun. Ri told the Americans that they had now seen his country's "deterrent."[10] But they had not seen a nuclear deterrent in the traditional sense, just that the North Koreans knew how to make plutonium. Building a nuclear weapon requires three main steps: producing fissile material, weaponizing this material, and integrating the weapon into a delivery system. Most scholars believe that completing all three steps and having a ready-to-fire weapon is a minimum requirement for a nuclear deterrent. Yet the North Koreans apparently believed that merely completing the first step – producing fissile material – was sufficient to convince Washington that they were nuclear-armed, thereby gaining influence over the United States.

This story underscores one of the book's key themes: Countries use bomb-making potential to gain international influence. Latent nuclear powers have used all three mechanisms of weaponless deterrence in pursuit of international influence. Sometimes leaders practicing latent nuclear deterrence are direct. In 1973, Spanish leader Luis Carrero Blanco went so far as to present US Secretary of State Henry Kissinger with an internal government report concluding that Spain had the capacity to build a bomb within two years. This bald-faced move, which occurred before Spain was a NATO member, was meant to convey a message: Do more to defend us or we will build nuclear weapons.[11] On other occasions, attempts to gain influence without arms are more subtle. The threat may be an implicit one communicated by developing certain types of nuclear technology. Either way, threats of this nature are widespread in world politics.

During the Cold War, Argentina, Brazil, Egypt, France, India, Pakistan, South Africa, Spain, and others embraced this approach. More recently, nonnuclear countries such as Iran, Japan, and Saudi Arabia have used the possibility of arming with nuclear weapons to gain political leverage. This tactic continues today. On January 11, 2023, South Korean president Yoon Suk-yeo said that his country could "acquire our own nuke" to deal with the growing nuclear threat from

---

[10] Quoted in Hecker and Serbin (2023, chapter 4).
[11] For a detailed study on this kind of threat, see Volpe (2017).

North Korea.[12] Yoon's statement seems calibrated to gain international influence. By threatening to build nuclear weapons if South Korea's security environment does not improve, Yoon may be hoping to induce greater caution among North Korean leaders, encourage China to rein-in its ally, or obtain stronger security commitments from the United States, including the possible reintroduction of US tactical nuclear weapons on South Korean soil.[13]

The United States has played this game too, leveraging an ally's bomb-making potential in the hope of moderating a common adversary's behavior. For example, when he was vice president, Joe Biden told Chinese leader Xi Jinping that Japan could go nuclear if China did not do more to restrain North Korea.[14]

Lesson #2: Nuclear Latency Sometimes Confers Political Influence

Countries try to gain influence from latent nuclear forces – but does it work? Many of the analysts who have commented on this issue express skepticism about weaponless nuclear deterrence. For these scholars, deterrence by proliferation, delayed attack, and doubt are wholly ineffective. As political scientists Rupal Mehta and Rachel Whitlark conclude, countries "suffer more burdens than benefits once they acquire nuclear latency."[15] Their research finds no evidence that building a latent nuclear capability lowers a country's vulnerability to military conflict.[16] Matthew Kroenig puts an even finer point on it, arguing that one must believe leaders "are stupid" to accept that countries such as Iran or Japan could achieve deterrence with their latent nuclear forces. He added, "To suggest ... that by stopping a screw-driver's turn away from the bomb, both countries can somewhat get what they want is ridiculous."[17]

This book tells a different story. A large number of policymakers around the world believe that latent deterrence works. The book has synthesized views about latent nuclear deterrence in ten countries representing most of the world's regions. Global leaders do not always make their thoughts readily discernible to outsiders. However, a deep look at the historical record reveals that confidence in weaponless deterrence runs deep among a diverse set of government officials. Seyed Mohammad Hossein Adeli, Iran's former ambassador to the United

---

[12] *The Economist* (2023).
[13] *The Economist* (2023).
[14] Adelstein (2018).
[15] Mehta and Whitlark (2017b).
[16] Mehta and Whitlark (2017a, 2016).
[17] Kroenig (2014b, 50–51).

Kingdom, exemplified this view in 2007, saying, "Iran would like to have the technology, and that is enough for deterrence."[18]

World leaders are correct that nuclear latency can confer political influence. But weaponless deterrence does not come easy, and latent nuclear forces are far from a magic pill that will cure any ailment. Even under ideal conditions, which include having a restrained nuclear program and high stakes, gaining a fissile-material production capacity does not always generate international influence.

The book's statistical analysis has examined how foreign-policy patterns changed in each of the ten years that followed the emergence of nuclear latency, in addition to the year of latency onset. The evidence revealed that states with full nuclear latency and restrained nuclear programs reaped foreign-policy benefits in some – but not all – of the years during their first decade as a latent nuclear power. Full nuclear latency reliably lowered the number of crises in an average of 3.58 years, changed the challenger's foreign-policy preferences an average of 6.86 years, led to greater foreign-policy similarity with adversaries in an average of 4.13 years, and increased the number of troops for US allies an average of 3.75 years.[19] The weakest evidence comes from fatal disputes, where fully latent states initially saw a reduction in two years but averaged a paltry 0.75 years across all of the tests.

The reduction in crises does not exhibit a clear time trend, as this benefit comes and goes over the ten-year postlatency period. The other benefits are concentrated in particular time periods. Changes in foreign-policy preferences – both the challenger's preferences and alignment with adversaries – typically start the year after full latency onset and then persist for a few years before fading away. By contrast, we start to see more reliable troop increases at the end of the ten-year period but not right away.[20] Full latency causes more troops to be deployed as soon as three years after full latency onset, but there is always a time delay of some kind.[21]

---

[18] Hirsh and Journal (2013).

[19] These numbers are based on my main analysis and all of the robustness tests carried out in Chapter 5. The averages increase when I remove cases where a change in research design makes the results less credible by worsening the covariate balance between latent and nonlatent states.

[20] In the rare tests where there was a reliable reduction in fatal disputes, this was also toward the later half of the period I examined.

[21] One limitation of my analysis is that it cannot tell us what happens after a decade of latency. The benefits could persist, reemerge, or disappear after this time. In the analysis of troop deployments, we saw that the ATTs remained positive and statistically significant for at least another five years after the first decade of being a fully latent state.

Based on these results, the dynamics of latent nuclear deterrence vary based on whether the latent nuclear power seeks to influence an ally or adversary.[22] Deterrence by proliferation is the primary mechanism in play for both foreign-policy preferences and US troop deployments – the outcomes where we see a strong time trend. With allies, this mechanism seems to become more effective over time as capabilities mature. When dealing with an adversary, though, the passage of time appears to weaken deterrence by proliferation. Yet, among adversaries, deterrence by delayed attack and doubt should strengthen over time as states make greater technological progress toward a bomb.

It is difficult to find "smoking gun" evidence for nuclear deterrence, whether countries use weapons-in-being or latent nuclear forces to gain influence. Heads of government generally want to appear strong, steadfast, and decisive. Admitting that they were deterred by a rival might cultivate a perception of weaknesses. Leaders may therefore deny that an adversary's nuclear program played any role in their decision making when it was, in fact, a key factor. They may also remain totally silent on the issue in public.[23] This makes things difficult for researchers trying to get inside leaders' heads.

However, a deep examination of the historical record has turned up evidence that deterrence by proliferation, delayed attack, and doubt influenced the target's foreign-policy behavior. For example, US officials from both Republican and Democratic administrations acknowledged that the possibility of fomenting an Iranian bomb contributed to their unwillingness to support airstrikes against Iran's nuclear facilities at various points over the past twenty years. During the 1990s, some US officials and foreign-policy commentators thought that attacking North Korea was too risky because Pyongyang *might* already be in possession of one to two nuclear weapons. Others worried less about this, believing that North Korea did not yet have nuclear weapons, but feared that backing North Korean officials into a corner would compel them to race toward a bomb – the very thing Washington was trying to stop. And officials in both Argentina and Brazil later admitted that they reined-in their nuclear ambitions at least partially to avoid fueling an arms race in Latin America.

South Africa's nuclear latency also helped curtail Communist expansion in the region during the 1970s, even if it did not totally eliminate this threat. As political scientist Peter Liberman argues, "South Africa's

---

[22] For more on bargaining dynamics among allies, see Volpe (2023).

[23] Leaders are more likely to express confidence that their own nuclear capabilities provide political leverage, as this acknowledgment does not carry the same reputation costs.

well-known uranium enrichment capability and test site by themselves had already" limited Soviet aggressiveness, rendering a full blown nuclear arsenal unnecessary.[24] Historian Anna-Mart van Wyk reached a similar conclusion, focusing on deterrence by doubt: "By keeping everyone guessing about whether it had 'a bomb in the basement,' Pretoria gained a degree of leverage in its relations with the outside world and within the geopolitical dynamics of southern Africa."[25]

The 1982 Falklands War provides another illustration, underscoring both the viability and limitations of weaponless deterrence. On April 2, 1982, Argentina seized the Falkland Islands, perhaps hoping that the United Kingdom would not risk war over a small piece of territory 8,000 miles from its homeland. But Britain launched a military campaign to reclaim the territory, achieving victory within two months.

The United States' actions during this conflict support two key dimensions of latent nuclear deterrence theory. First, the United States saw Argentine nuclear weapons proliferation as a potential form of punishment if the war got out of hand. As the conflict was heating up, US Secretary of State Alexander Haig asked his colleagues to prepare an "assessment of Argentina's potential for retaliation against U.S. interests," given American support for the United Kingdom during the conflict. A memo sent to Haig on April 13, eleven days after Argentina occupied the islands, indicated that Buenos Aires might punish Washington by "Reaching a national decision to use its unsafe-guarded nuclear facilities to develop a nuclear weapon."[26] The memo added that this might be done "both in defiance of US policy and to increase Argentine leverage in any future Falklands or Beagle crisis."[27] Second, deterrence by proliferation influenced US behavior. According to senior US officials, the possibility that Argentina might arm with nuclear weapons caused Haig to mediate the dispute.[28] By preventing Argentina from suffering a humiliating military defeat, these officials believed, Washington could stave off an Argentine bomb. The United States ultimately supported the United Kingdom during the war, but weaponless deterrence motivated Washington to control escalation.

At the same time, Argentina's nuclear latency did not stop the United Kingdom from fighting to reclaim the islands. Having latent nuclear forces, then, may not protect a country from retaliation if they seize

---

[24] Liberman (2001, 61).
[25] van Wyk (2019, 165).
[26] Foreign Relations of the United States (1984).
[27] Foreign Relations of the United States (1984). The Beagle crisis refers to a conflict with Chile over disputed islands that nearly led to war in 1978.
[28] Gwertzman (1982).

territory or initiate other aggressive foreign-policy actions. Some have argued that nuclear weapons are akin to a shield that enables military conflict.[29] Based on this line of thinking, countries can use military force and then raise the specter of nuclear punishment to limit retaliation or intervention by third parties. Russia's invasion of Ukraine in February 2022 has this flavor: After launching the invasion, Moscow threatened nuclear escalation if the United States or other countries joined the conflict. The Falklands War suggests that latent nuclear forces are ill suited for this kind of gambit – at least when deterrence by proliferation is the mechanism at play.

Lesson #3: Shorter Breakout Times Are Better for Deterrence

All latent nuclear powers have bomb-making potential. But they vary in their exact breakout times – how long it would take to obtain enough fissile material for a single nuclear bomb. For countries such as Japan, the breakout time is essentially zero because they already possess enough plutonium or highly enriched uranium to make at least one nuclear weapon. Others have demonstrated the ability to make fissile material on a small scale but may be a couple of years or more from having enough for one or more bombs. For example, Romania separated 100 milligrams of plutonium at the Pitesti Nuclear Research Institute during the 1980s. According to the International Atomic Energy Agency (IAEA), however, 8 kilograms is needed to make one bomb.

This book has accounted for this difference by measuring and analyzing two stages of nuclear latency: partial and full. Partially latent states, such as Australia, South Korea, and Sweden, had laboratory-scale ENR programs only. Fully latent countries go beyond the laboratory stage to build bigger ENR plants. These facilities are large enough to reasonable produce enough fissile material for a bomb but may not be commercial scale. Countries that made it to this stage include Brazil, Canada, and Germany.

Many policymakers and scholars see short breakout times as politically undesirable. Political scientist Tristan Volpe argues that getting too close to a bomb erodes a state's ability to coerce others with nuclear latency.[30] In this view, once countries produce fissile material on a large scale, giving them short breakout times, others will see nuclear proliferation as inevitable. Therefore, the latent nuclear power cannot credibly promise to refrain from arming if their demands are met, dooming coercion to

---

[29] For example, Beardsley and Asal (2009a) and Bell and Miller (2015).
[30] Volpe (2017).

fail. Others argue that it is better to have one's adversaries farther from a bomb. To illustrate, a key goal of the 2015 Joint Comprehensive Plan of Action (JCPOA), commonly known as the Iran Nuclear Deal, was to make Iran's breakout time at least one year. United States officials preferred a longer breakout time because it gave them adequate time to detect a mad dash to a bomb, and intervene to stop it. After President Donald Trump announced the US withdrawal from the JCPOA on May 8, 2018, Iran's breakout time began to shrink, reaching zero days in June 2022. In the United States, most people see this as an unwelcome trend. White House Press Secretary Jen Psaki said, it "definitely worries us."[31] Nuclear experts David Albright and Sarah Burkhard similarly concluded, "Iran has crossed a new, dangerous threshold."[32] For countries hoping to prevent a nuclear-armed Iran, this is indeed bad news.

From the standpoint of a latent nuclear power, however, a shorter breakout time is better. In general, latent nuclear deterrence strengthens as a country's ENR capabilities advance. The shift from partial to full latency is particularly important. Partial latency did relatively little to improve a country's foreign-policy fortunes. Once countries achieve full latency, however, they have a better chance at reaping political benefits.[33]

Latent nuclear deterrence theory helps explain why full latent states have advantages in gaining influence without arms. Getting closer to a bomb means that a latent nuclear power could inflict punishment sooner, if necessary. This makes it harder for countries to ignore a counterpart's bomb-making potential – a serious risk in weaponless deterrence. As a result of the short distance Japan would have to travel to build a nuclear weapon, the possibility of future armament looms in the background during Tokyo's interactions with Beijing and Seoul. By contrast, East Germany's reprocessing experiments during the 1980s did not foreground weapon proliferation in its relations with other countries. Having full nuclear latency also creates fewer opportunities to escape retaliation and lowers the discount rate on future costs, giving punishment more bite.

Lesson #4: Countries Covet Nuclear Latency for Political Leverage

Why countries build nuclear weapons is a central question in international relations.[34] Yet little research has theorized about why countries

---

[31] TOI staff (2022)

[32] Albright and Burkhard (2022)

[33] In addition, as discussed earlier, some benefits increase over time after states cross the full latency threshold.

[34] See, for example, Sagan (1996), Hymans (2006), Solingen (2007), Rublee (2009), Fuhrmann (2012a), Braut-Heggehammer (2016), Debs and Monteiro (2017).

obtain nuclear latency. This is partially because most scholars associate the development of ENR capabilities with having a nuclear weapons program. If a country has an ENR program, based on this line of thinking, it is probably because it wants a bomb. Political scientists Dong-Joon Jo and Erik Gartzke assume, for example, that a weapons program begins when "a suspect state's nuclear activities are seen to increase noticeably," identifying the construction of an ENR plant as one thing that counts as a noticeable increase.[35]

Analysts often apply this standard when assessing the intentions of individual countries. Argentina's ENR activities during the 1980s, for instance, led some to conclude that it had a concerted bomb program.[36] Others see Turkey's recent quest for a uranium enrichment program as evidence that it wants nuclear weapons.[37] And, according to the prevailing wisdom, Saudi Arabia's interest in ENR technology means that it wants a bomb. Referring to the importance of preventing this technology from falling into Riyadh's hands, US Congressperson Brad Sherman said in 2019, "If you can't trust a regime with a bone saw [the weapon used to assassinate journalist and dissident Jamal Khashoggi in a government-ordered killing], you shouldn't trust it with nuclear weapons."[38] In this view, once a state becomes ENR-capable, its nuclear program is like a train without brakes, steaming down the tracks toward a bomb.[39]

This perception is understandable given the tight connection between ENR programs and nuclear weapons. Some countries are indeed bent on getting nuclear weapons at the time they obtain a significant fissile material production capacity. Ten states, including China, Iraq, and the United States, fit this narrative. But the majority of latent nuclear powers – more than two-thirds – had flexible nuclear policies at the time they become ENR capable. This includes some that ultimately armed with nuclear weapons, such as South Africa.

There is growing recognition in scholarship that hedging plays a central role in nuclear politics.[40] Nuclear hedging is a deliberate strategy to shorten the time needed to make a nuclear bomb.[41] It combines the pursuit of a technological capability with an interest in potentially making nuclear weapons at some point in the future. Commentators

[35] See the codebook and data notes for Jo and Gartzke (2007).
[36] Singh and Way (2004) and Jo and Gartzke (2007).
[37] Rühle (2015).
[38] Bugos (2019).
[39] Former Iranian President Mahmoud Ahmadinejad once described Iran's nuclear program as "a train without brakes."
[40] See especially Narang (2022).
[41] Levite (2002).

sometimes describe hedging as "latency with intent."[42] Countries hedge to have an insurance policy in case their security environment deteriorates, necessitating swift nuclear armament. They may also pursue this strategy to gain stronger defense commitments from allies or influence their adversaries.[43]

This book provides evidence that hedging motivates countries to seek ENR technology, shortening their time to a bomb. Countries strive to become ENR-capable, in part, because they believe that having this technology will enhance their international influence even if they ultimately do not arm. As South Korean official Kim Tae-woo put it following indications that North Korea was unlikely to disarm, "our countermeasures should be to maximize the potential of arming ourselves ... to develop nuclear weapons on our own at any time."[44] Hedging was a strong motive for ten of the countries (43 percent) that achieved full nuclear latency, including lesser-studied cases like Norway and Spain. These countries sought ENR capabilities because they recognized that shortening the time to a bomb would benefit their national security. Yet not everyone did this explicitly to bolster weaponless deterrence. Some officials expressed a vague sense that being ENR-capable would be political advantageous but did not explain why they held this view. These policymakers may have wanted to keep their hands close to their chests, or they might have been acting instinctively without specific political objectives in mind.

Energy security, financial gain, and international status were also motives for obtaining ENR technology. In many cases, such as Japan, Brazil, and India, one or more of these motives existed alongside hedging. Very few countries became fully latent without a desire to hedge or actually race to a bomb. Belgium and the Netherlands stand out in this way.

Recognizing that many countries have flexible nuclear postures influences how we interpret the things leaders say and the actions they take in the future. Some leaders who seek ENR technology may be determined to build nuclear weapons at all costs. But the pursuit of ENR technology does not necessarily mean that a country is building bombs. When a leader seeking ENR technology makes public comments about nuclear weapons, their goal may be to influence an international audience rather than reveal an intent to swiftly arm. Saudi Crown Prince Mohammed bin Salman's suggestion in 2018 that his country could get nuclear weapons

---

[42] For example, Bowen and Moran (2014).

[43] For a discussion of these motives for hedging, see Narang (2017).

[44] Quoted in Oh (2019). Translated from Korean by Hankyeul Yang.

seems calibrated to convey a deterrent threat to Iran – if you build nuclear weapons we will too – not to reveal a Manhattan Project-like program in Saudi Arabia.[45]

Lesson #5: Racing to a Bomb Incites Instability

The idea that nuclear latency is dangerous has deep intellectual roots. In 1962, economist Thomas Schelling warned of instability in a world of near-nuclear states. He argued, "the side that believed it could be first to acquire a few dozen megatons ... would expect to dominate its opponent," leading to swift armament and a war to eliminate the enemy's nuclear infrastructure.[46] Over the next several decades, others echoed the view that latent nuclear forces trigger arms races and military conflict.[47] The destabilizing effects of nuclear latency continue to permeate scholarship today.[48]

When it comes to inviting international blowback, a country's intentions matter too, not just its capabilities. Scholars have long recognized that pursuing nuclear weapons is destabilizing. This is a central claim in a school of thought known as nuclear pessimism, which holds that the international spread of nuclear weapons is dangerous. In laying out the case for nuclear pessimism, political scientist Scott Sagan argues that there is a high risk of preventive war when a country is trying to build nuclear weapons but has not yet produced its first bomb.[49] Racing to build nuclear weapons is also widely believed to prompt other countries to follow suit, a phenomenon scholars call reactive proliferation.[50] However, most research on the political consequences of nuclear weapons pursuit does not focus specifically on whether a country possesses latent nuclear forces.

This book has shown that the intersection of a country's intentions and nuclear capabilities helps us understand when international blowback occurs. Launching an unrestrained nuclear program while possessing ENR technology can harm a country's foreign-policy interests for two reasons.

---

[45] Reuters (2018).

[46] Schelling (1962, 395).

[47] A prominent example is Waltz (1997).

[48] Fuhrmann and Tkach (2015), Mehta and Whitlark (2016), and Mehta and Whitlark (2017a).

[49] Sagan (1994). This is especially true, according to Sagan's argument, in regimes where the military has a big influence on decision making.

[50] See, for example, Sagan (1996), Miller (2014a), and Carnegie and Carson (2018).

First, these factors together reveal the capacity to build nuclear weapons and the political determination to do so. A crisis may emerge as countries hoping to stop the latent nuclear power from arming realize that their time is running out. By contrast, there is less urgency when an ENR-free country races to a bomb, making political or military interventions less likely at that stage.

Second, unrestrained nuclear programs take deterrence by proliferation off the table. Latent nuclear powers cannot gain influence by threatening to arm when others believe that they are already bent on doing so. Countries in this situation must rely on the other two means of influence, deterrence by delayed attack and doubt, to gain leverage from their latent nuclear forces. This is especially problematic when it comes to stopping a rival's armament, since deterrence by proliferation is the only viable mechanism in that context.

At the same time, unrestrained programs provide a key bargaining advantage: They strengthen deterrence by doubt and delayed attack by creating the impression that a country is closer to – or may already possess – a bomb. Since combining nuclear latency with an unrestrained program is both positive and negative for deterrence, their overall effects are likely to be more uncertain.

The evidence assembled in the preceding chapters offers considerable support for this view. The quantitative tests showed that full latency reduced crises and fatal disputes in the presence of an unrestrained nuclear program. Yet these benefits emerged less reliably than when a state had a restrained program – an average of 0.33 years for crises and 0.75 years for fatal disputes. In the best-case scenario, only two of the eleven causal effects were statistically significant. Partial nuclear latency reduced the number of crises in an average of 3.42 years but modestly increased the number of fatal disputes in an average of 1.08 years. The confidence intervals for the estimates of military conflict are much larger than when a program is restrained, underscoring that pairing latency with an unrestrained program generates greater uncertainty. This is consistent with the view that unrestrained programs simultaneously makes things worse and better for latent nuclear powers.

The consequences of unrestrained programs are particularly apparent when examining foreign-policy preferences. In the presence of an unrestrained nuclear program, full nuclear latency caused greater preference dissimilarity among adversaries in an average of 8.27 years.[51] Partial

---

[51] This is the only case from my main analysis in which all eleven of the causal effects were statistically significant.

latency is less consequential, producing an improvement in foreign-policy preference similarity an average of 1.13 years.[52]

The combination of nuclear latency and unrestrained programs also increases the likelihood that others will seriously consider preventive military attacks. Most cases of strike consideration fall into this category: the crisis over North Korea's nuclear program in 1993–94, India's plans to militarily destroy Pakistan's nuclear facilities during the 1980s, the Soviet Union's consideration of an attack against South Africa in the late 1970s, and others.

A similar story emerges for arms races. When a country has at least one ENR-capable rival with an unrestrained program, it is more likely to launch an unrestrained program of its own and ultimately build nuclear weapons. Pakistani officials, for example, perceived India's nuclear program as unrestrained, and this motivated Islamabad to seek its own nuclear weapons.

There is some good news for latent nuclear powers who launch unrestrained programs. Although these states provoke consideration of preventive strikes in other countries, those attacks are less likely to be carried out. The two most high-profile preventive attacks are Israel's strikes against Iraq in 1981 and Syria in 2007. In both of these cases, the target had an unrestrained program but was not yet producing fissile material. Preventive attacks against ENR-capable targets are less frequent, in part, because these countries can use deterrence by delayed attack or doubt to dissuade countries from striking. As Waltz argues, "To know for sure that the country attacked has not already produced or otherwise acquired some deliverable warheads becomes increasingly difficult" as a program advances.[53]

On top of this, latent nuclear powers generally have more survivable nuclear capabilities than their ENR-free counterparts. Countries that launch preventive attacks want to be confident that they can successfully erode the adversary's bomb-making capacity by destroying nuclear facilities and materials. They are less likely to have the requisite confidence when the target is already making fissile material. At that point, countries usually have a sprawling nuclear infrastructure. It would be necessary to destroy multiple facilities, not just a single "chokepoint." Moreover, ENR-capable countries possess substantial indigenous knowledge, giving them the means to rebuild facilities that are destroyed relatively quickly.

---

[52] This is the net effect, as the ATTs for partial latency are sometimes positive and sometimes negative.

[53] Waltz (1981, 15). For a counterargument, see Sagan (1994).

This brings us to a conundrum that I call the success–necessity tradeoff. As the need for a preventive strike becomes more urgent due to the target's advancing nuclear capabilities – particularly the production of fissile material – the likelihood of operational and political success declines. Countries could respond to this tradeoff in two ways. They could prioritize success, striking early in the course of the target's nuclear program even though it may not be clear that military force is needed at that point. Alternatively, an attacker could wait until a country is unambiguously making a final mad dash to a bomb. At that point, a strike may be necessary as a last ditch effort to stop nuclear armament but it is less likely to be successful. When carrying out attacks, countries have historically favored the former option, but the latter is possible in the future. Barack Obama bought into deterrence by proliferation but he was willing to attack Iran if it began a final sprint to arm. A future US leader may be, too.

Lesson #6: Secrecy Is a Blessing and a Curse

Secrecy plays a key role in international relations.[54] Many scholars see secrecy as counterproductive, viewing transparency as a path to greater international cooperation and less conflict. A key tenet of liberal institutionalism, which has shaped the field of international relations since the 1980s, is that the free flow of information is useful for reducing concerns about cheating, making countries more likely to enter into cooperative ventures.[55] The bargaining model of war similarly sees transparency as a conflict-mitigation tool, since military conflict arises from a lack of clear information about an adversary's capabilities or resolve.[56] However, a new wave of research over the past decade points to the virtues of secrecy.[57] Withholding information from other countries can be useful for gaining a tactical advantage, preventing escalation, preserving norms, and protecting national security.[58]

When it comes to nuclear latency, secrecy presents countries with opportunities and vulnerabilities. Prior research has shown that states may conceal their military capabilities to prevent others from taking counteractions.[59] This brings to light the main benefit of secrecy for

[54] For a recent overview of research on secrecy, see Carnegie (2021).
[55] Keohane (1984).
[56] Fearon (1995).
[57] Relevant examples include O'Rourke (2018), Carnegie and Carson (2018), Carnegie and Carson (2019), Coe and Vaynman (2020), and Poznansky (2020).
[58] Carnegie (2021, 220–222).
[59] Slantchev (2010).

a country seeking latent nuclear forces: It lowers the risk of preventive military strikes and reactive nuclear armament. Countries are well aware that their pursuit of sensitive nuclear technology could incite instability. To stop this from happening, a state may conceal its nuclear facilities from public view, developing them covertly. If they are successful, preventive strikes or arms races are unlikely since others cannot retaliate against nuclear programs about which they do not know.

Prior to 1981, Iraq developed its nuclear capabilities openly. It procured a nuclear reactor from France and declared the facility to the international community, subjecting it to IAEA safeguards. Baghdad also sought assistance in plutonium reprocessing from Italy and received nuclear materials from Brazil.[60] After Israeli bombed the French-supplied reactor, however, Iraq took its nuclear program underground, hoping to avoid another attack. It had some success in concealing its program. The United States severely underestimated Iraq's nuclear capabilities in the lead up to the 1991 Persian Gulf War. After the war, the *Gulf War Air Power Survey* concluded, "we now know that the Iraqis' program to amass enough enriched uranium to begin producing atomic bombs was more extensive, more redundant, further along, and considerably less vulnerable to air attack than was realized at the outset of Desert Storm."[61]

Yet keeping nuclear capabilities secret comes with a serious downside: It undermines deterrence. Stanley Kubrick's 1964 classic film *Dr. Strangelove* illustrates a key lesson for practitioners of deterrence: Capabilities that are unknown cannot deter.[62] In this fictional parody, the Soviet Union developed a machine to launch its nuclear missiles automatically, without intervention from humans, in the event of a US attack. This so-called *doomsday machine* was meant to bolster deterrence. But there was just one problem: The United States did not know about the device until it was too late. As the film's title character put it: "The whole point of the doomsday machine is lost ... if you keep it a secret! Why didn't you tell the world, eh?!" To have any hope of gaining leverage from latent nuclear forces, the country one hopes to influence must know about them.

Latent nuclear powers can address this quandary by pursuing secrecy and transparency simultaneously.[63] They could reveal one or more ENR plants but conceal others. This approach would let potential attackers

---

[60] Fuhrmann (2012a, 112–124). See also Kroenig (2010).
[61] Quoted in Kreps and Fuhrmann (2011).
[62] Green and Long (2017) analyze the problem of clandestine capabilities in deterrence.
[63] This strategy would not stop reactive nuclear proliferation, however.

know that the latent nuclear power could arm quickly, if necessary, while raising doubts about the aggressor's ability to wipe out the entire program in an attack. Iran may be pursuing a strategy along these lines. It has a number of known nuclear facilities that are relevant for bomb making. Given the scope of its program, it is possible that other facilities exist about which its adversaries do not know. If true, this would give an adversary pause before launching a preventive strike.

History shows that it is difficult to fully conceal a large-scale ENR capability. Foreign-intelligence services are adept at detecting programs that produce sufficient fissile material for a bomb, although they do not have a perfect track record. The United States and its European allies, for example, found Iran's enrichment plant in Qom, which the Iranians buried deep in a mountain, in 2006, three years before it was publicly revealed.[64] Laboratory-scale ENR programs are more likely to fly under the radar due to their small scale.

Lesson #7: Perceptions of Intentions Matter

The efficacy of weaponless deterrence hinges on a country's intentions. Countries that show nuclear restraint can gain foreign-policy leverage when they obtain ENR technology. When they race to arm with nuclear weapons, however, latent nuclear powers erode their ability to enhance their political influence. These claims rest on a key assumption: That other countries can correctly discern a latent nuclear power's true intentions. This may not always be the case.

I have identified unrestrained nuclear programs with the benefit of hindsight and access to materials that provide insights into decision making in countries with nuclear latency. In real time, however, it can be difficult for countries to assess the intentions of others. Whether a country is bent on building nuclear weapons is not directly observable to outsiders. Foreigners can often see the development of nuclear plants, but the same technology can serve peaceful or military ends. Moreover, latent nuclear powers have incentives to misrepresent their aims. When they are determined to arm, they may obfuscate this fact to avoid international blowback. On the other hand, they may want to cultivate doubt about their intentions in order to bolster deterrence by doubt. Either way, it can be hard for countries to deduce whether a counterpart's aims are threatening or innocuous.

---

[64] United States officials did not immediately know that the site they had detected was an enrichment plant (Ghosh, 2009).

As a result, countries often express uncertainty when sizing up a counterpart's nuclear intentions. For example, in the early 1990s, press reports indicated that Algeria had developed a nuclear reactor with assistance from China, prompting a debate within the US government over Algeria's intentions. Some in Washington viewed this revelation as evidence that Algeria intended to build nuclear weapons, but the reactor could also have been part of a legitimate program for nuclear research. This made it difficult for the United States to pinpoint the true purpose of the Algerian plant; the government's conclusions in formerly classified documents were generally guarded and tentative. As one State Department assessment put it, "we do not have sufficient information from which to conclude that the GOA [Algerian Government] has decided to pursue a military nuclear program."[65]

When there is uncertainty surrounding intentions, people may assume the worst, especially when assessing an adversary. A latent nuclear power might attempt to overcome this by communicating with words and deeds that its intentions are innocuous. But this leads to another problem: Leaders see what they expect to be present based on their image of the signaler.[66] There is a human tendency to see someone's intentions as hostile when we believe that they are aggressive or untrustworthy.

In November 1951, the football teams at Dartmouth College and Princeton University squared off in what would become a particularly rough game. A classic study by psychologists Albert Hastorf and Hadley Cantril found that students at the two universities perceived this game very differently.[67] Princeton students reported seeing the Dartmouth football team commit an average of nearly ten infractions – twice as many as students from Dartmouth reported seeing. Similarly, in international relations, leaders tend to assume the worst when assessing the intentions of their adversaries.[68]

This tendency can complicate latent nuclear deterrence. Countries may conclude that a rival is racing for a bomb when, in fact, the adversary is content to remain latent. Information suggestive of non-weaponization may be downplayed or ignored, leading to more threatening conclusions about an adversary's aims.[69] Leaders may not even seek out potentially helpful information, believing that they already

---

[65] US Department of State (1991).
[66] Jervis (1976, 68).
[67] Hastrof and Cantril (1954).
[68] See, for example, Levy (1983) and Mercer (1996).
[69] At the same time, decision-makers will latch on to information of questionable reliability – for example, cheap talk – if it supports their beliefs about the signaler (Yarhi-Milo, 2014, 4).

know that a rival's intentions are sinister. United States Vice President Dick Cheney argued in 2002, for instance, that more information about Saddam's Hussein's nuclear ambitions would be dangerous: "a return of [international] inspectors [in Iraq]," he contended, "would provide . . . false comfort that Saddam was somehow 'back in his box.'"[70] Ultimately, a formerly top secret US National Intelligence Estimate from October 2002 infamously concluded, "We judge that Iraq has continued its weapons of mass destruction (WMD) programs in defiance of UN resolutions and restrictions . . . if left unchecked, it probably will have a nuclear weapon during this decade."[71] This belief, which turned out to be wrong, contributed to a US-led war to invade Iraq and overthrow Saddam Hussein's government.

Countries sometimes reach different conclusions about the political aims of the same nuclear program. Over the past twenty years, Israeli officials such as Prime Minister Benjamin Netanyahu seem convinced that Iran is bent on building nuclear weapons. Some Americans think this too, but many see greater flexibility in Iran's nuclear policy. Likewise, during the George W. Bush administration, the US intelligence community was unsure if Syria's nuclear activities were part of a weapons program – but the Israelis had no doubt, and they ultimately bombed Syria's reactor in September 2007.

Lesson #8: Reconsidering What "Nuclear Power" Means

Robert Dahl gave us a classic definition of power back in 1957: The ability of A to make B behave in a way that B otherwise would not.[72] Power, then, is the ability to change someone else's behavior. In international relations, scholars and policymakers see power as stemming from a country's military capabilities. The ability to inflict pain on another country, in this view, provides greater influence. As Schelling wrote in his classic book *Arms and Influence*, "The power to hurt [through violence] is bargaining power. To exploit it is diplomacy – vicious diplomacy, but diplomacy."[73]

Nuclear weapons are unparalleled instruments of punishment. People refer to countries that possess them as "nuclear powers."[74] As this term implies, possessors of nuclear weapons are powerful – they have undue influence over other countries. States are nuclear powers, according to

---

[70] Quoted in Bush (2010, 91).
[71] US National Intelligence Council (2002).
[72] Dahl (1957).
[73] Schelling (1966, 2).
[74] For example, Waltz (1981).

conventional wisdom, when they have assembled nuclear weapons – or, as in the case of Israel, are widely believed to have done so. By this definition, there are nine nuclear powers in the world today, including such as China, Russia, and the United States.

This conception of a nuclear power is too narrow.[75] Powerful countries armed with nuclear arsenals are undoubtedly important in today's international environment. At the same time, in their own way, non-nuclear states that possess sensitive dual-use technology are nuclear powers, too. They cannot immediately launch a nuclear strike. Like the traditional nuclear weapons states, however, these countries can reap greater international influence from their possession of nuclear technology.

Iran does not (yet) have assembled nuclear weapons. However, this does not mean that it is truly nonnuclear. It has the technological capacity to build a bomb quickly, giving it a politically relevant nuclear capability. As Israeli diplomat Alon Pinkas wrote recently, "Iran is already a nuclear state" even though it does not have a military nuclear forces.[76] In this view, having a policy of "never allow[ing] Iran to become a nuclear power" is futile because the horse is already out of the barn.[77]

What matters is not just what nuclear capabilities countries presently possess – but also how long it would take to obtain a bomb. As Schelling wrote nearly fifty years ago, "Until recently, having or not having nuclear weapons appeared to be, and was treated as, a question of yes or no. From now on it will make more sense to describe a country's nuclear-weapon status not with a yes or a no but with a time schedule."[78] Echoing this argument, Albert Wohlstetter, Gregory Jones, and Roberta Wohlstetter wrote in 1979 that if a state were fighting a war against a nonnuclear country that could arm quickly, "it would be facing a government which to all practical effect had nuclear weapons." "[I]f there is no substantial elapsed time before a government may use nuclear weapons," they argued, "in effect it *has* them."[79]

Pakistani leader Zulfikar Ali Bhutto said in 1967, "It is dangerous to take aim with a gun loaded with blank cartridges."[80] This can indeed be a risky action, but the amount of time needed to load the gun also matters. Pointing an unloaded gun while having ammunition

---

[75] For an alternative perspective, see Hymans (2010).
[76] Pinkas (2022).
[77] Pinkas (2022).
[78] Schelling (1976, 79).
[79] Wohlstetter et al. (1979, 362). Emphasis in original.
[80] Quoted in Khan (2012, 69).

in your other hand or pocket means something different than lacking ammunition altogether.

Lesson #9: Nuclear Weapons Proliferation Should Continue at a Slow Clip

Pessimistic predictions about the pace of nuclear weapons proliferation are widespread in world politics. In 1960, John F. Kennedy, then a candidate for US president, predicted that twenty countries could have nuclear weapons within the next four years.[81] Mohamed ElBaradei, the former Director-General of the IAEA, similarly warned in 2005, "in the next 10–20 years, 20 or 30 countries will have nuclear weapons" if countries continue to rely on them for security.[82] Although these predictions did not materialize, similar claims appear in popular discussions about nuclear weapons today. As a headline in *Foreign Policy* put it, "In the Middle East, Soon Everyone Will Want the Bomb."[83]

This book leads to a more sanguine conclusion: Nuclear weapons will continue to spread internationally, but at a fairly slow clip. Some – but not all – countries will see latent nuclear forces as a substitute for full-blown arsenals. Countries facing serious but not existential threats will be most content to maintain nuclear latency, forgoing assembled weapons. These states can reap political and diplomatic benefits from their nuclear programs while dodging the costs of building and deploying weapons.

At the same time, there are limits to what states can do with latent nuclear forces. Nuclear latency may be unappealing for countries worried about full-scale invasions or leadership decapitation operations that could be completed in hours or days. North Korea perceived an existential threat from the United States and believed that nuclear weapons were essential to preserve the Kim regime. As the government-run Korean Central News Agency put it, "History proves that powerful nuclear deterrence serves as the strongest treasured sword for frustrating outsiders' aggression."[84] Pyongyang was determined to get a bomb as long as the United States had one. Future leaders facing an acute threat that they believe could result in their own near-instant death may see a reliance on latent nuclear forces as too risky.

---

[81] Carnegie Endowment for International Peace (2019).
[82] Kimball and Pemberton (2006).
[83] Sokolski (2018).
[84] Quoted in Shin and Pearson (2017).

The pace of ENR technology diffusion should exceed the rate of weapons proliferation in the coming years. Based on this book's conclusions, we would expect interest in ENR technology to continue. Signs are pointing in this direction. Jordan, Turkey, Saudi Arabia, Vietnam, and others have expressed an interest in obtaining the domestic capability to enrich uranium. History suggests that these states will face obstacles in gaining the ability to make fissile material, including pressure from the United States and others concerned about the military potential of the technology. A few of them may put the brakes on their ENR ambitions while others will probably move forward. Many of those that go on to achieve nuclear latency will be content to stop there for some period of time, eschewing nuclear warheads.

The international community has a say over whether latent nuclear powers ultimately arm. Attacking a country with nuclear latency or otherwise threatening its national security can foment weapons proliferation. The case of Israel offers a valuable lesson. Israel was on the fence about its nuclear future as late as 1966–67. By this point, although it could make enough fissile material for a bomb, armament was by no means guaranteed. According to historian Avner Cohen, "[Israeli Prime Minister Levi] Eshkol [was] reluctant to take the nuclear plunge, but he was apparently leaning to keep the option open yet not necessarily to go beyond it."[85] Things changed in May 1967 when Egypt deployed troops on the Sinai peninsula and carried out the flights over Dimona. As a result of the emerging threat, Israel swiftly assembled nuclear warheads before carrying out preemptive attacks against Egyptian forces on June 5.

Lesson #10: A Mixed Bag for Nuclear Disarmament

Weaponless deterrence may open the door to nuclear disarmament. Much of the thinking on this subject viewed latent nuclear forces as an arms control proposal. In the 1980s, journalist and disarmament advocate Jonathan Schell imagined a world where all countries eliminated their nuclear arsenals and used the prospect of rearmament to deter threats to international peace and stability.[86] At the heart of this idea is the notion that nuclear weapons can continue to exert influence over world politics even if no country has assembled weapons that could be launched instantly. One or more countries may be tempted to achieve a nuclear monopoly in a weapons-free world, giving it the means to dominate others. But any gains, Schell argued, would be temporary.

---

[85] Cohen (2007).
[86] Schell (1984).

Others would quickly match the first-mover's nuclear capabilities, and this possibility would deter anyone from attempting to arm first. As Schell put it, "factory would deter factory, blueprint would deter blueprint, equation would deter equation."[87] Moreover, the prospect of rearmament would deter war, just like assembled weapons have done for more than seventy years.

More recent writing referred to the use of rearmament in a disarmed world as a system of virtual nuclear arsenals (VNAs).[88] Some scholars and policymakers continue to see VNAs as offering a viable path toward eventual nuclear disarmament. Others view this idea as a dangerous recipe for global instability.[89]

What does this book teach us about the desirability of VNAs as a path to disarmament? Based on the book's conclusions, there is reason for optimism as well as cause for skepticism.

This book shows that it is possible for one country's possession of ENR capabilities to deter armament by another. Argentina and Brazil refrained from arming, in part, because officials understood that doing so would lead to reactive nuclear weapons proliferation. However, over a period of seventy-five years, this is the only country-pair that met the necessary requirements for success in latent nuclear deterrence. When it comes to preventing nuclear armament, three factors have made weaponless deterrence difficult.

First, nuclear threats from third parties have induced nuclear weapons proliferation. When scholars theorize about deterrence, they often assume that there are two relevant states: a challenger that seeks to change the status quo and a defender that wants to preserve it. In practice, though, third parties often complicate deterrence. Imagine a situation where there are two latent nuclear powers that are rivals (A and B) and a third country that is already armed with nuclear weapons (C). If A and C are also rivals, A may seek nuclear weapons to match C's capabilities, even if doing so compels B to follow suit. The possibility of fomenting an Indian bomb did not dissuade China from testing nuclear weapons in 1964 because Beijing was more concerned about two existing nuclear-armed adversaries: the Soviet Union and the United States. This, in turn, made India inclined to match China's achievement regardless of the implications for Pakistan's future nuclear policy. Similarly, North Korea surely does not want to see South

---

[87] Schell (1984).
[88] Mazarr (1997a) and Cohen and Pilat (1998).
[89] Waltz (1997) and Gray (1999).

Korea obtain its own nuclear forces but Pyongyang was more fixated on deterring the United States.

This problem would not exist in a hypothetical future world of VNAs. No one would possess nuclear weapons, eliminating the desire to match an existing nuclear power's capabilities. This suggests that deterrence by proliferation could work in a broader set of cases than it has in the past. However, the other two factors would still be daunting.

The second obstacle to success historically is the perception of hostile intentions. Countries worry that their latent rivals will arm with nuclear weapons, generating pressures to build nuclear weapons. Argentina and Brazil were able to overcome concerns about each other's nuclear intentions through a series of trust-building activities during the 1980s. Each country invited officials from the other to visit their most sensitive nuclear facilities. In the end, as Argentine official Roberto Ornstein put it, "both sides showed everything they had."[90] This degree of transparency increased confidence in both countries that the other side was not planning to build nuclear weapons, a belief that enabled deterrence by proliferation to operate.

Other countries might be reluctant to replicate this experience, fearing that too much transparency with an adversary would threaten national security. Indeed, an unwillingness to accept necessary verification measures is one reason formal arms control agreements are so rare.[91] For VNAs to be effective, however, confidence building and effective verification would be essential.

Third, some countries lack the capabilities to make armament threats credible. Nigeria's threat to build nuclear weapons, for example, could not have dissuaded South Africa from arming since Lagos lacked a viable ENR program. Nuclear parity between rivals is important for achieving successful deterrence by proliferation, not just having an ENR program. Weaponless deterrence becomes easier if two rivals are roughly the same distance to a bomb at a given point in time. If not, for both psychological and national security reasons, the state that is behind will be reluctant to stop its program until it catches up with the more-advanced rival. At the same time, the country with a shorter time to a bomb may not want to cede a perceived advantage by allowing the rival to catch up. This can result in a situation where both rivals continue to push toward a bomb, creating momentum toward a full blown arsenal. The experience of Argentina and Brazil underscores the importance of parity. The two countries did not reach a definitive nonproliferation deal until Brazil

---

[90] Mallea et al. (2012, 144).
[91] Coe and Vaynman (2020).

"tied the game," as Brazilian official Reubens Ricupero put it, matching Argentina's achievements in the area of uranium enrichment.[92]

Countries often strive to match their rival's capabilities. Former US Secretary of State George Schultz once said, "proliferation begets proliferation."[93] The book shows that latency begets latency: countries are more likely to obtain latent nuclear forces when one of their rivals does so. However, getting to parity is difficult. One state often ends up having a lead over the other in terms of fissile material production capacity. In a world of VNAs, it would be important for rivals to have similar breakout times.[94] Ensuring that this was the case at the outset would probably be essential to convince at least some countries to get on board.

What about the potential for VNAs to mitigate war and other forms of military conflict? As long as countries do not race to a bomb, this book has shown that developing ENR technology causes a reduction in crises and fatal disputes in some of the years that follow latency onset, although the latter benefit is particularly fragile. That at least some reduction in military conflict occurred provides reason for optimism that VNAs could deter disputes in a disarmed world. Yet, as in the case of deterring armament, there would be opportunities for deterrence to fail. A country that lacked an ENR capability or that had longer breakout times than its adversary may be vulnerable to attack. And war may ensue if one state believes that another has started a race to build a bomb.

Latent nuclear forces have limited political utility if they are not survivable, a fact that has long been understood in scholarship on VNAs.[95] If a country believes that it could wipe out its adversary's bomb-making capacity in a first-strike, it might be tempted to launch a preventive war.[96] This book shows that countries often see their adversaries' latent nuclear forces as survivable. Countries have historically increased the survivability of their bomb-making potential by dispersing key facilities, increasing the mobility of materials and technology, concealing parts of their ENR program, hardening plants that might be susceptible to attack, and surrounding those sites with air defenses. These measures have been at least partially effective, especially for countries that are already capable of producing fissile material.

The United States refrained from attacking Chinese nuclear plants in the early 1960s, in part, because it concluded that China's nuclear

---

[92] Mallea et al. (2012, 142).
[93] Quoted in Sagan (1996, 57).
[94] Schelling (1962, 395) makes a similar point.
[95] The earliest mention of this that I have seen is Schelling (1962).
[96] Schelling (1962, 395) called this "war of nuclear mobilization."

capabilities were likely survivable. As a formerly top secret assessment prepared by Robert Johnson of the State Department's Policy Planning Council in April 1964 concluded, "It is doubtful whether, even with completion of initial photographic coverage of the mainland, we will have anything like complete assurance that we will have identified all significant nuclear installations. Thus, even 'successful' action may not necessarily prevent the ChiComs [Chinese Communists] from detonating a nuclear device in the next few years."[97]

Ultimately, based on this book alone, I cannot say whether the international community should move toward a system of VNAs. Given the gravity of the stakes, no single study should drive future nuclear policy for the United States or other countries. Moreover, the book's conclusions rest on the types of nuclear latency that countries have pursued over the last seven decades.[98] Most latent nuclear powers have been at least a few months from a bomb. By contrast, VNA proponents envision a situation where a former nuclear weapons state could rearm quicker, perhaps in a matter of hours or days (at least initially). We do not fully understand the strategic implications this would carry since only one country – South Africa after it dismantled its weapons in the late 1980s – has so far fit that profile. Latent nuclear deterrence theory leads us to expect that a country's influence would grow with shorter times to a bomb, but we must be circumspect when generalizing beyond the types of cases I have examined in the book. On top of this, a complete assessment of VNAs must compare latent nuclear forces to assembled weapons. If nuclear weapons are superior for bringing peace and stability to the international system, moving toward a system of VNAs might be unwise even if latency confers benefits too.

Two modest conclusions about disarmament follow from the arguments and evidence presented in the preceding pages. First, the case for VNAs is stronger than the harshest critics would lead us to believe. That some countries have gained influence without arms in the past suggests, at the very least, that the idea of VNAs should not be dismissed out of hand. Second, by identifying how latent nuclear deterrence has failed in the past, this book puts the spotlight on issues that are worthy of further investigation. These issues include fissile material production capacity, foreign perceptions of intentions, verification, the survivability of latent nuclear capabilities, and parity in breakout times.[99]

---

[97] Johnson (1964, 3–4).

[98] For a discussion of different VNA types, see Ichimasa (2012, 26–29).

[99] Many of these issues are not new. On survivability, see Schelling (1962) and Wilson (1997). Kay (1997) lays out some key verification issues in a VNA context. An overview of some key issues appears in Mazarr (1997b).

Final Thoughts

This book has examined the issue of nuclear latency in international relations. Nuclear latency has traditionally been downplayed or ignored in scholarship. As the book has shown, however, latent nuclear forces influence the way that leaders think and shape critical issues affecting peace and stability in world politics.[100] Moving forward, scholars and policymakers should devote more attention to this issue. This book helps lay a broad foundation for understanding nuclear latency, but there is still much that we have left to learn.[101]

Future events will influence the salience of nuclear latency in world politics. Countries tend to draw lessons from the experiences of others. A few years after Libyan leader Muammar Qaddafi agreed to end his country's pursuit of nuclear weapons, he was ousted from power and killed following a NATO-led military intervention in Libya's civil war. This conveyed a message to leaders around the world: If you want to stop an invasion, get nuclear weapons. Russia's recent invasion of Ukraine has amplified this message, potentially generating further interest in nuclear weapons.[102]

Nuclear latency could quell some of the renewed desire for bombs as invasion insurance. Foreign leaders are watching events in Brazil, Iran, Japan, and other latent nuclear powers. What happens in those places will shape what the rest of the world thinks about the attractiveness of a latent nuclear deterrent. If others perceive that these countries are continuing to benefit from having latent nuclear forces, global interest in pursuing this path will probably increase. But if nuclear latency appears insufficient for addressing insecurity, others will find this option less attractive and may go all the way to assembled bombs instead. For example, if Israel or the United States launches a preventive war with Iran, other countries may not be content with mere latency.

The future nuclear energy landscape will also influence the importance of nuclear latency in the coming years and decades. As we know, ENR technology is dual-use in nature. Having nuclear power plants provides a commercial justification for producing fissile material.

---

[100] Other recent research points in this direction as well. See, for example, Fuhrmann and Tkach (2015), Mehta and Whitlark (2017a), Volpe (2017), Narang (2017), Pilat (2019), and Mattiacci et al. (2022).

[101] Promising areas for future research include: the optimal breakout time for deterrence, accounting for variation in perceptions of nuclear intentions among leaders, and how latency compares to assembled weapons.

[102] Ukraine inherited nuclear weapons that were on its soil when the Soviet Union collapsed but returned them to Moscow in the mid-1990s. It is unclear whether Ukraine ever had operational control over these weapons.

Without a nuclear energy program, a country would not have much hope of convincing others that its intentions are peaceful. Gaining political influence from latent nuclear forces, then, will probably require countries to make large investments in nuclear energy.

Some scholars and policymakers see nuclear energy as a partial solution to the problem of climate change.[103] Nuclear power plants are potentially helpful in this context because they do not emit greenhouse gasses, unlike their coal and gas counterparts. Concerns about climate change have contributed to renewed interest in nuclear power plants worldwide. About thirty countries are currently seeking to harness nuclear energy for the first time.[104] The list of nuclear energy aspirants includes Bangladesh, Chile, Poland, Ghana, Turkey, Qatar, and Uzbekistan.[105] However, nuclear energy is unpopular in some countries because of its potential for environmental disasters like the one that occurred at Japan's Fukushima nuclear plant in March 2011 following an earthquake and tsunami. Belgium and Germany previously decided to phase out nuclear energy completely. But Belgium reversed course after Russia's invasion of Ukraine. The war has renewed concerns about energy security in Europe and some in the region now seek to reduce their reliance on Russian oil and natural gas.[106]

It remains to be seen how many countries will join the ranks of the existing nuclear energy countries.[107] If the list of new nuclear energy states grows, so too would the number of countries that could seek the technology to produce fissile material. In that world, the international community would have to wrestle with the issue of nuclear latency more often. Even without a large-scale expansion in nuclear energy, however, this problem is unlikely to dissipate anytime soon. Countries such as Iran and Japan have placed nuclear latency on the center stage of world politics, and they will probably keep it there for years to come.

---

[103] See, for example, Knapp et al. (2010). Others, such as Muellner et al. (2021), conclude that nuclear energy is not a viable solution to this problem.

[104] Donovan (2021).

[105] World Nuclear Association (2022).

[106] Mufson and Parker (2022). Germany's nuclear future remains unclear. For a discussion of nuclear latency in Germany and its ties to nuclear energy, see Volpe and Kühn (2017).

[107] Past predictions of a "renaissance" in nuclear energy did not materialize. See Stulberg and Fuhrmann (2013).

References

AAP Newsfeed. 1999. FED: Gorton Admits Nuclear Decisions Kept Bomb Option Open, January 1.

ABC News. 2006. Nuclear Adviser Pushes Economic Benefits of Uranium Enrichment.

Abdenur, Roberto. 1985. Memorandum from Brazilian Ambassador Roberto Abdenur to Minister Saraiva Guerreiro, "Brazil–Argentina. Nuclear energy." Wilson Center Digital Archive, CPDOC Archives, Rubens Barbosa. Obtained and translated by Fundação Getúlio Vargas.

Abrams, Elliott. 2013. Bombing the Syrian Reactor: The Untold Story. *Commentary*, February 1.

Adelstein, Jake. 2018. Is Japan About to Hit Its Nuclear Tipping Point? *The Daily Beast*, February 15.

Albright, David. 1994. North Korean Plutonium Production. *Science and Global Security*, 5, 63–87.

Albright, David, and Burkhard, Sarah. 2022. Iranian Breakout Timeline Now at Zero. *Institute For Science and International Security*, June 1.

Allen, Michael A., Flynn, Michael E., and Machain, Carla Martinez. 2022. US Global Military Deployments, 1950–2020. *Conflict Management and Peace Science*, 39(3), 351–370.

Allison, Graham T., Carnesale, Albert, and Nye, Joseph S. 1985. *Hawks, Doves, and Owls: An Agenda for Avoiding Nuclear War*. New York: Norton.

Amanpour, Christiane. 2012. CNN'S Amanpour: Interview with Ehud Barak. CNN, April 19.

Anders, Therese, Fariss, Christopher J., and Markowitz, Jonathan N. 2020. Bread before Guns or Butter: Introducing Surplus Domestic Product (SDP). *International Studies Quarterly*, 64(2), 392–405.

Anderson, Jack. 1982. Argentines May Go Ahead With the Bomb. *The Washington Post*, June 7.

Angriest, Joshua D., and Pischke, Jorn-Steffen. 2009. *Mostly Harmless Econometrics*. Princeton, NJ: Princeton University Press.

Argentine Ministry of Foreign Relations. 1968. Nuclear Energy, January 15, 1968. Wilson Center Digital Archive, AMRECIC, Caja Brasil AH0124. Archives of the Ministry of External Relations and Culture, Argentina. Obtained and translated by Fundação Getúlio Vargas.

Argentine Naval Intelligence Service. 1967. Brazil: Prospects in the Field of Nuclear Energy. Wilson Center Digital Archive, Rodrigo Mallea Archives.

Associated Press. 1985. India to Review Nuclear Policy, Gandhi Says. *The Washington Post*, May 5.

Axelrod, Robert. 1984. *The Evolution of Cooperation*. New York: Basic Books.

Bailey, Michael A., Strezhnev, Anton, and Voeten, Erik. 2017. Estimating Dynamic State Preferences from United Nations Voting Data. *Journal of Conflict Resolution*, **61**(2), 430–456.

Bain, Alastair S., Boyd, Frederick C., Critoph, Eugene, et al. 1997. *Canada Enters the Nuclear Age: A Technical History of Atomic Energy of Canada Limited*. Montreal: McGill-Queen's University Press.

Baja, Farooq. 2013. *From Kutch to Tashkent: The Indo-Pakistan War of 1965*. London: Hurst.

Baker, Andrew C., Larcker, David F., and Wang, Charles C. Y. 2022. How Much Should We Trust Staggered Difference-in-Differences Estimates? *Journal of Financial Economics*, **144**(2), 370–395.

Baliga, Sandeep, and Sjostrom, Tomas. 2018. Strategic Ambiguity and Arms Proliferation. *Journal of Political Economy*, **116**(6), 1023–1057.

Barletta, Michael. 1997. *The Military Nuclear Program in Brazil*. Stanford University: Center for International Security and Arms Control.

Barnaby, Frank. 2004. *How to Build a Nuclear Bomb: And Other Weapons of Mass Destruction*. New York: Nation Books.

Bas, Muhammet A., and Coe, Andrew J. 2016. A Dynamic Theory of Nuclear Proliferation and Preventive War. *International Organization*, **70**(4), 655–685.

2018. Give Peace a (Second) Chance: A Theory of Nonproliferation Deals. *International Studies Quarterly*, **62**(3), 606–617.

Batista, Paulo Nogueira. 1980. Report from the President of Nuclebrás Paulo Nogueira Batista to Foreign Minister Saraiva Guerreiro, "Trip to Buenos Aires." Wilson Center Digital Archive, Paulo Nogueira Batista Archive/CPDOC. Critical Oral History Conference on the Argentine-Brazilian Nuclear Cooperation, Rio de Janeiro, March 2012.

Bayer, Resat. 2006. *Diplomatic Exchange Data set, v2006.1*. Correlates of War.

Beardsley, Kyle, and Asal, Victor. 2009a. Nuclear Weapons as Shields. *Conflict Management and Peace Science*, **26**(3), 235–255.

2009b. Winning with the Bomb. *Journal of Conflict Resolution*, **53**(2), 278–301.

Beardsley, Kyle, James, Patrick, Wilkenfeld, Jonathan, and Brecher, Michael. 2020. The International Crisis Behavior Project. *Oxford Research Encyclopedia of Politics*. https://doi.org/10.1093/acrefore/9780190228637.013.1638.

Beaton, Leonard. 1966. *Must the Bomb Spread?* Middlesex, England: Penguin Books.

Beccaria, Cesare. 2009. *On Crimes and Punishments*. Scotts Valley, CA: CreateSpace.

Bell, Mark S. 2015. Beyond Emboldenment: How Acquiring Nuclear Weapons Can Change Foreign Policy. *International Security*, **40**(1), 87–119.

Bell, Mark, and Miller, Nicholas. 2015. Questioning the Effect of Nuclear Weapons on Conflict. *Journal of Conflict Resolution*, **59**(1), 74–92.

Benjamin, Milton R. 1983. Argentina Claims to Build Plant for Enriched Uranium. *The Washington Post*, November 19.

Berrojo, Luis Castro. 2015. *La bomba atómica española: La energía nuclear en la transición*. Madrid: Paco Castro Creativos.

Beschloss, Michael R. 1991. *The Crisis Years: Kennedy and Khrushchev, 1960–1963*. New York: Harper Collins.

Betts, Richard K. 1987. *Nuclear Blackmail and Nuclear Balance*. Washington, DC: Brookings Institution.

Bildt, Carl, and Tuomioja, Erkki. 2012. The Only Option on Iran. *The New York Times*, March 20.

Bini, Elisabetta, and Londero, Igor (eds.). 2017. *Nuclear Italy: An International History of Italian Nuclear Policies during the Cold War*. Trieste: EUT-Edizioni Università di Trieste.

Birch, Douglas, and Smith, R. Jeffrey. 2015. U.S. Unease About Nuclear-Weapons Fuel Takes Aim at a South African Vault. *The Washington Post*, March 14.

Black, Samuel. 2010. *The Changing Political Utility of Nuclear Weapons: Nuclear Threats from 1970 to 2010*. Washington, DC: Stimson Center.

Blair, Bruce. 1993. *The Logic of Accidental Nuclear War*. Washington, DC: Brookings Institution.

Bleek, Philipp C. 2010. Why Do States Proliferate? Quantitative Analysis of the Exploration, Pursuit, and Acquisition of Nuclear Weapons. Pages 159–192 of: Potter, William C., and Makhatzhanova, Gaukar (eds.), *Forecasting Nuclear Proliferation in the 21st Century: The Role of Theory*. Palo Alto, CA: Stanford University Press.

2017. *When Did (and Didn't) States Proliferate? Chronicling the Spread of Nuclear Weapons*. Cambridge, MA: Project on Managing the Atom, Belfer Center for Science and International Affairs.

Bleek, Philipp C., and Lorber, Erik B. 2014. Security Guarantees and Allied Nuclear Proliferation. *Journal of Conflict Resolution*, **58**(3), 429–454.

Bob, Yonah Jeremy. 2022. Iran Could Have 4 "Crude" Nukes in 3 Months – Think Tank. *The Jerusalem Post*, June 2.

Bolaños, Roberto Muñoz. 2014. El Proyecto Islero. La bomba atómica española. *Anatomia de la Historia*. www.researchgate.net/publication/287210502_El_Proyecto_Islero_La_bomba_atomica_espanola/citation/download.

Bolton, John R. 2015. To Stop Iran's Bomb, Bomb Iran. *The New York Times*, March 26.

Bonnevier, Bjorn. 1970. Experimental Evidence of Element and Isotope Separation in a Rotating Plasma. *Plasma Physics*, **13**, 763–774.

Borger, Julian. 2004. Pakistan May Make Nigeria a Nuclear Power. *The Guardian*, March 3.

Bowen, Wyn, and Moran, Matthew. 2014. Iran's Nuclear Programme: A Case Study in Hedging? *Contemporary Security Policy*, **35**(1), 26–52.

Braut-Heggehammer, Malfrid. 2016. *Unclear Physics: Why Iraq and Libya Failed to Build Nuclear Weapons*. Ithaca, NY: Cornell University Press.

Braut-Hegghammer, Malfrid. 2019. Proliferating Bias? American Political Science, Nuclear Weapons, and Global Security. *Journal of Global Security Studies*, **4**(3), 384–392.

Brazilian Embassy. 1978. Telegram from the Brazilian Embassy in Buenos Aires to the Foreign Ministry, "External Policy. Argentina. Nuclear non-proliferation. Issue no. 132." Wilson Center Digital Archive, Argentine Foreign Ministry Archives.

Brazilian Foreign Ministry. 1977a. Brazilian Embassy Cable, Brazilian Ambassador to Bonn Reports on Soviet Pressure on West Germany, March 21. Wilson Center Digital Archive, Centro de Pesquisa e Documentação de História Contemporânea do Brasil (CPDOC), Fundação Getúlio Vargas (FGV), Azeredo da Silveira Archive, AAS mre pn 1974.08.15 pp. 589–591. Obtained and translated by Fundação Getúlio Vargas.

1977b. Memorandum from Brazilian Foreign Minister Silveira to President Geisel, US Threats and Promises and Brazilian Responses, February 25. Wilson Center Digital Archive, Centro de Pesquisa e Documentação de História Contemporânea do Brasil (CPDOC), Fundação Getúlio Vargas (FGV), Azeredo da Silveira Archive, AAS mre pn 1974.08.15 pp. 544–549. Obtained and translated by Fundação Getúlio Vargas.

Brazilian National Security Council. 1967. Minutes of the Fortieth Session of the Brazilian National Security Council. Wilson Center Digital Archive, Archive of the Brazilian Foreign Ministry (Brasilia). Obtained and translated by Fundação Getúlio Vargas.

Brecher, Michael, and Wilkenfeld, Jonathan. 1997. *A Study of Crisis*. Ann Arbor, MI: University of Michigan Press.

Brecher, Michael, Wilkenfeld, Jonathan, Beardsley, Kyle, James, Patrick, and Quinn, David. 2017. International Crisis Behavior Data Codebook, Version 12. *Journal of Peace Research*, Version 12.

Brennan, David. 2021. Iran Lawmaker Admits Nuclear Expansion Is Leverage for Joe Biden Talks. *Newsweek*, March 19.

Broad, William. 2012. How to Help Iran Build a Bomb. *The New York Times*, September 28.

Brodie, Bernard. 1946. *The Absolute Weapon: Atomic Power and World Order*. New York: Harcourt, Brace and Company.

1959. *Strategy in the Missile Age*. Princeton, NJ: Princeton University Press.

Browne, Malcolm W. 1977. Yugoslav Hints Atom Arm Goal. *The New York Times*, March 12.

Bugos, Shannon. 2019. Saudi Arabia Seeks to Enrich Uranium. *Arms Control Association*, October.

Bundy, McGeorge. 1991. Nuclear Weapons and the Gulf. *Foreign Affairs*, **70**(4), 83–94.

Bunn, Matthew, and Wier, Anthony. 2006. Terrorist Nuclear Weapon Construction: How Difficult? *The Annals of the American Academy of Political and Social Science*, **607**, 133–149.

Burns, William J. 2019. *The Back Channel: A Memoir of American Diplomacy and the Case for Its Renewal*. New York: Random House.

Burr, William. 2019. Kissinger State Department Insisted that South Koreans Break Contract with French for Reprocessing Plant. *The National Security Archive*.

Burr, William, and Richelson, Jeffrey T. 2000/2001. Whether to "Strangle the Baby in the Cradle": The United States and the Chinese Nuclear Program, 1960–64. *International Security*, **25**(3), 54–99.

Bush, George H. W. 1991. *Public Papers of the Presidents of the United States: George Bush, 1990, Book 2.* Washington, DC: National Archives and Records Service.

Bush, George W. 2010. *Decision Points.* New York: Crown.

Bush, George H. W., and Scowcroft, Brent. 1998. *A World Transformed.* New York: Alfred A. Knopf.

Canavan, Gregory H. 1998. *Advanced Techniques for the Analysis of Crisis Stability, Deterrence, and Latency.* Los Alamos, NM: Los Alamos National Laboratory.

Carnegie, Allison. 2021. Secrecy in International Relations and Foreign Policy. *Annual Review of Political Science,* 24(1), 213–233.

Carnegie, Allison, and Carson, Austin. 2018. The Spotlight's Harsh Glare: Rethinking Publicity and International Order. *International Organization,* 72(3), 627–657.

2019. The Disclosure Dilemma: Nuclear Intelligence and International Organizations. *American Journal of Political Science,* 63(2), 269–285.

Carnegie Endowment for International Peace. 2019. JFK on Nuclear Weapons and Non-Proliferation, October.

Carson, Austin. 2018. *Secret Wars: Covert Conflict in International Politics.* Princeton, NJ: Princeton University Press.

Carter, David, and Signorino, Curtis S. 2010. Back to the Future: Modeling Time Dependence in Binary Data. *Political Analysis,* 18(3), 271–292.

CBS News. 2007. Iran On Nukes: Full Speed Ahead, February 25.

Cervera, César. 2014. ¿Consiguió la España de Franco hacerse con la bomba atómica? ABC ESPAÑA.

Chakrov, Petr, and Hanlon, Thomas. 2018. Nigeria Converts Its Research Reactor from HEU to LEU Fuel. *International Atomic Energy Agency.*

Chang, Jae-soon. 2014. Park Asks China to Help Dissuade N. Korea from Nuclear Test. Yonhap News Agency, April 23.

Chari, P. R., Cheema, Pervaiz Iqbal, and Cohen, Stephen P. 2007. *Four Crises and a Peace Process: American Engagement in South Asia.* Washington, DC: Brookings Institution Press.

Cheney, Dick, and Cheney, Liz. 2011. *In My Time: A Personal and Political Memoir.* New York: Threshold Editions.

Churchill, Winston. 1955. Never Despair. March 1.

Cirincione, Joseph. 2023. Why Hasn't Putin Used Nuclear Weapons? *The Daily Beast,* February 9.

Clements, Richard. 2012. New Details of Israel's 2007 Attack on the Syrian Nuclear Reactor Emerge. *The Aviationist.*

Clinton, Bill. 2004. *My Life.* New York: Vintage.

Clinton, Hillary Rodham. 2014. *Hard Choices.* New York: Simon and Schuster.

CNN. 2003a. N. Korea "Admits Having Nukes," April 25.

2003b. Nuke Program Parts Unearthed in Baghdad Back Yard, June 26.

Coe, Andrew J., and Vaynman, Jane. 2015. Collusion and the Nuclear Nonproliferation Regime. *Journal of Politics,* 77(4), 983–997.

2020. Why Arms Control Is So Rare. *American Political Science Review,* 114(2), 342–355.

Cohen, Avner. 1998. *Israel and the Bomb.* New York: Columbia University Press.

2007. Crossing the Threshold: The Untold Nuclear Dimension of the 1967 Arab–Israeli War and Its Contemporary Lessons. *Arms Control Today*, **37**(5), 12–16.

Cohen, Avner, and Frankel, Benjamin. 1990. Opaque Nuclear Proliferation. *The Journal of Strategic Studies*, **13**(3), 14–44.

Cohen, Avner, and Pilat, Joseph. 1998. Assessing Virtual Nuclear Arsenals. *Survival*, **40**(1), 129–144.

Colaresi, Michael, Rasler, Karen, and Thompson, William R. 2007. *Strategic Rivalries in World Politics: Position, Space and Conflict Escalation*. New York: Cambridge University Press.

Cornejo, Robert M. 2000. When Sukarno Sought the Bomb: Indonesian Nuclear Aspirations in the Mid-1960s. *The Nonproliferation Review*, Summer.

Coutto, Tatiana. 2014. An International History of the Brazilian–Argentine Rapprochement. *The International History Review*, **36**(2), 302–323.

Crossette, Barbara. 1995. Crash Nuclear Program by Iraq Is Disclosed. *The New York Times*, August 26.

Dahl, Robert A. 1957. The Concept of Power. *Behavioral Science*, **2**, 201–215.

Danilovic, Vesna. 2002. *When the Stakes Are High: Deterrence and Conflict Among Major Powers*. Ann Arbor, MI: University of Michigan Press.

Dawson, Chester. 2011. In Japan, Provocative Case for Staying Nuclear; Some Say Bombs' Potential as Deterrent Argues for Keeping Power Plants Online. *Wall Street Journal*, October 27.

de Gaulle, Charles. 1975a. *Discours et Messages*. Vol. 3. Paris: PLON.

1975b. *Discours et Messages*. Vol. 2. Paris: PLON.

De la Cal, Juan C., and Garrido, Vincente. 2001. La Bomba Atómica que Franco Soñó. *El Mundo*, June 10.

Debs, Alexandre, and Monteiro, Nuno P. 2014. Known Unknowns: Power Shifts, Uncertainty, and War. *International Organization*, **68**(1), 7–52.

2017. *Nuclear Politics: The Strategic Causes of Proliferation*. New York: Cambridge University Press.

DeYoung, Karen. 1977. Rivals Argentina, Brazil Settle a "War" Over Dam. *The Washington Post*, December 16.

Donovan, Jeffrey. 2021. *Countries Detail Nuclear Power Climate Change Plans in COP26 Event with IAEA Director General*. Vienna: IAEA.

Downes, Alexander B., and Sechser, Todd S. 2012. The Illusion of Democratic Credibility. *International Organization*, **66**(3), 457–489.

Drell, Sidney D., and Goodby, James E. 2009. *A World Without Nuclear Weapons: End-State Issues*. Stanford, CA: Hoover Institution Press.

Dreyer, David, and Thompson, William R. 2011. *Handbook of International Rivalries, 1494–2010*. Washington, DC: CQ Press.

Dunlap, Christopher. 2018. Parallel Power Play: Building Nuclear Cooperation in Argentina and Brazil, 1974–1991. Unpublished manuscript.

Early, Bryan R. 2014. Exploring the Final Frontier: An Empirical Analysis of Global Civil Space Proliferation. *International Studies Quarterly*, **58**(1), 55–67.

Early, Bryan Robert, Fahrenkopf, Nolan, Horowitz, Michael C., and Walsh, James Igoe. 2022. Climbing the Ladder: Explaining the Vertical Proliferation of Cruise Missiles. *Journal of Conflict Resolution*, **66**(6), 955–982.

Eerkens, Jeff W., and Kim, Daewoo. 2010. Isotope Separation by Selective Laser-Assisted Repression of Condensation in Supersonic Free Jets. *American Institute of Chemical Engineers Journal*, **56**(9), 2331–2337.

Einhorn, Robert, and Kim, Duyeon. 2016. Will South Korea Go Nuclear? *Bulletin of the Atomic Scientists*. Available at https://thebulletin.org/2016/08/will-south-korea-go-nuclear/.

Eisenhower, Dwight D. 1953. *Address by Mr. Dwight D. Eisenhower, President of the United States of America, to the 470th Plenary Meeting of the United Nations General Assembly, December 8.*

Ejiogu, Amanze. 2013. A Nuclear Nigeria: How Feasible Is It? *Energy Strategy Reviews*, **1**(4), 261–265.

El País. 1987. La Tentación de la Bomba, February 1.

Fair, C. Christine. 2014. *Fighting to the End: The Pakistan Army's Way of War*. Oxford: Oxford University Press.

2017. Pakistan's Nuclear Program: Laying the Groundwork for Impunity. Pages 126–139 of: Liow, Joseph, Scobell, Andrew, and Gangly, Sumit (eds.), *Routledge Handbook of Asian Security Studies*, 2nd ed. Abingdon, Oxfordshire: Routledge.

FBIS. 1981. Worldwide Report: Nuclear Development and Proliferation.

1982a. CNEA Chairman Denies Plans for Atomic Bomb. *Buenos Aires DYN*, PY012356.

1982b. CNEA Chairman Discusses Nuclear Capabilities. *Jornal Do Brasil*, PY121621.

1982c. Nuclear Development for Military Purposes. *AFP*, PY241635.

Fearon, James D. 1995. Rationalist Explanations for War. *International Organization*, **49**(3), 379–414.

1997. Signaling Foreign Policy Interests: Tying Hands Versus Sinking Costs. *Journal of Conflict Resolution*, **41**(1), 68–90.

2002. Selection Effects and Deterrence. *International Interactions*, **28**(1), 5–29.

Feaver, Peter D., and Niou, Emerson M. S. 1996. Managing Nuclear Proliferation: Condemn, Strike, or Assist? *International Studies Quarterly*, **40**(2), 209–233.

Figueredo, Enrique. 2017. La Bomba Atómica Española que Nunca Llegó. *La Vanguardia*.

Fisher, Max. 2017. Fearing U.S. Withdrawal, Europe Considers Its Own Nuclear Deterrent. *The New York Times*, March 6.

Fitzpatrick, Mark. 2016. *Asia's Latent Nuclear Powers: Japan, South Korea and Taiwan*. London: International Institute for Strategic Studies.

Folha de São Paulo. 1986. Newspaper Article, "Serra Do Cachimbo May Be Nuclear Test Site." Wilson Center Digital Archive, Folha de São Paulo. Obtained and translated by Fundação Getúlio Vargas.

Fontaine, Roger W., Shoemaker, Christopher C., and Childress, Richard T. 1982. 309. Memorandum From Roger W. Fontaine, Christopher C. Shoemaker, and Richard T. Childress of the National Security Council Staff to the President's Deputy Assistant for National Security Affairs (McFarlane).

Ford, Christopher. 2005. NPT Article IV: Peaceful Uses of Nuclear Energy. *Statement to the 2005 Review Conference of the Treaty on the Nonproliferation of Nuclear Weapons New York, New York May 18.*

Ford, Christopher A. 2011. Nuclear Weapons Reconstitution and Its Discontents: Challenges of "Weaponless Deterrence." In: Schultz, George P., Drell, Sidney D., and Goodby, James E. (eds.), *Deterrence: Its Past and Future.* Stanford, CA: Hoover Institution Press.

Foreign Relations of the United States. 1984. Conflict in the South Atlantic, Vol. XIII.

Forland, Astrid. 1997. Norway's Nuclear Odyssey: From Optimistic Proponent to Nonproliferator. *The Nonproliferation Review*, 4(2), 1–16.

Friedman, Uri. 2017. Why One President Gave Up His Country's Nukes. *The Atlantic*, September 9.

Fuhrmann, Matthew. 2009a. Spreading Temptation: Proliferation and Peaceful Nuclear Cooperation Agreements. *International Security*, 34(1), 7–41.

2009b. Taking a Walk on the Supply Side: The Determinants of Civilian Nuclear Cooperation. *Journal of Conflict Resolution*, 53(2), 181–208.

2012a. *Atomic Assistance: How "Atoms for Peace" Programs Cause Nuclear Insecurity.* Ithaca, NY: Cornell University Press.

2012b. Splitting Atoms: Why Do Countries Build Nuclear Power Plants? *International Interactions*, 38(1), 29–57.

2013. A Diplomatic Endgame with Iran? The Case for Optimism. *The Washington Post Monkey Cage*, November 26.

2017. The Logic of Latent Nuclear Deterrence. Unpublished manuscript. Available at https://ssrn.com/abstract=3052231.

2018. When Preventive War Threats Work for Nuclear Nonproliferation. *The Washington Quarterly*, 41(3), 111–135.

Fuhrmann, Matthew, and Berejikian, Jeffrey D. 2012. Disaggregating Noncompliance: Abstention versus Predation in the Nuclear Nonproliferation Treaty. *Journal of Conflict Resolution*, 56(3), 355–381.

Fuhrmann, Matthew, and Horowitz, Michael C. 2015. When Leaders Matter: Rebel Experience and Nuclear Proliferation. *Journal of Politics*, 77(1), 72–87.

2017. Droning On: Explaining the Proliferation of Unmanned Aerial Vehicles. *International Organization*, 71(2), 397–418.

Fuhrmann, Matthew, and Kreps, Sarah. 2010. Targeting Nuclear Programs in War and Peace: A Quantitative Empirical Analysis, 1941–2000. *Journal of Conflict Resolution*, 54(6), 831–859.

Fuhrmann, Matthew, and Sechser, Todd S. 2014. Signaling Alliance Commitments: Hand-Tying and Sunk Costs in Extended Nuclear Deterrence. *American Journal of Political Science*, 58(4), 919–935.

Fuhrmann, Matthew, and Tkach, Benjamin. 2015. Almost Nuclear: Introducing the Nuclear Latency Dataset. *Conflict Management and Peace Science*, 32(4), 443–461.

Fukushima, Mayumi. 2021. No-Go Negotiations: Iran May Not Be in a Rush to Get Nuclear Weapons. *The National Interest*, June 27.

Fung, Brian. 2012. The Case for Letting Iran (Almost) Build a Bomb. *The Atlantic*, February 29.

Gaddis, John Lewis. 1986. The Long Peace: Elements of Stability in the Postwar International System. *International Security*, **10**(4), 99–142.

Gardner, John. 2022. Two-Stage Differences in Differences. Unpublished manuscript. Available at https://doi.org/10.48550/arXiv.2207.05943.

Gargan, Edward A. 1993. Demands Growing for an India That's Truly Hindu. *The New York Times*, January 24.

Gartzke, Erik. 2000. Preferences and the Democratic Peace. *International Studies Quarterly*, **44**(2), 191–212.

Gartzke, Erik, and Jo, Dong-Joon. 2009. Bargaining, Nuclear Proliferation, and Interstate Disputes. *Journal of Conflict Resolution*, **53**(2), 209–233.

Gartzke, Erik, and Kroenig, Matthew. 2016. Nukes with Numbers: Empirical Research on the Consequences of Nuclear Weapons for International Conflict. *Annual Review of Political Science*, **19**(1), 397–412.

Gates, Robert M. 2014. *Duty: Memoirs of a Secretary at War*. New York: Knopf.

Geller, Daniel S. 1990. Nuclear Weapons, Deterrence, and Crisis Escalation. *Journal of Conflict Resolution*, **34**(2), 291–310.

Gerzhoy, Gene. 2015. Alliance Coercion and Nuclear Restraint: How the United States Thwarted West Germany's Nuclear Ambitions. *International Security*, **39**(4), 91–129.

Gheorghe, Eliza. 2019. Proliferation and the Logic of the Nuclear Market. *International Security*, **43**(4), 88–127.

Ghosh, Bobby. 2009. CIA Knew About Iran's Secret Nuclear Plant Long Before Disclosure. *Time*.

Gibbs, Jack P. 1975. *Crime, Punishment, and Deterrence*. Amsterdam: Elsevier.

Gibler, Douglas M., Miller, Steven V., and Little, Erin K. 2017. An Analysis of the Militarized Interstate Dispute (MID) Dataset, 1816–2001. *International Studies Quarterly*, **60**(4), 719–730.

Ginor, Isabella, and Remez, Gideon. 2007. *Foxbats over Dimona: The Soviets' Nuclear Gamble in the Six-Day War*. New Haven, CT: Yale University Press.

Glaser, Charles L. 1990. *Analyzing Strategic Nuclear Policy*. Princeton, NJ: Princeton University Press.

2000. The Causes and Consequences of Arms Races. *Annual Review of Political Science*, **3**, 251–276.

Gleditsch, Nils Petter, Wallensteen, Peter, Eriksson, Mikael, Sollenberg, Margareta, and Strand, Havard. 2002. Armed Conflict 1946–2001: A New Dataset. *Journal of Peace Research*, **39**(5), 615–637.

Goldberg, Jeffrey. 2012. 7 Reasons Why Israel Should Not Attack Iran's Nuclear Facilities. *The Atlantic*, August 11.

Goldblat, Jozef. 2002. *Arms Control: The New Guide to Negotiations and Agreements*. Thousand Oaks, CA: Sage.

Goldstein, Lyle. 2006. *Preventive Attack and Weapons of Mass Destruction: A Comparative Historical Analysis*. Stanford, CA: Stanford University Press.

Goodman-Bacon, Andrew. 2021. Difference-in-Differences with Variation in Treatment Timing. *Journal of Econometrics*, **225**(2), 254–277.

Gordon, Michael R. 1994. Threats in the Gulf: The Military Buildup; At Least 36,000 U.S. Troops Going to Gulf in Response to Continued Iraqi Buildup. *The New York Times*, August 10.

Gordon, Michael R., and Trainor, Bernard E. 1995. *The Generals' War: The Inside Story of the Conflict in the Gulf.* New York: Little Brown & Co.

2006. *Cobra II: The Inside Story of the Invasion and Occupation of Iraq.* New York: Pantheon.

Gowing, Margaret. 1974. *Independence and Deterrence: Britain and Atomic Energy, 1945–1952, Vol. 1: Policy Making.* New York: St. Martin's Press.

Gray, Colin S. 1999. *The Second Nuclear Age.* Boulder, CO: Lynne Rienner.

Green, Brendan Rittenhouse, and Long, Austin. 2017. Invisible Doomsday Machines: The Challenge of Clandestine Capabilities and Deterrence. *War on the Rocks,* December 15.

Gwertzman, Bernard. 1982. U.S. Sees Setback to Its Latin Ties: Falkland Crisis Said to Create Shift Against Washington. *The New York Times,* May 23.

Hagerty, Devin T. 1993. The Power of Suggestion: Opaque Proliferation, Existential Deterrence, and the South Asian Nuclear Arms Competition. *Security Studies,* 2(3–4), 256–283.

1995. Nuclear Deterrence in South Asia: The 1990 Indo-Pakistani Crisis. *International Security,* 20(3), 79–114.

1998. *The Consequences of Nuclear Proliferation: Lessons from South Asia.* Cambridge, MA: MIT Press.

Harel, Amos, and Benn, Aluf. 2018. No Longer a Secret: How Israel Destroyed Syria's Nuclear Reactor. *Haaretz,* March 23.

Hastrof, A.H., and Cantril, H. 1954. They Saw a Game: A Case Study. *Journal of Abnormal and Social Psychology,* 129–134.

Hayden, Michael V. 2011. Correcting the Record about that Syrian Nuclear Reactor. *The Washington Post,* September 22.

Hecker, Sigfried S., and Serbin, Elliot A. 2023. *Hinge Points: An Inside Look at North Korea's Nuclear Program.* Stanford, CA: Stanford University Press.

Helms, Richard. 1974a. Iran's Intentions in Nuclear Matters. *Telegram from the Embassy in Iran, July 1.* Accessed via National Security Archive.

1974b. Shah's Alleged Statement on Nuclear Weapons. *Telegram from the Embassy in Iran, June 25.* Accessed via National Security Archive.

Herzog, Michael. 2018. Israel's 2007 Strike on Syrian Nuclear Reactor: Lessons Learned for Iran. *The Washington Institute for Near East Policy.*

Hirsh, Michael, and Journal, National. 2013. The Case for a Grand Bargain with Iran. *The Atlantic,* November 7.

Historical Archive of the Minister of Foreign Affairs of Brazil. 1985. Memorandum to President Sarney, "Brazil–Argentina. Cooperation on Nuclear Affairs." Wilson Center Digital Archive, AHMRE. Critical Oral History Conference on the Argentine-Brazilian Nuclear Cooperation, Rio de Janeiro, March 2012.

Hoag, Jim. 1977. S. Africa, With U.S. Aid, Near A-Bomb. *The Washington Post,* February 16.

Hoey, Fintan. 2016. Japan and Extended Nuclear Deterrence: Security and Non-proliferation. *Journal of Strategic Studies,* 39(4), 484–501.

Holdren, John P. 1997. *The Future of U.S. Nuclear Weapons Policy.* Washington, DC: National Academies of Sciences.

Holloway, David. 1981. Entering the Nuclear Arms Race: The Soviet Decision to Build the Atomic Bomb, 1939–45. *Social Studies of Science*, **11**(2), 159–197.

    1994. *Stalin and the Bomb: The Soviet Union and Atomic Energy, 1939–1956.* New Haven, CT: Yale University Press.

Hong, Sung Gul. 2011. The Search for Deterrence: Park's Nuclear Option. Pages 483–512 of: Kim, Byung-Kook, and Vogel, Ezra F. (eds.), *The Park Chung Hee Era: The Transformation of South Korea.* Cambridge, MA: Harvard University Press.

Horowitz, Michael C. 2010. *The Diffusion of Military Power: Causes and Consequences for International Politics.* Princeton, NJ: Princeton University Press.

    2013. Nuclear Power and Militarized Conflict: Is There a Link? Pages 288–312 of: Stulberg, Adam N., and Fuhrmann, Matthew (eds.), *The Nuclear Renaissance and International Security.* Stanford, CA: Stanford University Press.

Horowitz, Michael C., Schwartz, Joshua A., and Fuhrmann, Matthew. 2022. Who's Prone to Drone? A Global Time-Series Analysis of Armed Uninhabited Aerial Vehicle Proliferation. *Conflict Management and Peace Science*, **39**(2), 119–142.

Huth, Paul K. 1999. Deterrence and International Conflict: Empirical Findings and Theoretical Debates. *Annual Review of Political Science*, **2**, 25–48.

Hymans, Jacques. 2006. *The Psychology of Nuclear Proliferation: Emotions, Identity, and Foreign Policy.* New York: Cambridge University Press.

Hymans, Jacques E. C. 2010. When Does a State Become a 'Nuclear Weapon State'? *The Nonproliferation Review*, **17**(1), 161–180.

    2012. *Achieving Nuclear Ambitions: Scientists, Politicians, and Proliferation.* New York: Cambridge University Press.

IAEA. 1976a. *Experiencia Adquirida y Tecnologia Desarrollada en la JEN (Espana) en la Gestion de Desechos Radiactivos.* Vienna: International Atomic Energy Agency.

    1976b. *Management of Radioactive Wastes from the Nuclear Fuel Cycle.* Vienna: International Atomic Energy Agency.

    1990. Argentina–Brazilian Declaration on Common Nuclear Policy. International Atomic Energy Agency Information Circular: International Atomic Energy Agency.

    1991. Agreement Between the Rupublic of Argentina and the Rederative Republic of Brazil for the Exclusivelt Peaceful Use of Nuclear Energy. International Atomic Energy Agency Information Circular: International Atomic Energy Agency.

    2000. *Facilities Under Agency Safeguards Or Containing Safeguarded Material on 31 December 2000.* Vienna: International Atomic Energy Agency.

    2009. *Nuclear Fuel Cycle Information System: A Directory of Nuclear Fuel Cycle Facilities.* Vienna: IAEA-TECDOC-1613.

    2013. Country Nuclear Power Profiles. Vienna: International Atomic Energy Agency.

Ichimasa, Sukeyuki. 2012. The Concept of Virtual Nuclear Arsenals in a World without Nuclear Weapons. *NIDS Journal of Defense and Security*, **13**(3), 23–37.

Imai, Kosuke, and Kim, In Song. 2021. On the Use of Two-Way Fixed Effects Regression Models for Causal Inference with Panel Data. *Political Analysis*, **29**(3), 405–415.

Imai, Kosuke, Kim, In Song, and Wang, Erik H. 2023. Matching Methods for Causal Inference with Time-Series Cross-Sectional Data. *American Journal of Political Science*, **67**(3), 587–605.

Imamverdiyeva, Ulkar, and Shea, Patrick E. 2022. Re-examining Women Leaders and Military Spending. *Journal of Peace Research*, **59**(5), 679–693.

Jervis, Robert. 1976. *Perception and Misperception in International Politics*. Princeton, NJ: Princeton University Press.

Jervis, Robert. 1989. *The Meaning of the Nuclear Revolution: Statecraft and the Prospect of Armageddon*. Ithaca, NY: Cornell University Press.

Jo, Dong-Joon, and Gartzke, Erik. 2006. Codebook and Data Notes for "Determinants of Nuclear Weapons Proliferation: A Quantitative Model."

    2007. Determinants of Nuclear Weapons Proliferation. *Journal of Conflict Resolution*, **51**(1), 167–194.

Johansen, Mary Amelia. 2016. *The Nuclear Weapons Latency Value of the Joint Comprehensive Plan of Action with the Islamic Republic of Iran*. MS thesis, Texas A&M University.

Johnson, Robert. 1964. *An Exploration of the Possible Bases for Action Against the Chinese Communist Nuclear Facilities*. Washington, DC: US Department of State, Policy Planning Council.

Jones, Benjamin, Mattiacci, Eleonora, and Nordstrom, Timothy. 2023. How Leader's Type Shapes the Effect of Nuclear Latency on Dispute Involvement. *Conflict Management and Peace Science*, **41**(2), 177–193.

Joshi, Yogesh. 2017. Debating the Nuclear Legacy of India and One of Its Great Cold War Strategists. *War on the Rocks*, March 27.

Jurgensen, Céline, and Dominique, Mongin. 2020. *France and Nuclear Deterrence – A Spirit of Resistance*. Paris: Fondation pour la Recherche Stratégique.

Kahn, Herman. 1960. *On Thermonuclear War*. Princeton, NJ: Princeton University Press.

    1985. *Thinking about the Unthinkable in the 1980s*. New York: Simon and Schuster.

Kampani, Gaurav. 2014. New Delhi's Long Nuclear Journey: How Secrecy and Institutional Roadblocks Delayed India's Weaponization. *International Security*, **38**(4), 79–114.

Karami, Nasser. 2021. Iran May Pursue Nuclear Weapon, Intel Minister Warns West. AP News, February 9.

Kato, Norihiro. 2014. Ambiguities of Japan's Nuclear Policy. *The New York Times*, April 13.

Katz, Yaakov. 2019a. Israel Destroyed Syria's Nuclear Potential. What Would The World Look Like Now If They Hadn't? *Newsweek*, May 26.

    2019b. *Shadow Strike*. New York: St. Martin's Press.

Kay, David. 1997. The Challenge of Inspecting and Verifying Virtual Nuclear Arsenals. Pages 103–122 of: Mazarr, Michael J. (ed.), *Nuclear Weapons in a Transformed World*. New York: St. Martin's Press.

Kennedy, John F. 1961. State Department Telegram 5245 to U.S. Embassy United Kingdom, Top Secret, Sending Message from President Kennedy to Prime Minister Macmillan, 6 May 1961, Top Secret. Accessed via the National Security Archive.

Kennedy, John F., and de Gaulle, Charles. 1961. 30. Memorandum of Conversation, US/MC/1. Foreign Relations of the United States, 1961–1963, Vol. XIV, Berlin Crisis, 1961–1962.

Keohane, Robert O. 1984. *After Hegemony: Cooperation and Discord in the World Political Economy*. Princeton, NJ: Princeton University Press.

Kerry, John. 2018. *Every Day Is Extra*. New York: Simon & Schuster.

Khan, Feroz Hassan. 2012. *Eating Grass: The Making of the Pakistani Bomb*. Stanford, CA: Stanford University Press.

Kim, Tongfi. 2010. *The Alliance Market: American Security Relations Under Unipolarity*. PhD thesis, The Ohio State University.

Kimball, Daryl, and Pemberton, Miriam. 2006. Addressing the Nuclear Proliferation Challenge: Cooperation is Not Capitulation. *Foreign Policy in Focus*, January 12.

Kissinger, Henry. 2012. Henry Kissinger: Iran Must Be President Obama's Immediate Priority. *The Washington Post*, November 16.

Knapp, Vladimir, Pevec, Dubravko, and Matijevic, Mario. 2010. The Potential of Fission Nuclear Power in Resolving Global Climate Change Under the Constraints of Nuclear Fuel Resources and Once-Through Fuel Cycles. *Energy Policy*, **38**(1), 6793–6803.

Krastev, Nikola. 2009. IAEA Chief: Iran's Nuclear Program About Winning Recognition, Prestige. Radio Free Europe, November 5.

Kreps, Sarah E., and Fuhrmann, Matthew. 2011. Attacking the Atom: Does Bombing Nuclear Facilities Affect Proliferation? *Journal of Strategic Studies*, **34**(2), 161–187.

Kroenig, Matthew. 2009a. Exporting the Bomb: Why States Provide Sensitive Nuclear Assistance. *American Political Science Review*, **103**(1), 113–133.

2009b. Importing the Bomb: Sensitive Nuclear Assistance and Nuclear Proliferation. *Journal of Conflict Resolution*, **53**(2), 161–180.

2010. *Exporting the Bomb: Technology Transfer and the Spread of Nuclear Weapons*. Ithaca, NY: Cornell University Press.

2013. Nuclear Superiority and the Balance of Resolve: Explaining Nuclear Crisis Outcomes. *International Organization*, **67**(1), 141–171.

2014a. Force or Friendship? Explaining Great Power Nonproliferation Policy. *Security Studies*, **23**(1), 1–32.

2014b. *A Time to Attack: The Looming Iranian Nuclear Threat*. New York: Macmillan.

2018. *The Logic of American Nuclear Strategy: Why Strategic Superiority Matters*. New York: Oxford University Press.

Kydd, Andrew H., and McManus, Roseanne W. 2017. Threats and Assurances in Crisis Bargaining. *Journal of Conflict Resolution*, **61**(2), 325–348.

Lanoszka, Alexander. 2018. *Atomic Assurance: The Alliance Politics of Nuclear Proliferation*. Ithaca, NY: Cornell University Press.

Lee, Kyung Suk, Kim, James D., Jin, Hwalmin, and Fuhrmann, Matthew. 2022. Nuclear Weapons and Low-Level Military Conflict. *International Studies Quarterly*, **66**(5).

Leeds, Brett Ashley. 2003. Do Alliances Deter Aggression? The Influence of Military Alliances on the Initiation of Militarized Interstate Disputes. *American Journal of Political Science*, **47**(3), 427–439.

Leeds, Brett Ashley, Ritter, Jeffrey M., Mitchell, Sara McLaughlin, and Long, Andrew G. 2002. Alliance Treaty Obligations and Provisions, 1815–1944. *International Interactions*, **28**(3), 237–260.

Levite, Ariel. 2002. Never Say Never Again: Nuclear Reversal Revisited. *International Security*, **27**(3), 59–88.

Levy, Adrian, and Scott-Clark, Catherine. 2007. *Nuclear Deception: The Dangerous Relationship between the United States and Pakistan.* New York: Walker Books.

Levy, Herbert Victor. 1982. Note from Brazilian Congressman Herbert Levy. Wilson Center Digital Archive, Brazilian National Archives.

Levy, Jack S. 1983. Misperception and the Causes of War: Theoretical Linkages and Analytical Problems. *World Politics*, **36**(1), 76–99.

 2008. Case Studies: Types, Designs, and Logics of Inference. *Conflict Management and Peace Science*, **25**(1), 1–18.

Lewis, Jeffrey. 2014. If Japan Wanted to Build a Nuclear Bomb It'd Be Awesome at It. *Foreign Policy*, June 26.

Liberman, Peter. 2001. The Rise and Fall of the South African Bomb. *International Security*, **26**(2), 45–86.

Lipscy, Phillip Y., and Lee, Haillie Na-Kyung. 2019. The IMF As a Biased Global Insurance Mechanism: Asymmetrical Moral Hazard, Reserve Accumulation, and Financial Crises. *International Organization*, **73**(1), 35–64.

Los Angeles Times. 1987. Brazil Could Build Atomic Bomb in 2 Years, General Says, March 23.

Ludvik, Jan. 2019. Closing the Window of Vulnerability: Nuclear Proliferation and Conventional Retaliation. *Security Studies*, **28**(1), 87–115.

MacFarquhar, Neil. 2015. Putin Says He Weighed Nuclear Alert Over Crimea. *The New York Times*, March 15.

Makovsky, David. 2012. The Silent Strike. *The New Yorker*, September 10.

Mallea, Rodrigo. N.D. *Resolving the Dilemma of Nuclear Mistrust: From Foz do Iguacu to the Constitution of ABACC (1985–1991).* Washington, DC: Wilson Center.

Mallea, Rodrigo, Spektor, Matias, and Wheeler, Nicholas J. (eds.). 2012. *The Origins of Nuclear Cooperation: A Critical Oral History of Argentina and Brazil.* Washington DC, Rio de Janeiro: Woodrow Wilson International Center for Scholars, FGV.

Manning, Robert A. 1994. Clinton and Korea: From Cross-Recognition to Trilateral Package. *International Journal of Korean Unification Studies*, 63–78.

Marshall, Monty G., Gurr, Ted Robert, and Jaggers, Keith. 2009. *Polity IV Project: Political Regime Characteristics and Transitions, 1800–2009.*

Mattiacci, Eleonora, Mehta, Rupal N., and Whitlark, Rachel Elizabeth. 2022. Atomic Ambiguity: Event Data Evidence on Nuclear Latency and International Cooperation. *Journal of Conflict Resolution*, **66**(2), 272–296.

Mazarr, Michael J. 1995a. Virtual Nuclear Arsenals. *Survival*, **37**(3), 7–26.

1995b. *North Korea and the Bomb: A Case Study in Nonproliferation*. New York: St. Martin's Press.

1997a. The Notion of Virtual Arsenals. Pages 3–32 of: Mazarr, Michael J. (ed.), *Nuclear Weapons in a Transformed World*. New York: St. Martin's Press.

1997b. Virtual Nuclear Arsenals: A Second Look. In: Mazarr, Michael J. (ed.), *Nuclear Weapons in a Transformed World*. New York: St. Martin's Press.

(ed.). 1997c. *Nuclear Weapons in a Transformed World*. New York: Knopf.

Mearsheimer, John J. 1983. *Conventional Deterrence*. Ithaca, NY: Cornell University Press.

Mehta, Rupal N. 2020. *Delaying Doomsday: The Politics of Nuclear Reversal*. New York: Oxford University Press.

Mehta, Rupal, and Whitlark, Rachel. 2016. Unpacking the Iranian Nuclear Deal: Nuclear Latency and U.S. Foreign Policy. *The Washington Quarterly*, **39**(4), 45–61.

2017a. The Benefits and Burdens of Nuclear Latency. *International Studies Quarterly*, **61**(3), 517–528.

2017b. The Iran Nuclear Ideal Isn't So Great – for Iran. *The Washington Post Monkey Cage*, October 16.

Mercer, Jonathan. 1996. *Reputation and International Politics*. Ithaca, NY: Cornell University Press.

Meyer, Stephen. 1984. *The Dynamics of Nuclear Proliferation*. Chicago, IL: University of Chicago Press.

Mikhail, George. 2021. Egypt Postpones Nuclear Power Plant Amid Tensions with Russia over Nile Dam. *Al-Monitor*.

Milenky, Edward S. 1978. *Argentina's Foreign Policies*. Boulder, CO: Westview Press.

Miller, Nicholas L. 2014a. Nuclear Dominoes: A Self-Defeating Prophecy? *Security Studies*, **23**(1), 33–73.

2014b. The Secret Success of Nonproliferation Sanctions. *International Organization*, **68**(4), 913–944.

2018. *Stopping the Bomb: The Sources and Effectiveness of US Nonproliferation Policy*. Ithaca, NY: Cornell University Press.

Miller, Steven E. 1984. *Strategy and Nuclear Deterrence*. Princeton, NJ: Princeton University Press.

Moore, J. D. L. 1987. *South Africa and Nuclear Proliferation*. New York: Palgrave Macmillan.

Morgan, T. Clifton, Bapat, Navin, and Kobayashi, Yoshiharu. 2014. Threat and Imposition of Economic Sanctions 1945–2005: Updating the TIES Dataset. *Conflict Management and Peace Science*, **31**(5), 541–558.

Most, Benjamin, and Starr, Harvey. 1989. *Inquiry, Logic, and International Politics*. Columbia, SC: University of South Carolina Press.

Mount, Adam. 2014. Latent Deterrence: Sustainably Deterring Crises After the Cold War. Unpublished manuscript.

Mousavian, Seyed Hossein. 2012. *The Iranian Nuclear Crisis: A Memoir*. Washington, DC: Carnegie Endowment for International Peace.

Muellner, Nikolaus, Arnold, Nikolaus, Gufler, Klaus, et al. 2021. Nuclear Energy – The Solution to Climate Change? *Energy Policy*, **155**, 112363.

Mufson, Steven, and Parker, Claire. 2022. War in Ukraine Generates Interest in Nuclear Energy, Despite Danger. *The Washington Post*, April 15.

Muir, Jim. 1998. Tehran Puts Army on War Footing. *The Guardian*, September 16.

Muller, Harald, and Schmidt, Andreas. 2010. The Little-Known Story of Deproliferation: Why States Give Up Nuclear Weapons Activities. Pages 124–158 of: Potter, William C., and Mukhatzhanova, Gaukhar (eds.), *Forecasting Nuclear Proliferation in the 21st Century: The Role of Theory*. Stanford, CA: Stanford University Press.

Nagar, Dawn, and Paterson, Mark. N.D. The Eagle and the Springbok: Strengthening the Nigeria/South Africa Relation. History of Nigeria/South Africa Bilateral Relationship. Centre For Conflict Resolution (CCR).

Nagin, Daniel S., and Pogarsky, Greg. 2001. Integrating Celerity, Impulsivity, and Extralegal Sanction Threats Into a Model of General Deterrence: Theory and Evidence. *Criminology*, **39**(4), 865–892.

Narang, Neil, and Mehta, Rupal N. 2019. The Unforeseen Consequences of Extended Deterrence: Moral Hazard in a Nuclear Client State. *Journal of Conflict Resolution*, **63**(1), 218–250.

Narang, Vipin. 2009. Posturing for Peace: Pakistan's Nuclear Postures and South Asian Stability. *International Security*, **34**(3), 38–78.

    2014. *Nuclear Strategy in the Modern Era: Regional Power Nuclear Postures and International Conflict*. Princeton, NJ: Princeton University Press.

    2017. Strategies of Nuclear Proliferation: How States Pursue the Bomb. *International Security*, **41**(3), 110–150.

    2022. *Seeking the Bomb: Strategies of Nuclear Proliferation*. Princeton, NJ: Princeton University Press.

Neves, Luiz Augusto de Castro. 1979a. Memorandum DEM/89, Luiz Augusto de Castro Neves, Deputy Chief of the Energy and Mineral Resources Division, "Brazil-Argentina. Possibilities for Nuclear Cooperation." Wilson Center Digital Archive, AHMRE. Obtained and translated by Fundação Getúlio Vargas.

    1979b. Possible Brazil–Argentina Nuclear Cooperation. Wilson Center Digital Archive, AHMRE. Critical Oral History Conference on the Argentine-Brazilian Nuclear Cooperation, Rio de Janeiro, March 2012.

NPR. 2009. "How the US Knows What It Knows About Iran," *Talk of the Nation*, October 6.

NRC, US. 2018. Backgrounder on High Burnup Spent Nuclear Fuel.

Nuclear Threat Initiative. 2012. Nuclear Arms Talk Accompanies Japan Atomic Power Phaseout Debate. *The Nuclear Threat Initiative*, July 31.

Nuti, Leopoldo. 1993. "Me Too, Please": Italy and the Politics of Nuclear Weapons, 1945–1975. *Diplomacy & Statecraft*, **4**(1), 114–148.

    2019. Italy as a Hedging State? The Problematic Ratification of the Nonproliferation Treaty. Pages 119–154 of: Pilat, Joseph (ed.), *Nuclear Latency and Hedging: Concepts, History, and Issues*. Washington, DC: Wilson Center.

Obama, Barack. 2008. The First Presidential Debate. *The New York Times*, September 26.

  2009. *Remarks by President Barack Obama in Prague as Delivered, April 5.* Washington, DC: The White House.

  2012. Remarks by the President to the White House Press Corps. August 20.

  2015. Remarks by the President on the Iran Nuclear Deal, August 5.

  2020. *A Promised Land.* New York: Penguin.

Oh, Seoung-yeong. 2019. The Potential for Nuclear Armament . . . the Discussion Itself Works to Deter North Korean Nuclear Capabilities (in Korean). *New Daily.*

O'Rourke, Lindsey S. 2018. *Covert Regime Change: America's Secret Cold War.* Ithaca, NY: Cornell University Press.

Overly, Steven. 2014. Centrus Energy, Formerly Known as USEC, Emerges from Chapter 11 Bankruptcy. *The Washington Post*, September 30.

Palmer, Glenn, D'Orazio, Vito, Kenwick, Michael, and Lane, Matthew. 2015. The MID4 Dataset, 2002–2010: Procedures, Coding Rules, and Description. *Conflict Management and Peace Science*, **32**(2), 222–242.

Pape, Robert A. 1996. *Bombing to Win: Air Power and Coercion in War.* Ithaca, NY: Cornell University Press.

Paul, T. V. 2000. *Power versus Prudence: Why Nations Forgo Nuclear Weapons.* Montreal: McGill-Queens University Press.

Pauly, Reid. 2019. *Coercive Assurance in International Politics.* PhD dissertation, Massachusetts Institute of Technology.

PBS. 2003a. Interview with Ashton Carter, March 3.

  2003b. Interview with Robert Gallucci, March 5.

  2003c. Interview with William Perry, February 26.

Perkovich, George. 1999. *India's Nuclear Bomb: The Impact on Global Proliferation.* Berkeley, CA: University of California Press.

  2008. Nuclear Developments in the GCC: Risks and Trends. Pages 227–238 of: Sager, Abdulaziz, Christian Koch and Hasanain Tawfiq Ibrahim (eds.), *Gulf Yearbook 2007–2008.* Dubai: Gulf Research Center.

Perkovich, George, and Acton, James M. 2008. *Abolishing Nuclear Weapons* (Adelphi Paper No. 396). London: International Institute for Strategic Studies.

Perlmutter, Amos, Handel, Michael I., and Bar-Joseph, Uri. 2003. *Two Minutes Over Baghdad.* New York: Routledge.

Perry, William J. 1999. Review of United States Policy Toward North Korea: Findings and Recommendations. Washington, DC: Office of the North Korea Policy Coordinator, United States Department of State.

Perry, William. 2015. My Journey at the Nuclear Brink. In: *My Journey at the Nuclear Brink.* Stanford, CA: Stanford University Press.

Pifer, Steven, and O'Hanlon, Michael E. 2012. *The Opportunity: Next Steps in Reducing Nuclear Arms.* Washington, DC: Brookings Institution Press.

Pilat, Joseph F. 2014. *Report of a Workshop on Nuclear Latency.* Washington, DC: Woodrow Wilson International Center for Scholars.

  (ed.). 2019. *Nuclear Latency and Hedging: Concepts, History, and Issues.* Washington, DC: Wilson Center.

Pinkas, Alon. 2022. Israel Says Iran Should "Never Become a Nuclear Power." But What if It Already Is One? *Haaretz*, August 2.

Pollack, Kenneth M. 2013. *Unthinkable: Iran, the Bomb, and American Strategy*. New York: Simon and Schuster.

Potter, William C., and Mukhatzhanova, Gaukhar. 2008. Divining Nuclear Intentions: A Review Essay. *International Security*, **33**(1), 139–169.

Potter, William C., Miljanic, Djuro, and Slaus, Ivo. 2000. Tito's Nuclear Legacy. *Bulletin of the Atomic Scientists*, **56**(2), 63–70.

Powell, Colin. 1995. *My American Journey*. New York: Random House.

Powell, Robert. 1990. *Nuclear Deterrence Theory: The Search for Credibility*. New York: Cambridge University Press.

Poznansky, Michael. 2020. *In the Shadow of International Law: Secrecy and Regime Change in the Postwar World*. New York: Oxford University Press.

Prahladan, Vivek. 2017. Declassified: How Inida Tracked Pakistan's Development of a Nuclear Device. *The Diplomat*, January 6.

Puig, Albert Presas I. 2005. Science on the Periphery. The Spanish Reception of Nuclear Energy: an Attempt at Modernity? *Minerva*, **43**(2), 197–218.

Quester, George H. 1991. Conceptions of Nuclear Threshold Status. Pages 209–228 of: Karp, Regina Cowen (ed.), *Security with Nuclear Weapons? Different Perspectives on National Security*. New York: Oxford University Press.

Quinlan, Michael. 2007–08. Abolishing Nuclear Armouries: Policy or Pipedream. *Survival*, **49**(4), 7–16.

Radkau, Joachim. 1983. *Aufstieg und Krise der deutschen Atomwirtschaft. 1945–1975. Verdrängte Alternativen in der Kerntechnik und der Ursprung der nuklearen Kontroverse*. Reinbek: Rowohlt.

Ramberg, Bennett. 2006. Preemption Paradox. *Bulletin of the Atomic Scientists*, **62**(4), 48–56.

2017. North Korea's Other Nuclear Threat: Why We Have More to Fear Than Just Bombs. *Foreign Affairs*, August 28.

2019. Trump's New Iran Sanctions have put Airstrikes on Hold – but Nuclear Risks Remain. NBC News, June 24.

Rauchhaus, Robert. 2009. Evaluating the Nuclear Peace Hypothesis: A Quantitative Approach. *Journal of Conflict Resolution*, **53**(2), 258–77.

Reagan, Ronald. 1983. Address to the Nation on Defense and National Security. March 23.

Reid, David. 2019. US Will Not Open Door to Saudi Arabia Building Nuclear Weapons, Deputy Energy Secretary Says, *CNBC*, February 16.

Reiss, Mitchell. 1995. *Bridled Ambition: Why Countries Constrain their Nuclear Capabilities*. Washington, DC: Woodrow Wilson Center Press.

Reiter, Dan. 2006. Preventive Attacks against Nuclear, Biological, and Chemical Weapons Programs: The Track Record. In: Keller, William W., and Mitchell, Gordon R. (eds.), *Hitting First: Preventive Force in US Security Strategy*. Pittsburgh, PA: Pittsburgh University Press.

2014. Security Commitments and Nuclear Proliferation. *Foreign Policy Analysis*, **10**(1), 61–80.

Renshon, Jonathan. 2017. *Fighting for Status: Hierarchy and Conflict in World Politics*. Princeton, NJ: Princeton University Press.

Reuters. 2012. Iran Nuclear Sites May Be Beyond Reach of "Bunker Busters," January 12.

2013. Researchers Say Stuxnet Was Deployed against Iran in 2007, February 26.

2018. Saudi Crown Prince Says Will Develop Nuclear Bomb if Iran Does: CBS TV, March 15.

Rice, Condoleezza. 2011. *No Higher Honor: A Memoir of My Years in Washington*. New York: Crown.

Richelson, Jeffrey T. 2007. *Spying on the Bomb: American Nuclear Intelligence from Nazi Germany to Iran and North Korea*. New York: W. W. Norton.

Rider, Toby J. 2009. Understanding Arms Race Onset: Rivalry, Threat, and Territorial Competition. *The Journal of Politics*, 71(2), 693–703.

Roberts, Brad. 1997. VNAs and the Contemporary Latent Weapon State. Pages 263–288 of: Mazarr, Michael J. (ed.), *Nuclear Weapons in a Transformed World*. New York: St. Martin's Press.

Rogin, Josh. 2020. Iran's Retaliation for Soleimani Is to Race Toward a Bomb. *The Washington Post*, January 7.

Rothwell, Geoffrey. 2009. Market Power in Uranium Enrichment. *Science and Global Security*, 17, 132–154.

Rouanet, Pierre. 1965. *Mendès France au pouvoir – 1954–1955*. Paris: Robert Laffont.

Rublee, Maria Rost. 2009. *Nonproliferation Norms: Why States Choose Nuclear Restraint*. Athens, GA: University of Georgia Press.

Rühle, Hans. 2015. Is Turkey Secretly Working on Nuclear Weapons? *The National Interest*, September 22.

Sagan, Scott D. 1993. *The Limits of Safety: Organizations, Accidents, and Nuclear Weapons*. Princeton, NJ: Princeton University Press.

1994. The Perils of Proliferation: Organization Theory, Deterrence Theory, and the Spread of Nuclear Weapons. *International Security*, 18(4), 66–107.

1996. Why Do States Build Nuclear Weapons?: Three Models in Search of a Bomb. *International Security*, 21(3), 54–86.

2009. Shared Responsibilities for Nuclear Disarmament. *Daedalus*, 138(4), 157–168.

2010. Nuclear Latency and Nuclear Proliferation. Pages 80–101 of: Potter, William C., and Mukhatzhanova, Gaukhar (eds.), *Forecasting Nuclear Proliferation in the 21st Century: The Role of Theory*. Stanford, CA: Stanford University Press.

2011. The Causes of Nuclear Weapons Proliferation. *Annual Review of Political Science*, 17(14), 225–241.

Sagan, Scott D., and Waltz, Kenneth N. 2003. *The Spread of Nuclear Weapons: A Debate Renewed*. New York: W. W. Norton.

2012. *The Spread of Nuclear Weapons: An Enduring Debate*. New York: W. W. Norton.

Sagir, Dan. 2017. How the Fear of Israeli Nukes Helped Seal the Egypt Peace Deal. *Haaretz*, November 26.

Sample, Susan. 2021. Arms Races. Pages 63–80 of: Mitchell, Sara McLaughlin, and Vasquez, John A. (eds.), *What Do We Know about War?* Lanham, MD: Rowman and Littlefield.

Sánchez-Sánchez, Esther. 2017a. An Alternative Route? France's Position in the Spanish Nuclear Program, c. 1950s–1980s. Pages 155–186 of: M. d. Mar Rubio-Varas, De la Torre, Joseba (eds.), *The Economic History of Nuclear Energy in Spain: Governance, Business and Finance*. London: Palgrave Macmillan.

Sánchez-Sánchez, Esther M. 2017b. Review of Velarde Pinacho, Guillermo. Proyecto Islero. Cuando España pudo desarrollar armas nucleares. Córdoba, Guadalmazán, 2016, 378 páginas [ISBN: 978-84-94384-68-4]. *Asclepio. Revista de Historia de la Medicina y de la Ciencia*, **69**(1), 185–87.

Sang-Hun, Choe. 2017. Kim Jong-un Offers North Korea's Hand to South, While Chiding U.S. *The New York Times*, December 31.

Sanger, David E. 1993. North Korea, Fighting Inspection, Renounces Nuclear Arms Treaty. *The New York Times*, March 12.

1994. North Korea Quits Atom Agency In Wider Rift With U.S. and U.N. *The New York Times*, June 14.

2004. When a Virtual Bomb May Be Better Than the Real Thing. *The New York Times*, December 5.

2012. Obama Order Sped Up Wave of Cyberattacks Against Iran. *The New York Times*, June 1.

Sanger, David E., and Broad, William J. 2009. U.S. and Allies Warn Iran Over Nuclear "Deception." *The New York Times*, September 25.

2018. Saudis Want a U.S. Nuclear Deal. Can They Be Trusted Not to Build a Bomb? *The New York Times*, November 22.

Sarney, José, and Alfonsín, Raúl. 1985. Brazil–Argentina Foz do Iguaçu Joint Declaration on Regional Nuclear Policy. Wilson Center Digital Archive, Department of Energy and Mineral Resources of the Ministry of External Relations, AHMRE. Obtained and translated by Fundação Getúlio Vargas.

Sartori, Anne E. 2005. *Deterrence by Diplomacy*. Princeton, NJ: Princeton University Press.

Saunders, Elizabeth N. 2019. The Domestic Politics of Nuclear Choices – A Review Essay. *International Security*, **44**(2), 146–184.

Schell, Jonathan. 1984. *The Abolition*. New York: Knopf.

Schelling, Thomas C. 1960. *The Strategy of Conflict*. Cambridge, MA: Harvard University Press.

1962. The Role of Deterrence in Total Disarmament. *Foreign Affairs*, **40**(3), 392–406.

1966. *Arms and Influence*. New Haven, CT: Yale University Press.

1976. Who Will Have the Bomb? *International Security*, **1**(1), 77–91.

Schwartz, Stephen C. 1998. *Atomic Audit: The Costs and Consequences of U.S. Nuclear Weapons Since 1940*. Washington, DC: Brookings Institution Press.

Scowcroft, Brent, and Kanter, Arnold. 1994. Korea: Time for Action. *The Washington Post*, June 14.

Sechser, Todd S. 2011. Militarized Compellent Threats, 1918–2001. *Conflict Management and Peace Science*, **28**(4), 377–401.

Sechser, Todd S., and Fuhrmann, Matthew. 2017. *Nuclear Weapons and Coercive Diplomacy*. Cambridge: Cambridge University Press.

Setúbal, Olavo. 1985. Information to Mr. President of the Republic, Brazil–Argentina. Cooperation on Nuclear Energy. Wilson Center Digital Archive, AHMRE. Critical Oral History Conference on the Argentine–Brazilian Nuclear Cooperation, Rio de Janeiro, March 2012.

Shin, Hyonhee, and Pearson, James. 2017. The Thinking Behind Kim Jong Un's "Madness." Reuters, November 30.

Shipler, David K. 1981. Israeli Jets Destroy Iraqi Atomic Reactor; Attack Condemned by U.S. and Arab Nations. *The New York Times*, June 9.

Shultz, George P., Perry, William J., Kissinger, Henry A., and Nunn, Sam. 2007. A World Free of Nuclear Weapons. *Wall Street Journal*, January 4.

Sigal, Leon V. 1998. *Disarming Strangers: Nuclear Diplomacy with North Korea.* Princeton, NJ: Princeton University Press.

Sillah, Mohammed-Bassiru. 1985. The African Response to Nuclear Proliferation : A Case-Study of Nigeria. *Présence Africaine*, 10–30.

Silveira, Antonio Francisco Azeredo da. 1974a. Report from the Brazilian Foreign Ministry to President Ernesto Geisel, "Subject: the Indian Nuclear Test." Wilson Center Digital Archive, Brazilian Foreign Ministry Archives.

1974b. Memorandum, Foreign Minister Azeredo da Silveira, Information for the President of Brazil, "Uranium Enrichment." Wilson Center Digital Archive, CPDOC Archives, PNB ad 1973.10.05 pp. 100–108. Obtained and translated by Fundação Getúlio Vargas.

Silveira, Antonio Azeredo da. 1974c. Information for the President of the Republic. Wilson Center Digital Archive, CPDOC Archives, PNB ad 1973.10.05 pp. 100–108. Obtained and translated by Fundação Getúlio Vargas.

Simons, Howard. 1965. India Raises Possibility of Joining Nuclear Club. *The Washington Post*, November 17.

Singer, J. David, Bremer, Stuart A., and Stuckey, John. 1972. Capability Distribution, Uncertainty, and Major Power War. Pages 19–48 of: Russett, Bruce M. (ed.), *Peace, War, and Numbers*. Beverly Hills, CA: Sage.

Singh, Sonali, and Way, Christopher R. 2004. The Correlates of Nuclear Proliferation: A Quantitative Test. *Journal of Conflict Resolution*, **48**(6), 859–885.

Slantchev, Branislav L. 2010. Feigning Weakness. *International Organization*, **64**(3), 357–388.

Sloss, David. 2003. Forcible Arms Control: Preemptive Attacks on Nuclear Facilities. *Chicago Journal of International Law*, 4(1), 39–57.

Smith, Bradley C, and Spaniel, William. 2020. Introducing *v*-Clear: a Latent Variable Approach to Measuring Nuclear Proficiency. *Conflict Management and Peace Science*, **37**(2), 232–256.

Smith, R. Jeffrey. 2016. Nuclear Security: A Vital Goal but a Distant Prospect. The Center for Public Integrity, March 28.

Snyder, Glenn H. 1961. *Deterrence and Defense: Toward a Theory of National Security*. Princeton, NJ: Princeton University Press.

Sobek, David, Foster, Dennis M., and Robison, Samuel B. 2012. Conventional Wisdom? The Effect of Nuclear Proliferation on Armed Conflict, 1945–2001. *International Studies Quarterly*, **56**(1), 149–162.

Sokolski, Henry. 2018. In the Middle East, Soon Everyone Will Want the Bomb. *Foreign Policy*, May 21.

Solingen, Etel. 2007. *Nuclear Logics: Contrasting Paths in East Asia and the Middle East*. Princeton, NJ: Princeton University Press.

Soutou, Georges-Henri. 1996. *L'alliance Incertaine: Les Rapports Politico-Stratégiques Franco-Allemands, 1954–1996*. Paris: Fayard.

Spaniel, William. 2019. *Bargaining Over the Bomb: The Successes and Failures of Nuclear Negotiations*. Cambridge: Cambridge University Press.

Squassoni, Sharon (ed.). 2018. *Civil Plutonium Transparency in Asia*. Washington DC: Institute for International Science and Technology Policy.

Stacey, Kiran, and Bokhari, Farhan. 2017. Pakistan Vows Nuclear Retaliation of India Attacks. *Financial Times*, January 19.

Stoll, Richard J. 1996. *World Production of Latent Nuclear Capacity*. Houston, TX: Rice University.

Stulberg, Adam N., and Fuhrmann, Matthew (eds.). 2013. *The Nuclear Renaissance and International Security*. Stanford, CA: Stanford University Press.

Subiza, Héctor A. 1979. Memorandum, Héctor A. Subiza, Head of the Latin American Department of the Argentinian Foreign Ministry, "Cooperation with Brazil in the Nuclear Field." Wilson Center Digital Archive, AMRE-CIC. Obtained and translated by Fundação Getúlio Vargas.

Sweeney, David J. 2014. *Nuclear Weapons Latency*. PhD thesis, Texas A&M University.

Tait, Robert, and MacAskill, Ewen. 2006. Iran Declares: We Are in the Nuclear Club. *The Guardian*, April 11.

Tannenwald, Nina. 2007. *The Nuclear Taboo: The United States and the Nonuse of Nuclear Weapons Since 1945*. New York: Cambridge University Press.

Tau, Byron. 2012. Pentagon Brass Hedges on Iran Capabilities. *Politico*, January 8.

Tellis, Ashley J. 2001. *India's Emerging Nuclear Posture: Between Recessed Deterrent and Ready Arsenal*. Santa Monica, CA: RAND.

Tertrais, Bruno. 2007. Has Iran Decided to Build the Bomb? Lessons from the French Experience. *Carnegie Endowment for International Peace*, January 30.

The Economist. 2023. Why South Korea Is Talking about Getting Its Own Nukes, January 19.

The New York Times. 1964. Indonesia Asserts She Plans A-Bomb, November 16.

The New York Times. 1966. Nasser Cites Need for Nuclear Arms, May 9.

The New York Times. 1993. If North Korea Has Bombs, December 28.

Thornton, Richard C. 1998. *The Falklands Sting: Reagan, Thatcher, and Argentina's Bomb*. Washington, DC: Brassey's.

TOI staff. 2022. White House Says Iran Is "A Few Weeks Or Less" From Bomb Breakout. *The Times of Israel*, April 27.

Torgerson, David J., and Raftery, James. 1999. Discounting. *British Medical Journal*, **319**(7214), 914–915.

Trachtenberg, Marc. 2012. The de Gaulle Problem. *Journal of Cold War Studies*, 5, 81–92.

Trevithick, Joseph. 2018. Israel Details Long Secret Raid On Syrian Nuclear Reactor, Says It's Willing to Do It Again. *The War Zone*. March 21.

United Nations Security Council. 1981. Resolution 487, June 19.

US Central Intelligence Agency. 1957a. National Intelligence Estimate 100-6-57, "Nuclear Weapons Production in Fourth Countries – Likelihood and Consequences." Accessed via the Freedom of Information Act Electronic Reading Room.

1957b. *Questions on Nuclear Weapons Tests and Fourth Countries, March 26.* Accessed via the Freedom of Information Act Electronic Reading Room.

1958. *Development of Nuclear Capabilities by Fourth Countries: Likelihood and Consequences.* Washington, DC: Directorate of Intelligence. Accessed via the Freedom of Information Act Electronic Reading Room.

1961a. Central Intelligence Bulletin. Accessed via the Freedom of Information Act Electronic Reading Room.

1961b. Nuclear Weapons Production in Fourth Countries Likelihood and Consequences. Accessed via the Freedom of Information Act Electronic Reading Room.

(Director of Central Intelligence). 1963. National Intelligence Estimate 22-2-63. The French Nuclear Weapons Program. Accessed via the Freedom of Information Act Electronic Reading Room.

1964. Prospects for a Proliferation of Nuclear Weapons Over the Next Decade. Washington, DC: Wilson Center Digital Archive. Accessed via the Freedom of Information Act Electronic Reading Room.

1965. *Likelihood of Indian Development of Nuclear Weapons.* Washington, DC: National Intelligence Estimate 31-64. Accessed via the Freedom of Information Act Electronic Reading Room.

1966. The Likelihood of Further Nuclear Proliferation. Accessed via the Freedom of Information Act Electronic Reading Room.

1974. *Bhutto Seeks Nuclear Policy Assurances.* Washington, DC: The National Intelligence Daily, Copy No. 117. Accessed via the Freedom of Information Act Electronic Reading Room.

1975a. *Managing Nuclear Proliferation: The Politics of Limited Choice.* Washington, DC: Directorate of Intelligence, Office of Political Research. Accessed via the Freedom of Information Act Electronic Reading Room.

1975b. Memorandum to Holders of Special National Intelligence Estimat, SNIE 4-1-74: Prospects for Further Proliferation of Nuclear Weapons. Accessed via the National Security Archive.

1981a. *Request for Review of Draft Paper on the Security Dimension of Non-Proliferation.* Tech. rept. Accessed via the Freedom of Information Act Electronic Reading Room.

1981b. *Egypt: Nuclear Program and the Non-Proliferation Treaty.* Washington, DC: National Foreign Assessment Center. Accessed via the Freedom of Information Act Electronic Reading Room.

1981c. *Note For [Redacted].* Washington, DC: Deputy Director for National Foreign Assessment. Accessed via the Freedom of Information Act Electronic Reading Room.

1982a. Argentina's Nuclear Policies in Light of the Falklands Defeat. Accessed via the Freedom of Information Act Electronic Reading Room.

1982b. National Intelligence Estimate, NIE-4-82, "Nuclear Proliferation Trends Through 1987." Accessed via the Freedom of Information Act Electronic Reading Room.

1983. *Brazil's Changing Nuclear Goals: Motives and Constraints.* Washington, DC: Director of National Intelligence. Accessed via the Freedom of Information Act Electronic Reading Room.

1984a. *Argentine Nuclear Policy: Resisting International Controls.* Washington, DC: Directorate of Intelligence. Accessed via the Freedom of Information Act Electronic Reading Room.

1984b. National Intelligence Estimate, NIE 73/5-84, "Trends in South Africa's Nuclear Security Policies and Programs." Accessed via the Freedom of Information Act Electronic Reading Room.

1985a. *Brazil's Changing Nuclear Goals: Motives and Constraints: Memorandum to Holders of SNIE 93-83.* Washington, DC: Director of National Intelligence. Accessed via the Freedom of Information Act Electronic Reading Room.

1985b. *The Dynamics of Nuclear Proliferation: Balance of Incentives and Constraints.* Washington, DC: National Intelligence Council, NIC M 85-10001. Accessed via the Freedom of Information Act Electronic Reading Room.

2002. Untitled CIA Estimate Provided to Congress on November 19, 2002. Accessed via the Freedom of Information Act Electronic Reading Room.

US Department of Defense. 2010. *Nuclear Posture Review Report.* Washington, DC: Office of the Secretary of Defense.

1994. "SECDEF meeting with ROK Minister of Defense Rhee." Washington, DC: US Department of Defense. Accessed via the National Security Archive.

US Department of Energy. N.D.a. The Atomic Bombing of Hiroshima. In: *The Manhattan Project: An Interactive History.* Washington, DC: Office of History and Heritage Resources.

US Department of Energy. N.D.b. The Atomic Bombing of Nagasaki. In: *The Manhattan Project: An Interactive History.* Washington, DC: Office of History and Heritage Resources.

US Department of State. 1958a. Memorandum of Conversation with Dr. Friedrich Zimmermann, Secretary General of the CSU, February 11. In: *Foreign Service Despatch No. 1421.* Bonn: American Embassy.

1958b. Results of Paris Conference. *The Department of State Bulletin,* **31**(803), 719–736.

1968. Assessment of Brazilian Nuclear Device Capability. Wilson Center Digital Archive, RG 59, Subject-Numeric Files 1967–1969. Box 2895, AE 1 Brazil.

1974. India: Uncertainty over Nuclear Policy. In: Battle, Joyce (ed.), *India and Pakistan – On the Nuclear Threshold.* Washington, DC: The National Security Archive.

1975a. Korean Reprocessing – The Next Step, Action Memorandum from Philip C. Habib and Winston Lord to the Secretary of State, November 18. Washington, DC: The National Security Archive.

1975b. *US Department of State Cable, ROK Nuclear Reprocessing, December 10.* Washington, DC: History and Public Policy Program Digital Archive, Gerald Ford Presidential Library, National Security Adviser Presidential Country Files for East Asia and the Pacific, Box 11, Korea - State Department Telegrams, to SecState - NODIS (8). Obtained by Charles Kraus.

1979. US Department of State Cable 145139 to US Embassy India [Repeating Cable Sent to Embassy Pakistan], "Non-Proliferation in South [Asia]", June 6. Wilson Center Digital Archive, Mandatory Declassification Review request. Obtained and contributed by William Burr and included in NPIHP Research Update #6.

1981. *Cable to Secretary of State, 4 November: Visit of Principal Deputy Assistant Secretary Marshall with Chilean Officials Concerning Beagle Channel, LOS and Nuclear Cooperation.* Santiago, Chile: US Embassy. Accessed via the Freedom of Information Act Electronic Reading Room.

1982. Memorandum From Roger W. Fontaine, Christopher C. Shoemaker, and Richard T. Childress of the National Security Council Staff to the President's Deputy Assistant for National Security Affairs (McFarlane). *Foreign Relations of the United States, 1981–1988,* **13**(Document 309), https://history.state.gov/historicaldocuments/frus1981-88v13/d309.

1991. The Algerian Nuclear Program. Policy Coordinating Committee on Non-Proliferation, September 1. Available at http://nsarchive.gwu.edu/nukevault/ebb228/Algeria-20.pdf.

2001. U.S. Embassy Tehran airgram A-383 to State Department: Soviet Chicom Hostilities, 4 September 1969. In: Burr, William (ed.), *The Sino-Soviet Border Conflict, 1969: U.S. Reactions and Diplomatic Maneuvers.* Washington, DC: The National Security Archive.

2013. Implications of an Indian Nuclear Weapon Test. In: Burr, William (ed.), *U.S. Detected Indian Nuclear Test Preparations in 1995, but Photo Evidence was 'Clear As Mud'.* Washington, DC: The National Security Archive.

US National Intelligence Council. 2002. Iraq's Continuing Programs for Weapons of Mass Destruction. Available at http://fas.org/irp/cia/product/iraq-wmd-nie.pdf.

van Wyk, Anna-Mart. 2019. Apartheid's Bomb and Regional Liberation: Cold War Perspectives. *Journal of Cold War Studies,* **21**(1), 151–165.

Vance, Cyrus R. 1977. Brazil Scope Paper: Implications of the Argentina Visit. Wilson Center Digital Archive, Ernesto Geisel Archive/CPDOC. Critical Oral History Conference on the Argentine-Brazilian Nuclear Cooperation, Rio de Janeiro, March 2012.

Vazquez, Rafael. 1985. Cable from Rafael Vazquez, Argentinian Ambassador to Brazil, Requesting Meeting with the Brazilian Foreign Minister. Wilson Center Digital Archive, Archives of the Argentinian Ministry of Foreign Relations and Culture (AMRECIC), Caja Brasil, h0005B. Obtained and translated by Fundação Getúlio Vargas.

Venturini, Danilo. 1979. Notice No. 135/79 From the General Secretariat of the Brazilian National Security Council. Wilson Center Digital Archive,

Archive of the Brazilian Ministry of Foreign Affairs (Brasilia). Obtained and translated by Fundação Getúlio Vargas.

Volpe, Tristan. 2015. *Proliferation Persuasion: Coercive Bargaining with Nuclear Technology*. PhD thesis, George Washington University.

Volpe, Tristan. 2017. Atomic Leverage: Compellence with Nuclear Latency. *Security Studies*, 26(3), 517–544.

Volpe, Tristan A. 2023. *Leveraging Latency: How the Weak Compel the Strong with Nuclear Technology*. New York: Oxford University Press.

Volpe, Tristan, and Kühn, Ulrich. 2017. Germany's Nuclear Education: Why a Few Elites Are Testing a Taboo. *The Washington Quarterly*, 40(3), 7–27.

von Hippel, David, and Hayes, Peter. 2017. Potential Impacts of Accident at or Attack on the DPRK's Yonbyon Nuclear Reactors, NAPSNet Special Report, May 22.

von Hippel, Frank N. 2010. South Korean Reprocessing: An Unnecessary Threat to the Nonproliferation Regime. *Arms Control Today*, 40(2), 22–29.

Voute, Frederik Michiel. 2020. *Perceptions of Responsibility: Urenco and the Troika's Commercial and Nonproliferation Policies in Theoretical and Historical Perspective*. PhD thesis, Erasmus University Rotterdam.

Wald, Matthew L. 2002. Threats and Responses: Reactor Vulnerability; Experts Say Nuclear Plants Can Survive Jetliner Crash. *The New York Times*, August 20.

2011. Loan Request by Uranium-Enrichment Firm Upends Politics as Usual. *The New York Times*, November 24.

2013a. Kentucky Operator to Cease Enrichment of Uranium. *The New York Times*, May 24.

2013b. USEC, Enricher of Uranium for U.S., Seeks Bankruptcy. *The New York Times*, December 16.

Walker, Mark. 1989. *German National Socialism and the Quest for Nuclear Power, 1939–49*. New York: Cambridge University Press.

Waltz, Kenneth N. 1981. *The Spread of Nuclear Weapons: More May Be Better* (Adelphi Paper No. 171). London: International Institute for Strategic Studies.

1997. Thoughts about Virtual Nuclear Arsenals. *The Washington Quarterly*, 20(3), 153–161.

2012. Why Iran Should Get the Bomb: Nuclear Balancing Would Mean Stability. *Foreign Affairs*, 91(4), 2–5.

Warner, Margaret, and Elbaradei, Mohamed. 2004. Newsmaker: Mohamed Elbaradei. PBS, March 18.

Warrick, Joby, Nakashima, Ellen, and Fifield, Anna. 2017. North Korea Now Making Missile-Ready Nuclear Weapons, US Analysts Say. *The Washington Post*, August 8.

Way, Christopher, and Weeks, Jessica. 2014. Making It Personal: Regime Type and Nuclear Proliferation. *American Journal of Political Science*, 58, 705–719.

Weintraub, Richard M. 1987. Zia Says Pakistan Capable of Building A-Weapon. *The Washington Post*, March 23.

Weisman, Steven R. 1985. India Says It Has an Advanced Atom Reactor. *The New York Times*, August 11.

1987. On India's Border, A Huge Mock War. *The New York Times*, March 6.

Whitlark, Rachel. 2017. Nuclear Beliefs: A Leader-Focused Theory of Counter-Proliferation. *Security Studies*, 26(4), 545–574.

Whitlark, Rachel Elizabeth. 2021. *All Options on the Table: Leaders, Preventive War, and Nuclear Proliferation*. Ithaca, NY: Cornell University Press.

Wilson, Peter. 1997. Issues of Force Structure, Nuclear Infrastructure, and Survivability. Pages 77–102 of: Mazarr, Michael J. (ed.), *Nuclear Weapons in a Transformed World*. New York: St. Martin's Press.

Wilson, Ward. 2007. The Winning Weapon? Rethinking Nuclear Weapons in Light of Hiroshima. *International Security*, 31(4), 162–179.

Windrem, Robert. 2014. Japan Has Nuclear "Bomb in the Basement," and China Isn't Happy. *NBC News*, March 11.

Wit, Joel S., Poneman, Daniel B., and Gallucci, Robert L. 2004. *Going Critical: The First North Korean Nuclear Crisis*. Washington, DC: Brookings Institution Press.

Wohlstetter, Albert, Jones, Gregory, and Wohlstetter, Roberta. 1979. *Towards a New Consensus on Nuclear Technology*. Los Angeles: Pan Heuristics.

Woo, Seung Min, Chirayath, Sunil S., and Fuhrmann, Matthew. 2020. Nuclear Fuel Reprocessing: Can Pyro-Processing Reduce Nuclear Proliferation Risk? *Energy Policy*, 144, 111601.

World Nuclear Association. 2022. Emerging Nuclear Energy Countries, May.

Yarhi-Milo, Keren. 2014. *Knowing the Adversary: Leaders, Intelligence, and Assessments of Intentions in International Relations*. Princeton, NJ: Princeton University Press.

Zagare, Frank C., and Kilgour, D. Marc. 2000. *Perfect Deterrence*. New York: Cambridge University Press.

Zakaria, Fareed. 2011. Fareed Zakaria GPS: New Phase of Global Geopolitics; Interview with Ehud Barak; Interview with Bruce Bueno de Mesquita; A Look at Europe's Far Right. CNN, November 20.

Zentner, M. D., Coles, G. L., and Talbert, R. J. 2005. *Nuclear Proliferation Technology Trends Analysis*. Richland, WA: Pacific Northwest National Laboratory.

Index

A. Q. Khan Network, 84
Abdenur, Roberto
　Argentina–Brazil arms race and, 254,
　　265, 266
Abrams, Elliott, 234, 237
Abubakar, Iya
　Nigeria–South Africa arms race and,
　　269
Acheson–Lilienthal Report, 290
Adeli, Seyed Mohammad Hossein, 293
Adenauer, Konrad
　France–West Germany arms race and,
　　273–275
Agreed Framework, 222, 227, 291
Ahmadinejad, Mahmoud
　Iranian Nuclear Crisis and, 211
al Assad, Bashar, 26, 112
al Kibar attack, 59, 232–239
Alavi, Mahmoud, 86
Alfonsín, Raúl
　Argentina–Brazil arms race and, 256,
　　261
Algeria
　nuclear intentions and, 307
alliance leverage
　latent nuclear deterrence theory's
　　predictions about, 147–148
Amanpour, Christiane, 215
Areva, 120
Argentina
　Argentina–Brazil arms race and,
　　252–267
　Beagle Channel crisis and, 12
　beliefs about latent deterrence, 83–84
　enrichment and reprocessing (ENR)
　　facilities in, 53, 82, 254, 299
　Falklands War and, 296
　latent deterrence by, 11, 83
　nuclear intentions of, 82
　perception of Brazil's intentions, 313
　proliferation timeline of, 100, 257
　rivalry with Brazil, 253

arms race
　between Argentina and Brazil, 252–267
　between France and West Germany,
　　270–277
　between India and Pakistan, 277–283
　in international relations scholarship,
　　243
　in latent nuclear deterrence theory, 51
　between Nigeria and South Africa,
　　267–270
Australia
　enrichment and reprocessing (ENR)
　　facilities in, 98
　nuclear economics and, 121
　nuclear hedging in, 117
average effect of treatment reversal (ART),
　163
average treatment effect (ATE), 152
average treatment effect on the treated
　(ATT), 152, 162, 167

Baidatz, Yossi, 238
Bailey, Michael, 155
Baliga, Sandeep, 37
Barak, Ehud
　al Kibar attack and, 236
　Iranian Nuclear Crisis and, 216, 217
Barletta, Michael, 82
Baruch Plan, 6
Bas, Muhammet, 200, 201
Beaton, Leonard, 290
Beccaria, Cesare, 48
Begin Doctrine, 233
Begin, Menachem, 63, 194
Belgium
　enrichment and reprocessing (ENR)
　　facilities in, 56
　nuclear armament and, 15
Berlin crisis, 30
Bhutto, Zulfikar Ali, 309
　India–Pakistan arms race and, 277, 278,
　　282

Made in the USA
Middletown, DE
15 November 2024